SEQUELS

compiled by

Mandy E. Hicken

Volume I
Adult books

THE ASSOCIATION OF ASSISTANT LIBRARIANS
(GROUP OF THE LIBRARY ASSOCIATION)

THE AAL acknowledge the assistance of
REMPLOY LIMITED
in the production of this publication
1995

The Associaton of Assistant Librarians 1995

1st edition 1922 by Thomas Aldred
2nd edition 1928 by W. H. Parker
3rd edition 1947 by F. M. Gardner
4th edition 1955 by F. M. Gardner
5th edition 1967 by F. M. Gardner
6th edition 1974 by F. M. Gardner
7th edition 1982 by M. E. Hicken
8th edition 1986 by M. E. Hicken
9th edition 1986 by M. E. Hicken
10th edition 1991 by M. E. Hicken
11th edition 1995 by M. E. Hicken

British Library Cataloguing-in-Publication Data.

A catalogue record for this book is
available from the British Library.

ISBN 0-900092-91-2

Jacket design by Origin Studios, Stoke-on-Trent
Printed by Page Bros (Norwich) Ltd, Mile Cross Lane, Norwich
Bound by Remploy Limited, Leicester

ROYAL BOROUGH OF GREENWICH

Follow us on twitter 🐦 @greenwichlibs

Please return by the last date shown

Thank you! To renew, please contact any
Royal Greenwich library or renew online at
www.better.org.uk/greenwichlibraries

FOR
REFERENCE ONLY

PREFACE TO THE ELEVENTH EDITION

This edition of 'Sequels' has been compiled directly on to hard disk, and because much of the material has been inputted from the last edition, it has given me the opportunity to tidy-up entries, to do a certain amount of re-arrangement, and to delete many of the somewhat abstruse and scholarly notes made by the early compilers. I hope that the result will be easier to use.

There are some 3000 new entries, with a cut-off date of November 1994. As before the material included dates from approximately 1950. I have left in some of the earlier titles, since a lot of books, particularly detective stories, written in the 1930s and 1940s are being reprinted by publishers like Black Dagger. Any titles which could not be authenticated, or which did not appear to be sequels have been removed. They will, of course, still be found in earlier editions of the book.

The overall scheme of the book is, as always:
   a) novels in which the same characters appear
   b) sequences of books connected by a theme
   c) sequences with a geographical or historical connection
   d) non-fiction, particularly autobiographies, intended to be read
      in sequence

My thanks must, once more, go to all the people who have helped in the compilation of the book, particularly those people in and out of the library profession who have taken the trouble to write to me with corrections and suggestions for inclusion. I am always pleased to receive your comments, and I hope that you will continue to send them to me. Special thanks to Martin Underwood in Birmingham, to Holt Jackson, and to James Beaton and Remploy, who keep me to my deadline.

November 1994   Mandy Hicken

AARONS, E. S.
SAM DURRELL
1 Assignment disaster 1955
2 Assignment treason 1956
3 Assignment Budapest 1957
4 Assignment suicide 1957
5 Assignment Stella Marni 1957
6 Assignment Angelina 1958
7 Assignment Carlotta Cortez 1958
8 Assignment Cong Hai kill 1958
9 Assignment Ankara 1958
10 Assignment Madelaine 1958
11 Assignment Helene 1959
12 Assignment Lilli Lamaris 1959
13 Assignment Mara Tirana 1960
14 Assignment Burma girl 1961
15 Assignment Zoraya 1961
16 Assignment Lowlands 1961
17 Assignment school for spies 1961
18 Assignment Karachi 1962
19 Assignment Sorrento siren 1963
20 Assignment Manchurian doll 1963
21 Assignment the girl in the gondola 1964
22 Assignment the Cairo dancers 1965
23 Assignment Palermo 1966
24 Assignment Black Viking 1967
25 Assignment Moon girl 1967

ABBEY, L.
ULTIMA SAGA
1 The forge of virtue
2 The temper of wisdom
Paperback fantasy

ABBEY, L.
UNICORN AND DRAGON
1 Unicorn
2 Dragon
3 The green man
Paperback fantasy

ABRAHAM, C
THE ONEDIN LINE
1 The shipmaster 1973
2 The iron ships 1974
3 The high seas 1976
4 Trade winds 1977
5 The white ships 1979
6 Turning tide 1980
Adapted from the TV series. The last title is by B. Stewart.

ABSE, D.
1 Ash on a young man
2 There was a young man from Cardiff 1991

3 A poet in the family 1974
1 and 2 are autobiographical novels; 3 is autobiography.

ACHEBE, C.
AFRICAN TRILOGY
1 Things fall apart 1958
2 No longer at ease 1960
3 Arrow of gold 1964

ACTON, H.
1 Memoirs of an aesthete 1948
2 More memoirs of an aesthete 1970
N.F. Autobiography

ADAMS, D.
1 The hitch-hikers guide to the Galaxy 1979
2 The restaurant at the end of the Universe 1980
3 Life,the Universe and everything 1982
4 So long,and thanks for all the fish 1984
5 Mostly harmless 1992
Science fiction, originally written for radio

ADAMS, D.
DIRK GENTLY
1 Dirk Gently's Holistic Detective Agency 1987
2 The long dark teatime of the soul 1988

ADAMS, R.
1 Shardik 1974
2 Maia 1984
Fantasy

ADAMS, ROBERT.
HORSECLANS
1 The coming of the Horseclans 1985
2 The swords of the Horseclans 1985
3 The revenge of the Horseclans
4 A cat of silvery hue 1985
5 The savage mountains 1985
6 The patrimony 1985
7 Horseclans odyssey 1985
8 The death of a legend 1985
9 The witchgoddess 1985
10 Bili the axe 1985
11 Champion of the last battle 1985
12 A woman of the Horseclans 1985
A fantasy series published simultaneously in hardback and paperback.

ADAMSON, J.
1 Born free 1960
2 Living free 1961
3 Forever free 1962
4 Elsa and her cubs 1965
Republished in one vol., 'The story of Elsa' 1966

ADDIS, F.
1 The year of the cornflake 1983
2 Green behind the ears 1984
3 Buttered side down 1985
4 Down to earth 1987
5 Taking the biscuit 1989
N.F. Life on a smallholding in Devon

ADLARD, M.
1 Interface 1970
2 Volteface 1972
S. F.

AGRY, E.
O'REILLY
1 Assault force O
2 O'Reilly:blowtorch 1982

AHERN, J.
THE SURVIVALIST
1 Total war
2 The nightmare begins
3 The quest
4 The doomsayer
5 The web
6 The savage horde
7 The prophet
8 The end is coming
9 Earth fire
10
11 The reprisal
12 The rebellion
13 Pursuit
14 The terror
15 Overlord
16 The arsenal
17 The ordeal
18 The struggle
19 Final rain

AIKEN, JOAN
1 The smile of the stranger 1970
2 The lightning tree 1980
Gothic romances set in the 19th century

AIKMAN, A.
BOYET RHODES
1 The caves of Segonda 1985
2 The eye of Itza 1986
3 The brokers of doom 1987

AINSWORTH, P.
1 The flickering candle 1966
2 The candle rekindled 1968
3 Steady burns the candle 1970

AIRD, C.
INSPECTOR C.D.SLOAN
1 The religious body 1966
2 A most contagious crime 1967
3 Henrietta who? 1968
4 The complete steel 1969
5 A late phoenix 1970
6 His burial too 1973
7 Slight mourning 1975
8 Parting breath 1977
9 Some die eloquent 1979
10 Passing strange 1980
11 Last respects 1982
12 Harm's way 1984
13 A dead liberty 1986
14 The body politic 1990
15 A going concern 1993
16 Injury time:short stories 1994

ALBANY, J.
S.A.S.
1 Warrior caste 1982
2 Mailed fist 1983
3 Deacon's dagger 1983
4 Close combat 1983
5 Marching fire 1984
6 Last bastion 1984
7 Borneo story 1985

ALBERT, M.
PETE SAWYER
1 Stone angel 1986
2 Back in the real world 1987
3 Get off at Babylon 1988
4 Long teeth 1988
5 The midnight sister 1989
6 Bimbo heaven 1990
7 The last smile 1989
8 The zig-zag man 1991
9 The Riviera contract 1992

ALDING, P.
C.I.D. ROOM
1 The C.I.D. room 1967
2 Circle of danger 1968
3 Murder among thieves 1969
4 Guilt without proof 1970
5 Despite the evidence 1971
6 Call back to crime 1972
7 Field of fire 1973
8 The murder line 1974
9 Six days to death 1975
10 Murder is suspected 1977
11 Ransom town 1979

12 A man condemned 1981
13 Betrayal by death 1982
14 One man's justice 1983

ALDISS, B.
1 The hand-reared boy 1970
2 A soldier erect 1971
3 A rude awakening 1978

ALDISS, B.
HELLICONIA TRILOGY
1 Helliconia Spring 1982
2 Helliconia Summer 1983
3 Helliconia Winter 1985
(*Science fiction*)

ALDRIDGE, J.
RUPERT ROYCE
1 A captive in the land 1963
2 The statesman's game 1966

ALEICHEM, S.
1 The old country 1966
2 Tevye's daughters 1973
*Stories on which 'Fiddler on the Roof'
was based*

ALEXANDER, D.
PHOENIX
1 Dark Messiah
2 Ground zero
Paperback fantasy

ALEXANDER, L.
CHRONICLES OF PRYDAIN
1 The book of three
2 The black cauldron
3 Castle of Llyr
4 Taran wanderer
5 The High King
Paperback fantasy

ALEXANDER, M.
THE WELLS OF YTHAN
1 Ancient dreams
2 Magic casements
3 Shadow realm
Paperback fantasy

ALEXANDER, S.
MICHELANGELO BUONAROTTI
1 Michelangelo, the Florentine 1957
2 The hand of Michelangelo 1965
3 Nicodemus 1985

ALLBEURY, T.
TAD ANDERS
1 Snowball 1974
2 The Judas factor 1984

ALLBURY, A.
1 You'll die in Singapore 1953
2 Bamboo and Bushido 1955
N.F. War in the Far East.

ALLDRITT, K.
BLACK COUNTRY SERIES
1 The good pit man 1976
2 The lover next door 1978
3 Elgar on the journey to Hanley
1979

ALLEGRETTO, M.
JACOB LOMAX
1 Death on the rocks 1988
2 Blood stone 1989
3 Dead of winter 1990

ALLEN, C. V.
1 Leftover dreams 1992
2 Chasing rainbows 1993

ALLEN, M.
DET.SERGEANT SPENCE
1 Spence in Petal Park 1975
2 Spence in the Blue Bazaar 1976

ALLEN, R. B.
VENERA
1 The torch of honour
2 Rogue powers
Paperback fantasy

ALLEN, R. M.
1 Caliban 1993
2 Isaac Asimov's inferno 1994

ALLINGHAM, M.
ALBERT CAMPION
1 The crime at Black Dudley 1929
2 Mystery mile 1929
3 Look to the lady 1931
4 Police at the funeral 1931
5 Sweet danger 1933
6 Death of a ghost 1934
7 Flowers for the judge 1936
8 The case of the late pig 1937
9 Dancers in mourning 1937
10 The fashion in shrouds 1938
11 Mr.Campion and others 1939
12 Black plumes 1940
13 Traitor's purse 1941
14 Coroner's pidgin 1945
15 More work for the undertaker
1948
16 Tiger in the smoke 1952
17 The beckoning lady 1955
18 Hide my eyes 1958
19 The china governess 1963

20 The mind readers 1965
21 Cargo of eagles (completed by
   P.Y.Carter) 1967
22 Mr.Campion's farthing,by
   P.Y.Carter 1968
23 Mr.Campion's falcon, by
   P.Y.Carter 1969
24 Mr.Campion's lucky day and
   other stories 1973
   *P. Youngman Carter was Margery
   Allingham's husband and collaborated
   on many of her books. The 'Allingham
   minibus', 1973, contains some
   Campion stories.*

ALLIS, M.
ASHBEL FIELD
1 Now we are free 1952
2 To keep us free 1953
3 Brave pursuit 1954
4 Rising storm 1955
5 Free soil 1960
   *A family chronicle set in 19th century
   America.*

ALLISON, E. S.
1 Kiwi at large 1967
2 Kiwi vagabond 1969
   N.F. Autobiography

ALLISON-WILLIAMS, J.
THE TABARD
1 Mistress of 'The Tabard' 1983
2 Simon of 'The Tabard' 1984
   *Novels set in a 15th century London
   tavern*

ALLYSON, A.
MARTIN ROSS
1 Don't mess with murder 1972
2 Do you deal in murder? 1973

ALMEDINGEN, E. M.
1 Tomorrow will come 1948
2 The almond tree
3 Within the harbour 1955
   M. F. Autobiography

ALMEDINGEN, E. M.
THORNGOLD FAMILY
1 Fair haven 1959
2 Dark splendour 1961
   Set in 18th century Russia.

AMBLER, E.
ARTHUR ABDEL SIMPSON
1 Light of day 1962
2 Dirty story 1967

AMBLER, E.
CHARLES LATIMER
1 The mask of Dimitrios 1939
2 The intercom conspiracy 1970

AMERY, L. S.
1 England before the storm,1896-
   1914 1953
2 War and peace,1914-1929 1954
3 The unforgiving years 1955
   N.F. Autobiography of a politician.

AMES, D.
DAGOBERT BROWN
1 She shall have murder 1948
2 Murder begins at home 1949
3 Death of a fellow traveller 1950
4 Corpse diplomatique 1950
5 The body on page one 1951
6 Murder, maestro please 1952
7 No mourning for the Matador
   1953
8 Crime, gentlemen please 1954
9 Landscape with corpse 1955
10 Crime out of mind 1956
11 She wouldn't say who 1957
12 Lucky Jane 1959

AMES, D.
SERGEANT JUAN LLORCA
1 The man in the tricorn hat 1962
2 The man with three Jaguars 1963
3 The man with three chins 1964
4 The man with three passports
   1967

AMIS, K.
PATRICK STANDISH
1 Take a girl like you 1960
2 Difficulties with girls 1988

ANAND, V.
BRIDGES OVER TIME
1 The proud villeins 1990
2 The ruthless yeoman 1991
3 Women of Ashdon 1992
4 The faithful lovers 1993
5 The cherished wives 1994

ANAND, V.
NORMAN TRILOGY
1 Gildenford 1979
2 The Norman pretender 1980
3 Disputed crown 1982

ANDERSON, J.
1 Assassin 1972
2 Abolition of death 1974

ANDERSON, J. R. L.
PIET DEVENTER
1 A sprig of sea lavender 1978
2 Festival 1979
3 Late delivery 1982

ANDERSON, O.
GUY RANDOM
1 Random rendezvous 1955
2 Random mating 1956
3 Random at random 1958
4 Random rapture 1959
5 Random all round 1960

ANDERSON, P.
EARTHBOOK OF STORMGATE
*3 vols. in paperback, without
individual titles*

ANDERSON, P.
FLANDRY
1 Ensign Flandry 1977
2 A circus of Hells 1978
3 The rebel worlds
4 Tiger by the tail
5 Honourable enemies
6 Flandry of Terra
7 Commander Flandry 1979
8 A handful of stars
9 Knight Flandry 1980
10 A stone in Heaven 1981
11 The game of Empire 1994

ANDERSON, P.
POLESOTECHNIC LEAGUE
1 The Earthbook of Stormgate
2 The trouble twisters
3 War of the wingmen
4 Trader to the stars
5 Satan's world
6 Mirkheim

ANDERSON, P.
THE KING OF YS
1 Roma mater
2 Gallicenae
3 Dahut
4 The dog and the wolf
Paperback fantasy

ANDERSON, V.
1 Spam tomorrow 1956
2 Our Square 1957
3 Beware of children 1958
4 Daughters of divinity 1959
5 The Flo affair 1963
6 The Northrepps grandchildren
1968

7 Scrambled eggs for Christmas
1970
N.F. Autobiography

ANDREWS, L.
ST. MARTHA'S HOSPITAL
1 The light in the ward 1984
2 The healing time 1986
3 Front line,1940 1990

ANDREWS, L.
ST. BARNABAS HOSPITAL
1 The young doctor downstairs 1978
2 The new Sister Theatre 1979

ANDREWS, L.
THE GARDEN
1 One night in London 1980
2 Weekend in the Garden 1981
3 In an Edinburgh drawing room
1983
4 The phoenix syndrome 1987
*The story of a London teaching
hospital bombed in WW2, and its
rebuilding to 1980*

ANDREWS, V.
CASTEEL FAMILY
1 Heaven 1986
2 Dark angel 1987
3 Fallen hearts 1989
4 Gates of paradise 1989
5 Web of dreams 1990

ANDREWS, V.
CUTLER FAMILY
1 Dawn 1990
2 Secrets of the morning 1991
3 Twilight's child 1992
4 Midnight whispers 1992
5 Darkest hour 1993

ANDREWS, V.
DOLLENGAGER FAMILY
1 Garden of shadows 1987
2 Petals on the wind 1980
3 If there be thorns 1981
4 Seeds of yesterday 1984
5 Flowers in the attic 1980
6 Fallen hearts 1989
*Both series were completed by Andrew
Niederman after Virginia Andrews'
death.*

ANDREWS, V.
LANDRY FAMILY
1 Ruby 1994
2 Pearl in the mist 1994

ANDRIC, L.
YUGOSLAVIAN TRILOGY
1 The bridge on the Drina 1959
2 Bosnian story 1959
3 The woman from Sarajevo 1956

ANGELOU, M.
1 I know why the caged bird sings 1984
2 Gather together in my name 1985
3 Singin'and swingin'and makin'merry like Christmas 1985
4 The heart of a woman 1986
5 All God's children need travelling shoes 1987
N.F. Autobiography of a black American woman

ANGOFF, C.
POLONSKY FAMILY
1 Journey to the dawn 1951
2 In the morning light 1952
3 The sun at dawn 1955
4 Between day and dark 1959
5 The bitter spring 1961
6 Summer storm 1963
7 Memory of autumn 1968
8 Winter twilight 1970
9 Season of mists 1971
10 Mid-century 1974
11 Toward the horizon 1980
The story of a Jewish family who emigrated from Czarist Russia to the USA, and their life there

ANTHONY, D.
MORGAN BUTLER
1 The midnight lady and the morning 1970
2 Blood on the harvest moon 1973
3 The long hard cure 1979

ANTHONY, D.
STANLEY BASS
1 The organisation 1974
2 Stud game 1977

ANTHONY, E.
1 Imperial Highness 1953
2 Curse not the King 1954
3 Far fly the eagles 1955

ANTHONY, E.
DAVINA GRAHAM
1 The defector 1980
2 Avenue of the dead 1981
3 Albatross 1982
4 The company of saints 1983
Spy stories

ANTHONY, P.
1 Chthon 1967
2 Phthor 1970
Paperback only in this country.

ANTHONY, P.
BATTLE CIRCLE
1 Sos the rope 1968
2 Var the stick 1971
3 Neq the sword 1971
Science fiction. Also published in one volume

ANTHONY, P.
BIO OF A SPACE TYRANT
1 Refugee
2 Mercenary
3 Politician
4 Executive
5 Statesman

ANTHONY, P.
CLUSTER
1 Vicinity 1979
2 Chaining the lady 1979
3 Kirlian quest 1979
4 Thousandstar
5 Viscous circle 1981
Fantasy

ANTHONY, P.
INCARNATIONS OF IMMORTALITY
1 On a pale horse 1986
2 Bearing an hour glass 1986
3 With a tangled skein 1987
4 Wielding a red sword 1987
5 Being a green mother 1988
6 For love of evil 1990
7 And eternity 1990

ANTHONY, P.
MODE
1 Virtual mode 1991
2 Fractual mode 1992
3 Chaos mode 1994

ANTHONY, P.
OF MAN AND MANTA
1 Omnivore
2 Orn
3 Ox

ANTHONY, P.
TAROT TRILOGY
1 God of Tarot
2 Vision of Tarot
3 Faith of Tarot
Paperback fantasy, 1982

ANTHONY, P.
THE APPRENTICE ADEPT
1 Split infinity 1981
2 Blue adept 1981
3 Juxtaposition 1983
4 Out of phaze 1988
5 Phaze doubt 1991
Science fiction

ANTHONY, P.
THE MAGIC OF XANTH
1 A spell for the chameleon 1977
2 A source of magic 1979
3 Castle Roogna 1979
4 Centaur Aisle 1982
5 Ogre,Ogre 1982
6 Night mare 1983
7 Dragon on a pedestal 1985
8 Crewel Lye 1988
9 Golem in the gears
10 Vale of the vole 1988
11 Heaven cent 1989
12 Man from Mundania 1990
13 Isle of view 1991
14 Question quest 1992
15 The colour of her panties 1992
16 Demons don't dream 1993
17 Harpy thyme 1993
18 Geis of the gargoyle 1994

ANTHONY, P. & MARGROFF, R. E.
1 Dragon's gold 1
2 Serpent's silver 1992
3 Chimaera's copper 1993
4 Orc's opal 1993
5 Mouvar's magic 1994

ANTONIUS, S.
1 The Lord 1986
2 Where the Jinn consult 1987

ANTONY, J.
1 Wisteria Street will soon be gone 1970
2 The young stranger 1971

ANTONY, J.
MRS DALE
1 Mrs.Dale's bedside book 1951
2 Mrs.Dale at home 1955
3 The Dales of Parkwood Hill 1959
4 Dear Dr.Dale 1970

APPIAH, A.
SIR PATRICK SCOTT
1 Avenging angel 1990
2 Nobody likes Letitia 1994

APPIGNANESI, R.
ITALIA PERVASA
1 Stalin's orphans 1982
2 The mosque 1985
3 Destroying America 1987

ARCHER, F.
1 The distant scene 1967
2 Under the parish lantern 1969
3 Hawthorn hedge country 1970
4 Secrets of Bredon Hill 1971
5 A lad of Evesham Vale 1972
6 Muddy boots and Sunday suits 1973
7 Golden sheaves,black horses 1974
8 When village bells were silent 1975
9 Poacher's pie 1976
10 By hook and by crook 1978
11 When Adam was a boy 1979
12 Fred Archer,farmer's son 1986
13 The village of my childhood 1989

ARCHER, J.
1 Kane and Abel 1980
2 The prodigal daughter 1982

ARDEN, W.
KANE JACKSON
1 A dark power 1969
2 Deal in violence 1971

ARDIES, T.
CHARLIE SPARROW
1 Their man in the White House 1971
2 This suitcase is going to explode 1972

ARLEN, L.
THE BORODINS
1 Love and honour 1984
2 War and passion 1984
A family saga originally published in paperback

ARMITAGE, A.
EVA BOWER
1 Chapter of innocence 1988
2 Chapter of echoes 1989
3 Chapter of shadows 1990

ARMITAGE, A.
HAWKSMOOR
1 Hawksmoor 1981
2 Hunter's moon 1985
3 Touchstone 1987

4 Hawkrise 1988
*Novels set in Yorkshire from the 18th
century to*

ARMSTRONG, C.
DET.FRANK PAGAN
1 Jig 1987
2 Mazurka 1988
3 Mambo 190
4 Jigsaw 1994

ARMSTRONG, E. S.
1 Daughter of Valdoro 1975
2 Valdoro's mistress 1976

ARMSTRONG, R.
CHIEF INSPECTOR MASON
1 Dangerous limelight 1947
2 Sinister playhouse 1949
3 Sinister widow 1951
4 Sinister widow again 1952
5 Sinister widow returns 1953
6 Sinister widow comes back 1956
7 Widow and the cavalier 1956
8 Sinister widow down under 1958
9 Sinister widow at sea 1959

ARMSTRONG, R.
ROCKINGHAM STONE
1 Cavalier of the night 1955
2 The widow and the cavalier 1956

ARMSTRONG, S.
CLACHAN
1 A croft in Clachan 1976
2 Clachan days 1977
3 A hotel by Clachan 1978
4 The electrics come to Clachan 1979
5 Jamie in Clachan 1980
*N.F. Autobiography, set in the
Scottish Highlands*

ARMSTRONG, T.
THE CROWTHER CHRONICLES
1 The Crowthers of Bankdam 1940
2 Pilling always pays 1954
3 Sue Crowther's marriage 1961
4 Our London office 1966

ARNOLD, B.
COPPINGER TETRALOGY
1 A singer at the wedding 1979
2 The song of the nightingale 1980
3 The muted swan 1981
4 Running to Paradise 1983

ARNOLD, R.
1 A very quiet war 1962

2 Orange Street and Brickhole Lane
1963
N.F. Autobiography

ARNOTHY, C.
1 I am fifteen and I do not want to
die 1963
2 It is not so easy to live 1965
N.F. Autobiography

ARTHUR, F.
INSPECTOR SPEARPOINT
1 Who killed Netta Maul? 1940
2 Another mystery in Suva 1956
3 Murder in the tropic night 1961
4 The throbbing dark 1962

ARVAY, H.
TRIAD
1 Triad 21 1977
2 Society of fear 1979
Novels about international drug traffic

ASCH, S.
1 The Nazarene 1939
2 The Apostle 1943
3 Mary 1949
4 Moses 1951
5 The Prophet 1955

ASHFORD, J.
DET.INSPECTOR DON KERRY
1 Counsel for the defence 1961
2 Investigations are proceeding 1963
3 Enquiries are continuing 1964
4 Will anyone who saw the
accident? 1964
5 Superintendent's room 1965
6 Forget what you saw 1967

ASHTON, H.
WILCHESTER CHRONICLES
1 Tadpole Hall 1941
2 Joanna at Littlefold 1945
3 Yeoman's hospital 1949
4 Captain comes home 1950
5 Half-crown house 1956

ASHWORTH, S.
1 A matter of fat 1992
2 Personal growth 1993

ASIMOV, I.
BLACK WIDOWERS DINING CLUB
1 Tales of the Black Widowers 1975
2 More tales of the Black Widowers
1977
3 Casebook of the Black Widowers
1980

4 Puzzles of the Black Widowers
1990
Detective stories

ASIMOV, I.
DAVID STARR - SPACE RANGER
1 Space ranger 1972
2 Pirates of the asteroids 1972
3 The big sun of Mercury 1972
4 The oceans of Venus 1972
5 The rings of Saturn 1973
6 The moon of Jupiter 1973

ASIMOV, I.
ELIJAH BALEY
1 The caves of steel 1954
2 The naked sun 1958
3 The robots of dawn 1983
4 Robots and Empire 1985
Science fiction

ASIMOV, I.
FANTASTIC VOYAGE
1 Fantastic voyage 1966
2 Destination brain 1987

ASIMOV, I.
FOUNDATION
1 Prelude to Foundation 1988
2 Foundation and Empire 1952
3 Second Foundation 1953
4 Foundation's edge 1983
5 Foundation 1951
6 Foundation and Earth 1986
7 Forward the foundation 1993
Science fiction

ASIMOV, I.
ROBOTS
1 I,Robot 1950
2 The rest of the robots 1967
3 The positronic man, with
R.Silverberg 1992
4 Caliban, by R.M.Allen 1993

ASPINALL, R.
MALINSON BROTHERS
1 Yesterday's kingdom 1961
2 The promise of his return 1962
3 Echo sounding 1965

ASPRIN, R.
MYTH
1 Mythnomers and imperfections
2 Another fine myth
3 Myth directions
4 Hit or myth
5 Myth conceptions
6 Myth-ing persons

7 Little myth marker
8 M.Y.T.H. INC. link
9 Myth Inc. in action
Paperback fantasy/humour

ASPRIN, R.
PHULE
1 Phule's company
2 Phule's paradise

ASPRIN, R. EDITOR
SANCTUARY
1 Thieves world
2 Tales from the vulgar unicorn
3 Shadows of Sanctuary
4 Storm season
5 The face of chaos
*Stories by different authors, using the
same characters and setting.
Paperback only.*

ASQUITH, LADY C.
1 Haply I may remember 1950
2 Remember and be glad 1952
N.F. Autobiography

ASTLEY, J.
1 Fall of Midas 1976
2 Copsi Castle 1978
*Written by Norah Lofts under a
pseudonym*

ASTOR, BROOKE.
1 Patchwork child
2 Footprints 1986

ASTURIAS, M. A.
1 The cyclone 1967
2 The Green Pope 1971
3 The eyes of the interred 1974
*About the relations between a Central
American Republic and an American
fruit company.*

ATKINS, E.
1 We bought an island 1976
2 Tales from our Cornish island
1986

ATKINS, M. E.
IRIS SERIES
1 By the north door
2 Palimpsest 1981
3 Samain 1977
4 Tangle 1988

ATTANASIO, A.
RADIX
1 In other worlds

9

2 Radix

AUDEMARS, P.
M. PINAUD
1 The two imposters 1959
2 The fire and the clay 1960
3 The turns of time 1961
4 The crown of night 1962
5 The dream and the dead 1963
6 The wings of darkness 1963
7 Fair maids missing 1964
8 Dead with sorrow 1965
9 Time of temptation 1966
10 A thorn in the dust 1966
11 The veins of compassion 1967
12 The white leaves of death 1968
13 The flame in the mist 1969
14 A host for dying 1970
15 Stolen like magic away 1971
16 The delicate dust of death 1973
17 No tears for the dead 1974
18 Nightmare in rust 1975
19 And one for the dead 1975
20 Healing hands of death 1977
21 Now dead is any man 1977
22 A sad and savage dying 1978
23 Slay me a sinner 1979
24 Gone to her death 1981
25 The bitter path of death 1982
26 The red rust of death 1983
27 A small slain body 1985

AUEL, J.
EARTH'S CHILDREN
1 Clan of the cave bear 1980
2 The valley of horses 1983
3 The mammoth hunters 1985
4 Plains of passage 1990

AUSTEN, J.
The following titles are miscellaneous items of Austen memorabilia. 'Old friends and new fancies' by S. G. Brinton; 'The Watsons:a fragment', concluded by L. Oulton; 'The Watsons', completed by John Coates 1958; 'Lady Susan', by P. A. Karr, is an adaptation of an unfinished novel; 'Truth and Rumour', by J. Gillespie 1993, is a recreation of the world of Jane Austen.

AUSTEN, J.
EMMA
1 Emma 1815
2 The journal of Miss Jane Fairfax,by C.Grey 1984
3 Jane Fairfax, by Joan Aiken 1990

AUSTEN, J.
MANSFIELD PARK
1 Mansfield Park 1814
2 Ladysmead, by J.Gillespie 1982
3 Mansfield revisited, by Joan Aiken 1984
4 Mrs.Rushworth, by V.Gordon 1989

AUSTEN, J.
NORTHANGER ABBEY
1 Northanger Abbey 1816
2 Uninvited guests, by J.Gillespie 1994

AUSTEN, J.
PERSUASION
1 Persuasion 1818
2 Sir Willy, by Jane Fairfax 1992

AUSTEN, J.
PRIDE AND PREJUDICE
1 Pride and prejudice 1813
2 Pemberley shades, by D.Bonavia-Hunt 1970
3 Teverton Hall, by J.Gillespie 1983
4 Pemberley, by E.Tennant 1993
5 Presumption, by J.Barrett 1994
6 The unequal marriage, by E.Tennant 1994

AUSTEN, J.
SENSE AND SENSIBILITY
1 Sense and sensibility 1811
2 Margaret Dashwood, by F.Brown
3 Susan Price, by F.Brown
4 Brightsea, by J.Gillespie 1987
5 Eliza's daughter, by Joan Aiken 1994

AUSTER, P.
NEW YORK TRILOGY
1 City of glass 1986
2 Ghosts 1986
3 The locked room 1986

AUSTIN, DEE.
1 Reckless heart
2 Wild prairie sky

AUSTWICK, J.
1 Murder in the Borough Library 1959
2 The County Library murders 1962
3 The Mobile Library murders 1963
4 The Borough Council murders 1965

AVALLONE, M.
ED MOON
1 The tall Dolores 1956
2 The spitting ikmage 1957
3 Dead game 1954
4 Violence in velvet 1958
5 The alarming clock 1962
6 The bouncing Betty 1960
7 The violent virgin 1960
8 The crazy mixed-up corpse 1957
9 The voodoo murders 1959
10 Meanwhile back at the morgue 1964
11 The living bomb 1963
12 There is something about a dame 1963
13 The brutal kook 1965
14 The bedroom bolero 1964
15 The fat death 1966
16 The February doll murders 1966
17 Assassins don't die in bed 1965
18 The horrible man 1968
19 The flower covered corpse 1970
20 The doomsday bag 1970
21 Death dives deep 1971
22 Little Miss Murder
23 Shoot it again Sam
24 London, bloody London
25 The girl in the cockpit
26 Kill her, you'll like it
27 Killer on the keys
28 The hot body
29 The x-rated corpse
30 Blues for Sophia Loren
Not all published in UK.

AVALLONE, M.
SUITE POLICIERE
1 The passenger on the U 1968
2 The fountains at Marlieux 1949
3 The double death of Frederick Belot 1949
4 Carriage 7, Seat 16 1963
5 Cat's eye 1972
The author's chronological order

AVERY, E.
1 The Margaret days 1959
2 The Marigold summer 1960

AVERY, G.
1 The lost railway 1980
2 The onlookers 1983
Not direct sequels, but the same characters appear

AVERY, V.
1 London morning 1980
2 London shadows 1981

3 London spring 1982
N.F. Autobiography

AWLINSON, R.
AVATAR TRILOGY
1 Shadowdale
2 Tantras
3 Waterdeep
Paperback fantasy Prince of lies, by J. Lowden is a pendant to the series.

AYER, A. J.
1 Part of my life 1977
2 More of my life 1984
N.F. Autobiography

BABSON, M.
1 A trail of ashes 1983
2 Death swap 1984

BABSON, M.
PERKINS & TATE LTD
1 Cover up story 1970
2 Murder on show 1972

BABSON, M.
TRIXIE DOLAN
1 Reel murder 1986
2 Encore murder 1989
3 Shadows in their blood 1991
4 Even yuppies die 1993

BACCHELLI, R.
1 Mill on the Po 1952
2 Nothing new under the sun 1956

BACHMANN, L. P.
BEN CLANCY
1 The legend of Joseph Nokato 1971
2 The ultimate act 1972

BADDOCK, J.
CORMACK & WOODWARD
1 The radar job 1986
2 Emerald 1987

BAGBY, G.
INSPECTOR SCHMIDT
1 Bachelor's widow 1935
2 Murder at the piano 1936
3 Murder half-baked 1938
4 Murder on the nose 1939
5 Bird walking weather 1940
6 Corpse with the purple thighs 1941
7 The corpse wore a wig 1942
8 Here comes the corpse 1943
9 Red is for killing 1944
10 Original carcase 1946

11 Dead drunk 1954
12 The body in the basket 1956
13 Murder in wonderland 1965
14 Corpse candle 1967
15 Another day another death 1969
16 Honest reliable corpse 1970
17 Killer boy was here 1971
18 Two in the bush 1976
19 My dead body 1976
20 Innocent bystander 1977
21 The tough get going 1978
22 Better dead 1978
23 Guaranteed to fade 1979
24 I could have died 1979
25 Mugger's day 1980
26 Country and fatal 1981
27 A question of quarry 1981
28 The sitting duck 1982
29 The golden creep 1982
30 The most wanted 1984

BAGLEY, D.
CURTIS AND HARDIN
1 Flyaway 1978
2 Windfall 1982

BAGLEY, D.
SLADE
1 Running blind 1970
2 The freedom trap 1971

BAGNOLD, E.
VELVET BROWN
1 National Velvet 1939
2 International Velvet, by B.Forbes
  1978

BAILEY, A.
1 America lost and found 1980
2 England first and last 1985
  N.F. Autobiography

BAILEY, HILARY.
1 Polly put the kettle on 1975
2 As time goes by 1988

BAILEY, P.
1 The raw Pearl 1970
2 Talking to myself 1972
  N.F.Autobiography

BAILEY, PAUL
1 Gabriel's lament 1986
2 Sugar cane 1993
  *Not direct sequels, but characters
  recur*

BAILEY, R.
BROTHERS OF THE DRAGON
1 Brothers of the dragon
2 Straight on til mourning
  Paperback fantasy

BAKER, D. VAL
1 The sea's in the kitchen 1963
2 The door is always open 1965
3 We'll go round the world
  tomorrow 1966
4 To sea with 'Sanu' 1968
5 Life up the creek 1971
6 The petrified mariner 1972
7 Old mill by the stream 1973
8 Spring at Land's End 1974
9 Sunset over the Scillies 1975
10 A view from the valley 1976
11 A long way to Land's End 1977
12 The wind blows from the West
   1978
13 All this and Cornwall too 1979
14 A family for all seasons 1979
15 As the stream flows by 1980
16 Upstream at the mill 1981
17 A family at sea 1981
18 Summer at the mill 1982
19 Down a Cornish lane 1983
20 Family circles 1984
21 When Cornish skies are smiling
   1984
22 My Cornish world 1985
23 The waterwheel turns 1983
24 The mill in the valley 1984
25 Cornish prelude 1985
   *N.F.Autobiography. Nos. 1-4
   published in one volume*

BAKER, DAISY
1 Travels in a donkey trap 1974
2 More travels in a donkey trap
  1976
  N.F.Autobiography

BAKER, DONNA
WEAVERS
1 The weaver's daughter 1991
2 The weaver's dream 1991
3 The weaver's glory 1992

BAKER, DONNA.
GLASSMAKERS SAGA
1 Crystal 1987
2 Black cameo 1988
3 Chalice 1989

BAKER, H.
1 All the gods are dead 1984
2 Alive to the burning 1985

BAKER, S.
ASHLU CYCLE
1 Drink the fire from the flames
2 Firedance

BAKER, W. H.
RICHARD QUINTAIN
1 Take death for a lover 1964
2 Strike north 1965
3 Destination Dieppe 1965
4 The dogs of war 1966
5 The inexpendable 1966
6 The rape of Berlin 1966
7 The guardians 1967
8 The girl in asses' milk 1967
9 The dead and the damned 1967
10 The girl, the city and the soldier 1968
11 The dirty game 1968
12 The night of the wolf 1969
13 The Judas diary 1969
14 The charge is treason 1973

BALAAM
1 Chalk in my hair 1953
2 Chalk gets in your eyes 1956
N.F. Autobiography

BALDWIN, A.
MEN AT WAR
1 The last heroes 1986
2 The secret warriors 1987
3 The soldier spies 1988
4 The fighting agents 1988

BALDWIN, J.
1 Notes of a native son 1955
2 Nobody knows my name 1961
N.F. Autobiography

BALDWIN, M.
1 Grandad with snails 1958
2 In step with a goat 1962
3 Goose in the jungle 1965
N.F. Autobiography

BALDWIN, M.
PATRICK MATSON & THE COMMITTEE
1 Exit wounds 1988
2 Holofernes 1989

BALL, B.
KEEGAN
1 The no-option contract 1975
2 The one-way deal 1976

BALL, B.
TIME
1 Timepiece 19
2 Timepit 1971
S. F.

BALL, J.
JACK TALLON
1 Police chief 1982
2 Trouble for Tallon 1982

BALL, J.
VIRGIL TIBBS
1 In the heat of the night 1966
2 The cool cottontail 1967
3 Johnny get your gun 1970
4 Five pieces of jade 1972
5 The eyes of the Buddha 1976
6 Then came violence 1980

BALLARD, J. G.
1 Empire of the sun 1984
2 The kindness of women 1991

BALLINGER, W. A.
1 The voyageurs 1975
2 There and back again 1977
Sea stories

BANIS, V. J.
BRUSSAC FAMILY
1 This splendid earth 1978
2 The earth and all it holds 1980

BANKS, L. R.
1 The L-shaped room 1968
2 The backward shadow 1970
3 Two is lonely 1974
A trilogy about an single mother

BANKS, L. R.
THE BRONTES
1 Dark quartet 1976
2 Path to the silent country 1977

BANKS, O.
AMOS HATCHER
1 The Rembrandt panel 1984
2 The Caravaggio obsession 1985
Thrillers set in the word of art dealing

BANNERMAN, B.
DAVE WOOLF
1 Orbach's judgement
2 The judge's song
3 Controlling interest
4 The last Wednesday
Paperback thrillers

BANNISTER, J.
DET.CHIEF INSPECTOR FRANK
SHAPIRO
1 A bleeding of innocents 1993
2 Sins of the heart 1994

BANVILLE, J.
1 Dr.Copernicus
2 Kepler
3 The Newton letter
4 Mefisto 1986

BAR-ZOHAR, M.
JEFF SAUNDERS
1 The third truth 1974
2 The spy who died twice 1975

BARBER, A. V.
1 Days at Wickham 1966
2 Childhood in Egypt 1971
N.F. Autobiography

BARBETTE, J.
HARVEY BRITTEN
1 Final copy 1952
2 Dear dead days 1954

BARCLAY, T.
CORVILL FAMILY
1 Web of dreams 1988
2 Broken threads 1989
3 The final pattern 1990

BARCLAY, T.
CRAIGALLAN FAMILY
1 A sower went forth 1980
2 The stony places 1981
3 Harvest of thorns 1983
4 The good ground 1984
A family saga set in the mid-western USA

BARCLAY, T.
TRAMONT SERIES
1 The wine widow 1985
2 The champagne girls 1986
3 The last heiress 1987
A family saga about the wine trade in France

BARD'S TALE
1 Castle of deception, by M.Lackey & J.Sherman
2 Fortress of frost and fire,by M.Lackey & J.Sherman
3 Prison of souls, by M.Lackey & M.Shepherd

4 The chaos gate, by J.Sherman
Paperback fantasies based on the fantasy game.

BARD, M.
1 the doctor wears three faces 1949
2 Forty odd 1952
3 Just be yourself 1957
N.F. Autobiography

BARDSLEY, M.
SUPT. DONALD MARTIN
1 Murder on fire 1969
2 Murder for sale 1970
3 Murder on ice 1972
4 Hit it rich 1972

BARKE, J.
ROBERT BURNS
1 The wind that shakes the barl;ey 1946
2 The song in the green thorn tree 1947
3 The wonder of all the gay world 1949
4 The crest of the broken wave 1953
5 The well of the silent harp 1954
6 Bonnie Jean 1958
6 is the story of Burns's widow, Jean

BARKER, C.
BOOK OF THE ART
1 The great and secret show 1989
2 Everville 1994

BARKER, P.
1 Regeneration 1991
2 The eye in the door 1993
2 contains some of the characters from 1.

BARLING, M. V. M.
INSPECTOR HENDERSON
1 Accessory to murder (as Pamela Barrington) 1968
2 Death of a shrew 1968

BARLING, M. V. M.
INSPECTOR MARSHALL
1 The rest is silence 1951
2 Account rendered 1953
3 Night of violence 1959
4 By some person unknown 1960
5 Motive for murder 1963
6 Afternoon with violence 1963
7 Appointment with death 1964
8 Time to kill 1965
9 Cage without bars 1966
10 Slow poison 1967

11 A game of murder 1967
12 Confession of murder 1967
13 A marked man 1968
*Some of the series was originally
written under the name of Pamela
Barrington.*

BARLING, M. V. M.
INSPECTOR TRAVERS
1 The Mortimer story 1952
2 Among those present 1953
3 The gentle killer (as Pamela
  Barrington) 1961

BARLING, T.
CHARLIE DANCE
1 The smoke 1986
2 Smoke dragon 1988
3 Smoke dance 1991
Thrillers about drug trafficking

BARNARD, R.
SUPT. PERRY TRETHOWAN
1 Sheer torture 1981
2 Death and the princess 1982
3 The missing Bronte 1983
4 Bodies 1986
5 Death in purple prose 1987

BARNES, G. M.
JONATHAN MARK
1 Murder is a gamble 1954
2 Murder walks the stairs 1956
3 Murder is insane 1958

BARNES, L.
MICHAEL SPRAGUE
1 Bitter finish 1983
2 Dead heat 1984
3 Cities of the dead 1986

BARNES, LINDA
CARLOTTA CARLYLE
1 A trouble of fools 1988
2 The snake tattoo 1989
3 Coyote 1991
4 Steel guitar 1992
5 Snapshot 1993

BARNES, R.
1 A licence to live 1975
2 Coronation cups and jamjars 1977
  N.F. A story of East End family life

BARNES, T.
DET.SUPT.BLANCHE HAMPTON
1 A midsummer killing 1990
2 Dead meat 1991
3 Taped 1992

BARNETT, J.
SUPT. OWEN SMITH
1 Marked for destruction 1982
2 Diminished responsibility 1984

BARNWELL, W.
BLESSING TRILOGY
1 The Blessing papers 1981
2 The Sigma curve 1982

BARON, A.
HARRYBOY BOAS
1 The lowlife 1964
2 Strip Jack naked 1966

BARR, N.
ANNE PIGEON
1 Track of the cat 1993
2 A superior death 1994

BARR, P.
1 The coming of the barbarians 1967
2 The deer cry pavilion 196
  *The opening of Japan in the 19th
  century, and the impact of Western
  society.*

BARR, P.
ALICE GREENWOOD
1 Chinese Alice 1981
2 Uncut Jade 1983
  *Missionary life in 19thC China, based
  on fact*

BARREN, C.
STEMSTON FAMILY
1 Eighty North 1959
2 Jamestown 1960

BARRETT, A.
1 Lucid stars 1989
2 Secret harmonies 1990

BARRETT, J. G.
CHIEF INSPECTOR BLESSINGAY
1 He died twice 1968
2 Guilty be damned 1968
3 A cup that kills 1969
4 His own funeral 1972

BARRY, C.
1 The spear-grinner 1968
2 Fly Jamskoni 1969
  *About an airline in a newly
  independent country*

BARSTOW, S.
ELLA LINDLEY
1 Just you wait and see 1987

2 Give us this day 1989
3 Next of kin 1991

BARSTOW, S.
VIC BROWN
1 A kind of loving 1962
2 The watchers on the shore 1965
3 The right true end 1976

BARTH, J.
1 Sabbatical 1982
2 More Tidewater tales 1988

BARTH, R.
MARGARET BINTON
1 The rag bag clan 1983
2 One dollar death 1985
3 A ragged plot 1984
4 The co-op kill 1986

BARTLETT, V.
1 This is my life 1958
2 And now, tomorrow 1962
3 Tuscan retreat 1964
N.F. Autobiography

BARTON, A.
1 Two lamps in our street 1965
2 The penny world 1969
3 School for love 1976
N.F. Autobiography

BARTON, J.
WASTEWORLD
1 Aftermath
2 Resurrection
3 Angels
4 My way
Paperback science fiction

BASS, T. J.
1 Half-past human
2 The god-whale
Paperback science fiction

BASSANI, G.
1 A prospect of Ferrara 1965
2 The gold-rimmed spectacles 1965
3 The garden of the Finz-Continias 1965
4 Behind the door 1973
A sequence set in Ferrara, linked by location and character, rather than events.

BASSETT, R.
1 Tinfish run 1977
2 Pier head jump 1978

3 The Neptune landing 1979
About the Royal Navy in World War 1.

BASSETT, R.
MARGERY FAMILY
1 Witchfinder General 1967
2 Amorous trooper 1968
3 Rebecca's brat 1969
4 Kill the Stuart 1970
The story of an English family from the time of Cromwell to the Jacobite Rising in 1745.

BASSO, H.
1 Light Infantry ball 1959
2 Pompey's head 1954
3 The view from Pompey's Head 1958

BATCHELOR, D.
DET. INSPECTOR JOHNSON
1 The man who loved chocolates 1962
2 On the brink 1964
3 The sedulous ape 1965

BATCHELOR, R.
SERGEANT FENWICK
1 The murder game 1970
2 Murderer's row 1970

BATES, H. E.
1 The vanished world 1969
2 The blossoming world 1971
3 The world in ripeness 1972
N.F. Autobiography

BATES, H. E.
THE LARKINS
1 The darling buds of May 1958
2 A breath of French air 1959
3 When the green woods laugh 1961
4 Oh! to be in England 1963
5 A little of what you fancy 1970
Published in one volume, 1991, as 'The Larkin Chronicles'

BATES, H. E.
UNCLE SILAS
1 My Uncle Silas 1953
2 Sugar for the horse 1957

BATESON, D.
LARRY VERNON
1 It's murder, Senorita 1954
2 The man from the rock 1955
3 The big tomorrow 1956
4 The Soho jungle 1957

5 The night is for violence 1958
6 I'll go anywhere 1959
7 I'll do anything 1960

BATTISON, B.
DET. CHIEF INSPECTOR JIM
ASHWORTH
1 The Christmas bow murder 1994
2 Fool's ransom 1994

BATTLETECH
1 Way of the clans, by R.N.Charrette
2 Bloodname, by R.N.Charrette
3 Falcon guard by R.Thurston
4 Wolf pack, by R.N.Charrette
5 Natural selection, by M.Stackpole
6 Mercenary's son, by W.H.Keith
7 The price of glory,by W.H.Keith
8 Decision at Thunder Rift, by
  W.H.Keith
9 Ideal war, by C.Kubasik
10 Blood of heroes, by A.Keith
11 Assumption of risk, by M.A
  Stackpole
  Paperback science fiction

BAUMAN, J.
1 Winter in the morning 1986
2 A dream of belonging 1988
  N.F. Autobiography of a Polish girl

BAXT, G.
1 A parade of cockeyed creatures
  1968
2 'I!', said the demon 1969

BAXTER, A.
1 Flat on my back 1974
2 Up to my neck 1975
3 Out onmy ear 1976
4 Upside down under 1977
  N.F. Humorous autobiography

BAYER, W.
LT.FRANK JANEK
1 Switch 1985
2 Wallflower 1992
3 Mirror maze 1994

BAYLEY, B.
CHRONOS
1 Collison with Chronos
2 The fall of Chronopolis
3 The knights of the limits
  Paperback science fiction

BAYLEY, B. J.
JASPERODUS
1 The soul of the robot 1974

2 The rod of light 1984
  Science fiction

BEAR, G.
1 Infinity concerto 1988
2 The serpent mage 1988
  Science fiction Published in one
  volume as 'Songs of earth and power'
  1992

BEARDSWORTH, M.
CHARLES I
1 The King's friend 1968
2 The King's endeavour 1969
3 The King's servant 1970
4 The King's adversary 1972
5 The King's contest 1975
6 The King's victory 1978

BEARE, G.
VICTOR STALLARD
1 The bloody sun at noon 1970
2 The very breath of hell 1971
3 The bee sting deal 1972

BEATON, C.
1 The wandering years, 1922-39 1964
2 The years between 1939-44 1966
3 The happy years, 1944-48 1972
4 The strenuous years, 1948-55 1973
5 The restless years, 1955-63 1976
6 The parting years, 1963-74 1978
  N.F. Autobiography

BEATON, M. C.
1 Death of a gossip 1989
2 Death of a cad 1990
  Detective stories set in rural Scotland.
  The author writes historical romance
  as M. Chesney.

BEAUVOIR, S. DE
1 Memoirs of a dutiful daughter
  1959
2 The prime of life 1963
3 Force of circumstances 1965
4 All said and done 1974
  N.F. Autobiography

BECKER, J.
1 The keep 1967
2 The union 1971
  Set in South Africa

BECKER, S.
1 The Chinese bandit 1975
2 The last mandarin 1979
3 The blue-eyed Shan 1982
  A trilogy set in the Far East, linked

by setting and contemporary
attitudes, rather than characters

BECKETT, S.
1 Molloy 1955
2 Malone dies 1956
3 The unnamable 1958
Published in one volume, 1959

BECKWITH, L.
1 About my father's business 1971
2 The hills is lonely 1959
3 The sea for breakfast 1961
4 The loud halo 1964
5 A rope in case 1968
6 Lightly poached 1973
7 Beautiful just 1975
8 Bruach blend 1978
9 The bay of strangers 1988
N.F. Autobiography. 1 is about the
author's childhood; 2-9 about her
retirement in the Hebrides.

BEDFORD, S.
1 Compass error 1968
2 A favourite of the Gods 1967
The main characters are mother and
daughter

BEDFORD, W.
1 Happiland 1990
2 All shook up 1992

BEEBEE, C.
THE HUB
1 The hub 1987
2 The main event 1989
Science fiction

BEEBY, O.
TOBY SPENCER
1 Blank cheque for murder 1968
2 The faceless men 1969
3 No profit in dying 1970
4 Too many innocents 1972

BEERE, P.
TRAUMA 2020
1 Urban prey
2 The crucifixion squad
Paperback fantasy

BEHAN, B.
1 Borstal boy 1959
2 The confessions of an Irish rebel
1965
N.F. Autobiography

BEHRMAN, S. N.
1 The Worcester account 1968
2 Tribulations and laughter 1972
N.F. Autobiography

BELL, A.
1 Corduroy 1930
2 Silver ley 1931
3 The cherry tree 1932
4 Apple acre 1942
5 Sunrise to sunset 1944

BELL, A.
ROLAND PACE
1 The balcony 1934
2 Young man's fancy 1956
3 The mill house 1958

BELL, J.
CIVIL WAR
1 To serve a Queen 1971
2 In the King's absence 1973

BELL, J.
CLAUDE WARRINGTON-REEVE, Q.C.
1 A well-known face 1960
2 A flat tyre in Fulham 1963

BELL, J.
DR.DAVID WINTRINGHAM
1 Murder in hospital 1949
2 The summer school mystery 1950
3 Death on the Borough Council
1954
4 Fall over cliff 1956
5 Death at half-term 1957
6 From natural causes 1957
7 All is vanity 1958
8 Death at the Medical Board 1959
9 Death in clairvoyance 1959
10 Bones in the barrow 1960

BELL, J.
JACOBEAN TRILOGY
1 Jacobean adventure 1969
2 Over the seas 1970
3 The dark and the light 1971
About Scottish immigrants in
Jamestown, Virginia

BELL, P.
DET.CHIEF INSPECTOR BROWNE
1 The dead do not praise 1990
2 Feast into mourning 1991
3 No pleasure in death 1992
4 The way of a serpent 1993
5 Downhill to death 1994

BELL, V.
1 The dodo 1950
2 This way home 1951
N.F. Autobiography

BELL, V.
DR. BAYNES
1 Death under the stars 1949
2 Two by day and one by night 1950
3 Death has two doors 1950
4 Death darkens council 1952
5 Death o' the night watches 1959
6 Death walks by the river 1960

BELLAIRS, G.
DET.INSPECTOR LITTLEJOHN
1 Littlejohn on leave 1941
2 Four unfaithfulservants 1941
3 Death of a busybody 1942
4 The dead shall be raised 1942
5 Murder of a quack 1943
6 Calamity at Harwood 1943
7 He'd rather be dead 1944
8 Death in the night watches 1944
9 Crime at Halfpenny Bridge 1945
10 The case of the scared rabbits 1945
11 Death on the last train 1946
12 Outrage on Gallows Hill 1946
13 The case of the seven whistlers 1947
14 The case of the famished parson 1947
15 The case of the demented spiv 1948
16 The case of the headless Jesuit 1949
17 Dead march for Penelope Blow 1949
18 Death in dark glasses 1950
19 Crime in Leper's Hollow 1950
20 A knife for Harry Dodd 1951
21 Half mast for Deemster 1952
22 Corpses in Enderby 1953
23 The cursing stones murder 1953
24 Death in Room 5 1954
25 Death treads softly 1954
26 Death drops the pilot 1955
27 Death in High Provence 1956
28 Death sends for the doctor 1956
29 Corpse at the carnival 1957
30 Murder makes mistakes 1957
31 Bones in the wilderness 1958
32 Toll the bell for murder 1959
33 Death in the fearful night 1959
34 Death in despair 1960
35 Death of a tin god 1960
36 The body in the Dumb River 1961
37 Death before breakfast 1961
38 The tormentors 1962

39 Death in the wasteland 1963
40 Surfeit of suspects 1964
41 Death of a shadow 1965
42 Death spins the wheel 1965
43 Intruder in the dark 1966
44 Strangers among the dead 1966
45 Death in desolation 1967
46 Single ticket to death 1967
47 Fatal alibi 1968
48 Murder gone mad 1969
49 Tycoon's death bed 1970
50 The night they killed Joss Varron 1971
51 Murder adrift 1972
52 Pomeroy deceased 1972
53 Devious murder 1973
54 Fear round about 1975
55 Close all roads to Sospel 1977
56 An old man dies 1980

BELLE, P.
HERON FAMILY
1 The moon in the water 1984
2 The chains of fate 1984
3 Alathea 1985 (pb) 1989 (hb)
A series set at the time of the English Civil War

BELLE, P.
WINTERCOMBE
1 Wintercombe 1988
2 Herald of joy 1989
3 A falling star 1990
4 Treason's gift 1992

BENFORD, G.
GALACTIC CENTRE
1 Great sky river 1987
2 Tides of light 1989
3 Furious gulf 1994
Science fiction

BENNETT, D.
ALLARDYCE
1 Chaos makers 1968
2 Operation chaos 1970

BENNETT, P.
CALLADINE FAMILY
1 There is a season 1976
2 The beggar's virtue 1978
3 A rough music 1980

BENNETT, W. R.
ADAM KANE
1 Man from checkmate 1971
2 Dossier on a mantis 1972

BENNETTS, P.
CESARE BORGIA
1 Borgia bull 1966
2 Borgia prince 1968

BENNETTS, P.
EDWARD I
1 A dragon for Edward 1975
2 The she-wolf 1975

BENSON, B.
RALPH LINDSAY
1 The girl in the cage 1954
2 The silver cobweb 1955
3 Broken shield 1955
4 The running man 1957
5 The end of violence 1959
6 Seven steps East 1959

BENSON, E. F.
LUCIA
1 Queen Lucia 1922
2 Miss Mapp 1922
3 Lucia in London 1927
4 Mapp and Lucia 1935
5 Lucia's progress 1935
6 Trouble for Lucia 1939
'Lucia in Wartime' (1985) and 'Lucia Triumphant' (1986), both by Tom Holt, are continuations

BENTLEY, J.
1 Proud Riley's daughter 1988
2 Sing me a new song 1990

BENTLEY, P.
TALES OF THE WEST RIDING
1 Panorama 1952
2 Take courage 1940
3 Manhold 1941
4 The house of Moreys 1953
5 Inheritance 1932
6 Carr 1929
7 Life story 1952
8 The spinner of the years 1928
9 A modern tragedy 1934
10 Sleep in peace 1938
11 The rise of Henry Morcar 1946
12 Quorum 1950
13 Noble in reason 1955
14 Love and money 1957
15 Crescendo 1958
16 Kith and Kin 1960
17 Tales ofthe West Riding 1965
18 A man of his times 1966
19 Ring in the new 1969
20 More tales of the West Riding 1974
This is the author's own arrangement.

Except for 5, 11, 18 and 19, which are sequels, characters do not reappear, but the whole gives a picture of West Riding life from the 17th century onwards.

BENTON, K.
PETER CRAIG
1 Twentyfourth level 1969
2 Sole agent 1970
3 Spy in chancery 1972
4 Craig and the Jaguar 1973
5 Craig and the Tunisian tangle 1974

BENZONI, J.
CATHERINE
1 One love is enough 1963
2 Catherine 1963
3 Belle Catherine 1966
4 Catherine and Arnaud 1967
5 Catherine and a time for love 1968
6 A snare for Catherine 1974
Historical romances set in France during the Hundred Years' War

BENZONI, J.
FALCON
1 Lure of the Falcon 1978
2 The devil's diamonds 1980

BENZONI, J.
MARIANNE
1 Marianne 1969
2 Marianne and the masked prince 1971
3 Marianne and the privateer 1972
4 Marianne and the rebels 1973
5 Marianne and the Lords of the East 1975
6 Marianne and the crown of fire 1976
Set in France during the Napoleonic Wars

BERGER, J.
1 The foot of Clive 1963
2 Corker's freedom 1964

BERGER, J.
INTO THEIR LABOURS
1 Pig earth 1979
2 Once in Europa 1987
3 Lilac and Flag

BERGER, J.
REINHART
1 Crazy in Berlin 1958
2 Reinhart in love 1963
3 Vital parts 1971

4 Reinhart's women 1982

BERGMAN, A.
JACK LEVINE
1 The big kiss-off of 1944 1975
2 Hollywood and Levine 1976

BERGMAN, I.
1 The best intentions 1993
2 Sunday's child 1994

BERKELEY, T.
1 We kept a pub 1955
2 I go on the films 1958
3 We cope with the kids 1960
   N.F. Autobiography

BERNIERES, L. DE
MACONDO
1 The war of Don Emmanual's
   nether parts 1990
2 Senor Vivo and the Coca lord 1991
3 The troublesome offspring of
   Cardinal Guzman 1992

BERRY, A.
1 Koyana
2 Labyrinth of lies 1985
   Science fiction

BEST, R.
YARROW
1 The house called Yarrow 1961
2 The honest rogue 1962
3 High tide 1964
4 Idle rainbow 1955
5 Greenwood 1967

BICKERS, R. T.
DAEDALUS QUARTET
1 The gifts of Jove 1983
2 A time for haste 1984
3 Too late the morrow 1984
4 The sure recompense 1985

BIDERMAN, B.
JOSEPH RUDKIN
1 The Genesis files 1988
2 Judgement of death 1989

BIELENBERG, C.
1 The past is myself 1984
2 The road ahead 1992
   N.F. Autobiography

BIGGINS, J.
OTTO PROHASKA
1 A sailor of Austria 1991
2 The Emperor's coloured coat 1992

3 The two-headed eagle 1993
4 Tomorrow the world 1994

BIGGLE, L. J.
JAN DARZEK
1 This darkening universe 1979
2 All the colours of darkness 1964
3 Watchers of the dark 1968
4 Silence is deadly 1980

BINCHY, D.
BRULAGH
1 The last Madonna 1991
2 The last resort 1992
3 Fireballs 1993
   Humorous stories, set in Ireland

BINGHAM, C.
1 Belgravia 1983
2 Country life 1985
3 At home 1986
   Satires on upper-class life

BINGHAM, C.
CORONET
1 Coronet among the weeds 1969
2 Coronet among the grass 1971
   N.F. Autobiography

BINGHAM, J.
SUPT. BROCK
1 Brock 1981
2 Brock and the defector 1982

BIRDSALL, J.
1 The boys and the butterflies 1988
2 Moths in the memory 1990
   N.F. Autobiography

BIRMINGHAM, M.
KATE WEATHERLEY
1 You can help me 1974
2 The heat of the sun 1976
3 Sleep in a ditch 1978
   Detective stories about a CAB adviser

BIRMINGHAM, S.
1 Our crowd 1968
2 The rest of us 1985
   N.F. Jewish immigrants in New York

BISHOP, S. P.
TRACK
1 Track
2 Partners in death
3 Apache gold
   Paperback Westerns

BISSET, SIR J.
1 Sail ho! 1958
2 Tramps and ladies 1959
3 Commodore's farewell 1960
N.F. Autobiography

BJORN, T. F.
1 Papa's wife 1953
2 Papa's daughter 1958
3 Mama's way 1959
4 Dear papa 1963
Stories of a Swedish-American pastor

BLACK, G.
PAUL HARRIS
1 Suddenly at Singapore 1959
2 Dead man calling 1961
3 A dragon for Christmas 1962
4 A wind of death 1967
5 The cold jungle 1969
6 A time for pirates 1970
7 The bitter tea 1973
8 The golden cockatrice 1974
9 A big wind forsummer 1975
10 A moon for killers 1976
11 A path for serpents 1991

BLACK, L.
EMMA GREAVES
1 The bait 1965
2 Two ladies in Verona 1967

BLACK, L.
KATE THEOBALD
1 The penny murders 1979
2 The eve of the wedding 1980
3 The Rumanian circle 1981

BLACK, V.
SISTER JOAN
1 A vow of silence 1992
2 A vow of chastity 1992
3 A vow of sanctity 1993
4 A vow of obedience 1993
5 Vow of penance 1994
6 Vow of devotion 1994
Thrillers set amongst an Order of nuns

BLACKBURN, J.
GENERAL KIRK
1 The gaunt woman 1962
2 Colonel Bogus 1964
3 A ring of roses 1965
4 Nothing but the night 1968
5 The young man from Lima 1970
6 Broken boy 1973

BLACKER, I.
GENERAL LE GRANDE & GENOPS
1 Chain of command 1965
2 The valley of Hanoi 1966
3 To hell in a basket 1967

BLACKLOCK, J. P.
1 The elfin ship
2 The disappearing dwarf

BLAIR, A.
1 A tree in the West 1979
2 The rowan on the ridge 1980

BLAISDELL, A. [E. LININGTON]
SGT. IVOR MADDOX & WILCOX ST. PRECINCT
1 Greenmask 1965
2 No evil angel 1966
3 Date with death 1967
4 Something wrong 1968
5 Policeman's lot 1969
6 Practice to deceive 1971
7 Crime by chance 1974
8 Perchance of death 1978
9 No villain need be 1979
10 Consequence of death 1981
11 Skeleton in the closet 1983
12 Felony report 1985
13 Strange felony 1986

BLAKE'S SEVEN
1 Blake's Seven, by T.Nation 1980
2 Project Avalon, by T.Hoyle 1981
3 Scorpio attack, by T. Hoyle 1981
4 Afterlife 1984
Paperback science fiction, based on the TV series

BLAKE, M. G.
AYESTHORPE SERIES
1 The Peterloo weaver 1981
2 The Peterloo inheritance 1981
3 Bitter legacy 1982
The Lancashire cotton trade in the Industrial Revolution

BLAKE, N. [C. DAY LEWIS]
NIGEL STRANGEWAYS
1 A question of proof 1935
2 Thou shell of death 1936
3 There's trouble brewing 1937
4 The beast must die 1938
5 The smiler with the knife 1939
6 Malice in wonderland 1940
7 The case of the abominable snowman 1941
8 Minute for murder 1947
9 Head of a traveller 1949

10 The dreadful hollow 1953
11 The whisper in the gloom 1954
12 End of a chapter 1958
13 Widow's cruise 1959
14 The worm of death 1960
15 The morning after death 1966

BLAKESTON, O.
1 And then the screaming started 1968
2 For crying out loud 1970

BLAMIRES, H.
TRILOGY OF HEAVEN AND HELL
1 The devil's hunting ground 1954
2 Cold war in hell 1955
3 Blessing unbounded 1956

BLANC, S.
MIGUEL MERNANDES
1 The green stone 1963
2 The yellow villa 1964
3 The rose window 1968

BLATTY, W.
1 The exorcist 1971
2 Legion 1983

BLEASDALE, A.
SCULLY
1 Scully 1975
2 Who's been sleeping in my bed? 1977

BLEECK, O.
PHILIP ST.IVES
1 Brass go-between 1970
2 Protocol for a kidnapping 1971
3 The thief who painted sunlight 1973
4 The highbinders 1974
5 No questions asked 1976

BLISH, J.
AFTER SUCH KNOWLEDGE
1 A case of conscience 1959
2 Dr.Mirabilis 1962
3 Black easter 1969
4 The day after judgement 1972

BLISH, J.
CITIES IN FLIGHT
1 They shall have stars
2 A life for the stars
3 Earthman come home
4 A clash of cymbals
Paperback science fiction

BLISHEN, E.
1 Roaring boys 1964
2 This right soft lot 1969
3 A cack-handed war 1972
4 Uncommon entrance 1974
5 Sorry,Dad 1977
6 A nest of teachers 1980
7 Shaky relations 1981
8 Lizzie Pye 1982
9 Donkey work 1983
10 A second skin 1984
11 Outside contributor 1986
12 The disturbance fee 1988
13 The penny world 1990
N.F. The author calls it 'Recycling my memories'

BLOCH, R.
1 Psycho 1960
2 Psycho 2 1986

BLOCK, L.
BERNIE RHODENBARR
1 Burglars can't be choosers 1979
2 The burglar in the closet 1980
3 The burglar who liked to quote Kipling 1981
4 The burglar who studied Spinoza 1982
5 The burglar who painted like Mondrian 1984

BLOCK, L.
EVAN TANNER
1 The thief who couldn't sleep
2 The cancelled Czech
3 Tanner's twelve swingers
4 Two for Tanner
5 Tanner's tiger
6 Here comes a hero
7 Me Tanner, you Jane

BLOCK, L.
LEO HAIG
1 Five little rich girls 1984
2 The topless tulip caper 1984

BLOCK, L.
MATTHEW SCUDDER
1 Sins of the fathers 1978
2 Time to murder and create 1979
3 In the midst of death 1980
4 A stab in the dark 1982
5 Eight million ways to die 1983
6 When the sacred ginmill closes 1987
7 Out on the cutting edge 1988
8 A ticket to the boneyard 1990

9 A dance at the slaughterhouse 1991
10 A walk among the tombstones 1992
11 The devil knows you're dead 1994

BLOOM, U.
1 Victorian vinaigrette 1956
2 The elegant Edwardian 1957
3 Youth at the gate 1959
4 Down to the sea in ships 1957
5 War isn't wonderful 1961
6 Life is no fairytale 1976
N.F. Autobiography

BLOOM, U.
NO LADY
1 Log on no lady 1940
2 No lady buys a cot 1943
3 No lady in bed 1944
4 No lady with a pen 1947
5 No lady meets a gentleman 1947
6 No lady in the cart 1949
7 Mum's girl was no lady 1950
8 No lady on the spree 1954
9 No lady has a dog's day 1956
N.F. Autobiography

BLOOM, U.
PALESTINE TRILOGY
1 Now Barabbas was a robber 1977
2 Pilate's wife 1978
3 Song of Salome 1978

BLOOM, U.
REVEREND BLOOM
1 Parson extraordinary 1963
2 Price above rubies 1965
N.F. Biography of her father

BLOOM, U.
ROSEMARY
1 Rosemary for Stratford on Avon 1966
2 Rosemary for Frinton 1970
3 Rosemary for Chelsea 1971
N.F. Reminiscences of the places in which the author has lived.

BLUMENFELD, J.
1 Pin a rose on me 1960
2 See me dance the polka 1962
N.F. Autobiography

BLUNT, B.
1 Treacherous moon
2 Deep ran the river 1986
3 Star sapphire 1988

BLUNT, W.
1 Married to a single life 1983
2 Slow on the feather 1986
N.F. Autobiography

BOAST, P.
1 London's child 1987
2 The millionaire 1989
3 London's daughter 1992

BOGARDE, D.
1 A postillion struck by lightning 1977
2 Snakes and ladders 1978
3 An orderly man 1983
4 Backcloth 1986
5 A particular friendship 1989
N.F.Autobiography

BOGGIS, D.
1 Killer instinct 1980
2 A time to betray 1981

BOISSARD, J.
MOREAU FAMILY
1 A matter of feeling 1979
2 Christmas lessons 1984
3 A time to choose 1986

BOLAND, J.
COUNTERPOL
1 Counterpol 1963
2 Counterpol in Paris 1964

BOLAND, J.
THE GENTLEMEN
1 The League of Gentlemen 1960
2 The gentlemen reform 1961
3 The gentlemen at large 1962

BOLITHO, J.
DET.CHIEF INSPECTOR IAN ROPER
1 Kindness can kill 1993
2 Ripe for revenge 1994
3 Motive for murder 1994

BOLTON, M.
LAWSON OF SPECIAL BRANCH
1 The softener 1986
2 The testing 1987

BOND, M.
M.PAMPLEMOUSSE
1 Monsieur Pamplemousse 1983
2 Monsieur Pamplemousse and the secret mission 1985
3 Monsieur Pamplemousse on the spot 1986

4 Monsieur Pamplemousse takes the cure 1987
5 Monsieur Pamplemousse aloft 1988
6 Monsieur Pamplemousse investigates 1990
7 Monsieur Pamplemousse rests his case 1991
8 Monsieur Pamplemousse on location 1992
9 Monsieur Pamplemousse takes the train 1993

BONE, E.
1 Thirty years hard 1964
2 Seven years solitary 1960
N.F. Autobiography

BONETT, J. & E.
INSPECTOR BORGES
1 Better dead 1964
2 The private face of murder 1965
3 This side murder 1967
4 The sound of murder 1970
5 No time to kill 1972

BONFIGLIOLI, C.
CHARLIE MORTDECAI
1 Don't point that thing at me 1974
2 Something nasty in the woodshed 1977
3 After you with the pistol 1979

BONINGTON, C.
1 I chose to climb 1966
2 The next horizon 1973
N.F. Autobiography

BOONE, J. C.
REMINGTON
1 Lawman's justice 1988
2 Showdown at Comanche Butte 1988
3 West of the Pecos 1989
4
5 Wyoming blood trail 1990

BORG, J.
HOGLEG BAILEY
1 Hellbent trail 1953
2 Sheriff of Clinton 1954
3 Cannon Kid 1955
4 Big Cherokee 1956
5 Sheriff's deputy 1956
6 Bushwhack Canyon 1956
7 Bronco justice 1957
8 Gunsmoke feud 1957
9 Rawhide tenderfoot 1958
10 Cherokee trail 1958

11 Kansas trail 1958
12 Badlands fury 1959
13 Rustler's range 1959
14 Range wolves 1960
15 Saddle tramp 1960
16 Horsethieves hang high 1961
17 Kid with a Colt 1961
18 Guns of the lawless 1962
19 Cast a wide loop 1963
20 Texas wolves 1963
21 Gun feud at Sun Creek 1964
22 Rope for a rustler 1965
23 Stagecoach to Concho 1966
24 Owlhooter 1968
25 Dry Valley war 1968

BORGEN, J.
WILFRED SAGEN
1 Lillelord 1955
2 The dark springs 1956
3 We've got him now 1957
A trilogy about a Norwegian adolescent and his awakening social conscience. Vol. 1 only in English

BORGES, J. L.
1 Six problems for Don Isidro Parodi 1981
2 Chronicles of Bustos Domecq 1982
Short stories featuring the same characters

BOSSE, M.
ASIAN SAGA
1 The warlord 1984
2 Fire in Heaven 1986

BOTTOME, P.
1 Search for a soul 1947
2 Challenge 1952
N.F. Autobiography

BOURNE, P.
1 Black saga 1953
2 Ten thousand shall die 1954

BOVA, B.
KINSMAN SAGA
1 Kinsman 1965
2 Millenium 1976
3 Colony 1979

BOVA, B.
ORION
1 Orion 1984
2 Vengeance of Orion 1988
3 Orion in the dying time 1991

BOVA, B.
VOYAGERS
1 Voyagers 1986
2 The alien within 1987
3 Star brothers 1990
Science fiction

BOWDEN, J.
DAN MCCOY
1 Return of the Sheriff
2 Wayman's Ford
3 Two gun justice
4 Roaring Valley
5 Revenge in Red Springs
6 Black Water Canyon
7 Brazo feud
8 Guns along the Brazo
9 Gun loose

BOWERS, E.
MEG LACEY
1 Ladies night 1990
2 No forwarding address 1993

BOWIE, J.
1 Penny buff 1975
2 Penny boss 1976
3 Penny change 1977
*N.F. Autobiography of a Clydeside
teacher*

BOWLES, C.
MIKE HAZZARD
1 Flying blind 1986
2 Flying Hazzard 1987

BOWLING, H.
1 Gaslight in Page Street 1991
2 The girl from Cotton Lane 1992

BOWRING, M.
1 The animals came first 1976
2 Animals before breakfast 1978
3 Animals round the clock 1981
N.F.Autobiography of a vet

BOX, E. [G. VIDAL]
PETER CUTLER
1 Death in the fifth position 1954
2 Death before bedtime 1955
3 Death likes it hot 1955

BOYD, M.
THE LANGTONS
1 The cardboard clown 1952
2 A difficult young man 1955
3 Outbreak of love 1957

4 Much in evidence 1957
*Novels about an Anglo-Australian
family*

BOYD, N.
FATHER DUDDLESWELL
1 Bless me,Father 1976
2 A Father before Christmas 1978
3 Father in a fix 1979
4 Father under fire 1980
5 Bless me again, Father 1981
Stories about a Catholic priest

BOYER, E. H.
WORLD OF THE ALFAR
1 The sword and the satchel
2 The elves and the otterskin
3 The thrall and the dragon's heart
4 The wizard and the warlord
5 The troll's grindstone
6 The curse of Slagfid
Paperback fantasy

BOYER, R.
DOC ADAMS
1 Billingsgate shoal 1985
2 Penny Ferry 1985
3 Moscow metal 1988

BOYLAN, C.
1 Home rule 1992
2 Holy pictures 1989

BOYLE, D.
COMMANDER MORETON SHADE
1 Strange corpse on Murder Mile
1960
2 Death at Devil-Fish Point 1961

BOYLE, J.
1 A sense of freedom 1977
2 The pain of confinement 1984
N.F.Prison diaries

BOYLE, T.
DET.FRANCIS DE SALES
1 Only the dead know Brooklyn
1987
2 Post-mortem effects 1988
3 Brooklyn three 1991

BRADDON, R.
1 The naked island 1951
2 End of a hate 1958
*N.F. Autobiography of a former
P. O. W. in Japan*

BRADFORD, B. T.
EMMA HARTE
1 A woman of substance 1979
2 Hold the dream 1985
3 To be the best 1988

BRADLEY, H.
1 And Miss Carter wore pink 1971
2 Miss Carter came with us 1973
3 In the beginning,said Great Aunt Jane 1975
4 The Queen who came to tea 1978
   N.F.Reminiscences of Lancashire in Edwardian days, told mainly in pictures.

BRADLEY, J.
BATTLESQUAD
1 Alamein attack 1982
2 Slaughter in Sicily 1983
3 Killer winter 1983
4 Bloody bridgehead 1984

BRADLEY, M. Z.
DARKOVER
1 Darkover landfall
2 The spell sword 1990
3 Star of danger 1993
4 Shattered chain
5 The winds of Darkover
6 The bloody sun
7 Sword of Aldones
8 Heritage of Hastur
9 The planet savers
10 The world wreckers 1989
11 Hunters of the red moon
12 The forbidden tower 1994
13 Stormqueen 1989
14 Two to conquer
15 Sharra's exile
16 Thendara House
17 City of sorcery 1990
18 The heirs of Hammerfell 1991
   Fantasy. Dates given are for hardback editions

BRADSHAW, G.
ARTHUR AND GAWAIN
1 Hawk of May 1981
2 Kingdom of summer 1982
3 In Winter's shadow 1982

BRADY, J.
MATT MINOGUE
1 A stone of the heart 1988
2 Unholy ground 1989
3 Kaddish in Dublin 1990

BRADY, T. & BINGHAM, C.
1 Victoria 1972
2 Victoria and company 1974

BRADY, W. S.
HAWK
1 The sudden guns
2 Blood money
3 Death's bounty
4 Killing time
5 Fool's gold
6 Blood kin
7 The gates of death
8 Desperadoes
9 The widowmaker
10 Dead man's hand
11 Sierra gold
12 Death and Jack Shade
13 Killer's breed
14 Border war
   Paperback Westerns

BRADY, W. S.
PEACEMAKER
1 Comanche
2 Outlaws
3 Whiplash
4 Lynch law
5 Blood run
6 War party
7 $1000 death
8
9 Shootout
   Paperback Westerns

BRAGG, M.
TALLENTIRE FAMILY
1 The hired man 1968
2 A place in England 1970
3 Kingdom come 1980
   A family chronicle set in Cumbria

BRAINE, J.
1 One and last love 1981
2 These golden days 1985
   Novels based on incidents in the author's life

BRAINE, J.
CLIVE AND ROBIN LENDRICK
1 Stay with me till morning 1970
2 The two of us 1984
3 My one true love 1985

BRAINE, J.
JOE LAMPTON
1 Room at the top 1959
2 Life at the top 1962

BRAINE, J.
XAVIER FLYNN
1 The pious agent 1975
2 Finger of fire 1977

BRAITHWAITE, E. R.
1 To Sir, with love 1959
2 Paid servant 1962
   N.F. Autobiography

BRAITHWAITE, R.
A YORKSHIRE TRILOGY
1 Martha 1983
2 Ben 1984
3 The house in Kingston Square
   1985
   The history of a Bridlington family

BRAMBLE, F.
1 Regent Square 1978
2 The iron roads 1982
   Set in 18th century England

BRAND, C.
INSPECTOR COCKERILL
1 Death in high heels 1939
2 Heads you lose 1944
3 Green for danger 1945
4 Suddenly at his residence 1947
5 Death of Jezebel 1948
6 Cat and mouse 1950
7 London particular 1954
8 Tour de force 1955

BRANDNER, G.
THE HOWLING
1 The howling
2 The return
3 Echoes
   Paperback horror stories

BRANDON, J. G.
A.S.PENNINGTON
1 The Cork Street crime
2 Death in the ditch
3 Mr. Pennington goes nap
4 Mr.Pennington comes through
5 Mr.Pennington barges in
6 Mr.Pennington sees red
7 The riverside mystery 1950
8 Murder in Mayfair
9 One-minute murder
10 The pawnshop murder
11 The snatch game
12 The Bond Street murders
13 Death in D Division
14 Death in Downing Street

15 Death in Jermyn Street
16 Death foils the gang
17 M is for murder
18 The call-girl murders 1954
19 The case of the would-be widow
   1955
20 The coffin rode on 1955
21 Murderer's stands 1956
22 Murder on the beam 1956
23 Death of a Greek 1957
24 Death of a socialite 1957
25 Death stalks in Soho 1958
26 Murder in Pimlico 1958
27 Murder comes smiling 1959
28 Death of a mermaid 1960

BRANDON, J. G.
INSPECTOR MCCARTHY
1 The blue print murders
2 Candidate for a coffin
3 The crooked fire
4 The case of the withering hand
5 Death burns swiftly
6 Death in the quarry
7 Death in duplicate
8 Death on delivery
9 The dragnet
10 The espionage killings
11 The 50 marriage case
12 The frame up
13 Fingerprints never lie
14 The hand of Seeta
15 The mail van mystery
16 The mark of Fang
17 Murder at the Yard
18 Murder in Soho
19 Murder for a million
20 McCarthy, C.I.D.
21 The night club murder
22 The Regent Street raid
23 A scream in Soho
24 The transport murders 1955
25 Yellow gods 1956
26 Bonus for murder 1957
27 The corpse from the City 1958

BRANDON, R.
ANDREW TAGGART
1 Mind out 1991
2 The gorgon's smile 1992

BRASON, J.
1 Secret army 1978
2 Secret army dossier 1979
3 End of the line 1980
4 Kessler 1981
   *Novels about the Belgian Resistance
   in WW2. No. 4 is about their*

*attempts to trace war criminals 30
years later.*

BRASON, J.
HOWARD'S WAY
1 Howard's way 1986
2 Howard's way 2 1987
3 Howard's way 3 1988
Based on the TV series

BRATA, S.
1 My god died young 1968
2 Confessions of an Indian woman-
  eater 1971
3 A traitor to India 1976
*N.F. Autobiography of an Indian
Brahmin*

BRAUN, L. J.
QWILLERAN AND KOKO
1 The cat who could read
  backwards 1966
2 The cat who ate Danish modern
  1967
3 The cat who turned on and off
  1968
4 The cat who played Brahms 1970
5 The cat who played Post Office
  1987
6 The cat who knew Shakespeare
  1989
7 The cat who saw red 1990
8 The cat who sniffed glue 1990
9 The cat who had 14 tales 1990
10 The cat who went underground
  1990
11 The cat who talked to ghosts 1990
12 The cat who lived high 1991
13 The cat who knew a Cardinal 1991
14 The cat who moved a mountain
  1992
15 The cat who wasn't there 1993
16 The cat who went into the closet
  1993
17 The cat who came to breakfast
  1994

BRAUN, M.
LUKE STARBUCK
1 Hangman's Creek
2 Jury of six
3 The spoilers
4 Tombstone
5 Manhunter
6 Deadwood
7 The Judas tree
Paperback Westerns

BRAY, D.
CAPTAIN DAVY
1 Between two shores 1984
2 The captain
*Naval adventure stories set in the
18th C.*

BREAM, F.
REV.JABAL JARRETT
1 The Vicar done it 1982
2 The Vicar investigates 1983
3 Sealed and despatched 1984
4 With murder in mind 1985
5 The problem at Piha 1986

BREEN, J.
JERRY BROGAN
1 Vicar's roses 1984
2 The gathering place 1984
3 Triple crown 1985
4 Loose lips 1990

BREESE, A.
1 Setting out 1981
2 A loving imprint 1982

BREEZE, P.
1 While my guitar gently weeps
  1979
2 Back street runner 1980

BREMOND D'ARS, Y DE
1 In the heart of Paris 1959
2 An antique dealer's tale 1961
3 The chest with a secret 1964
*N.F. Anecdotes of an antique dealer in
Paris*

BRENNAN, C. M.
INNER PLANETS TRILOGY
1 First power play
2 Two prime squared
3 Matrix cubed

BRENNAN, C. M.
INVADERS OF CHARON
1 The genesis web
2 Nomads of the sky
Paperback fantasy

BRENNAN, C. M.
MARTIAN WARS TRILOGY
1 Rebellion 2456
2 Hammer of Mars
3 Armageddon of Vesta
Paperback s. f.

BRENNAN, J. H.
DEMONSPAWN
1 Firewolf
2 Crypts of terror
Paperback horror stories

BRENT, N.
BARNEY HYDE
1 The scarlet lily
2 Motive for murder
3 Blood in the bank
4 Dig the grave deep
5 Murder swings high
6 The leopard died too 1957
7 The golden angel 1959
8 Badger in the dusk 1960
9 No space for murder 1960
10 Spider in the web 1961

BRETT, S.
CHARLES PARIS SERIES
1 Cast in order of disappearance 1975
2 So much blood 1976
3 Star trap 1977
4 An amateur corpse 1978
5 A comedian dies 1979
6 Dead side of the mike 1980
7 Situation tragedy 1981
8 Murder unprompted 1982
9 Murder in the title 1983
10 Not dead only resting 1984
11 Dead giveaway 1985
12 What bloody man is that? 1987
13 A series of murders 1989
14 Corporate bodies 1991
15 A reconstructed corpse 1993

BRETT, S.
MRS.PARGETER SERIES
1 A nice class of corpse 1986
2 Mrs.,presumed dead 1988
3 Mrs.Pargeter's package 1990
4 Mrs.Pargeter's pound of flesh 1992

BRIDGE, A.
JULIA PROBYN
1 The lighthearted quest 1956
2 The Portuguese quest 1956
3 The numbered account 1960
4 The dangerous islands 1964
5 Emergency in the Pyrenees 1965
6 The episode at Toledo 1967
7 The malady in Madeira 1969
2 and 6 are direct sequels

BRIDGWOOD, C.
STEINS OF GRAYLINGS
1 This wicked generation 1987

2 The dew of heaven 1989

BRIERLEY, D.
CODY
1 Cold war 1979
2 Blood group O 1980
3 Skorpion's death 1985
4 Snowline 1986

BRIGGS, V.
THE WAY AHEAD
1 Sacred ground 1975
2 Reap the harvest 1976
3 Yours is the earth 1977
A family saga set in Bristol and the Cotswolds

BRIGHT, P.
1 Life in our hands 1955
2 Breakfast at night 1956
3 The day's end 1959
N.F. Autobiography of a nurse

BRIN, D.
1 Startide rising
2 The uplift war
Paperback science fiction

BRINDLEY, L.
1 They must have seen me coming 1980
2 There's one born every minute 1982
3 Vicky and I 1984
Semi-autobiographical stories about the warden of an Old Peoples' Home

BRINDLEY, L.
TANQUILLAN
1 Tanquillan 1986
2 The tender leaves of hope 1987
3 Our summer faces 1988

BRINTON, H.
JOHN& SALLY STRANG
1 Death to windward 1952
2 One down and two to slay 1953
3 Now like to die 1955
4 Coppers and gold 1957
5 Drug on the market 1958

BRITTAIN, V.
1 Testament of youth 1933
2 Testament of experience 1957
N.F. Autobiography

BRITTAIN, V.
DIARIES
1 Chronicle of youth 1984

2 Chronicle of friendship 1986
3 Wartime chronicle 1989

BROCH, H.
THE SLEEPWALKERS
1 The romantic 1888
2 The anarchist 1903
3 The realist 1918
Reprinted under the title of the series in 1986

BROCKWAY, F., LORD
1 Inside the left 1960
2 Outside the right 1962
N.F. Autobiography

BROD, D. C.
QUINT MCCAULEY
1 Murder in store 1990
2 Error in judgement 1991
3 Masquerade in blue 1992

BRODE, A.
1 Picture of a country vicarage 1952
2 To bed on Thursday 1958
N.F. Autobiography

BRODIE, G.
JOHN BORHAM
1 The lady had a tiger 1967
2 Poison of poppies 1968
3 Who called diamonds? 1969

BROMIGE, I.
THE RAINWOOD FAMILY
1 The quiet hills 1966
2 The stepdaughter 1967
3 An April girl 1969
4 The tangled wood 1969
5 A sheltering tree 1970
6 A magic place 1971
7 A bend in the river 1975
8 The distant song 1977
9 The happy fortress 1978
10 The years between 1991

BROMLEY, G.
INSPECTOR SEVERN
1 In the absence of the body 1972
2 Chance to poison 1973

BRONTE, C.
JANE EYRE
'The quiet stranger' by R. Kydd, 1991 is a pendant. The main characters are Richard Mason and his sister who becomes Rochester's mad wife.

BRONTE, E.
1 Wuthering Heights
Heathcliff: the return to Wuthering Heights, by L. Haire-Sargeant 1992

BROOKE, CASSANDRA
1 Dear Venus 1992
2 With much love 1993

BROOKE, J.
ORCHID TRILOGY
1 The military orchid
2 A mine of serpents
3 The goose cathedral
Autobiographical novels. Published in 1 vol., 1981

BROOKE, K.
EXPATRIA
1 Expatria 1991
2 Expatria incorporated 1992

BROOKE-ROSE, C.
JIB AND JAB
1 Xorandor 1986
2 Verbivore 1990

BROOKS, J.
1 Jampot Smith 1962
2 Smith as hero 1964
Thre diary of a young man, as an adolescent and as a Naval Officer

BROOKS, T.
MAGIC KINGDOM OF LANDOVER
1 Magic kingdom for sale/sold 1986
2 The black unicorn 1988
3 Wizard at large 1988
4 The tangle box 1994
Fantasy

BROOKS, T.
SHANNARA
1 Sword of Shannara 1981
2 Elfstones of Shannara 1982
3 Wishsong of Shannara 1984
Fantasy, originally published in paperback

BROOKS, T.
THE HERITAGE OF SHANNARA
1 The scions of Shannara 1990
2 The Druid of Shannara 1991
3 The Elf-Queen of Shannara 1992
4 The talismans of Shannara 1993

BROSNAN, J.
SKY LORDS TRILOGY
1 The sky lords 1988
2 War of the sky lords 1989
3 The fall of the sky lords 1991
Science fiction

BROUN, D.
HARRY EGYPT, MASTER CRIMINAL
1 The subject of Harry Egypt 1963
2 Egypt's choice 1964

BROWN, CARTER
AL WHEELER
1 Girl in a shroud
2 The dame 1959
3 The passionate 1959
4 The temptress 1960
5 The velvet vixen 1964
6 A corpse for Christmas 1965
7 The corpse 1966
8 Target for their dark desire 1968
Paperback thrillers

BROWN, CARTER
DANNY BOYD
1 Nymph to the slaughter
2 Wayward wahine
3 Siren signs off 1958
4 Walk softly, witch 1959
5 The sometimes wife 1965
6 Catch me a phoenix 1965
7 Terror comes creeping 1967

BROWN, CARTER
MAVIS SEIDLITZ
1 None but the lethal heart 1959
2 Lament for a lousy lover 1968

BROWN, CARTER
RICK HELMAN
1 Who killed Dr.Sex?
2 Blonde on a broomstick 1963
3 Murder is a package deal 1964
4 The white bikini 1965
5 The girl from outer space 1965
6 Nude - with a view 1965
7 No tears from the widow 1968

BROWN, D.
MAJOR PAT MCLANAHAN
1 Flight of the old dog 1988
2 Day of the Cheetah 1989
3 Night of the hawk 1992
Aviation thrillers

BROWN, D.
REAR ADMIRAL IAN HARDCASTLE
1 Hammerheads 1988

2 Storming heaven 1994

BROWN, EDWARD
MAJOR TITTERTON
1 A penny to spend 1966
2 Vandersely 1967

BROWN, FRANCES
ROMANY SERIES
1 The haresfoot legacy 1990
2 Dancing on the rainbow 1991
3 The other sister 1992

BROWN, FREDERIC
ED HUNTER
1 The fabulous clipjoint 1947
2 The dead ringer 1948
3 Murder in moonlight 1950
4 Death has many doors 1952
5 Compliments of a friend 1951
6 The late lamented 1957
7 Mrs.Murphy's underpants 1964

BROWN, HOSANNA
FRANK LE ROUX
1 Ispy, you die 1984
2 Death upon a spear 1986

BROWN, M.
1 Playing the Jack 1988
2 The heart has its reasons 1992
Not true sequels, but some of the characters appear in both novels.

BROWN, R.
1 Then the woods became the trees 1965
2 A forest is a long time growing 1967

BROWNE, D. G.
MR.HARVEY TUKE
1 What beckoning ghost 1947
2 Too many cousins 1953
3 Rustling end 1954
4 Death in perpetuity 1956
5 Death in seven volumes 1958
6 Sergeant Death 1961

BRUCE, J.
SECRET AGENT OSS17
1 Deep freeze 1963
2 Short wave 1964
3 Double take 1964
4 Flash point 1965
5 Pole reaction 1965
6 Shock tactics 1965
7 Live wire 1966
8 Softsell 1966

9 Photo finish 1967
10 Hot line 1967
11 High treason 1968
12 Top secret 1968
13 Cold spell 1968
14 Dead silence 1969
15 Strip tease 1969

BRUCE, L.
CAROLUS DEENE
1 Cold blood 1952
2 At death's door 1955
3 Death of cold 1956
4 Dead for a ducat 1956
5 Dead man's shoes 1958
6 A louse for the hangman 1959
7 Our jubilee is death 1959
8 Jack on the gallows tree 1960
9 Furious old women 1960
10 A bone and a hank of hair 1960
11 Die all, die merrily 1961
12 Nothing like blood 1961
13 Crack of doom 1962
14 Death in Albert Park 1963
15 Death at Hallows End 1963
16 Death in the Black Sands 1964
17 Death at St.Asprey's School 1967
18 Death of a commuter 1967
19 Death on Romney Marsh 1968
20 Death with blue ribbon 1969
21 Death on All-Hallowe'en 1970
22 Death by the lake 1971
23 Death in the middle watch 1974
24 Death of a bovver boy 1974

BRUCE, L.
SERGEANT BEEF
1 The case of three detectives 1935
2 The case wothout a corpse 1937
3 The case with no conclusion 1939
4 The case with four clowns 1939
5 The case with ropes and rings 1939
6 The case of Sergeant Beef 1947

BRUNNER, J.
1 Stand at Zanzibar 1972
2 The sheep look up 1974

BRUNNER, J.
MAX CURFEW
1 A plague on both your causes 1969
2 God men do nothing 1970
3 Honky in the woodpile 1971

BRUST, S.
VLAD TALTOS
1 Jhereg 1990

2 Yeudi 1990
3 Teckla 1990
4 Taltos 1990

BRUTON, E.
CITY OF LONDON POLICE
1 The laughing policeman 1963
2 The Finsbury mob 1964
3 The Smithfield slayer 1965
4 The wicked saint 1965
5 The firebug 1967

BRYAN, J.
RICHARD SARET
1 The difference to me 1956
2 The contessa came too 1957
3 The man who came back 1958

BRYANT, SIR A.
NAPOLEONIC WARS
1 The years of endurance (1793-1802) 1942
2 The years of victory (1802-1812) 1944
3 The age of elegance (1812-1822) 1950
   N.F. *History of England*

BRYANT, SIR A.
SAMUEL PEPYS
1 The man in the making 1933
2 The years of peril 1935
3 The saviour of the Navy 1938
   N.F.

BRYANT, SIR A.
THE STORY OF ENGLAND
1 Makers of the realm 1953
2 The age of chivalry 1963

BRYCE, I.
1 Canals are my home 1979
2 Canals are my life 1982
   N.F.Autobiography

BUCHAN, S. C.
VICTORIAN TRILOGY
1 Cousin Harriet 1959
2 Dashbury Park 1960
3 A stone in a pool 1961

BUCKLEY, E.
1 For benefits received 1959
2 Fiorana 1961

BUCKLEY, E.
SANDOR RAIMANN
1 They walk on earth 1966
2 The man on the rope 1966

3 Diamonds in the family 1967
4 The flaming sword 1969
Novels about a musician-healer

BUCKLEY, E.
VIENNESE SAGA
1 Blue Danube
2 Family from Vienna

BUCKLEY, W. F.
BLACKFORD OAKES
1 Saving the Queen 1976
2 Stained glass 1978
3 Who's on first? 1980
4 The story of Henri Tod 1984
5 Marco polo if you can 1982
6 See you later,alligator 1986
7 High jinx 1987
8 Mongoose R.I.P. 1988
9 Tucker's last stand 1991

BUDD, M.
1 Dust to dust 1966
2 Prospect of love 1969
3 Fit for a duchess 1970
N.F. Family history

BUDE, J.
DET.INSPECTOR MEREDITH
1 The Cornish coast murder
2 The Cheltenham Square murder
3 Hand on the alibi
4 Loss of a head
5 Death on paper
6 Death of a cad
7 Death knows no calendar
8 Death deals a double
9 Slow vengeance
10 Death in ambush
11 Death in white pyjamas
12 Trouble brewing
13 Death makes a prophet
14 Dangerous sunlight
15 A glint of red herrings
16 Death steals the show
17 The constable and the lady
18 Death on the Riviera
19 When the case was opened
20 Twice dead
21 So much is dark 1954
22 Two ends to the town 1955
23 Shift of guilt 1957
24 Telegram from Le Touquet 1956
25 Another man's shadow 1957

BUDE, J.
INSPECTOR SHERWOOD
1 The night the fog came down 1958
2 A twist of the rope 1958

BUECHNER, T. F.
LEO BEBB,EVANGELIST
1 Lion country 1971
2 Open heart 1972
3 The love feast 1975
4 Treasure hunt 1978

BULL, P.
1 To sea in a sieve 1956
2 Bulls in the meadows 1957
3 I know the face but... 1959
4 I say, look here 1965
5 It isn't all Greek to me 1967
6 Life is a cucumber 1973
N.F. Autobiography

BULLETT, G.
1 The daughter of Mrs.Peacock 1956
2 The Peacock brides 1958

BULMER, K.
SEA WOLF
1 Steel shark
2 Shark north
3 Shark pack
4 Shark hunt
5 Shark Africa
6 Shark raid
7 Shark America
8 Shark trap
*Originally in paperback, under
Krauss, B. Most published in
hardback 1983-5*

BUNTING, J.
BRITISH INTERNATIONAL AIRWAYS
1 Devil mountain 1968
2 Flight of the lobster 1970
3 Vapour trail 1972

BURDEN, P.
DET.CHIEF SUPT.BASSETT
1 Screaming bones 1989
2 Wreath of honesty 1990
3 Bury him kindly 1991
4 Father,forgive me 1993

BURGESS, A.
ENDERBY
1 Inside Mr.Enderby 1964
2 Enderby outside 1968
3 The clockwork testament,or
Enderby's end 1974
4 Enderby's dark lady or No end to
Enderby 1984

BURGESS, E.
HARRY TONG
1 A killing frost 1961

2 Deadly deceit 1963
3 Closely confined 1968

BURGH, A.
DAUGHTERS OF A GRANITE LAND
1 The azure bowl 1989
2 The golden butterfly 1990
3 The stone mistress 1991
   A family chronicle set in Cornwall

BURKE, J.
DR.CASPIAN
1 The devil's footsteps 1976
2 Black charade 1977
3 Ladygrove 1978
   Supernatural stories

BURKE, J.
MIKE MERRIMAN
1 Fear by instalments 1960
2 Deadly downbeat 1962

BURKE, J. L.
DAVE ROBICHEAUX
1 The neon rain 1989
2 Heaven's prisoners 1990
3 Black cherry blues 1991
4 In the electric mist with the
   Confederate dead 1993
5 Dixie city jam 1994

BURKHOLZ, H.
1 The sensitives 1988
2 Strange bedfellows 1989
3 Brain damage 1992

BURKHOLZ, H. & IRVING, C.
MANCUSO AND BORGNEFF
1 The death freak 1983
2 The sleeping spy 1984

BURLAND, B.
JAMES BERKELEY
1 A fall from aloft 1968
2 A few flowers for St.George 1969

BURLEY, W. J.
DET.SUPT.WYCLIFFE
1 Three-toed pussy 1969
2 To kill a cat 1970
3 Guilt edged 1971
4 Death in a salubrious place 1972
5 Death in Stanley Street 1973
6 Wycliffe and the pea green boat
   1975
7 Wycliffe and the schoolgirls 1976
8 Wycliffe and the scapegoat 1978
9 Wycliffe in Paul's Court 1980
10 Wycliffe's wild goose chase 1982

11 Wycliffe and the Beales 1983
12 Wycliffe and the four Jacks 1985
13 Wycliffe and the quiet virgin 1986
14 Wycliffe and the Winsor Blue 1987
15 Wycliffe and the tangled web 1988
16 Wycliffe and the cycle of death
   1990
17 Wycliffe and the dead flautist 1991
18 Wycliffe and the last rites 1992
19 Wycliffe and the dunes mystery
   1993

BURLEY, W. J.
DR. PYM
1 A taste of power 1966
2 Death in willow pattern 1969

BURNETT, W. R.
1 Adobe walls 1955
2 Pale moon 1957

BURNLEY, J.
1 The wife 1977
2 Unrepentant women 1982
3 The woman herself 1986

BURNS, P.
1 Stacey's flyer 1986
2 Kezzy 1988

BURNS, R.
GABE WAGER
1 The Alvarez journal
2 The Farnsworth score
3 Speak for the dead
4 Angle of attack
5 The avenging angel
6 Strip search
7 Ground money

BURR, S.
LISA LONGLAND
1 Life with Lisa 1958
2 Leave it to Lisa 1959

BURROUGHS, E. R.
MARTIAN SERIES
1 A princess of Mars
2 The gods of Mars
3 The warlord of Mars
4 Thuvia, maid of Mars
5 Chessmen of Mars
6 A fighting man of Mars
7 Master mind of Mars
8 Synthetic men of Mars
9 Swords of Mars
10 Llana of Gathol
11 John Carter of Mars
   Available in paperback only.

BURROUGHS, E. R.
PELLUCIDAR SERIES
1 At the earth's core
2 Pellucidar
3 Tarzan at the earth's core 1930
4 Tarzan of Pellucidar
5 Back to the Stone-age
6 Land of terror

BURROUGHS, E. R.
TARZAN
1 Tarzan of the apes 1914
2 The return of Tarzan 1915
3 The beasts of Tarzan 1916
4 The son of Tarzan 1917
5 Tarzan and the jewels of Opar 1918
6 Jungle tales of Tarzan 1919
7 Tarzan the untamed 1920
8 Tarzan the terrible 1921
9 Tarzan and the golden lion 1923
10 Tarzan and the Antmen 1924
11 Tarzan,Lord of the jungle 1928
12 Tarzan and the lost empire 1929
13 Tarzan at the Earth
14 Tarzan the invincible 1931
15 Tarzan triumphant 1932
16 Tarzan and the city of gold 1933
17 Tarzan and the lion man 1934
18 Tarzan and the leopard men 1935
19 Tarzan's quest 1936
20 Tarzan and the forbidden city 1938
21 Tarzan the magnificent 1939
22 Tarzan and the Foreign Legion 1947
23 Tarzan and the madman 1965
24 Tarzan and the castaways 1965
25 Ta
26 Tarzan lives, by P.J.Farmer 1974
Nos. 1 - 24 reprinted in paperback

BURROUGHS, E. R.
VENUS SERIES
1 Pirates of Venus
2 Lost on Venus
3 Carson of Venus
4 Escape on Venus
5 Planet Venus
6 Wizard of Venus

BURROUGHS, W.
1 Cities of red night 1981
2 The place of dead woods 1984
3 The western lands 1988

BURROWES, J.
GORBALS TRILOGY
1 Jamsie's people 1984

2 Incomers 1988
3 Mother Glasgow 1991

BURROWS, J.
SUPT.BOWMAN
1 No need for violence 1970
2 Like an evening gone 1971

BURTON, A.
THE NAVIGATORS
1 The master idol 1975
2 The navigators 1976
3 A place to stand 1977
A trilogy about the canal builders

BURTON, B.
NUGENT FAMILY
1 Jude 1986
2 Jaen 1986
3 Women of no account 1988
4 Hard loves,easy riches 1989

BURTON, M.
INDSPECTOR ARNOLD & DESMOND MERRION
1 The Hardway diamond mystery 1930
2 The secret of High Eldersham 1930
3 The three crimes 1931
4 Menace on the downs 1931
5 Death of Mr.Gantley 1932
6 Murder at the moorings 1932
7 Fate at the fair 1933
8 Tragedy at the thirteenth hole 1933
9 Death at the crossroads 1933
10 The charabanc mystery 1934
11 To catch a thief 1934
12 The Deveraux Court mystery 1935
13 The milk churn murders 1935
14 Death in the tunnel 1936
15 Murder of a chemist 1936
16 Where is Barbara Prentice? 1936
17 Death at the club 1937
18 Murder in Crown Passage 1937
19 Death at low tide 1938
20 The platinum cat 1938
21 Death leaves no card 1939
22 Mr.Babbacombe dies 1939
23 Murder in the coal hole 1940
24 Mr.Westerby missing 1940
25 Death takes a flat 1940
26 Death of two brothers 1941
27 Up the garden path 1941
28 This undesirable residence 1942
29 Dead stop 1943
30 Murder M.D. 1943
31 Four ply yarn 1944
32 The three corpse trick 1944

33 No leg to stand on 1945
34 Early morning murder 1945
35 The cat jumps 1946
36 Situation vacant 1946
37 Heir of Lucifer 1947
38 A will in the way 1947
39 Death in shallow water 1948
40 Devil's reckoning 1948
41 Death takes the living 1949
42 Look alive 1949
43 Ground for suspicion 1950
44 A village afraid 1950
45 Beware your neighbour 1951
46 Murder out of school 1951
47 Murder on duty 1952
48 Something to hide 1953
49 Heir to murder 1953
50 Murder in absence 1954
51 Unwanted corpse 1954
52 Murder unrecognised 1955
53 Found drowned 1956
54 A crime in turn 1956
55 Death in a duffle coat 1956
56 The Chinese puzzle 1957
57 The moth-watch murder 1957
58 Bones in the brickfield 1958
59 Death takes a detour 1958
60 Return from the dead 1959
61 A smell of smoke 1959
62 Death takes a picture 1960
63 Legacy of death 1961

BUSBY, R.
DET.SERGEANT LERIC
1 Robbery blue 1969
2 The frighteners 1970
3 Deadlock 1971
4 A reasonable man 1972
5 Pattern of violence 1973

BUSCH, N.
1 California Street 1959
2 The San Franciscans 1962

BUSH, C.
LUDOVIC TRAVERS
1 The perfect murder case
2 Dancing death
3 Dead man's music
4 Dead man twice
5 Murder at Fenwold
6 Cut-throat
7 The case of the green felt hat
8 The case of the unfortunate village
9 The case of the April Fools
10 The case of the three strange faces
11 The case of the 100% alibis
12 The case of the dead shepherd
13 The case of the Chinese gong

14 The case of the Monday murders
15 The caseof the bonfire body
16 The case of the missing minutes
17 The case of the hanging rope
18 The case of the Tudor Queen
19 The case of the leaning man
20 The case of the flying ass
21 The case of the fighting soldier
22 The case of the climbing rat
23 The case of the kidnapped colonel
24 The case of the murdered major
25 The case of the magic mirror
26 The case of the running mouse
27 The case of the platinum blonde
28 The case of the ccorporal's leave
29 The case of the missing men
30 The case of the second chance
31 The case of the curious client
32 The case of the Haven Hotel
33 The case of the housekeeper's hair
34 The case of the seven bells
35 The case of the purloined picture
36 The case of the happy warrior
37 The case of the corner cottage
38 The case of the fourth detective
39 The case of the happy medium
40 The case of the counterfeit colonel
41 The case of the burnt Bohemian
42 The case of the silken petticoat
43 The case of the red brunette
44 The case of the three lost letters
45 The case of the benevolent bookie
46 The case of the amateur actor 1955
47 The case of the extra man 1956
48 The case of the flowery corpse 1956
49 The case of the Russian cross 1957
50 The case of the treble twist 1958
51 The case of the running man 1958
52 The case of the careless thieves 1959
53 The case of the sapphire brooch 1960
54 The case of the extra grave 1961
55 The case of the dead man gone 1961
56 Three ring puzzle 1962
57 Heavenly twins 1963
58 The case of the grand alliance 1964
59 The case of the jumbo sandwich 1965
60 The case of the good employer 1966
61 The case of the deadly diamonds 1966
62 The case of the prodigal daughter 1967

BUSHBY, J.
CAPT. JAMES ROLLO
1 The Spanish General 1982
2 Mondego Bay 1983
Sea stories set at the time of the Napoleonic Wars

BUTLER, D.
1 We'll meet again 1982
2 The end of an era 1983
Based on the TV series about the USAAF in Britain during WW2.

BUTLER, G.
INSPECTOR COFFIN
1 The murdering kind 1958
2 The interloper 1959
3 Death lives next door 1960
4 Make me a murderer 1961
5 Coffin in Oxford 1962
6 Coffin on the water 1986
7 Coffin for baby 1963
8 Coffin waiting 1964
9 Coffin in Malta 1964
10 A nameless Coffin 1966
11 Coffin following 1968
12 Coffin's dark number 1969
13 A Coffin from the past 1970
14 A Coffin for the canary 1974
15 Coffin in fashion 1987
16 Coffin underground 1988
17 Coffin in the Black Museum 1989
18 Coffin and the paper man 1990
19 Coffin on Murder Street 1991
20 Cracking open a Coffin 1992
21 A Coffin for Charley 1993
22 The Coffin tree 1994
Coffin first appears as a Sergeant in 'The Dull Dead' 1958

BUTLER, M.
HENRY II
1 Lion of England 1974
2 The lion of justice 1975
3 This turbulent priest 1977

BUTLER, O.
XENOGENESIS
1 Dawn 1987
2 Adulthood rites 1988
3 Imago 1989

BUTLER, RAGAN
CAPTAIN NASH
1 Captain Nash and the Wroth inheritance 1975
2 Captain Nash and the honour of England 1977

BUTLER, RICHARD
MAX FARNE
1 Where all the girls are sweeter 1975
2 Italian assets 1976

BUTLER, W. V.
OLD IRELAND YARD
1 Scarepower 1968
2 The lie witnesses 1969
3 Clampdown 1971

BYAM, W.
1 The road to Harley Street 1963
2 Dr. Byam in Harley Street 1961
N.F. Autobiography

BYATT, A. S.
1 The virgin in the garden 1978
2 Still life 1985

BYRD, M.
MIKE HALLER
1 California thriller 1984
2 Fly away Jill 1984
3 Finders weepers 1985

BYRNE, B.
MENDOZA FAMILY TRILOGY
1 The lasting fire 1992
2 The flames of vengeance 1992

CADELL, E.
WAYNES OF WOODMOUNT
1 The lark shall sing 1952
2 Blue sky of spring 1956
3 Six impossible things 1961

CAERNARVON, HENRY, EARL OF
1 No regrets 1976
2 Ermine tales 1980
N.F. Autobiography

CAIDIN, M.
STEVE AUSTIN, BIONIC MAN
1 Cyborg 1973
2 Operation Nuke 1974
3 High crystal 1975
4 Cyborg IV 1976

CALDECOTT, M.
1 The tall stones 1976
2 The temple of the sun 1977
3 Shadow on the stones 1978

CALDECOTT, M.
EGYPTIAN SERIES
1 Daughter of Amun 1989
2 The son of the sun 1986

3 Daughter of the Ra 1990

CALDERINI, P.
1 Mount Subasio 1985
2 Borderland 1987

CALDWELL, T.
1 Dynasty of death 1938
2 The eagles gather 1940
3 The final hour 1944

CALDWELL, T.
SANCTUARY
1 The man who listens 1961
2 No-one hears but him 1967

CALHOUN, W
CHULO
1 Chulo 1988
2 At Muerto Springs 1989
3 Texas nighthawks 1990
4 Sierra trail 1993

CALLISON, B.
BREVET CABLE
1 A plague of sailors 1971
2 A frenzy of merchantmen 1977

CALLISON, B.
CAPT.EDWARD TRAPP
1 Trapp's war 1973
2 Trapp's peace 1979
3 Trapp and World War Three 1988
4 Crocodile Trapp 1993

CALLOW, P.
COLIN PATON
1 Going to the moon 1967
2 The Bliss body 1969
3 Flesh of morning 1971

CALLOWAY SISTERS
1 Mariah, by Sandra Canfield 1989
2 Jo, by Tracy Hughes 1989
3 Tess, by Katherine Burton 1990
4 Eden, by Penny Richards 1990

CALVINO, I.
QFWFQ
1 Cosmicomics 1969
2 Time and the hunter 1970

CAMERON, D.
1 The field of sighing 1966
2 Sons of Eldorado 1968
   N.F. Autobiography

CAMERON, D. K.
1 The ballad and the plough 1978

2 Willie Gavin,Crofterman 1980
3 The cornkister days 1984
   N.F.Farming life in 19thC Scotland

CAMERON, J.
1 Point of departure 1967
2 An Indian summer 1974
   N.F. Autobiography

CAMP, J.
KIDD
1 The fool's run 1990
2 The empress file 1992

CAMPBELL, D.
HOPEWELL SAGA
1 Broken promises
2 Silent dreams
3 Stolen passions
4 Tomorrow
   Paperback

CAMPBELL, K.
MIKE BRETT
1 Goodbye, gorgeous
2 Listen lovely
3 Born beautiful
4 Darling, don't
5 That was no lady
6 Pardon my gun

CAMPBELL, M.
1 Peter Perry 1856
2 Nothing doing 1970

CAMPBELL, ROBERT
JIMMY FLANNERY
1 The junkyard dog 1989
2 The cat's meow 1990
3 Thinning the turkey herd 1990
4 The gift horse's mouth 1992
5 Nibbled to death by ducks 1991
6 In a pig's eye 1993

CAMPBELL, ROBERT.
WHISTLER
1 In La-La land we trust 1987
2 Alice in La-La land 1988
3 Sweet La-La land 1990

CANDY, E. [A. NEVILLE]
BURNIVEL
1 Which doctor 1953
2 Bones of contention 1954

CANETTI, E.
1 Earwitness 1979
2 The torch in my ear 1989
   N.F. Autobiography

CANNAM, H.
1 The last ballad 1991
2 A stranger in the land 1992

CANNELL, D.
ELLIE HASKELL
1 The thin woman 1990
2 Mum's the word 1991
3 Femmes fatal 1993

CANNING, V.
ARTHURIAN TRILOGY
1 The crimson chalice 1976
2 Circle of the Gods 1977
3 The immortal wound 1978

CANNING, V.
BIRDCAGE
1 Birdcage 1977
2 The Satan sampler 1979
3 Vanishing point 1982

CANNING, V.
MR.FINCHLEY
1 Mr.Finchley discovers his England 1934
2 Mr.Finchley goes to Paris 1936
3 Mr.Finchley takes the road 1939

CANNING, V.
REX CARVER
1 Whiphand 1965
2 Doubled in diamonds 1966
3 Python project 1967
4 The melting man 1968

CANNING, V.
SMILER MILES TRILOGY
1 The runaways 1970
2 Flight of the grey goose 1973
3 The painted tent 1974

CAO, XUEGIN
THE STORY OF THE STONE
1 Golden days
2 The crab-flower club
3 The warning voice
4 The debt of tears
5 The dreamer wakes

CAPE, T.
DEREK SMAILES
1 The Cambridge theorem 1990
2 The last defector 1991

CARD, O. S.
1 Ender's game 1985
2 Speaker for the dead 1987
Science fiction

CARD, O. S.
HOMECOMING
1 The memory of earth 1992
2 The call of earth 1993
3 The ships of earth 1994

CARD, O. S.
TALES OF ALVIN MAKER
1 Seventh son 1988
2 Red prophet 1989
3 Prentice Alvin 1989

CARLON, P.
JEFFERSON SHIELDS
1 The souvenir 1970
2 Death by demonstration 1970

CARMICHAEL, H.
PIPER & QUINN
1 Death leaves a diary 1952
2 The vanishing trick 1952
3 Deadly nightcap 1953
4 School for murder 1953
5 Why kill Johnnie? 1954
6 Death counts three 1954
7 Noose for a lady 1955
8 Justice enough 1956
9 Emergency exit 1957
10 Put out that star 1957
11 James Knowland, Dec. 1958
12 Or be he dead 1959
13 Stranglehold 1959
14 The seeds of hate 1960
15 Requiem for Charles 1960
16 Alibi 1961
17 The link 1962
18 Of unsound mind 1962
19 Vendetta 1963
20 Flashback 1964
21 Post mortem 1965
22 Suicide clause 1966
23 The condemned 1967
24 Murder by proxy 1967
25 Remote control 1970
26 Death trap 1970
27 The quiet woman 1971
28 Most deadly hate 1971
29 Naked to the grave 1972
30 Too late for tears 1973
31 Candles for the dead 1973
32 The motive 1974
33 False evidence 1975
34 Grave for two 1977
35 Life cycle 1978

CARNAC, C.
INSPECTOR STRANG
1 Doubleturn 1956
2 Death of a ladykiller 1958

CARNAC, C.
JULIAN RIVERS
1 A double for detection 1945
2 The striped suitcase 1946
3 When the devil was sick 1946
4 Clue sinister 1947
5 Over the garden wall 1947
6 Copy for crime 1947
7 Upstairs downstairs 1950
8 It's her own funeral 1951
9 Crossed skis 1952
10 Murder among members 1957
11 Long shadows 1958
12 A policeman at the door 1959

CARNEGIE, S.
MAJOR GAIR MAINWEARING
1 Noble purpose
2 Sunset in the East

CARNEGIE, S.
THE DESTINY OF EAGLES SEQUENCE
1 The banners of love 1967
2 The banners of war 1970
3 The banners of power 1972
4 The banners of courage 1976
5 The banners of revolt 1977
A series of novels about the history of Poland

CARNEY, D.
1 The wild geese 1977
2 The square circle 1983

CARR, G.
SIR ABERCROMBIE LEWKER
1 Murder on the Matterhorn 1951
2 The Youth Hostel murders 1952
3 The corpse in the crevasse 1952
4 Death on Milestone Buttress 1953
5 Death under Snowdon 1954
6 Death finds a foothold 1954
7 Holiday with murder 1955
8 A corpse at Camp 2 1955
9 Murder of an owl 1956
10 The ice-axe murders 1958
11 Swing away climber 1959
12 Lewker in Norway 1963
13 Death of a weirdy 1965
14 Lewker in Tyrol 1967
15 Fat man's agony 1969

CARR, J. D.
BENCOLIN
1 It walks by night 1930
2 Castle skull 1931
3 Lost gallows 1931
4 The four false weapons 1937
5 The waxworks murder 1952

CARR, J. D.
DR.GIDEON FELL
1 Hag's Nook 1933
2 The mad hatter mystery 1933
3 The eight of swords 1934
4 The blind barber 1934
5 Death watch 1935
6 The hollow man 1935
7 To wake the dead 1937
8 The crooked hinge 1938
9 The man who could not shudder 1940
10 Theblack spectacles 1940
11 The problem of the wire cage 1940
12 The case of the constant suicides 1941
13 Till death do us part 1944
14 He who whispers 1946
15 Below suspicion 1950
16 The dead man's knock 1958
17 In spite of thunder 1960
18 The house at Satan's Elbow 1965
19 Panic in Box C 1966
20 The dark of the moon 1968
The men who explained miracles, 1964, has two Dr. Fell stories.

CARR, J. D.
METROPOLITAN POLICE
1 Fire burn! 1957
2 The seat of the scornful 1959
3 The witch of the lowtide 1961

CARR, J. L.
HETTY BEAUCHAMP
1 What Hetty did 1988
2 Harpole and Foxberrow 1992

CARR, P.
DAUGHTERS OF ENGLAND
1 The miracle at St. Bruno
2 The lion triumphant 1974
3 The witch from the sea 1975
4 Saraband for two sisters 1976
5 Lament for a lost lover 1977
6 The lovechild 1978
7 Song of the siren 1980
8 The drop of the dice 1981
9 The adulteress 1982
10 Zipporah's daughter 1983
11 Voices in a haunted room 1984
12 The return of the gypsy 1985
13 Midsummer's eve 1986
14 The pool of St.Branok 1987
15 The changeling 1989
16 Black swan 1990
17 A time for silence 1991
18 The gossamer cord 1992
19 We'll meet again 1993

CARREL, M.
AMDREW MCCALL
1 The blood pit 1965
2 The shadow of a hawk 1966
3 Tears of blood 1967
4 A sword of silk 1968
5 The dark age of violence 1969

CARRIER, J. G.
1 My father's house 1974
2 Family 1977
3 A cage of bone 1979

CARRINGTON, C.
1 A subaltern's war 1929
2 Soldier from the wars returning 1965
N.F. Autobiography

CARSON, A.
1 The adventures of Mr.Quick 1965
2 The golden kiss 1967

CARSON, M.
MARTIN BENSON
1 Sucking sherbet lemons 1988
2 Stripping penguins bare 1991
3 Yanking up the yo-yo 1992

CARSON, R.
1 Silent spring 1966
2 Since silent spring, by F.Graham
*N.F. 1 is a warning against pollution;
2 a follow- up after ten years.*

CARSTAIRS, J. P.
GARWAY TRENTON
1 Gardenias bruise easily 1959
2 No wooden overcoat 1959
3 The concrete kimono 1964
4 Touch of a French pom-pom 1965
5 Pardon my gun 1966
6 A smell of peardrops 1966
7 No thanks for the shroud 1967

CARTER, A.
BLACKOAKS
1 Master of Blackoaks 1977
2 Sword of the golden stud 1978
3 Secrets of Blackoaks 1980
4 Heritage of Blackoaks 1982
5 A farewell to Blackoaks 1984
*A series about plantation life, closely
linked to the 'Falconhurst' series,
which he also writes. See the entry
under Onstott, K.*

CARTER, F.
JOSEY WALES
1 The outlaw Josey Wales
2 The vengeance trail of Josey Wales
Paperback Westerns

CARTER, L.
THONGOR
1 Thongor of Lemmuria
2 Wizard of Lemmuria
3 Thongor fights the pirates of Taracus
4 Thongor against the Gods
5 Thongor at the end of time
6 Thongor in the city of magicians
Paperback fantasy

CARTER, N.
NICK CARTER
1 The sea trap
2 Macao
3 The N3 conspiracy
4 The Arab plague
5 Operation snake
6 Assignment intercept
7 The ebony cross
8 The terrible ones
9 Cambodia
10 Rhodesia
11 The mark of Cosa Nostra
12 Code name Werewolf
13 The death strain
14 The death's head conspiracy
15 The defector
16 The executioners
17 The human time bomb
18 The Omega terror
19 The ultimate code
20 The Red Guard
21 Deadly doubles
22 Safari for spies
23 The man who sold death
24 Time clock of death
25 The cobra kill
26 The Jerusalem file
27 Trouble in Paradise
28 Thunderstrike in Syria
29 Hawaii
30 The Pamplona affair
31 Race of death
32 Reich 4
33 The Satan trap
34 Tropical death pact
35 Under the Wall
Paperback adventure stories

CARTLAND, B.
1 The isthmus years, 1919-39 1943

2 The years of opportunity, 1939-45 1947
3 I search for rainbows. 1945-66 1967
4 We danced all night 1970
5 I reach for the stars 1994
N.F. Reminiscences

CARVIC, H.
MISS SEETON
1 Picture Miss Seeton 1968
2 Miss Seeton draws the line 1970
3 Miss Seeton bewitched 1971
4 Miss Seeton sings 1974
5 Odds on Miss Seeton 1976

CARY, J.
GULLEY JIMSON
1 Herself surprised 1948
2 To be a pilgrim 1949
3 The horse's mouth 1950

CARY, J.
THE LIFE OF CHESTER NIMMO
1 Except the Lord 1953
2 Prisoner of grace 1952
3 Not honour more 1955

CASEY, M.
1 An Australian story 1964
2 Tides and eddies 1966
N.F. Autobiography

CASLEY, D.
CHIEF INSPECTOR JAMES ODHIAMBO
1 Death underfoot 1993
2 Death undertow 1994

CASSELLS, J.
CHIEF INSPECTOR FLAGG
1 The doctor deals with murder 1944
2 Murder comes to Rothesay 1949
3 Master in the dark 1949
4 The castle of sin 1949
5 The league of nameless men 1951
6 The clue of the purple asters 1952
7 Waters of sadness 1952
8 Death comes to Lady's Step 1952
9 The circle of dust 1952
10 The grey ghost 1952
11 The second Mrs. Locke 1952
12 The rattler 1953
13 Salute Inspector Flagg 1953
14 Case for Inspector Flagg 1954
15 Inspector Flagg and the scarlet skeleton 1955
16 Again Inspector Flagg 1956
17 Presenting Supt. Flagg 1959
18 Case 29 1959

19 Enter Supt. Flagg 1960
20 Score for Supt. Flagg 1960
21 Problem for Supt. Flagg 1961
22 The brothers of benevolence 1962
23 The council of the rat 1963
24 Blue mask 1964
25 Grey face 1965
26 Black fingers 1966
27 The room in Quiver Court 1967
28 Call for Supt. Flagg 1968
29 The double crosser 1969
30 The grafter 1970
31 The hatchet man 1971
32 The enforcer 1973
33 Killer's rope 1974
34 Quest for Supt. Flagg 1975

CASSELLS, J.
LUDOVIC SAXON(PICAROON)
1 Enter the Picaroon 1954
2 The avenging Picaroon 1956
3 Beware the Picaroon 1956
4 Meet the Picaroon 1957
5 The engaging Picaroon 1958
6 The enterprising Picaroon 1958
7 Salute the Picaroon 1960
8 The Picaroon goes west 1962
9 Prey for the Picaroon 1962
10 Challenge for the Picaroon 1965
11 The benevolent Picaroon 1965
12 Plunder for the Picaroon 1967
13 The audacious Picaroon 1967
14 The elusive Picaroon 1968
15 Night ofthe Picaroon 1969
16 Quest for the Picaroon 1970
17 The Picaroon collects 1970
18 Profit for the Picaroon 1972
19 The Picaroon laughs last 1973
20 Action for the Picaroon 1975
21 The Picaroon gets the runaround 1976

CASTANEDA, C.
1 The teachings of Don Juan 1968
2 A separate relaity 1970
3 Journey to Ixtlan 1973
4 Tales of power 1975
5 The second ring of power 1978
N.F. Cult books on sorcery and Mexican witchcraft

CASUALTY
1 The early years, by L.Waring
2 Swings and roundabouts, by L.del Sasso
3 One day at a time, by M.Walker
4 How it all began, by E.Christie
5 Lost and found, by M.Walker

6 On dangerous ground, by
   M.Walker
   *Paperback novels based on the
   television series*

CATLING, P. S.
1 The experiment 1969
2 The surrogate 1972

CATO, N.
AUSTRALIAN TRILOGY
1 All the rivers run 1958
2 Time, flow softly 1960
3 But still the stream 1962

CATTO, M.
LIMPIE
1 Mister Midas 1976
2 The empty tiger 1976

CATTON, B.
AMERICAN CIVIL WAR
1 The coming fury 1961
2 Terrible swift sword 1963
3 Never call retreat 1965
   N.F.

CATTON, B.
THE POTOMAC
1 Mr.Lincoln's army 1951
2 Glory road 1952
3 A stillness at Appomattox 1953
   N.F.

CAUDWELL, S.
PROFESSOR HILARY TAMAR
1 Thus was Adonis murdered 1981
2 The shortest way to Hades 1984
3 The sirens sang of murder 1989

CECIL, H.
ROGER THURSBY
1 Brothers in law 1955
2 Friends at court 1956
3 Sober as a judge 1957

CELINE, L-F.
1 Journey to the end of the night
   1932
2 Death on credit 1936

CHABER, M. E.
MILO MARCH
1 No grave for March 1954
2 The man inside 1954
3 The splintered man 1955
4 A lonely walk 1957
5 The gallows garden 1958
6 A hearse of another colour 1959

7 So dead the rose 1960
8 Jade for a lady 1961
9 Softly in the night 1962
10 Hangman's harvest 1962
11 As old as Cain 1963
12 Uneasy lies the dead 1964
13 Six who ran 1964
14 Wanted: dead men 1966
15 The day it rained diamonds 1966
16 The flaming man 1970
17 Green grow the graves 1971
18 The loaded dead 1972

CHADWICK, E.
1 The wild hunt 1990
2 The running vixen 1991
3 The leopard unleashed 1992

CHALKER, J. L.
CHANGEWINDS
1 When the changewinds blow
2 Riders of the winds
3 War of the maelstrom

CHALKER, J. L.
DANCING GODS
1 Demons of the Dancing Gods
2 Vengeance of the Dancing Gods
3 The river of the Dancing Gods

CHALKER, J. L.
FOUR LORDS OF THE DIAMOND
1 Lilith
2 Cerberus
3 Charon
4 Medusa

CHALKER, J. L.
GOD INC.
1 The labyrinth of dreams
2 The shadow dancers
3 The maze in the mirrors
   Paperback fantasy

CHALKER, J. L.
RINGS OF THE MASTER
1 Lords of the middle dark
2 Pirates of the thunder
3 Warriors of the storm
4 Marks of the martyrs
   *Paperback fantasy 1 and 2 published
   in hardback 1989*

CHALKER, J. L.
SOUL RIDER
1 Spirits of Flux and Anchor
2 Empires of Flux and Anchor
3 Masters of Flux and Anchor
4 The birth of Flux and Anchor

5 Children of Flux and Anchor

CHALKER, J. L.
THE WELLWORLD SAGA
1 Midnight at the Well of Souls
2 Exiles at the Well of Souls
3 Quest for the Well of Souls
4 The return of Nathan Brazil
5 Twilight at the Well of Souls
6 Echoes of the Well of Souls
7 Shadows of the Well of Souls
Paperback fantasy

CHALLONER, R.
COMMANDER LORD CHARLES
OAKSHOTT
1 Run out the guns 1984
2 Give fire! 1986
3 Into battle! 1987
*Naval stories set in the Napoleonic
War period*

CHAMBERS, P.
MARK PRESTON
1 This'll kill you 1963
2 Nobody lives forever 1964
3 You're better off dead 1966
4 Always take the big ones 1966
5 No gold where you go 1966
6 The bad die young 1967
7 Don't bother to knock 1968
8 The blonde wore black 1968
9 No peace for the wicked 1968
10 Speak ill of the dead 1968
11 They call it murder 1969
12 Somebody has to lose 1975
13 The deader they fall 1976
14 Lady,you're killing me 1977
15 The day of the big dollar 1978
16 The beautiful golden frame 1979
17 Nothing personal 1980
18 The deep blue cradle 1980
19 A long time dead 1980
20 The lady who never was 1981
21 Female - handle with care 1981
22 Murder is its own reward 1982
23 The highly explosive case 1982
24 A miniature murder mystery 1982
25 Jail bait 1983
26 Dragons can be dangerous 1983
27 Bomb scare - Flight 147 1984
28 The moving picture writes 1984
29 The vanishing holes murders 1985

CHAMBERS, R.
HANK MOODY
1 Moth in a rag shop 1969
2 The lesser evil 1971

CHANCE, J. N.
CHANCE
1 Screaming fog 1944
2 The eye in darkness 1946
3 The man in my shoes 1955

CHANCE, J. N.
JASON
1 The Jason affair 1954
2 Jason and the sleep game 1954
3 The Jason murders 1954
4 Jason goes west 1955

CHANCE, J. N.
JOHN MARSH & LOHM
1 The case of the death computer 1967
2 The caseof the fear makers 1968
3 Thug executive 1969
4 The three masks of death 1970

CHANCE, J. N.
JONATHAN BLAKE
1 The affair at Dead End 1966
2 The double death 1966
3 The mask of pursuit 1966
4 The death woman 1967
5 The hurricane drift 1967
6 Dead men's shoes 1968
7 Man trap 1968
8 Death of the wild bird 1968
9 Fate of the lying jade 1968
10 The rogue aunt 1968
11 The Hallowe'en murders 1968
12 Involvement in Austria 1969
13 The Abel coincidence 1969
14 The killer reaction 1969
15 The killing experiment 1969
16 The ice maidens 1969
17 The mists of treason 1970
18 The mirror train 1970
19 A ring of liars 1970
20 A wreath of bones 1971
21 The cat watchers 1971
22 The faces of a bad girl 1971
23 The man with two heads 1972
24 Last train to Limbo 1972
25 The dead take tellers 1972
26 A bad dream of death 1973
27 The farm villains 1973
28 The grab operation 1973
29 The starfish affair 1974
30 Girl in the crime belt 1974
31 The shadows of the killer 1975
32 Hill fog 1975
33 The monstrous regiment 1975
34 The devil's edge 1975
35 The murder makers 1976
36 Return to Death Alley 1976

37 A fall out of thieves 1976
38 House of dead ones 1977
39 The frightened fisherman 1977
40 Mists of treason 1977
41 The Ducrow folly 1978
42 A drop of hot gold 1978
43 The guilty witnesses 1979
44 The death watch ladies 1980
45 Mayhem Madchen 1980
46 The reluctant agent 1988

CHANCE, J. N.
MR.DE HAVILLAND
1 Wheels in the forest 1935
2 Maiden possessed 1937
3 Death of an innocent 1938
4 The red knight 1945
5 The knight and the castle
6 The black highway 1947
7 Coven gibbet 1948
8 The brandy pole 1949
9 Night of the full moon 1950
10 Alarm at Black Brake 1960
11 The forest affair 1962
12 Stormlight 1965

CHANDLER, B.
RIM RUNNERS
1 The rim of space 1981
2 When the dream dies 1981
3 Bring back yesterday 1982
4 Beyond the galactic rim 1982

CHANDLER, R.
PHILIP MARLOWE
1 The big sleep 1939
2 Farewell my lovely 1940
3 The high window 1942
4 Lady in the lake 1944
5 Little sister 1949
6 The simple art of murder 1950
7 The long goodbye 1953
8 Playback 1958
9 Poodle Springs, by R.B.Parker 1990
10 Perchance to dream, completed by R.B.Parker 1991
The smell of fear (1965) contains some short stories about Marlowe

CHAPMAN, J.
1 The long weekend 1984
2 Regretting it 1987

CHAPMAN, R.
REX BANNER
1 One jump ahead 1951
2 Crime on my hands 1952
3 Winter wears a shroud 1953

4 Murder for a million 1953
5 Behind the headlines 1955
6 Frozen stiff 1956

CHARLES, K.
DAVID MIDDLETON-BROWN
1 A drink of deadly wine 1991
2 The snares of death 1992
3 Appointed to die 1993
4 A dead man out of mind 1994
Detective stories with an ecclesiastical setting.

CHARLES, R.
SIMON LARREN
1 Nothing to lose 1963
2 One must survive 1963
3 Dark vendetta 1964
4 Mission of murder 1965
5 Arctic assignment 1966
6 The fourth shadow 1968
7 Assassins for peace 1968
8 Stamboul intrigue 1969
9 The big fish 1969
10 Strikefast 1969

CHARLIE'S ANGELS
1 Charlie's angels
2 The killing kind
3 Angels on a string
4 Angels in chains
5 Angels on ice
Paperbacks based on the TV series

CHARNOS, S. M.
ALLDERA
1 Walk to the end of the world
2 Motherlines 1980
Science fiction

CHARRIERE, H.
1 Papillon 1968
2 Banco 1973
N.F. Autobiography

CHARTERIS, L.
THE SAINT
1 Meet the tiger 1928
2 Enter the Saint 1936
3 The Saint closes the case 1936
4 Knight Templar 1936
5 Featuring the Saint 1936
6 Alias the Saint 1936
7 The Saint meets his match 1936
8 The Saint versus Scotland Yard 1936
9 Getaway 1936
10 The Saint and Mr.Teal 1936
11 The brighter buccaneer 1936

12 The Saint in London 1936
13 The Saint intervenes 1936
14 The Saint goes on 1936
15 The Saint in New York 1936
16 Saint overboard 1936
17 The ace of knaves 1037
18 The Saint bids diamonds 1937
19 The Saint plays with fire 1938
20 Follow the Saint 1938
21 The happy highwayman 1939
22 The Saint in Miami 1941
23 The Saint goes west 1942
24 The Saint steps in 1944
25 TheSaint on guard 1945
26 The Saint sees it through 1946
27 Call for the Saint 1948
28 Saint errant 1948
29 The Saint in Europe 1954
30 The Saint in theSpanish Main 1955
31 Saint around the world 1959
32 Thanks to the Saint 1961
33 Senor Saint 1961
34 Trust the Saint 1962
35 The Saint in the sun 1963
36 Vendetta for the Saint 1964
37 The Saint on TV 1968
38 The Saint returns 1969
39 The Saint and the fiction makers 1969
40 The Saint abroad 1969
41 The Saint in pursuit 1971
42 The Saint and the people importers 1971
43 Saints alive 1974
44 Catch the Saint 1975
45 The Saint and the Habsburg necklace 1977
46 Send for the Saint 1978
47 The Saint in trouble 1978
48 The Saint and the Templar treasure 1979
49 Count on the Saint 1980
50 The fantastic Saint 1981
From 36, the stories are adaptations of TV series revised by the author, but not actually written by him. Each contains two episodes.

CHARYN, J.
ISAAC SIDEL
1 Marilyn the wild 1991
2 The good policeman 1991
3 Blue eyes
4 The education of Patrick Silver
5 Secret Isaac

CHASE, J. H.
CORRIDON
1 Mallory 1950

2 Why pick on me 1951

CHASE, J. H.
HELGA ROLFE
1 An ace up my sleeve 1971
2 The joker in the pack 1975
3 I hold the four aces 1977

CHASE, J. H.
MADDOX
1 Shock treatment 1961
2 The double shuffle 1962
3 Tell it to the birds 1963

CHASE, J. H.
MARK GIRLAND
1 This is for real 1965
2 You have yourself a deal 1960
3 Have this one on me 1967
4 The whiff of money 1969

CHAUDHURI, N. C.
1 Autobiography of an unknown Indian 1951
2 A passage to England 1963
3 Thy hand, great Anarch 1987
N.F. Autobiography

CHEEK, M.
1 Pause between acts 1988
2 Parlour games 1989

CHEEVER, J.
1 The Wapshott chronicle 1962
2 The Wapshott scandal 1964

CHERRYH, C. J.
1 The dreamstone
2 The tree of swords and jewels
Paperback fantasy

CHERRYH, C. J.
CHANUR
1 Pride of Chanur
2 Chanur's venture
3 Chanur's homecoming
Paperback fantasy

CHERRYH, C. J.
MERCHANTER
1 Downbelow station
2 Cyteen
3 Merchanter's luck
4 Rimrunners
5 Heavy time
6 Hellburner
Paperback fantasy

CHERRYH, C. J.
MORGAINE CHRONICLES
1 Gate of Ivrel 1981
2 Well of Shuian
3 The fires of Azeroth
Paperback fantasy

CHERRYH, C. J.
RUSALKA
1 Chernevog 1991
2 Rusalka 1989
3 Yvgenie 1992

CHESBRO, G. C.
MONGO MYSTERIES
1 City of whispering sto
2 An affair of sorcerers 1980
3 Shadow of a broken man 1981

CHESNEY, M.
A HOUSE FOR THE SEASON
1 The miser of Mayfair 1987
2 Plain Jane 1987
3 The wicked godmother 1988
4 Rakes progress 1988
5 The adventuress 1989
6 Rainbird's revenge 1989

CHESNEY, M.
SCHOOL FOR MANNERS
1 Refining Felicity 1989
2 Perfecting Fiona 1990
3 Enlightened Delilah 1990
4 Finessing Clarissa 1991
5 Animating Maria 1991
6 Marrying Harriet 1992

CHESNEY, M.
SIX SISTERS
1 Minerva 1983
2 The taming of Annabelle 1983
3 Deirdre and desire 1984
4 Daphne 1984
5 Diana the huntress 1985
6 Frederica in fashion 1986

CHETWYND-HAYES, R.
CLAVERING GRANGE
1 Tales of darkness 1981
2 Tales of the other side 1983
3 Ghosts from the mists of time 1985
4 The King's ghost 1985
5 Tales from the haunted house
1987
6 Tales from the hidden world 1988
*Supernatural stories, centred around
an old house*

CHEYNEY, P.
LEMMY CAUTION
1 This man is dangerous
2 Poison Ivy
3 Dames don't care
4 Can ladies kill?
5 Don't get me wrong
6 You'd be surprised
7 Mr.Caution - Mr.Callaghan
8 Your deal, my lovely
9 Never a dull moment
10 You can always duck
11 I'll say she does
12 G2 man at the Yard

CHEYNEY, P.
SECRET SERVICE
1 Dark duet
2 The stars are dark
3 The dark street
4 Sinister errand
5 Dark hero
6 Dark interlude
7 Dark wanton
8 But ladies won't wait
9 You can call it s day
10 Dark Bahama

CHEYNEY, P.
SLIM CALLAGHAN
1 The urgent hangman
2 Dangerous curves
3 You can't keep the change
4 Mr.Caution - Mr.Callaghan
5 It couldn't matter less
6 Sorry you've been troubled
7 They never say when
8 Uneasy terms

CHISHOLM, M.
BLADE
1 The Indian incident
2 The Tucson conspiracy
3 The Lareda assignment
4 The Pecos manhunt
5 The Colorado virgins
6 The Mexican proposition
7 The Arizona climax
8 The Nevada mustang
9 The Montana deadlock
10 The Cheyenne trap
11 The Navajo trail

CHISHOLM, M.
MACALLISTER
1 MacAllister
2 MacAllister rides
3 MacAllister makes war
4 Kill MacAllister

5 MacAllister's fury
6 MacAllister fights
7 MacAllister strikes
8 MacAllister runs wild
9 MacAllister:the hard man
10 Death at noon
11 MacAllister justice
12 On the Comanche crossing
13 The hangman rides tall
14 Hell for MacAllister
15 MacAllister:tough to kill
16 Macallister and the Spanish gold
17 Macallister never surrenders
18 Macallister and the Cheyenne death
19 Macallister:quarry
20 Diehard
21 Wolfbait
22 Firebrand
A new series in paperback

CHRISTIAN, F. H.
FRANK ANGEL
1 Kill Angel 1973
2 Send Angel 1973
3 Find Angel 1975
4 Trap Angel 1976
5 Hang Angel 1975

CHRISTIAN, J.
RICHARD DEUTSCH
1 Five gates to Armageddon 1971
2 The Persian death trap 1976

CHRISTIE, A.
MISS MARPLE
1 Murder at the vicarage 1930
2 The body in the library 1942
3 The thirteen problems 1942
4 The moving finger 1943
5 A murder is announced 1950
6 They do it with mirrors 1952
7 A pocket full of rye 1953
8 The 4.50 from Paddington 1957
9 The mirror crack'd from side to side 1962
10 A Caribbean mystery 1964
11 At Bertram's Hotel 1965
12 Nemesis 1971
13 Sleeping murder 1976
14 Miss Marple's final cases 1979
'The life and times of Miss Jane Marple', by Anne Hart, is a fictional biography(1986).

CHRISTIE, A.
POIROT
1 The mysterious affair at Styles 1920

2 The murder on the links 1923
3 Poirot investigates 1924
4 The murder of Roger Ackroyd 1926
5 The big four 1927
6 The mystery of the Blue Train 1928
7 Peril at End House 1932
8 Lord Edgeware dies 1933
9 Murder on the Orient Express 1934
10 The ABC murders 1935
11 Three act tragedy 1935
12 Death in the clouds 1935
13 Murder in Mesopotamia 1936
14 Cards on the table 1936
15 Dumb witness 1937
16 Death on the Nile 1937
17 Appointment with death 1938
18 Murder in the mews 1938
19 Hercule Poirot's Christmas 1939
20 Sad cypress 1940
21 One two, buckle my shoe 1940
22 Evil under the sun 1941
23 Five little pigs 1943
24 The hollow 1946
25 Labours of Hercules 1947
26 Taken at the flood 1948
27 Mrs.McGinty's dead 1952
28 After the funeral 1953
29 Hickory, dickory dock 1955
30 Dead man's folly 1956
31 Cat among the pigeons 1959
32 The adventure of the Christmas pudding 1959
33 The clocks 1963
34 Third girl 1966
35 Hallowe'en party 1969
36 Elephants can remember 1972
37 Poirot's early cases 1974
38 Curtain:Poirot's last case 1976
Life and times of Hercule Poirot, by A. Hart 1990

CHRISTIE, A.
SUPT.BATTLE
1 The secret of Chimneys 1925
2 Murder is easy 1939
3 Towards zero 1944
4 The seven dials mystery

CHRISTIE, A.
TOMMY AND TUPPENCE BERESFORD
1 The secret adversary 1922
2 Partners in crime 1929
3 N or M 1941
4 By the pricking of my thumbs 1968
5 Postern of fate 1973

CHRISTIE, ANNE
1 First act 1983
2 My secret gorilla 1981
3 A time to weep 1987

CHRISTIE, K.
1 Smith 1954
2 Harold in London 1956

CHUN CHAN YEH
QUIET ARE THE MOUNTAINS
1 The mountain village
2 The open fields 1988

CHURCH, R.
1 Over the bridge 1956
2 The golden sovereign 1957
3 The voyage home 1964
N.F. *Autobiography*

CHURCH, R.
JOHN QUICKSHOTT
1 The porch 1955
2 The stronghold 1959
3 The room within 1961

CHURCHILL, P.
1 Of their own choice 1952
2 Duel of wits 1953
3 The spirit in the cage 1954
N.F. *War memoirs*

CIRNI, J.
FRANK FONTANA
1 The kiss off 1988
2 The come on 1989

CLANCY, TOM
JOHN KELLY
1 The hunt for Red October 1985
2 Clear and present danger 1989
3 The sum of all fears 1991
4 Without remorse 1993

CLANCY, TOM.
JACK RYAN
1 Patriot games 1987
2 The Cardinal of the Kremlin 1988
3 Debt of honour 1994

CLAPTON, P.
TOY
1 Toy 1968
2 Truffles for Toy 1971

CLARIDGE, M.
P.C.MCMORRAN
1 Nobody's fool 1993
2 Slow burn 1994

CLARK, C. H.
REGAN REILLY
1 Decked 1992
2 Snagged 1993

CLARK, D.
CHIEF INSPECTOR MASTERS
1 Nobody's perfect 1969
2 Death after evensong 1969
3 Deadly pattern 1970
4 Sweet poison 1970
5 Sick to death 1971
6 The miracle makers 1971
7 Premedicated murder 1975
8 Dread and water 1976
9 Table d'hote 1977
10 The gimmel flask 1977
11 The Libertines 1978
12 Heberden's seat 1979
13 Poacher's bag 1979
14 Golden rain 1980
15 Roast eggs 1981
16 The longest pleasure 1981
17 Shelf life 1982
18 Doone walk 1982
19 Vicious circle 1983
20 The Monday theory 1983
21 Bouquet garni 1984
22 Dead letter 1984
23 Performance 1985
24 Jewelled eye 1985
25 Storm centre 1986
26 The big grouse 1986
27 Plain sailing 1987

CLARKE, A.
1 Twice round the black church 1965
2 A penny in the clouds 1967
N.F. *Autobiography*

CLARKE, A. C.
1 2001:a space odyssey 1968
2 2010:odyssey 2 1982
3 2061:odyssey 3 1988

CLARKE, A. C.
RAMA
1 Rendezvous with Rama 1973
2 Rama II (with Lee Gentry) 1989
3 The garden of Rama (with Lee Gentry) 1991
4 Rama revealed (with Lee Gentry) 1993

CLARKE, A. C.
THE FALL OF NIGHT
1 Against the fall of night 1953

2 Beyond the fall of night, by
G.Benford 1991

CLARKE, R.
SUMMER WINE CHRONICLES
1 Gala Week 1986
2 The moonbather 1987
Based on the TV series

CLAVELL, J.
ASIAN SAGA
1 Shogun 1975
2 Tai-pan 1966
3 King Rat 1962
4 Noble house 1981
5 Gai-jin 1993
*Not direct sequels, but linked by
theme and location.*

CLAYTON, C. G.
THE BLAKENEY PAPERS
1 Daughter of the Revolution 1984
2 Such mighty rage 1985
3 Bordeaux red 1986
*A series following Baroness
Orczy, about Lady Blakeney, wife of
the Scarlet Pimpernel*

CLEARY, D.
THEODORE J.CASH
1 Shameful 1970
2 The rattler 1972

CLEARY, D. & MAHER, F.
BREAKENRIDGE
1 The hook 1980
2 Sahara strike 1981
3 Break-out 1981

CLEARY, J.
SCOBIE MALONE
1 The High Commissioner 1970
2 Helga's web 1971
3 Ransom 1972
4 Dragons at the party 1987
5 Now and then, Amen 1988
6 Babylon south 1989
7 Murder song 1990
8 Pride's harvest 1991
9 Bleak spring 1993
10 Autumn maze 1994

CLEEVE, B.
SEAN RYAN
1 Dark blood, dark terror 1966
2 Judas goat 1966

CLEEVES, A.
GEORGE PALMER-JONES
1 A bird in the hand 1986
2 Come death and high water 1987
3 Murder in Paradise 1988
4 A prey to murder 1989
5 Another man's poison 1992
6 Sea fever 1993
7 The mill on the shore 1994
*Detective stories with a background of
birdwatching*

CLEEVES, A.
INSPECTOR RAMSAY
1 A lesson in dying 1990
2 Murder in my back yard 1991
3 A day in the death of Dorothea
Cassidy 1992
4 Killjoy 1993

CLEIFE, P.
MARTYN FINCH
1 The pinchbeck masterpiece 1971
2 The slick and the dead 1972

CLEMENT, D. & LA FRENAIS, I.
PORRIDGE
1 Porridge 1977
2 Another stretch of porridge 1977
3 A further stir of porridge 1977
4 Going straight 1978

CLEMENT, D. & LA FRENAIS, I.
THE LIKELY LADS
1 The likely lads 1974
2 Whatever happened to the likely
lads 1975

CLEMENTS, E. H.
ALISTER WOODHEAD
1 The other island 1956
2 Back in daylight 1956
3 Uncommon cold 1958
4 High tension 1959
5 Honey for the marshal 1960
6 A note of enchantments 1961

CLEVELEY, H.
1 Justin Kelly 1961
2 Garland of valour 1963

CLEWES, D.
GRANT FAMILY
1 Missing from home 1975
2 Testing year 1977

CLEWS, R.
1 Young Jethro 1975
2 King's bounty 1976

3 The drums of war 1978

CLIFFORD, J. L.
1 Young Samuel Johnson 1955
2 Dictionary Johnson 1979
N.F. Biography

CLIFFORD, R.
1 Just here doctor 1976
2 Not there,doctor 1978
3 What next,doctor? 1979
4 Oh dear,doctor 1980
5 Look out,doctor 1983
6 Surely not,doctor 1985
7 There you are, doctor 1986
8 On holiday again, doctor? 1987
9 You're still a doctor, Doctor 1989
N.F. Humorous autobiography
Published in three omnibus volumes;
'Three times a day, doctor'(1-3);
'Only when I laugh, doctor' (4-6);
'It's a long story, doctor' (7-9) 1993

CLINTON-BADDELEY, V. C.
DR. DAVIE
1 Death's bright dart 1966
2 My foe outstretch'd beneath the
tree 1967
3 Only a matter of time 1968
4 No case for the polkice 1970
5 To study a long silence 1972

CLIVE, W.
RIFLEMAN JOSEPH DANDO
1 Dando on Delhi Ridge 1971
2 Dando and the Summer Palace
1972
3 The tunes that they play 1973
4 Dando and the mad Emperor 1974
5 Blood of an Englishman 1975

CLOAKMASTER CYCLE
1 Beyond the moons, by D.Cook
2 Into the void, by D.Findley
3 The maelstrom's eye, by R.Moore
4 The radiant dragon, by
E.Cunningham
5 The broken sphere, by
E.Cunningham
6 The ultimate helm,by R.T.Howard
Paperback fantasy

CLOETE, S.
1 A Victorian son (1897-1922) 1972
2 The gambler (1920-1939) 1973
N.F. Autobiography

CLOETE, S.
JEAN MACAQUE
1 The thousand and one nights of
Jean Macaque 1967
2 More nights of Jean Macaque 1975

CLOETE, S.
VANDERBERG FAMILY
1 The turning wheels 1937
2 Watch for the dawn 1939
3 The hill of doves 1941
4 The mask 1958
Novels about the early Boer
settlements

CLOSS, H.
THE ALBIGENSIAN CRUSADE
1 High are the mountains 1959
2 And sombre the valleys 1960
3 The silent tarn 1963

CLYNES, M.
SIR ROGER SHALLOTT
1 The white rose murders 1991
2 The poisoned chalice 1992
3 The Grail murders 1993
4 A brood of vipers 1994
Spy stories set in the reign of Henry
VIII

COBB, B.
CHEVIOT BURMANN
1 No alibi 1936
2 The poisoner's mistake 1937
3 Fatal dose 1938
4 Quickly dead 1938
5 Like a guilty thing 1938
6 The fatal holiday 1938
7 Inspector Burmann's busiest day
1939
8 Death defied the doctor 1939
9 Inspector Burmann's blackout 1941
10 Double detection 1946
11 Death in the 13th dose 1950
12 No mercy for Margaret 1952
13 Next door to death 1952
14 Detective in distress 1953
15 Corpse incognito 1953
16 Need a body tell? 1954
17 The willing witness 1955
18 Corpse at Casablanca 1956
19 Drink alone and die 1956
20 Doubly dead 1956
21 Poisoner's base 1956
22 The missing scapegoat 1957
23 With intent to kill 1958
24 Don't lie to the police 1959
25 Death with a difference 1960
26 Search for Sergeant Baxter 1961

27 Corpse in the cargo 1961
28 Murder:men only 1962
29 No shame for the devil 1962
30 Death of a peeping Tom 1964
31 Dead girl's shoes 1964
32 I never miss twice 1965
33 Last drop 1965
34 Some must watch 1966
35 Stone for his head 1966
36 Lost without trace 1966
37 Security secrets sold here 1967
38 Secret inquiry 1968
39 Silence under threat 1968
40 Food for felony 1969
41 Scandal at Scotland Yard 1969
42 The horrible man in Heron's Wood 1970
43 Catch me if you can 1970
44 Suspicion in triplicate 1971

COBB, B.
SUPT. MANNING
1 Early morning poison
2 The secret of Superintendent Manning
3 The framing of Carol Woan
4 No last words
5 Stolen strychnine
6 No charge for the poison 1950
7 Sergeant Ross in disguise
8 The Home Guard mystery
9 The lunatic, the lover 1950

COBB, R.
1 Still life 1983
2 A classical education 1986
3 Something to hold on to 1988
N.F. Autobiography of an Oxford Don

COBURN, W.
CALEB THORN
1 First shot
2 The raiders
3 Brotherly death
4 Bloody Shiloh
5 Death river
Paperback Westerns

COCCIOLI, C.
1 Heaven and earth 1958
2 The white stone 1961

COCKBURN, C.
1 In time of trouble 1956
2 Crossing the line 1958
3 Views from the west 1961
N.F. Autobiography

CODY, L.
ANNA LEE AND BRIERLEY SECURITY
1 Head case 1985
2 Dupe 1980
3 Bad company 1982
4 Stalker 1984
5 Under contract 1986
6 Backhand 1991

CODY, L.
EVA WYLIE
1 Bucket nut 1992
2 Monkey wrench 1994

CODY, S.
CACTUS CLANCY
1 Trouble shooter 1964
2 The gunslick code 1965
3 Sinister valley 1966

COE, T.
MITCHELL TOBIN
1 Kinds of love, kinds ofdeath 1966
2 Murder among children 1967
3 Wax apple 1970
4 A jade in Aries 1970
5 Don't lie to me 1974
See also the entry under the author's real name, Donald WESTLAKE

COFFEY, B.
MICK TUCKER
1 Blood risk 1974
2 Surrounded 1975

COFFMAN, V.
1 The Gaynor women 1981
2 Dinah Faire 1982
A family saga set in Virginia

COFFMAN, V.
ANNE WICKLOW
1 Moura 1959
2 The beckoning 1965

COFFMAN, V.
LOMBARD FAMILY
1 Pacific cavalcade 1986
2 The Lombard cavalcade 1986
3 The Lombard heiress 1986
Publication dates are for UK editions

COFFMAN, V.
NAPOLEONIC TRILOGY
1 Veronique 1978
2 Marsanne 1979
3 Careen 1989

COFFMAN, V.
THE ROYLES
1 The Royles 1992
2 Dangerous loyalties 1993
3 The Princess Royal 1994

COGGIN, J.
DUBLIN TRILOGY
1 McIlhenney 1989
2 Leaving 1989
3 Northside 1990

COHEN, ANTHEA
NURSE CARMICHAEL
1 Angel without mercy 1981
2 Angel of vengeance 1982
3 Angel of death 1983
4 Fallen angel 1984
5 Guardian angel 1985
6 Hell's angel 1986
7 Ministering angel 1987
8 Destroying angel 1988
9 Angel dust 1990
10 Recording angel 1991
11 Angel in action 1992
12 Angel in love 1993
Thrillers with a hospital setting

COLE, A.
OMARAN SAGA
1 A place among the fallen 1986
2 Throne of fools 1987
3 The King of light and shadows 1988
4 The gods in anger 1988
Paperback fantasy

COLE, A.
STAR REQUIEM
1 Mother of storms 1989
2 Thief of dreams 1989
3 Warlord of heaven 1990
4 Labyrinth of worlds 1990

COLE, A. & BUNCH, C.
1 The far kingdoms 1993
2 The warrior's tale 1994

COLE, HARRY
1 Policeman's patch
2 Policeman's lot
3 Policeman's progress
4 Policeman's patrol
5 Policeman's story
6 Policeman's prelude
7 Policeman's gazette 1987
*N.F. Autobiography of a Police
Constable. Paperback though some*

*titles have been published in hard-
back and large print format in 1987-8*

COLE, HUBERT
SIR JOHN HAWKWOOD
1 Hawkwood 1967
2 Hawkwood in Paris 1969
3 Hawkwood and the towers of Pisa
1973
*Novels about an English mercenary
during the Hundred Years' War*

COLE, J.
CHEYENNE
1 Arrow keeper
2 Death chant
3 Renegade justice
4 Vision quest
5 Blood on the plains
6 Comanche raid
7 Comancheros
8 War party
9 Pathfinder
10 Buffalo hiders
Paperback Westerns

COLEGATE, I.
ORLANDO KING
1 Orlando King 1969
2 Orlando at the brazen threshold
1971
3 Agatha 1973

COLEMAN, L.
BEULAH LAND
1 Beulah land 1973
2 Look away, Beulah Land 1977
3 The legacy of Beulah Land 1980
*A trilogy set in the American Deep
South*

COLES, M.
HAMBLEDON
1 Drink to yesterday
2 Pray silence
3 They tell no tales
4 Without lawful authority
5 Green hazard
6 Fifth man
7 Brother for Hugh
8 Among those absent
9 Not negotiable
10 Let the tiger die
11 Diamonds to Amsterdam
12 Dangerous by nature
13 Now or never
14 Night train to Paris
15 Alias Uncle Hugo
16 Knife for a juggler

17 Not for export
18 The man in the green hat 1955
19 Basle Express 1956
20 The three beans 1957
21 Death of an ambassador 1958
22 No entry 1958
23 Crime in concrete 1960
24 Search for a sultan 1961
25 The house at Pluck's Gutter 1962

COLES, P. J. C.
CHAMPION
1 Champion's folly 1984
2 Champion's chariot 1985
3 Champion's calamity 1987
Humorous novels

COLLARD, T.
DET. SUPT. JAMES BYRD
1 Murder at the Tower 1991
2 Murder at Hampton Court Palace 1992
3 Murder at the Royal Shakespeare 1994

COLLENETTE, E. J.
BEN GRANT
1 90 feet to the sun 1984
2 The Gemini plot 1985
3 The secret of the Kara Sea 1986
4 The Monday mutiny 1987
5 A capful of glory 1988
6 Sea wolf hunter 1989
Sea stories about submarines

COLLIER, C.
1 Hearts of gold 1991
2 One blue moon 1993

COLLINS, J
1 Chances 1982
2 Lucky 1985

COLLINS, M.
DAN FORTUNE
1 Act of fear 1969
2 The brass rainbow 1970
3 Night of the toads 1971
4 Walk a black wind 1973
5 Shadow of a tiger 1974
6 The silent scream 1975
7 Blue death 1975
8 Blood red dream 1976
9 The slasher 1981

COLLINS, M. A.
MALLORY
1 The baby-blue ripoff 1984
2 Cure for death 1985

COLLINS, M. A.
NATHAN HELLER
1 True detective
2 True crime
3 The million-dollar wound 1989
4 Neon mirage 1989

COLLINS, W.
1 Challenge 1990
2 New world 1991
3 Death of an angel 1992

COLSON, J.
1 The Goose and I 1863
2 The Goose up the creek 1864
3 Goose at sea 1965

COMMON, J.
1 Kiddar's luck 1951
2 The ampersand 1954

COMPTON, R.
TRAIL DRIVE
1 The goodnight trail
2 The Western trail
3 The Chisholm trail
4 The Bandera trail
5 The California trail
6 The Shawnee trail
Paperbacks about cattle drives.

CONDON, R.
PRIZZI
1 Prizzi's honour 1984
2 Prizzi's family 1986
3 Prizzi's glory 1988
4 Prizzi's money 1994

CONEY, M.
1 The celestial steam locomotive 1984
2 Gods of the greataway 1986
Science fiction

CONLON, K.
1 A forgotten season 1980
2 Consequences 1981

CONNELL, E.
1 Mrs.Bridge 1967
2 Mr.Bridge 1969

CONNELLY, M.
DET.HARRY BOSCH
1 The black echo 1992
2 The black ice 1993

CONRAD, P.
1 Down home 1988

2 Where I fell to earth 1990
N.F. Autobiography of an Australian.

CONRAN, S.
1 Lace 1982
2 Lace II 1985

CONSTANTINE, K. C.
MARIO BALZIC
1 The Rocksburg railroad murders
2 The man who liked to look at himself 1986
3 The blank page
4 A fix like this
5 The man who liked to grow tomatoes 1984
6 Always a body to trade 1985
7 Upon some midnight's clear 1986
8 Joey's case 1988
9 Sunshine enemies 1990
Not all have been published in UK

CONSTANTINE, S.
WRAETHTHU
1 The enchantments of flesh and spirit 1987
2 The bewitchments of love and hate 1988
3 The fulfilments of fate and desire 1989
Fantasies

CONWAY, P.
INSPECTOR NEWTON
1 Victims of circumstance 1977
2 30 days to live 1979
3 Nut case 1980
4 Needle track 1981
5 Dead drunk 1982
6 Cryptic clue 1984

CONYNGHAM, J.
1 The arrowing of the cane 1988
2 The desecration of the graves 1992

COOK, BOB
MICHAEL WYMAN
1 Disorderly elements 1986
2 Questions of identity 1987

COOK, D.
1 Walter 1978
2 Winter doves 1979
Novels about a boy with learning difficulties

COOK, G.
THE BLACK COMPANY
1 The Black Company

2 Shadows linger
3 The white rose
Paperback fantasy

COOK, GLORIA
PENGARRON
1 Pengarron land 1992
2 Pengarron pride 1993
3 Pengarron's children 1993

COOK, H.
CHRONICLES OF AN AGE OF DARKNESS
1 The wizards and the warriors 1987
2 The wordsmiths and the warguild 1987
3 The women and the warlords 1988
4 The walrus and the warwolf 1988
5 The wicked and the witless 1989
6 The wishstone and the wonderworkers 1990
7 The Wazir and the witch 1990
8 The werewolf and the wormlord 1991
9 The worshippers and the way 1992
Fantasies

COOK, T. H.
1 Sacrificial ground 1988
2 Flesh and blood 1989
3 Streets of fire 1990
4 Night secrets 1991

COOKE, C.
1 The winged assassin
2 Realm of the gods
Paperback fantasy

COOKE, D. C.
PETER ROURKE
1 C/O American Embassy 1969
2 The 14th agent 1969
3 Sleep with nightmares 1969

COOKE, G. W.
PETER MITCHELL
1 Death can wait 1957
2 Death takes a dive 1962
3 Death is the end 1965

COOKSON, C.
BILL BAILEY
1 Bill Bailey 1986
2 Bill Bailey's lot 1987
3 Bill Bailey's daughter 1988

COOKSON, C.
HAMILTON
1 Hamilton 1983
2 Goodbye Hamilton 1984
3 Harold 1985

COOKSON, C.
MALLEN FAMILY
1 The Mallen streak 1973
2 The Mallen girl 1973
3 The Mallen litter 1974

COOKSON, C.
MARY ANN SHAUGHNESSY
1 A grand man 1954
2 The Lord and Mary Ann 1956
3 The devil and Mary Ann 1958
4 Love and Mary Ann 1961
5 Life and Mary Ann 1962
6 Marriage and Mary Ann 1964
7 Mary Ann's angels 1965
8 Mary Ann and Bill 1967

COOKSON, C.
TILLY TROTTER
1 Tilly Trotter 1980
2 Tilly Trotter wed 1981
3 Tilly Trotter widowed 1982

COONEY, M.
THE QUEEN'S INVESTIGATOR
1 Doomsday England 1967
2 Ten days to oblivion 1968

COONTS, S.
JAKE GRAFTON
1 Flight of the intruder 1987
2 Final flight 1989
3 The minotaur 1990
4 Under siege 1990
5 The intruders 1994
Aviation thrillers

COOPER, BRIAN
JOHN LUBBOCK
1 The cross of San Vincente 1991
2 The singing stones 1993
3 Covenant with death 1994

COOPER, C.
MATT SAVAGE
1 Blackmail is murder 1966
2 Dame in distress 1967
3 What's funny about murder 1968
4 You'll die laughing 1968
5 Catch and squeeze 1969
6 Who killed Honey Bee? 1970

COOPER, DIANA
1 Animal hotel 1979
2 Up to scratch 1981
3 Mere folly 1982
N.F.Adventures with animals

COOPER, E.
1 The expendables 1975
2 The Rings of Tantalus 1977
Science fiction

COOPER, L.
DET. CHIEF INSPECTOR CORBY
1 Tea on Sunday 1973
2 Unusual behaviour 1986

COOPER, LADY DIANA
1 The rainbow comes and goes 1957
2 The light of common day 1959
3 Trumpets from the steep 1960
N.F. Autobiography. Reprinted in one vol. 1979

COOPER, LOUISE
CHAD'S GATE
1 The deceiver
2 The pretender
3 The avenger

COOPER, LOUISE
INDIGO
1 Nemesis (hardback 1993)
2 Inferno
3 Infanta
4 Nocturne
5 Troika
6 Avatar
7 Revenant
8 Aisling
Paperback fantasy

COOPER, LOUISE
TIME MASTER TRILOGY
1 The initiate 1986
2 The outcast 1986
3 The master 1987
Paperback fantasies

COOPER, N.
WILLOW KING
1 Festering lilies 1990
2 Poison flowers 1991
3 Bloody roses 1993
4 Bitter herbs 1993
Detective stories featuring a Civil Servant. The author also writes under her real name, Daphne Wright.

COOPER, W.
1 Scenes from provincial life 1950
2 Scenes from married life 1961
3 Scenes from metropolitan life 1982
4 Scenes from later life 1983

COPPER, B.
MIKE FARADAY
1 The dark mirror 1965
2 Night frost 1966
3 No flowers for the general 1967
4 Scratch on the dark 1967
5 Die now,live later 1967
6 Don't bleed on me 1968
7 The marble orchard 1969
8 Dead file 1970
9 No letters from the grave 1971
10 Big chill 1972
11 Strong-arm 1972
12 A great year for dying 1973
13 shockwave 1973
14 The breaking point 1974
15 A voice from the dead 1974
16 Feedback 1974
17 Ricochet 1974
18 The high wall 1975
19 Impact 1975
20 A good place to die 1976
21 The lonely place 1976
22 Crack in the sidewalk 1976
23 Tight corner 1976
24 The year of the dragon 1977
25 Death squad 1977
26 Murder one 1977
27 A quiet room in Hell 1978
28 The big ripoff 1978
29 The Caligari complex 1979
30 Flip-side 1980
31 The long rest 1981
32 The empty silence 1981
33 Dark entry 1981
34 Hang loose 1982
35 Shoot-out 1982
36 The far horizon 1982
37 Trigger-man 1983
38 Pressure point 1983
39 The narrow corner 1983
40 Hard contract 1984
41 The hook 1984
42 You only die once 1984
43 Tuxedo Park 1985
44 The far side of fear 1985
45 Snow job 1985
46 Jet-lag 1986
47 Blood on the moon 1986
48 Heavy iron 1987
49 Turn down an empty glass 1987
50 Bad scene 1987
51 House-dick 1988

52 Print-out 1988

COPPER, B.
SOLAR PONS
1 The dossier of Solar Pons
2 The further adventures of Solar Pons
3 The secret files of Solar Pons
4 The exploits of Solar Pons
5 Some uncollected cases of Solar Pons
6 The recollections of Solar Pons
7 The further recollections of Solar Pons

CORDELL, A.
1 This proud and savage land 1988
2 Rape of the fair country 1966
3 Song of the earth 1969
4 The fire people 1972
5 This sweet and bitter earth 1977
6 Land of my fathers 1983
7 Beloved exile 1993
Two separate trilogies, covering the years of Industrial Revolution in Wales, 1826-1913 No. 1 is a prequel to the series

CORDER, E.
1 Slave ship 1969
2 Slave 1971

CORK, B.
INSPECTOR ANGUS STRAUN
1 Dead ball 1988
2 Unnatural hazard 1989
3 Laid dead 1990
4 Winter rules 1991
5 Endangered species 1992
Detective stories set around the golf course.

CORNWELL, B.
NATHANIEL STARBUCK
1 Rebel 1993
2 Copperhead 1994
3 Battle flag 1994
Novels set during the American War of Independence

CORNWELL, B.
RICHARD SHARPE
1 Sharpe's rifles (Galicia 1809) 1988
2 Sharpe's eagle (Talavera 1809) 1980
3 Sharpe's gold (Almeida 1810) 1981
4 Sharpe's company (Badajoz 1812) 1982

5 Sharpe's sword (Salamanca 1812) 1983
6 Sharpe's enemy (Defence of Portugal 1812) 1984
7 Sharpe's honour (Vitoria 1813) 1985
8 Sharpe's regiment (1813) 1985
9 Sharpe's siege (1814) 1987
10 Sharpe's revenge (1814) 1989
11 Sharpe's Waterloo (1815) 1990
12 Sharpe's devil(Sharpe and the Emperor 1820-21)1992
Novels about the British Army in the Peninsular War

CORNWELL, P. D.
DR. KAY SCARPETTA
1 Post mortem 1991
2 Body of evidence 1991
3 All that remains 1992
4 Cruel and unusual 1993
5 The body farm 1994
Detective stories about a forensic scientist

CORRIGAN, M.
CORRIGAN & TUCKER
1 Bullets and brown eyes 1948
2 Sinner takes all 1949
3 Lovely lady 1949
4 Wayward blonde 1950
5 Golden angel , 1950
6 Shanghai Jezebel 1951
7 Madam Sly 1951
8 Baby face 1952
9 Lady of China Street 1952
10 All brides are beautiful 1952
11 Sweet and deadly 1953
12 The naked lady 1954
13 Madam and Eve 1955
14 The big squeeze 1955
15 Big boys don't cry 1956
16 Sydney for sin 1956
17 The cruel lady 1957
18 Dumb as they come 1957
19 Menace in Siam 1958
20 Honolulu snatch 1958
21 Singapore downbeat 1959
22 Sin of Hong Kong 1960
23 Lady from Tokyo 1960
24 Girl from Moscow 1961
25 Danger's green eyes 1961
26 The riddle of Double Island 1962
27 Why do women 1963
28 The riddle of the Spanish circus 1964

CORY, D.
DEE
1 Stranglehold 1962
2 The name of the game 1964

CORY, D.
JOHNNY FEDORA
1 Secret ministry 1951
2 This traitor death 1952
3 Dead man falling 1953
4 Intrigue 1954
5 Height of day 1955
6 High requiem 1955
7 Johnny goes north 1956
8 Johnny goes east 1959
9 Johnny goes west 1959
10 Johnny goes south 1959
11 The head 1960
12 Undertow 1961
13 Hammerhead (retitled Shockwave) 1962
14 Feramontov 1966
15 Timelock 1967
16 Sunburst 1971

CORY, D.
LINDA GRAY
1 Begin, murderer 1951
2 This is Jezebel 1952
3 Lady lost 1953

CORY, D.
MIKE PILGRIM
1 Pilgrim at the gate 1958
2 Pilgrim on the island 1961

CORY, D.
PROFESSOR DOBIE
1 The strange attractor 1991
2 The mask of Zeus 1992
3 The Dobie paradox 1993

COSGRAVE, P.
COLONEL CHEYNEY
1 Cheyney's law 1977
2 The three Colonels 1979
3 Adventure of state 1984

COUGHLIN, W. J.
1 Shadow of a doubt 1992
2 Death penalty 1993

COULTER, C.
SHERBROOKE FAMILY
1 The Sherbrooke bride 1994
2 The heiress bride 1994
3 The hellion bride 1994

COURTENAY, B.
1 The power of one 1989
2 Tandia 1991

COURTER, G.
HANNAH SOKOLOW
1 The midwife 1986
2 The midwife's advice 1993

COURTNEY, E.
KIT HEMSWORTHY
1 The price of loving 1987
2 Over the bridge 1988

COWPER, R.
BIRD OF KINSHIP SAGA
1 Piper at the gates of dawn 1976
2 The road to Corlay 1978
3 A dream of Kinship 1981
4 A tapestry of time 1982
Fantasy

COX, J.
1 Her father's sins 1987
2 Let loose the tigers 1988

COX, J.
EMMA GRADY
1 Outcast 1990
2 Alley urchin 1991
3 Vagabonds 1992

COXE, G. H.
KENT MURDOCH
1 The camera clue 1937
2 The frightened woman 1939
3 The lady is afraid 1940
4 Murder is for the asking 1940
5 The Jade Venus 1946
6 The fifth key 1950
7 The hollow needle 1951
8 Eye witness 1953
9 The widow had a gun 1954
10 Lady killer 1955
11 The crimson clue 1955
12 Focus on murder 1956
13 Murder on their minds 1958
14 The big gamble 1960
15 The last commandment 1961
16 The hidden key 1964
17 The reluctant heiress 1965
18 With intent to kill 1966
19 The ring of truth 1967
20 An easy way to go 1968

CRADDOCK, M.
1 A north country maid 1965
2 Return to Rainton 1968
N.F. Autobiography

CRADOCK, F.
THE LORMES OF CASTLE RISING
1 The Lormes of Castle Rising 1975
2 Shadows over Castle Rising 1977
3 War comes to Castle Rising 1977
4 Wind of change over Castle Rising 1978
5 Uneasy peace at Castle Rising 1979
6 Thunder over Castle Rising 1980
7 Gathering clouds at Castle Rising 1981
8 Fateful years at Castle Rising 1982
9 The defence of Castle Rising 1984
10 The loneliness of Castle Rising 1986

CRAGOE, E.
1 Buttercups and Daisy 1974
2 Cowslips and clover 1978
3 Yorkshire relish 1979
4 Sweet nothings 1980
5 The untidy gardener 1982
N.F. The first three are about the author country childhood, the last two about the creation of a Welsh garden.

CRAIG, D.
PETER GALE
1 The Albion case 1975
2 Faith hope and death 1976

CRAIG, D.
ROY RICKMAN
1 The alias man 1969
2 Message ends 1969
3 Contact lost 1970

CRAIG, D.
SHEILA ROATH
1 Young men may die 1970
2 A walk by night 1971

CRAIS, R.
ELVIS COLE
1 The monkey's raincoat 1988
2 Stalking the angel 1990
3 Lullaby town 1992

CRANE, F.
PAT ABBOTT
1 The turquoise shop 1943
2 The golden box 1944
3 The yellow violet 1944
4 The pink umbrella 1944
5 The apple green cat 1945
6 The amethyst spectacles 1946
7 The indigo necklace 1946
8 The shocking pink hat 1948

9 The cinnamon murder 1949
10 Murder on the purple water 1949
11 Black cypress 1950
12 Flying red horse 1951
13 The daffodil blonde 1951
14 The polkadot murder 1952
15 Death in the blue hour 1952
16 Thirteen white tulips 1953
17 Murder in bright red 1954
18 The coral princess murders 1955
19 Death in lilac time 1955
20 Horror on the Ruby X 1956
21 Th ultra-violet window 1957
22 The grey stranger 1958
23 The buttercup case 1958
24 Death-wish green 1960
25 Amber eyes 1962
26 Body beneath a mandarin tree 1965

CRANE, T.
1 Tomorrow, Jerusalem 1989
2 Green and pleasant land 1991

CRAWFORD, R.
SALISBURY & SHEARER
1 Cockleburr 1969
2 Kiss the boss goodbye 1970
3 The Badger's daughter 1971

CRAWLEY, A.
SULEIMAN THE MAGNIFICENT
1 The bride of Suleiman 1981
2 The shadow of God 1982
3 The house of war 1984

CREASEY, J.
DEPARTMENT Z
1 The death miser 1932
2 Redhead 1933
3 First came murder 1934
4 Death around the corner 1935
5 Mark ofthe crescent 1935
6 Thunder in Europe 1936
7 Terror trap 1936
8 Carriers of death 1937
9 Days of danger 1937
10 Death stands by 1938
11 Menace 1938
12 Murder must wait 1939
13 Panic! 1939
14 Death by night 1940
15 The island of peril 1941
16 Sabotage 1941
17 Go away death 1942
18 Day of disaster 1942
19 Prepare for action 1943
20 No darker crime 1943
21 Dark peril 1944

22 The peril ahead 1945
23 League of dark men 1947
24 The department of death 1949
25 The enemy within 1950
26 Dead or alive 1951
27 A kind of prisoner 1954
28 The black spiders 1957

CREASEY, J.
DR. PALFREY
1 Traitor's doom 1942
2 The valley of fear 1943
3 The legion of the lost 1943
4 Dangerous quest 1944
5 The hounds of vengeance 1944
6 Death in the rising sun 1945
7 Shadow of doom 1946
8 The house of the bears 1947
9 Sons of Satan 1947
10 Dark harvest 1947
11 The wings of peace 1948
12 The dawn of darkness 1949
13 The league of light 1949
14 The man who shook the world 1950
15 The prophet of fire 1951
16 The children of hate 1952
17 The touch of death 1954
18 The mists of fear 1957
19 The flood 1958
20 The plague of silence 1958
21 The drought 1959
22 The terror:the return of Dr.Palfrey 1962
23 The depths 1963
24 The sleep 1964
25 The inferno 1965
26 The famine 1967
27 The blight 1968
28 The oasis 1970
29 The smog 1970
30 The unbegotten 1971
31 The insulators 1972
32 The voiceless one 1973

CREASEY, J.
INSPECTOR WEST
1 Inspector West takes charge 1942
2 Inspector West leaves town 1943
3 Inspector West at home 1944
4 Inspector West regrets 1945
5 Holiday for Inspector West 1946
6 Triumph for Inspector West 1948
7 Battle for Inspector West 1948
8 Inspector West kicks off 1949
9 Inspector West cries wolf 1950
10 Inspector West alone 1950
11 Puzzle for Inspector West 1951
12 Case for Inspector West 1952

13 Inspector West at bay 1952
14 Send Inspector West 1953
15 A gun for Inspector West 1953
16 A beauty for Inspector West 1954
17 Inspector West makes haste 1954
18 Two for Inspector West 1956
19 A prince for Inspector West 1956
20 Parcels for Inspector West 1956
21 Accident for Inspector West 1957
22 Find Inspector West 1957
23 Strike for death 1958
24 Murder London - New York 195
25 Death of a racehorse 1959
26 The case of the innocent victims
   1959
27 Murder on the line 1960
28 The scene of the crime 1960
29 Death in cold print 1961
30 Policeman's dread 1962
31 Hang the little man 1963
32 Look three ways at murder 1964
33 Murder London - Australia 1965
34 Murder London - South Africa
   1966
35 The executioners 1967
36 So young to burn 1968
37 Murder London - Miami 1969
38 A part for a policeman 1970
39 Alibi? 1971
40 Splinter of glass 1972
41 The theft of Magna Carta 1973
42 The extortioners 1974
43 A sharp rise in crime 1978

CREASEY, J.
THE TOFF
1 Introducing the Toff 1938
2 The Toff steps out 1939
3 TheToff goes on 1939
4 The Toff breaks in 1940
5 Here comes the Toff 1940
6 Salute the Toff 1941
7 The Toff proceeds 1941
8 The Toff is back 1942
9 The Toff goes to market 1942
10 Accuse the Toff 1943
11 The Toff among the millions 1943
12 The Toff and the great illusion
   1944
13 The Toff and the curate 1944
14 Feathers for the Toff 1945
15 The Toff and the lady 1946
16 Hammer the Toff 1947
17 The Toff on ice 1947
18 The Toff in town 1948
19 The Toff takes a share 1948
20 The Toff and Old Harry 1949
21 The Toff on board 1949
22 Kill the Toff 1950

23 Fool the Toff 1950
24 The Toff goes gay 1951
25 Knife for the Toff 1951
26 Hunt the Toff 1952
27 Call the Toff 1953
28 The Toff down under 1953
29 The Toff at Butlins 1954
30 The Toff at the fair 1954
31 A six for the Toff 1955
32 The Toff and the deep blue sea
   1955
33 Make up for the Toff 1956
34 The Toff in New York 1956
35 The Toff on fire 1956
36 Model for the Toff 1957
37 The Toff and the stolen tresses
   1957
38 The Toff on the farm 1958
39 The Toff and the runaway bride
   1958
40 Double for the Toff 1959
41 The Toff and the kidnapped child
   1959
42 A rocket for the Toff 1960
43 Follow the Toff 1961
44 The Toff and the Teds 1961
45 Leave it to the Toff 1962
46 A doll for the Toff 1964
47 The Toff and the spider 1965
48 The Toff in wax 1966
49 A bundle for the Toff 1967
50 Stars for the Toff 1968
51 The Toff and the golden boy 1969
52 The Toff and the fallen angels
   1970
53 Vote for the Toff 1971
54 The Toff and the trip-trip triplets
   1972
55 The Toff and the terrified taxman
   1973
56 The Toff and the sleepy cowboy
   1974
57 The Toff and the crooked copper
   1977
58 The Toff and the dead man's
   finger 1978

CREASEY, J. (AS A. MORTON)
THE BARON
1 Meet the Baron 1937
2 The Baron returns 1937
3 The Baron at bay 1938
4 The Baron again 1938
5 The Baron at large 1939
6 Alias the Baron 1939
7 Versus the Baron 1939
8 Call forthe Baron 1940
9 The Baron comes back 1943
10 A case for the Baron 1945

11 Reward for the Baron 1945
12 A career for the Baron 1946
13 The Baron and the beggar 1947
14 A rope for the Baron 1948
15 Blame the Baron 1949
16 Books for the Baron 1949
17 Cry for the Baron 1950
18 Trap theBaron 1950
19 Shadow theBaron 1951
20 Attack the Baron 1951
21 Warn the Baron 1952
22 TheBaron goes east 1953
23 Danger for the Baron 1953
24 The Baron in France 1953
25 The Baron goes fast 1954
26 Nest egg for the Baron 1954
27 Help from the Baron 1955
28 Hide the Baron 1956
29 Frame the Baron 1957
30 Red eye for the Baron 1958
31 Black for the Baron 1959
32 Salute to the Baron 1960
33 A branch for the Baron 1961
34 Bad for the Baron 1962
35 A sword for the Baron 1963
36 The Baron on board 1964
37 The Baron and the Chinese puzzle 1965
38 Sport for the Baron 1966
39 Affair for theBaron 1967
40 The Baron and the missing Old Masters 1968
41 The Baron and the unfinished portrait 1969
42 Last laugh for the Baron 1970
43 The Baron goes a-buying 1971
44 The Baron and the arrogant artist 1972
45 Burgle theBaron 1973
46 The Baron - Kingmaker 1975
47 Love for the Baron 1979

CREASEY, J. (AS G. ASHE)
PATRICK DAWLISH
1 The speaker 1939
2 Death on demand 1939
3 Terror by day 1940
4 Secret murder 1940
5 'Ware danger 1941
6 Murder most foul 1941
7 There goes death 1941
8 Death in high places 1941
9 Death in flames 1943
10 Two men missing 1943
11 Rogues rampant 1944
12 Death on the move 1945
13 Invitation to adventure 1946
14 Here is danger 1946
15 Give me murder 1947

16 Murder too late 1947
17 Engagement with death 1947
18 Dark mystery 1948
19 A puzzle in pearls 1949
20 Kill or be killed 1949
21 The dark circle 1951
22 Murder with mushrooms 1950
23 Death in diamonds 1952
24 Missing or dead 1952
25 Death in a hurry 1952
26 Sleepy death 1953
27 The long search 1953
28 Death in the trees 1954
29 Double for death 1954
30 The kidnapped child 1955
31 Day of fear 1956
32 Wait for death 1957
33 Come home to death 1958
34 Elope to death 1959
35 Don't let him kill 1960
36 The crime haters 1961
37 Rogue's ransom 1961
38 Death from below 1963
39 The big call 1964
40 A promise of diamonds 1965
41 A taste of treasure 1965
42 A clutch of coppers 1967
43 A shadow of death 1968
44 A scream of murder 1969
45 A nest of traitors 1970
46 A rabble of rebels 1971
47 A life for a death 1973
48 A blast of trumpets 1975
49 A plague of demons 1976

CREASEY, J. (AS J. J. MARRIC)
COMMANDER GIDEON
1 Gideon's day 1955
2 Gideon's week 1956
3 Gideon's night 1957
4 Gideon's month 1958
5 Gideon's staff 1959
6 Gideon's risk 1960
7 Gideon's fire 1961
8 Gideon's march 1962
9 Gideon's ride 1963
10 Gideon's vote 1964
11 Gideon's lot 1965
12 Gideon's badge 1966
13 Gideon's wrath 1967
14 Gideon's river 1968
15 Gideon's power 1969
16 Gideon's sport 1970
17 Gideon's art 1971
18 Gideon's men 1972
19 Gideon's press 1973
20 Gideon's fog 1974
21 Gideon's drive 1976
22 Gideon's law, by W.V.Butler 1981

23 Gideon's raid, by W.V.Butler 1986

CREASEY, J. (AS J. YORK)
SUPT.FOLLY
1 Find the body 1946
2 Runaway to murder 1947
3 Close the door on murder 1947
4 Let's kill Uncle Lionel 1949
5 The gallows are waiting 1949

CREASEY, J. (AS M. HALLIDAY)
DR. CELLINI
1 Cunning as a fox 1965
2 Wicked as the devil 1966
3 Sly as a serpent 1967
4 Cruel as a cat 1968
5 Too good to be true 1969
6 A period of evil 1970
7 As lonely as the damned 1971
8 As empty as hate 1972
9 As merry as hell 1973
10 This man did I kill 1973
11 The man who was not himself 1976

CREASEY, J. (AS M. HALLIDAY)
FANE BROTHERS
1 Take the body 1952
2 The lame dog murder 1952
3 Murder in the stars 1953
4 Man on the run 1953

CREASEY, J. (AS N. DEANE)
BRUCE MURDOCH
1 Secret errand 1939
2 Dangerous journey 1939
3 Unknown mission 1940
4 The withered man 1940
5 I am the withered man 1941
6 Where is the withered man? 1942

CREASEY, J. (AS N. DEANE)
LIBERATOR
1 Return to adventure 1943
2 Gateway to escape 1944
3 Come home to crime 1945

CREATON, D.
1 The beasts of my field 1976
2 Beasts and babies 1978
3 The beasts go west 1979
N.F. Autobiography of a farmer

CREMER, J.
1 I, Jan Cremer 1965
2 Jan Cremer 1967

CRISP, J. H.
SOE
1 Dragon's spoor 1979
2 Final act 1979

CRISP, W.
WESTFALL
1 Spytrap 1984
2 Vengeance is thine 1986

CRISPIN, A. C.
V
1 V:East Coast crisis
2 V

CRISPIN, E.
GERVASE FEN
1 The case of the gilded fly 1944
2 Holy disorders 1945
3 The moving toyshop 1846
4 Swan song 1947
5 Love lies bleeding 1948
6 Buried for pleasure 1949
7 Frequent hearses 1950
8 The long divorce 1951
9 Beware of the trains 1953
10 Glimpses of the moon 1977
11 Fen country 1979

CROFT-COOKE, R.
THE SENSUAL LIFE
1 The gardens of Camelot 1958
2 The altar in the loft 1960
3 The drums of morning 1961
4 The glittering pastures 1962
5 The numbers came 1963
6 The last of Spring 1964
7 The purple streak 1966
8 The wild hills 1966
9 The happy highways 1967
10 The sound of revelry 1969
11 The moon in my pocket 1970
12 The licentious soldiery 1971
13 The blood red island 1967
14 The gorgeous east 1965
15 The dogs of peace 1968
16 The life for me 1970
17 The verdict of you all 1970
18 The tangerine house 1956
19 The quest for Quixote 1961
20 The wintry sea 1964
21 The ghost of June 1969
22 The caves of Hercules 1974
23 The long way home 1974
24 The green, green grass 1977
N.F. Autobiography. This is the author's preferred arrangement

CRONIN, A. J.
1 The green years 1944
2 Shannon's way 1948

CRONIN, A. J.
LAWRENCE CARROLL
1 A song of sixpence 1967
2 A pocketful of rye 1969

CRONIN, M.
JAMES HELLIER
1 Man alive 1968
2 Dead loss 1970
3 Emergency exit 1970
4 The long memory 1971
5 Escape at sunrise 1972
6 Nobody needs a corpse 1972
7 The big C 1973

CRONIN, M.
MR. PILGRIM
1 Paid in full 1956
2 Sweet water 1958
3 Begin with a gun 1959
4 Curtain call 1960

CRONIN, M.
SAM HARRIS
1 A proper carve up 1970
2 A black leather case 1971
3 The con game 1972
4 The big tickle 1974
5 Strictly private business 1975
6 The final instalment 1976
7 A pair of knaves 1977
8 Unfinished business 1978
9 Epitaph for a lady 1980

CROSBY, J.
HORATIO CASSIDY
1 An affair of strangers 1975
2 The company of friends 1977
3 Party of the year 1980
4 Men at arms 1984
5 Take no prisoners 1986

CROSS, A.
KATE FANSLER
1 In the last analysis 1966
2 The James Joyce murder 1967
3 Poetic justice 1970
4 The Theban mysteries 1972
5 The question of Max 1976
6 A death in the faculty 1981
7 Sweet death,kind death 1984
8 No word from Winifred 1987
9 A trap for fools 1990

CROSS, M.
DAPHNE WRAY
1 The shadow of the four
2 The grip of the four
3 The hand of the four
4 The way of the four
5 The mark of the four
6 The four strike home
7 Surprise for the four
8 The four make holiday
9 The four get going
10 Challenge to the four
11 The four at bay
12 It couldn't be murder
13 Find the Professor
14 Murder in the pool
15 How was it done?
16 The mystery of Gruden's Gap
17 The green circle
18 Murder as arranged
19 Murder in the air
20 Murder in black
21 The mystery of Joan Marryat
22 Secret of the Grange
23 Strange affair at Greylands
24 Other than natural causes
25 Missing from his home
26 On the night of the 14th
27 Who killed Henry Wickenston?
28 Jaws of darkness
29 The black spider
30 The circle of freedom
31 Murder will speak
32 The strange case of Pamela Wilson
33 In the dead of night
34 The best laid schemes
35 When thieves fall out 1956
36 The mystery of the corded box 1956
37 Desperate steps 1957
38 When danger threatens 1957
39 Over thin ice 1958
40 Foul deeds will rise 1958
41 Not long to live 1959
42 Third time
43 Wanted for questioning 1960
44 Once too often 1960
45 Once upon a time 1961
46 Perilous hazard 1961

CROSSLEY, B.
ANNA KNIGHT
1 Candyfloss coast 1993
2 Rollercoaster 1994

CROW, D.
SIMON IRE
1 The first summer 1967
2 The crimson petal 1969

CROWDER, H.
DAVID LLEWELLYN
1 Ambush at Osirak 1990
2 Missile zone 1991

CROWLEY, E.
O'HARA FAMILY
1 Dreams of other days 1984
2 Waves upon the shore 1989

CROZIER, B.
1 The warrior 1973
2 The statesman 1974
  N.F. Biography of Charles de Gaulle

CRUISE, T. E.
WINGS OF GOLD
1 Wings of gold 1989
2 Skies of gold 1990
3 Pilots of gold 1991
  Aviation stories

CRUMLEY, J.
C. W. SUGHRUE
1 The last good kiss 1991
2 The Mexican tree duck 1994

CRUMLEY, J.
MILO MILOGRADOVITCH
1 The wrong case 1975
2 Dancing bear 1983

CUDDON, J. A.
GOTOBED TRILOGY
1 Gotobed dawn 1962
2 Gotobedlam 1963
3 John Gotobed alone 1963

CULLEN, S.
1 A noose of light
2 The Sultan's turret
  Paperback fantasy

CULPAN, M.
INSOECTOR HOUGHTON
1 A nice place to die 1965
2 The Minister of Injustice 1966
3 In a deadly vein 1967
4 The Vasiliko affair 1968
5 Bloody success 1969

CUMBERLAND, M.
SATURNIN DAX
1 Someone must die
2 Questionable shape
3 Quislings over Paris
4 The knife will fall
5 Steps in the dark
6 Not expected to live

7 A lovely corpse
8 Hearsed in death
9 And worms have eaten them
10 And then came fear
11 Policeman's nightmare
12 On a danger list
13 Confetti can be red
14 The man who covered mirrors
15 One foot in the grave
16 Booked for death
17 Fade out the stars
18 Which of us is safe
19 Etched in violence
20 The frightened brides
21 Unto death utterly
22 The charge is murder 1956
23 Lying at death's door 1956
24 Far better dead 1957
25 Hate for sale 1958
26 Out of this world 1958
27 Murmurs in the Rue Morgue 1959
28 Remains to be seen 1960
29 There must be victims 1961
30 Attention! Saturnin Dax! 1962
31 Postscript to a death 1963
32 The dice were loaded 1965
33 No sentiment in murder 1966

CUNNINGHAM, E. V.
MASAO MASUTO
1 The case of the one-penny orange 1978
2 The case of the Russian diplomat 1979
3 The case of the poisoned eclairs 1980
4 The case of the sliding pool 1982
5 The case of the kidnapped angel 1983
6 The case of the murdered Mackenzie 1985

CURRY, G.
SADDLER
1 A dirty way to die
2 Colorado crossing
3 Hot as a pistol
4 Wild wild women
  Paperback Westerns

CURZON, C.
DET.SUPT.MIKE YEADINGS
1 I give you five days 1983
2 Masks and faces 1984
3 The Trojan hearse 1985
4 Cat's cradle 1991
5 First wife, twice removed 1992
6 Death prone 1992
7 Nice people 1993

8 Past mischief 1994

CUSSLER, C.
DIRK PITT
1 Pacific vortex 1983
2 Raise the Titanic 1980
3 Night probe 1981
4 Deep six 1984
5 Cyclops 1986
6 Treasure 1988
7 Dragon 1990
8 Sahara 1992
9 Inca gold 1994

D'ORMESSON, J.
1 The winds of evening 1987
2 Mad about the girl 1988

DACRE, R.
SAM HOSKINS
1 The blood runs hot 1987
2 Scream blue murder 1988
3 Money with menaces 1989

DAHL, R.
1 Boy 1984
2 Going solo 1986
N.F. Autobiography

DAILEY, J.
CALDERS
1 This Calder range 1983
2 The Calder sky 1982
3 Stands a Calder man 1983
4 Calder born,Calder bred 1984

DAISH, E.
COPPINS BRIDGE
1 The shop on Coppins Bridge 1985
2 The family on Coppins Bridge 1986
3 Ebbtide at Coppins Bridge 1988
Emma's War, 1989, contains some of the characters 1 - 3 published in one vol., 'The Coppins Bridge Saga' 1991

DALEY, B.
ALACRITY FITZHUGH AND HOBART FLOYT
1 Requiem for a ruler of worlds
2 Jinx on a terran inheritance
3 Fall of the white ship Avatar

DALEY, B.
CORAMONDE
1 The doomfarers of Coramonde
2 The starfollowers of Coramonde
Paperback fantasies

DALTON, H., 1ST BARON
1 Call back yesterday 1953
2 The fateful years 1957
3 High tide and after 1962
N.F. Autobiography

DALY, E.
HENRY GAMADGE
1 Unexpected night 1940
2 Murders in Vol. 2 1941
3 Three house without the door 1942
4 Nothing can rescue me 1945
5 Evidence of things seen 1946
6 An arrow pointing nowhere 1946
7 The book of the dead 1946
8 Deadly nightshade 1948
9 Any shape or form 1949
10 Somewhere in the house 1949
11 Wrong way down 1950
12 Night walk 1950
13 The book of the lion 1951
14 And dangerous to know 1952
15 Death and letters 1953
16 The book of the crime 1954

DANE, E.
SCHROEDER FAMILY
1 Shadows in the fire 1976
2 A lion by the mane 1977
3 The Vaaldorp diamond 1978
Set in the Transvaal

DANIEL, J.
DESERT TRILOGY
1 The siege 1979
2 Dispatch rider 1980

DANIELSON, P.
1 Children of the lion 1985
2 The shepherd kings 1985
3 Vengeance of the lion 1985
4 The lion in Egypt 1985

DANIKEN, E. VON
1 Chariots of the Gods 1969
2 Return to the stars 1971
3 The gold of the Gods 1973
4 In search of Ancient Gods 1974
5 Miracles of the Gods 1975
6 Signs of the Gods 1980

DANISCHENSKY, M.
1 White Russian - red face 1970
2 Out of my mind 1972
N.F. Autobiography

DANKS, D.
GEORGINA POWERS
1 The pizza house crash 1990
2 Better off dead 1991
3 Frame grabber 1992
4 Wink a hopeful eye 1993

DARBY, C.
FALCONS
1 Falcon for a witch 1975
2 Game for a Falcon 1976
3 Falcon's claw 1986
4 Falcon to the lure 1981
5 Fortune for a Falcon 1976
6 Season of the Falcon 1976
7 A pride of Falcons 1977
8 The Falcon tree 1977
9 The Falcon and the moon 1977
10 Falcon rising 1978
11 Falcon sunset 1978
12 Seed of the Falcons 1981

DARBY, C.
ROWAN SERIES
1 Rowan Garth 1982
2 Rowan for a Queen 1983
3 A scent of Rowan 1983
4 A circle of Rowan 1983
5 The Rowan maid 1984
6 Song of the Rowan 1984

DARBY, C.
SABRE
1 Sabre 1984
2 Sabre's child 1985
3 The silken sabre 1985
4 House of Sabre 1986
5 A breed of Sabres
6 Morning of a Sabre 1987
7 Fruit of the Sabre 1988
8 Gentle Sabre 1988

DARBY, L.
EYE OF TIME TRILOGY
1 Crystal and steel 1988
2 Bloodshed 1988
3 Phoenixfire
Paperback fantasy

DARBYSHIRE, S.
MELBURY TRILOGY
1 Journey to melbury 1950
2 The years at Melbury 1952
3 High noon at Melbury 1954

DARK, E.
MANNION FAMILY
1 The timeless land 1941
2 Storm of time 1948

68

3 No barrier 1953
Novels on the history of Australia

DARKE, J.
THE WITCHES
1 The prisoner
2 The trial
3 The torture
4 No escape
5 The meeting
6 The killing
Paperback horror stories

DARRELL, E.
SHERIDAN FAMILY
1 At the going down of the sun 1984
2 And in the morning 1988
About a family in World War II

DART, I. R.
1 Beaches 1985
2 I'll be there 1992

DAVENAT, C.
DEBORAH
1 Deborah: the springtime of love 1973
2 Deborah:the many faces of love 1974
3 Deborah:the siege of Paris 1975
Historical romances

DAVEY, D.
KATE ENGLAND
1 Caravanserai for Kate 1986
2 Keyhole for Kate 1987
3 Coronet for Kate 1987

DAVEY, D.
VICTOR ARLISS (THE VICAR)
1 The case of the golden coins 1990
2 The death of a Wimbledon finalist 1990

DAVEY, J.
AMBROSE USHER
1 The undoubted deed 1956
2 The naked villainy 1958
3 A touch of stage fright 1960
4 A killing in hats 1965

DAVID, J.
1 A square of sky 1965
2 A touch of earth 1966
3 A part of the main 1969
Semi-autobiographical novels

DAVIES, A.
1 A very peculiar practice 1987

2 The new frontier 1988

DAVIES, F.
1 Death of a hitman 1982
2 Snow in Venice 1983

DAVIES, P.
1 Mare's milk and wild honey 1987
2 A corner of Paradise 1992
N.F. Autobiography N.F.
Autobiography

DAVIES, R.
CORNISH TRILOGY
1 Rebel angels 1981
2 What's bred in the bone 1985
3 The lyre of Orpheus 1988

DAVIES, R.
EISENGRIN TRILOGY
1 The fifth business 1971
2 The Manticore 1973
3 World of wonders 1977
Published as one volume called 'The
Deptford Trilogy' in 1983

DAVIES, R.
SALTERTON TRILOGY
1 Tempest-tost
2 Leaven of malice
3 Mixture of frailties

DAVIES, T.
1 One winter of the Holy Spirit 1985
2 Fire in the bay 1989
3 The dragon's war NYP
4 Black sunlight 1987
A chronicle of 20th C. Wales

DAVIS, BART
PETER MACKENZIE
1 Raise the Red Dawn 1991
2 Destroy the Kentucky 1994

DAVIS, D. S.
JIMMIE JARVIS
1 Death of an old sinner 1958
2 A gentleman called 1959
3 Old sinners never die 1960

DAVIS, D. S.
JULIE HAYES
1 A death in the life 1980
2 Scarlet night 1981
3 Lullaby of murder 1984

DAVIS, G.
ROAG'S CRIME SYNDICATE
1 Roag's syndicate 1960

2 Toledano 1962
3 Friday before Bank Holiday 1964
4 Crime in Threadneedle Street 1968
5 The killer grew tired 1971
6 Death ofa fire-raiser 1973

DAVIS, G.
THE SERGEANT
1 Death train
2 Hell harbour
3 Bloody bush
4 The liberation of Paris
5 Doom river
6 Slaughter city
7 Bullet bridge
8 Bloody Bastogne
9 Hammerhead
Paperback war stories

DAVIS, J.
MACLEODS OF VIRGINIA
1 Cloud on the land 1954
2 Bridle the wind 1955
3 Eagle on the sun 1957
Novels about the development of the
Shenendoah Valley in the 1920s

DAVIS, J. G.
1 Hold my hand,I'm dying 1980
2 Seize the reckless wind 1984

DAVIS, L.
FALCO
1 The silver pigs 1989
2 Shadows in bronze 1990
3 Venus in copper 1991
4 The iron hand of Mars 1992
5 Poseidon's gold 1993
6 Last act in Palmyra 1994
Detective stories set in Ancient Rome

DAVIS, M. T.
1 Rag woman, rich woman 1987
2 Daughters and mothers 1988
3 Wounds of war 1989

DAVIS, M. T.
GLASGOW TRILOGY
1 The breadmakers 1971
2 A baby might be crying 1973
3 A sort of peace 1974

DAVIS, M. T.
MONKTON FAMILY
1 A woman of property 1991
2 A sense of belonging 1993

DAVIS, M. T.
SCOTTISH TRILOGY
1 The prince and the tobacco lords 1975
2 The roots of bondage 1976
3 Scorpion in the fire 1977
Set in the 18th century

DAVISON, G.
STEPHEN FLETCHER
1 The spy who swapped shoes 1966
2 Nest of spies 1968
3 The chessboard spies 1969

DAWES, F. V.
COLE FAMILY
1 A family album 1982
2 Inheritance 1984

DAWSON, D.
1 Vet in the vale
2 Vet in the paddock
N.F. Autobiography of a vet

DAWSON, J.
JERI HOWARD
1 Kindred crimes 1990
2 Till the old men die 1992
3 Don't turn your back on the ocean 1993
4 Take a number 1994

DAY, M.
CLAUDIA VALENTINE
1 The life and crimes of Harry Valentine 1988
2 The case of the Chinese boxes 1990
3 The last tango of Dolores Delgada 1992

DAYUS, K.
1 Her people 1982
2 Where there's life 1985
3 All my days 1988
4 The best of times 1991
5 The people of Lavender Court 1993
N.F.Working class life in Birmingham in the early 1900s

DE BOISSIERE, R.
1 Crown jewel 1982
2 Rum and coca-cola 1984
Novels set in contemporary Trinidad

DE BORN, E.
DE KAILERN FAMILY
1 Schloss Fielding

2 The house in Vienna
3 The flat in Paris
4 A question of age

DE BORN, E.
JIMMY CHESTER
1 The disintegrator 1969
2 The fight for Pelignano 1970
3 The end of the struggle 1972

DE CHAIR, S.
1 The golden carpet 1945
2 Buried pleasures 1986
N.F. Autobiography of a soldier/ diplomat

DE HAAN, T.
BRYCHMACHRYE
1 A mirror for princes 1988
2 The child of good fortune 1989

DE HAVEN, T.
CHRONICLES OF THE KING'S TRAMP
1 Walker of worlds
2 The end of everything man
Paperback fantasy

DE LA ROCHE, M.
WHITEOAKS
1 The building of Jalna 1944
2 Morning in Jalna 1960
3 Mary Wakefield 1949
4 Young Renny 1935
5 Whiteoak heritage 1940
6 Whiteoak brothers 1953
7 Jalna 1927
8 Whiteoaks 1929
9 Finch's fortune 1931
10 Master of Jalna 1933
11 Whiteoak harvest 1936
12 Wakefield's course 1941
13 Return to Jalna 1946
14 Renny's daughter 1937
15 Variable winds at Jalna 1954
16 Centenary at Jalna 1958
Listed in order of reading

DE MANIO, J.
1 To Auntie, with love 1968
2 Life begins too early 1970
N.F. Autobiography

DE MILLE, A.
1 Dance to the piper 1952
2 And promenade home 1958
N.F. Autobiography

DE POLNAY, P.
1 Death and tomorrow 1942

2 Fools of choice 1955
3 A door ajar 1959
4 Rough childhood 1960
N.F. Autobiography

DE SILVA, C.
1 The winds of Sinhala 1982
2 Founts of Sinhala 1984
3 The fires of Sinhala 1986
4 The last Sinhala lions 1987

DEAL, P.
1 Nurse! Nurse! Nurse! 1956
2 Forward Staff Nurse 1958
3 Nurse at Butlins 1959
4 Surgery nurse 1960
5 Village nurse 1960
6 Factory nurse 1962
N.F. Autobiography

DEAN, S.
DON CADEE
1 Merchant of murder 1954
2 The frightened fingers 1955
3 The scent of fear 1956
4 Marked down for murder 1958
5 Murder on delivery 1958
6 Dishonour among thieves 1959

DEAN, S. F. X.
NEIL KELLY
1 By frequent anguish 1982
2 Such pretty toys 1983
3 It can't be my grave 1983
4 Ceremony of innocence 1985
5 Death and the mad heroine 1986

DEFOE, D.
1 Robinson Crusoe
2 The return of Robinson Crusoe, by H.Treece 1958
3 Foe, by J.M.Coetzee 1987

DEFORGES, R.
THE BLUE BICYCLE
1 The blue bicycle 1985
2 101 Avenue Henri-Martin 1986
3 The devil is still laughing 1987

DEIGHTON, B.
FELICITY TRAVERS
1 A little learning 1987
2 Good intentions 1988
Thrillers about a polytechnic lecturer

DEIGHTON, L.
BERNARD SAMSON
1 Berlin game 1983
2 Mexico set 1984

3 London match 1985
4 Spy hook 1988
5 Spy line 1989
6 Spy sinker 1990
7 Faith 1994
1-3 Published in one volume in 1987 as 'Game, set and Match'. 'Winter:a Berlin family'(1987) is a pendant to the first trilogy, with some of the same characters. 4-6 comprise a second trilogy, 'Hook, line and sinker'

DEIGHTON, L.
HARRY PALMER
1 The Ipcress file 1962
2 Horse under water 1963
3 Funeral in Berlin 1964
4 Billion dollar brain 1966
5 An expensive place to die 1969

DELACORTA
GORODISH AND ALBA
1 Nana 1984
2 Diva 1984
3 Luna 1985
4 Lola 1986
5 Vida 1986

DELANEY, F.
1 The sins of the mothers 1992
2 Telling the pictures 1993
Linked novels about Ireland.

DELANY, J.
1 No starch in my coat 1970
2 Smile at me, doctor 1972
3 Pass the happy pills 1978
4 It's my nerves, doctor 1980
N.F. A doctor's life in a mental hospital

DELANY, S. R.
1 Fall of the towers 1971
2 Out of the dead city 1966
3 The towers of Toron

DELANY, S. R.
NEVERYON
1 Tales of Neveryon
2 Neveryone
3 Flight from Neveryon
4 Return to Neveryon

DELDERFIELD, R. F.

1 For my own amusement 1968
2 Overture for beginners 1971
N.F. Autobiography

DELDERFIELD, R. F.
DIANA
1 There was a fair maid dwelling
1960
2 The unjust skies 1962

DELDERFIELD, R. F.
NAPOLEON BONAPARTE
1 Napoleon in love 1964
2 The march of the 26 1966
3 The retreat from Moscow 1967
4 Imperial sunset 1969
N.F.

DELDERFIELD, R. F.
THE AVENUE STORY
1 The dreaming suburb 1958
2 The avenue goes to war 1959
*Reprinted in one vol. as 'The Avenue
story' 1964*

DELDERFIELD, R. F.
THE CRADDOCKS OF SHALLOWFORD
1 The horseman riding by 1966
2 The green gauntlet 1968
*The paperback edition is in three
volumes, 'Long summer's day', 'Post
of honour', 'Green gauntlet'*

DELDERFIELD, R. F.
THE SWANN SAGA
1 God is an Englishman(1857-1866)
1970
2 Theirs was the kingdom(1878-
1897) 1971
3 Give us this day(1900-1914) 1973

DELISLE, F.
1 Francoise: in love with love 1963
2 Friendship's Odyssey 1946
(rev.1962)
N.F. *Autobiography. 2 tels the story
of her life with Havelock Ellis*

DELMAN, D.
JACOB & HELEN HOROWITZ
1 Sudden death 1973
2 One man's murder 1975
3 The nice murderers 1977
4 Death of a nymph 1986
5 Dead faces laughing 1987
6 The liar's league 1989
7 Last gambit 1990
8 Bye-bye baby 1992

DELVING, M.
EDISON & CANNON
1 Smiling the boy fell dead 1969
2 The devil finds work 1970

3 Die like a man 1970
4 A shadow of himself 1972
5 A wave of fatalities 1976
6 No sign of life 1978
7 The China expert 1979

DENHAM, B.
DEREK THYRDE
1 The man who lost his shadow
1985
2 Two Thyrdes 1986
3 Foxhunt 1988

DENIS, C.
1 King's wench 1977
2 King's bastard 1977

DENISON, M.
1 Overture and beginners 1973
2 Double act 1985
N.F. *Autobiography of the actor and
his wife*

DENKER, H.
HOROWITZ
1 Horowitz and Mrs.Washington
1990
2 Mrs.Washington and Horowitz too
1994

DENNING, T.
PRISM PENTAD
1 The verdant passage
2 The crimson legion
3 The amber enchantress
4 The obsidian oracle
5 The cerulean storm
Paperback fantasy

DENNIS, I.
THE PRINCE OF STARS IN THE
CAVERN OF TIME
1 Baghdad
2 The Prince of Stars
Paperback science fiction

DENNIS, P.
AUNTIE MAME
1 Auntie Mame 1955
2 Around the world with Auntie
Mame 1957

DENNIS, R. C.
READERS, PSYCHIC DETECTIVE
1 Sweat of fear 1973
2 Conversations with a corpse 1974

DENTINGER, J.
JOCELYN O'ROURKE
1 First hit of the season 1986
2 Death mask 1988
3 Murder on cue 1985

DENVER, L.
CHEYENNE JONES
1 The gun code of Cheyenne Jones 1969
2 Cheyenne swings a wide loop 1970
3 Three slugs for Cheyenne 1971
4 Cheyene pays in lead 1972
5 Lone trail for Cheyenne 1973
6 Cheyenne Jones maverick marshal 1977
7 Cheyenne's sixgun justice 1980
8 Cheyenne's trail to perdition 1982
9 Cheyenne's two-gun shootout 1983
10 Cheyenne at Dull Knife Pass 1984

DERWENT, L.
1 A breath of Border air 1975
2 Another breath of Border air 1977
3 A Border bairn 1979
4 God bless the Borders 1981
5 Lady of the Manse 1983
6 A mouse in the Manse 1985
N.F.Autobiography set in the Scottish Borders

DESSAU, J.
ELIZABETH I
1 The red haired brat 1978
2 Absolute Elizabeth 1978
3 Fantastical, marvellous Queen 1979

DEUTSCH, D.
THE EQUALISER
1 The equaliser
2 To even the odds
3 Blood and wine
Paperbacks, based on the TV series

DEVERAUX, J.
CHANDLER TWINS
1 Twin of ice
2 Twin of fire
Paperback

DEVERAUX, J.
JAMES RIVER TRILOGY
1 Counterfeit lady
2 Lost lady
3 River lady
Paperback

DEVERAUX, J.
MONTGOMERY FAMILY
1 The velvet promise
2 Highland velvet
3 Velvet angel
4 Velvet song
5 The temptress
6 The princess
7 The raider 1988
Paperbacks 7 is in hardback.

DEVINE, R.
FLESHTRADERS
1 Master of Black River
2 Black River affair
3 Black River breed

DEWES, S.
1 A Suffolk childhood
2 Essex schooldays
3 When all the world was young
N.F. Autobiography

DEWEY, T. B.
PETE SCHOFIELD
1 Go to sleep, Jeannie 1960
2 I.O.U. murder 1961
3 Mexican slayride 1961
4 Go, Honeylou! 1962
5 Too hot for Hawaii 1963
6 The girl with the sweet plump knees 1963
7 Only on Tuesdays 1963
8 The girl in the punchbowl 1965
9 Nude in Nevada 1966

DEWEY, T. B.
PRIVATE EYE MAC
1 The mean street 1955
2 Prey for me 1955
3 The brave bad girls 1957
4 The chased and the unchaste 1960
5 You've got him cold 1960
6 The girl who wasn't there 1960
7 How hard to kill 1963
8 A sad song for singing 1964
9 Don't cry for long 1964
10 Portrait of a dead heiress 1965
11 Every bet's a sure thing 1965
12 Deadline 1966
13 Death and taxes 1969
14 Death turns right 1969
15 The Taurus trip 1972

DEWEY, T. B.
SINGER BATTS
1 Every bet's a sure thing
2 Mourning after
3 Handle with fear

DEWHURST, E.
HELEN JOHNSON
1 Whoever I am 1981
2 Playing safe 1985

DEWHURST, E.
NEIL CARTER
1 Trio in three flats 1982
2 There was a little girl 1984
3 Nice little business 1990

DEXTER, C.
DET. CHIEF INSPECTOR MORSE
1 Last bus to Woodstock 1975
2 Last seen wearing 1976
3 The silent world of Nicholas Quinn 1977
4 Service of all the dead 1979
5 The dead of Jericho 1981
6 The riddle of the third mile 1983
7 The secret of Annexe 3 1986
8 The wench is dead 1989
9 The jewel that was ours 1991
10 The way through the woods 1992
11 Morse's greatest mystery and other stories 1993
12 The daughters of Cain 1994

DEXTER, S.
THE WINTER KING'S WAR
1 The ring of Allaire 1987
2 The sword of Calandra 1987
3 The mountains of Channadran 1987
Fantasy

DEXTER, T. & MAKINS, C.
JACK STENTON
1 Test kill 1978
2 Deadly putter 1979

DIBBA, E.
1 Chaff in the wind 1984
2 Fafa 1989

DIBDIN, M.
AURELIO ZEN
1 Ratking 1988
2 Vendetta 1990
3 Cabal 1992

DICKASON, C.
1 The dragon riders 1988
2 The years of the tiger 1989

DICKENS, C.
1 Great expectations
'Magwitch' by M. Noonan covers the adventures of Magwitch in Australia.

1982 'Estella:her expectations', by S. Roe is based on the character of Miss Havisham. 1982 'Estella', by Alanna Knight (1986) follows 'Great Expectations'.

DICKENS, C.
EDWIN DROOD
The disappearance of Edwin Drood, by P. Rowland (1991) also concerns Sherlock Holmes

DICKINSON, B.
LORD IFFY BOATRACE
1 The adventures of Lord Iffy Boatrace 1990
2 The missionary position 1992

DICKINSON, M.
ABBEYFORD TRILOGY
1 Sarah 1981
2 Adeline 1981
3 Carrie 1982

DICKINSON, P.
ALTERNATIVE ROYAL FAMILY
1 King and joker 1976
2 Skeleton-in-waiting 1989

DICKINSON, P.
DET.SUPT.PIBBLE
1 Skin deep 1968
2 A pride of heroes 1969
3 The seals 1970
4 Sleep and his brother 1971
5 The lizard in the cup 1972
6 One foot in the grave 1979

DICKSON, C. [J. D. CARR]
SIR HENRY MERIVALE
1 The bowstring murders 1933
2 The Plague Court murders 1935
3 The White Priory murders 1935
4 The red widow murders 1935
5 The unicorn murders 1936
6 The magic lantern murders 1936
7 The ten teacups 1937
8 The Judas window 1938
9 Death in five boxes 1938
10 The reader is warned 1939
11 Murder in the submarine zone 1940
12 The Department of Queer Complaints 1940
13 And so to murder 1941
14 Seeing is believing 1942
15 The gilded man 1942
16 She died a lady 1943
17 He wouldn't kill Patience 1944

18 Lord of the sorcerers 1946
19 My late wives 1947
20 Skeleton in the clock 1949
21 Graveyard to let 1950
22 Night at the Mocking Widow 1951
23 Behind the crimson blind 1952
24 Cavalier's cup 1954

DICKSON, G.
DORSAI
1 Tactics of mistake
2 Dorsai
3 Soldier,ask not
4 The spirit of Dorsai
5 Lost Dorsai
Paperback science fiction

DICKSON, G. R.
CHILDE CYCLE
1 The final encyclopaedia
2 Chantry guild
3 Young Bleys
Linked to the Dorsai series

DICKSON, G. R.
DRAGON SERIES
1 The dragon and the George
2 The dragon knight
3 The dragon at war

DICKSON, G. R.
SEA PEOPLE
1 Home from the shore
2 The Space swimmers
Paperback science fiction

DIDELOT, F.
COMMANDER BIGNON
1 The tenth leper 1961
2 Death on the Champs Elysee 1965

DILLON, A.
1 Seasons 1990
2 Another time,another season 1991
3 Season's end 1991

DILLON, E.
1 Wild geese 1981
2 Citizen Burke 1984
Novels set in present-day Ireland

DILLON, E.
IRISH SAGA
1 Across the bitter sea 1974
2 Blood relation 1978

DIMENT, A.
PHILIP MACALPINE
1 The dolly dolly spy 1966
2 The great spy race 1967
3 The bang bang birds 1968

DINES, M.
JOHNNY MANNING
1 Operation - deadline 1961
2 Operation - to kill a man 1968
3 Operation - kill or be killed 1969

DISCH, T. M.
1 The ruins of Earth 1973
2 Bad moon rising 1974
3 The new improved sun 1976
Science fiction

DIXON, R.
1 The Messiah 1974
2 Christ on trial 1972
Novels on the life of Jesus

DJEBAR, A.
ALGERIAN QUARTET
1 Fantasia 1989
2 A sister to Scheherezade 1989

DOBBS, M.
FRANCIS URQUHART
1 House of cards 1989
2 To play the King 1992
3 The final cut 1994

DOBLIN, A.
NOVEMBER 1918:A GERMAN
REVOLUTION
1 A people betrayed 1986
2 The troops return 1986
3 Karl and Rosa 1986
Originally published 1948-50.

DOBYNS, S.
CHARLIE BRADSHAW
1 Saratoga swimmer 1986
2 Saratoga headhunter 1986
3 Saratoga longshot 1988
4 Saratoga snapper 1988
5 Saratoga bestiary 1989
6 Saratoga hexameter 1990

DODGE, D.
JOHN ABRAHAM LINCOLN
1 Hatchet man 1970
2 Troubleshooter 1972

DOELL, E. W.
1 Doctor against witch doctor 1956
2 Hospital in the bush 1958

3 Mission doctor sees the wind of change 1960
N.F. Autobiography

DOHERTY, L.
1 The good lion 1958
2 The good husband 1959

DOHERTY, P. C.
1 The Prince of Drakulya 1986
2 The Lord Count Drakulya 1986

DOHERTY, P. C.
CANTERBURY TALES
1 An ancient evil 1993
2 A tapestry of murders 1994
Mystery stories set among Chaucer's pilgrims

DOHERTY, P. C.
HUGH CORBETT
1 Satan in St.Mary's 1986
2 Spy in chancery 1988
3 Crown in darkness 1991
4 The angel of death 1991
5 The prince of darkness 1992
6 Murder wears a cowl 1992
7 The assassin in the greenwood 1993
8 The song of a dark angel 1994
Mediaeval mystery stories

DOMINIC, R. B. [E. LATHEN]
CONGRESSMAN BEN SAFFORD
1 Murder in high places 1970
2 Murder out of court 1971
3 Epitaph for a lobbyist 1974
4 Murder out of commission 1976
5 Attending physician 1980
6 A flaw in the system 1983

DONACHIE, D.
HARRY LUDLOW
1 The devil's own luck (1792) 1991
2 A dying trade (1794) 1993
3 A hanging matter (1795) 1994
4 An element of chance 1994
Sea stories

DONALD, A.
ALEX TANNER
1 An uncommon murder 1992
2 In at the deep end 1993
3 The glass ceiling 1994

DONALDSON, S. R.
MORDANT'S NEED
1 A mirror for her dreams 1986
2 A man rides through 1988

DONALDSON, S. R.
THE CHRONICLES OF THOMAS COVENANT,UNBELIEVER
1 Lord Foulbane 1980
2 The Illearth war 1980
3 The power that preserves 1980
4 The wounded land 1980
5 The one tree 1982
6 White gold wielder 1983
'Gildfire', 1983, links with 2. 4-6 were sub- titled 'The second chronicles. . . '

DONALDSON, S. R.
THE GAP
1 The gap into conflict:the real story 1990
2 The gap into vision:forbidden knowledge 1991
3 Gap into power:a dark and hungry god arises 1992
4 The gap into madness:chaos and order 1994

DONALDSON, W.
1 Both the ladies and the gentlemen 1975
2 The balloons in the black bag 1975
3 The English way of doing things 1984
2 was reissued in 1985 as 'Nicknames only'

DONLEAVY, J. P.
DARCY DANCER
1 The destinies of Darcy Dancer,gentleman 1978
2 Leila 1983
3 That Darcy,that Dancer,that gentleman 1990

DONLEAVY, J. P.
SCHULTZ
1 Schultz
2 Are you listening, Rabbi Low? 1987

DOOLITTLE, J.
TOM BETHANY
1 Body scissors 1991
2 Strangle hold 1992
3 Bear hug 1994

DOUGLAS, A.
JONATHAN CRAYTHORNE
1 Last rights 1986
2 A very wrong number 1987
3 The goods 1985
4 A worm turns 1987

DOUGLAS, C. N.
SWORD AND CIRCLET
1 Keepers of Edenvant
2 Heir of Rengarth
3 Seven of swords

DOUGLAS, COLIN
1 The Houseman's tale 1975
2 The greatest breakthrough since lunchtime 1977
3 Bleeders come first 1979
4 Wellies from the Queen 1981
5 A cure from living 1983
6 For services to medicine 1985
7 Ethics made easy 1986
8 Hazards of the profession 1987
A series of novels about young doctors in a Scottish hospital

DOUGLAS, D. MCNEIL
BOLIVAR MANCHENIL
1 Rebecca's pride
2 Many brave hearts 1959
3 Saba's treasure 1963

DOUGLAS, E.
1 Family's affairs 1962
2 Black cloud, white cloud 1964

DOUGLAS, GEORGE
DET.SUPT.HALLAM & SGT.SPRATT
1 Odd woman out 1965
2 Unwanted witness 1963
3 Death went hunting 1966
4 Death unheralded 1967
5 Death in duplicate 1968
6 Gunmanat large 1968
7 Devil to pay 1969
8 Dead reckoning 1970
9 Murder unmourned 1971
10 Crime most foul 1971
11 Time to die 1971
12 One to jump 1972
13 Death in darkness 1973
14 Death on the doorstep 1974
15 Dead on the dot 1974
16 Crime without reason 1975
17 Final score 1975
18 Death in retreat 1976
19 Dead on delivery 1976
20 Luckless lady 1976
21 Double cross 1977
22 End of the line 1979
23 Death of a big shot 1981

DOUGLAS, KIRK
1 Dance with the devil 1990
2 The gift 1992

DOUGLAS, P.
1 Down the village street 1979
2 About this village 1980
N.F. Village life in Norfolk

DOWNE, P.
1 Dear doctor 1958
2 The doctor calls again 1959
3 Come in, doctor 1960
N.F. Autobiography

DOYLE, A. C.
SHERLOCK HOLMES
1 A study in scarlet 1888
2 The sign of four 1890
3 Adventures of Sherlock Holmes 1892
4 The memoirs of Sherlock Holmes 1894
5 The hound of the Baskervilles 1902
6 The return of Sherlock Holmes 1905
7 The valley of fear 1915
8 His last bow 1917
9 The casebook of Sherlock Holmes 1927
10 The seven per cent solution, by N.Meyer 1975
11 The West End horror, by N.Meyer 1976
12 The giant rat of Sumatra, by R.L.Boyer 1977
13 Exit Sherlock Holmes, by R.L.Hall 1977
14 Tangled skein, by D.S.Davies 1978
15 The last Sherlock Holmes story, by M.Dibdin 1978
16 S.Holmes versus Dracula, by L.D.Estleman 1978
17 Prisoner of the devil, by M.Hardwick 1979
18 Advs.of the stalwart companions, by H.Jeffers 1979
19 Infernal device, by M.Kurland 1979
20 Puzzle for S.Holmes, by R.Newman 1979
21 Case of the philosopher's ring,by R.Collins 1980
22 Curse of the Nibelungen,by M.D'Agreau 1981
23 Final advs. of S.Holmes, by P.Haining 1983
24 The Mycroft memoranda, by R.Walsh 1984
25 Sherlock Holmes, by M.Hardwick 1984

26 Ten years beyond Baker St.,by
    C.Van Ash 1985
27 S.Holmes at the 1902 5th Test,by
    S.Shaw 1985
28 Private life of Dr.Watson,by
    M.Hardwick 1985
29 S.Holmes meets Annie Oakley,by
    S.Shaw 1986
30 The Kentish Manor murders, by
    J.Symons 1988
31 Revenge of the hound, by
    M.Hardwick 1988
32 My dearest Holmes, by R.Piercy
    1988
33 S.H.and the eminent Thespian, by
    V.Andrews 1988
34 S.H.investigates the murder in
    Euston Sq. 1989
35 S.H.and the Brighton Pavilion
    mystery 1990
36 Sherlock Holmes revisited, by
    C.Brooks 1990
37 Secret files of Sherlock Holmes, by
    J.Thomson 1990
38 Disappearance of Edwin Drood,
    by P.Rowland 1991
39 S.H.and the Hentzau affair, by
    D.S.Davies 1991
40 Secret chronicles of S.Holmes, by
    J.Thomson 1992
41 Unopened casebook of
    S.Holmes,by J.Thomson 1993
42 The case of Emily V., by K.Oatley
    1993
43 S.H. and the Egyptian Hall adv,by
    V.Andrews 1993
44 S.H. and the railway maniac,by
    B.Roberts 1994
45 Singular case of the duplicate
    Holmes, by J.Walker
46 S.H. and the earthquake machine,
    by A.Mitchelson 1994

DOYLE, D. & MACDONALD, J. D.
MAGEWORLDS
1 The price of the stars
2 Starpilot's grave
   Paperback fantasy

DOYLE, R.
RABBITTE FAMILY
1 The commitments 1987
2 The snapper 1990
3 The van 1991
   *Published in one vol., 'The Barrytown
   trilogy' 1992*

DRABBLE, M.
1 The radiant way 1988

2 A natural curiosity 1989
3 The gates of ivory 1991

DRABBLE, P.
1 Country scene 1975
2 Country seasons 1976
3 Badgers at my window 1976
4 A weasel in my meatsafe 1977
5 No badgers in my wood 1979
   *N.F. About the author's work with
   wild animals*

DRAGONLANCE
DEFENDERS OF MAGIC TRILOGY
1 Night of the eye
2 The medusa plague

DRAGONLANCE
DRAGONLANCE PRELUDES
1 Darkness and light,by
   P.B.Thompson
2 Kendermore, by M.Kirchoff
3 Brothers Majere, by K.Stein

DRAGONLANCE
DRAGONLANCE PRELUDES II
1 Riverwind the plainsman, by
   P.B.Thompson
2 Flint the king, by M.Kirchoff
3 Tanis, the shadow years

DRAGONLANCE
DRAGONLANCE SAGA HEROES
1 The legend of Huma, by
   R.A.Kraak
2 Stormblade
3 Weasel's luck, by M.Williams

DRAGONLANCE
DRAGONLANCE SAGA HEROES II
1 Kaz the monster, by R.A.Kraak
2 The gates of Thorbarden, by
   D.Parkinson
3 Galen benighted

DRAGONLANCE
DWARVEN NATIONS TRILOGY
1 The covenant of the forge, by
   D.Parkinson
2 Hammer and axe, by D.Parkinson

DRAGONLANCE
ELVEN NATIONS TRILOGY
1 Firstborn
2 The kinslayer wars
3 The Qualinesti

DRAGONLANCE
MEETINGS SEXTET
1 Kindred spirits
2 Wanderlust
3 Dark heart
4 The oath and the measure
5 Steel and stone
6 The companions

DRAGONLANCE
THE DRAGONLANCE CHRONICLES
1 Dragons of autumn twilight
2 Dragons of winter night
3 Dragons of spring dawning
Written by M. Weis and T. Hickman

DRAGONLANCE
THE DRAGONLANCE LEGENDS
1 Time of the twins
2 War of the twins
3 Test of the twins

DRAGONLANCE
THE DRAGONLANCE TALES
1 The magic of Krynn
2 Kenders, Gully Dwarfs and
  Gnomes
3 Love and war

DRAGONLANCE
THE DRAGONLANCE TALES II
1 The reign of Istar
2 The cataclysm
3 The war of the lance

DRAGONLANCE
VILLAINS
1 Before the mask, by M.T.Williams
2 The black wing, by M.Kirchoff
3 Emperor of Ansalon, by D.Niles
4 Hederick the theocrat, by
  E.D.Sevenson
5 Lord Toede, by J.Grubb
6 The dark queen, by M.&T.
  Williams
*Dragonlance is a cult series based on
the Dungeons and Dragons games,
with pendants in the form of maps,
guides, etc. The series is confusing
because of the number of authors
involved, hence its entry under series
rather than authors.*

DRAPER, A.
CRISPIN PATON,R.N.
1 Grey seal 1982
2 The restless waves 1983
3 The raging deep 1985
4 Storm over Singapore 1986

5 The great avenging day 1988

DREHER, S.
STONER MCTAVISH
1 Stoner McTavish 1987
2 Something shady 1988
3 Grey magic 1990
4 Captive time 1991
5 Other world 1993

DRUMMOND, C.
SERGEANT REED
1 Death at the furlong post 1967
2 Death and the leaping ladies 1968
3 Odds on death 1969
4 Stab in the back 1970
5 Death at the bar 1972

DRUMMOND, E.
KNIGHTSHILL
1 That sweet savage land 1992
2 A distant hero 1994

DRUMMOND, I.
LADY JENNIFER, SANDRO & COLLY
1 The man with the tiny head 1969
2 The priest of the abomination 1970
3 The frog in the moonflower 1972
4 The jaws of the watchdog 1973
5 The power of the bug 1974
6 The tank of sacred eels 1976
7 The necklace of skulls 1977
8 A stench of poppies 1978
9 The diamonds of Loreta 1980

DRUON, M.
THE ACCURSED KINGS
1 The iron King 1956
2 The strangled Queen 1956
3 The poisoned crown 1957
4 The royal succession 1958
5 The she-wolf of France 1960
6 The lily and the lion 1961
*A series about France in the 14th
century, under the Capetan and
Valois Kings.*

DRUON, M.
THE CURTAIN FALLS
1 The magnates 1948
2 Feet of clay 1949
3 Rendezvous in hell 1951
*Published in one vol. as 'The curtain
falls' 1959*

DRURY, A.
1 Advise and consent 1962
2 A shade of difference 1964
3 Capable of honour 1966

4 Preserve and protect 1968
5 Come Nineveh,come Tyre 1974
6 Promise of joy 1975
7 Anna Hastings 1978
Novels about American political life.

DRURY, A.
EGYPTIAN DYNASTY
1 A god against Gods 1976
2 Return to Thebes 1977

DRURY, A.
SOVIET CONQUEST
1 The hill of summer 1983
2 The roads of earth 1985

DRURY, A.
UNIVERSITY SERIES
1 Toward what bright glory? 1990
2 Into what far harbour? 1993

DRYSDALE, A.
1 Faint heart never kissed a pig 1982
2 Sows ears and silk purses 1984
3 Pearls before swine 1985
N.F. Autobiography of a hill farmer

DRYSDALE, MARGARET
ROBERT DUDLEY,EARL OF LEICESTER
1 Quest for a crown 1982
2 Heir for the Earl 1983
3

DU BARRY, M.
THE LOVES OF ANGELA CARLYLE
1 Into passion
2 Across captive seas
3 Towards love
Paperback bodice rippers

DU MAURIER, A/
1 It's only the sister 1951
2 Old maids remember 1966
N.F. Autobiography

DU MAURIER, D.
1 Rebecca 1938
2 Mrs.De Winter, by Susan Hill 1993

DUANE, D.
TALE OF THE FIVE
1 The door into fire
2 The door into shadow
3 The door into sunset
Paperback fantasy

DUBUS, E. N.
1 Where love rules 1986

2 To love and to dream 1987
A family saga set in America's Deep South

DUDLEY, E.
DR.MORELLE
1 Meet Dr.Morelle 1944
2 Dr.Morelle again 1947
3 Menace for Dr.Morelle 1947
4 Dr.Morelle and the drummer girl 1950
5 Dr.Morelle takes a bow 1957
6 Callers for Dr.Morelle 1957
7 The mind of Dr.Morelle 1958
8 Dr.Morelle and destiny 1958
9 Confess to Dr.Morelle 1958
10 Dr.Morelle at midnight 1959
11 Alibi for Dr.Morelle 1960
12 Dr.Morelle and the doll 1960

DUFFY, M.
PATRICK & INGRID LANGLEY
1 A murder of crows 1987
2 Death of a raven 1988
3 Brass eagle 1988
4 Who killed Cock Robin? 1990
5 Rook-shoot 1991
6 Gallows bird 1993

DUFFY, MAUREEN
METROPOLITAN TRILOGY
1 Wounds 1969
2 Capital 1975
3 Londoners 1983

DUGGAN, A.
SAXON TRILOGY
1 Conscience of the King 1948
2 Cunning of the dove 1950
3 The King of Athelney 1961

DUKE, M.
1 Sobaka 1968
2 The lethal innocents 1970
3 Because of fear in the night 1973

DUKE, M.
DR.NORAH NORTH
1 Death at the wedding 1975
2 Death of a holy murderer 1976
3 Death of a Dandie Dinmont 1978

DUKE, M.
THE SUNDMANS
1 A city built to music 1960
2 Ride the brooding wind 1961
3 The sovereign lords 1963

DUNANT, S.
HANNAH WOLFE
1 Birth marks 1991
2 Fatlands 1993

DUNCAN, A.
1 It's a vet's life 1962
2 The vet has nine lives 1962
3 Vets in the belfry 1963
4 A vet exposed 1977
5 Vets in congress 1978
6 Vets in the manger 1979
7 Vet among the pigeons 1979
8 Vet in a state 1980
9 Vet on vacation 1980

DUNCAN, A.
COUNTRY DOCTOR
1 To be a country doctor 1980
2 God and the doctor 1981
3 Diary of a country doctor 1982
4 The doctor's affairs all told 1983

DUNCAN, D.
A MAN OF HIS WORD
1 Magic casement
2 Faery lands forlorn
3 Perilous seas
4 Emperor and clown
Paperback fantasy

DUNCAN, J.
REACHFAR
1 My friends the Miss Boyds 1958
2 My friend Muriel 1959
3 My friend Monica 1960
4 My friend Annie 1960
5 My friend Sandy 1961
6 My friend Martha's aunt 1961
7 My friend Flora 1962
8 My friend Madame Zora 1963
9 My friend Rose 1964
10 My friend Emmie 1964
11 My friends the Mrs.Millers 1965
12 My friend from Cairnton 1966
13 My friend my father 1966
14 My friends the Macleans 1967
15 My friends the hungry generation 1968
16 My friend the swallow 1969
17 My friend Sachie 1970
18 My friends the Misses Kindness 1974
19 My friends George and Tom 1976

DUNCAN, R.
1 All men are islands 1964
2 How to make enemies 1968

3 Obsessed 1977
N.F. Autobiography

DUNCAN, W. M.
GREENSLEEVES
1 Mystery on the Clyde
2 Straight ahead for danger
3 The cult of queer people

DUNCAN, W. M.
SUPT.DONALD REAMER
1 Meet the Dreamer 1963
2 Again the Dreamer 1964
3 Presenting the Dreamer 1966
4 Case for the Dreamer 1966
5 Problem for the Dreamer 1967
6 The Dreamer intervenes 1968
7 Salute the Dreamer 1968
8 Challenge for the Dreamer 1969
9 The Dreamer deals with murder 1970
10 Detail for the Dreamer 1971
11 The Dreamer at large 1972
12 Prey for the Dreamer 1974
13 Laurels for the Dreamer 1975

DUNCAN, W. M.
SUPT.LESLIE
1 The council of comforters 1968
2 The green triangle 1969

DUNDAS, L.
SALMOND
1 He liked them murderous 1964
2 The strange smell of murder 1965

DUNN, M.
1 Lady Addle at home 1986
2 Lady Addle remembers 1985
3 The memoirs of Mipsie 1986
Paperback humour

DUNNE, C.
JOE HUSSEY
1 Retrieval 1984
2 Ratcatcher 1985
3 Hooligan 1987

DUNNETT, D.
FRANCIS CRAWFORD OF LYMOND
1 The game of kings 1965
2 Queen's play 1966
3 The disorderly knights 1968
4 Pawn in frankincense 1969
5 The ringed castle 1971
6 Checkmate 1975
Novels set in Scotland and Europe in the 16th century

DUNNETT, D.
JOHNSON JOHNSON
1 Tropical issue 1983
2 Rum affair 1968
3 Ibiza surprise 1970
4 Operation Nassau 1971
5 Roman nights 1973
6 Split code 1977
7 Moroccan traffic 1991
Formerly published under the name of
Dorothy Halliday, with different titles.
All reprinted in paperback in 1991.
For the original titles, see under
HALLIDAY, D.

DUNNETT, D.
THE HOUSE OF NICCOLO
1 Niccolo rising 1986
2 The spring of the ram 1987
3 Race of scorpions 1989
4 Scales of gold 1991
5 The unicorn hunt 1993

DURACK, M.
1 Kings in grass castles 1959
2 Sons in the saddles 1983
N.F. Australian pioneering history

DURBRIDGE, F.
PAUL TEMPLE
1 Send for Paul Temple
2 Paul Temple and the front page
  men
3 Paul Temple intervenes
4 News of Paul Temple
5 Send for Paul Temple again 1948
6 Paul Temple and the Kelby affair
  1970
7 Paul Temple and the Harkdale
  robbery 1970
8 The Geneva mystery 1972
9 The Curzon case 1972
10 Paul Temple and the Margo
   mystery 1986
11 Paul Temple and the Madison
   case 1988

DURBRIDGE, F.
TIM FRAZER
1 The world of Tim Frazer 1961
2 Tim Frazer again 1964
3 Tim Frazer gets the message 1979

DURRANT, D.
1 With my little eye 1975
2 Trunch 1978
3 Addle 1980

DURRELL, G.
1 My family and other animals 1956
2 Birds, beasts and relatives 1969
3 The garden of the Gods 1978
N.F. Autobiography

DURRELL, L.
1 Prospero's cell 1945
2 Reflections on a marine Venus
  1953
3 Bitter lemons of Cyprus 1957
N.F. Autobiography and travel in the
islands of the Mediterranean

DURRELL, L.
ALEXANDRIA QUARTET
1 Justine 1957
2 Balthazar 1958
3 Mountolive 1958
4 Clea 1960

DURRELL, L.
ANTROBUS
1 Esprit de corps 1957
2 Stiff upper lip 1958
3 Sauve qui peut 1966
4 Antrobus complete 1985

DURRELL, L.
AVIGNON QUINTET
1 Monsieur 1974
2 Livia or Buried alive 1978
3 Constance 1982
4 Sebastien 1983
5 Quinx 1985

DURRELL, L.
REVOLT OF APHRODITE
1 Tunc 1967
2 Nunquam 1970

DURST, P.
MICHAEL CARMICHAEL
1 Backlash 1967
2 Badge of infamy 1968

DWYER-JOYCE, A.
DR. ROSS
1 Dr.Ross of Harton 1966
2 The story of Dr Esmond Ross 1967
3 Verdict of Dr.Esmond Ross 1968
4 Dial emergency for Dr.Ross 1969

DYMOKE, J.
FRENCH REVOLUTION SERIES
1 The white cockade 1979
2 The Queen
3 The march to Corunna 1985
4 Two flags for France 1986

DYMOKE, J.
HENRY I
1 The ring of Earls 1970
2 Henry of the high rock 1971
3 The lion's legacy 1972

DYMOKE, J.
HOLLANDER FAMILY
1 Hollander's House 1990
2 Cry of the peacock 1992
3 Winter's daughter 1994

DYMOKE, J.
THE PLANTAGENETS
1 A pride of Kings 1978
2 The royal griffin 1978
3 The lion of Mortimer 1979
4 The Lord of Greenwich 1980
5 The sun in splendour 1980

EAMES, M.
1 The secret room 1975
2 Fair wilderness 1976

EARLY, R. E.
1 The apprentice 1977
2 Master Weaver 1980
3 Weavers and war 1984
Novels about the blanket-weaving
industry

EASTON, N.
BILL BANNING
1 Always the wolf 1956
2 One good turn 1957
3 Bill for damages 1958
4 Mistake me not 1959
5 A book for Banning 1959
6 Right for trouble 1960
7 Quick tempo 1960
8 Moment on ice 1960

EASTWOOD, J.
ANNA ZORDAN
1 The Chinese visitor 1965
2 Little dragon from Peking 1967
3 Come die with me 1969

EBDON, J.
1 Ebdon's Odyssey 1979
2 Ebdon's Iliad 1983
3 Ebdon's England 1985
N.F. Autobiography of a broadcaster

EBEL, S.
SIR ROBERT WARING
1 A name in lights 1967
2 A most auspicious star 1969
3 To seek a star 1973

EBERSOHN, W.
YUDEL GORDON
1 A lonely place to die 1979
2 Divide the night 1980
3 Closed circle 1990

EBERT, A.
TIERNAN FAMILY
1 Traditions 1982
2 The long way home 1985

ECCLES, M.
INSPECTOR GIL MAYO
1 Death of a good woman 1989
2 Requiem for a dove 1990
3 More deaths than one 1991
4 Late of this parish 1992
5 The company she kept 1993

ECKHARDT, K.
SS DIVISION VATERLAND
1 Heroes without honour 1980
2 Stalingrad heroes 1981
3 Heroes of Cassino 1982
4 Achtung Normandy 1982

EDDINGS, D.
ELENIUM
1 The diamond throne 1989
2 The ruby knight 1990
3 The sapphire rose 1991

EDDINGS, D.
TAMULI
1 Domes of fire 1992
2 The shining ones 1993
3 The hidden city 1994
Linked to 'Elenium'

EDDINGS, D.
THE BELGARIAD
1 Pawn of prophecy 1982
2 Queen of sorcery 1982
3 Magician
4 Castle of wizardry 1984
5 Enchanter
Fantasy

EDDINGS, D.
THE MALLOREON
1 Guardians of the West 1987
2 King of the Murgos 1988
3 Demon Lord of Karanda 1988
4 Sorceress of Darshiva 1989
5 Seeress of Kell 1991

EDEL, L.
1 The untried years 1959
2 The conquest of London 1961

3 The middle years 1884-18984 1963
4 The treacherous years 1895-1901 1969
N.F. Biography of Henry James

EDELMAN, M.
1 The minister 1963
2 The Prime Minister's daughter 1964

EDELMAN, M.
DISRAELI
1 Disraeli in love 1972
2 Disraeli rising 1975

EDEN, M.
MARC SAVAGE
1 Countdown to crisis 1968
2 Dangerous exchange 1969
3 Flight of hawks 1969
4 The man who fell 1970

EDEN, R. A., 1ST EARL OF AVON
1 Facing the dictators 1962
2 The reckoning 1965
3 Full circle 1960
N.F. Autobiography

EDGAR, J
1 Margaret Normanby 1983
2 A dark and alien rose 1991

EDGAR, J.
1 Duchess 1976
2 Countess 1978

EDMONDS, J.
LINUS RINTOUL
1 Dog's body 1988
2 Dead spit 1989
3 Judge and be damned 1990
4 Let sleeping dogs lie 1992
5 Death has a cold nose 1993
Thrillers set in the world of dog showing

EDSON, J. T.
ALVIN DUSTINE FOG
1 You're a Texas Ranger,Alvin Fog
2 Rapido Clint
3 The instice of Company K
4 Cap Fog, Texas Ranger, meet Mr.J.G.Reeder
5 Decision for Dusty Fog

EDSON, J. T.
BUNDUKI
1 Bunduki
2 Bunduki and dawn

3 Sacrifice for the Quagga God
4 Fearless master of the jungle

EDSON, J. T.
CALAMITY JANE
1 Cold deck, hot lead
2 The bull whip breed
3 Trouble trail
4 The cow thieves
5 Calamity spells trouble
6 White stallion, red mare
7 The remittance kid
8 The whip and the war lance
9 The big hunt

EDSON, J. T.
OLE DEVIL HARDIN
1 Young Ole Devil
2 Ole Devil and the Caplocks
3 Ole Devil and the mule train
4 Ole Devil at San Jacinta
5 Get Urrea

EDSON, J. T.
ROCKABY COUNTY
1 The sixteen dollar shooter
2 The professional killers
3 The quarter second draw
4 The deputies
5 Point of contact
6 The owlhoot
7 Run for the border
8 Bad hombre

EDSON, J. T.
THE CIVIL WAR
1 Comanche
2 You're in command now, Mr.Fog
3 The big gun
4 Under the stars and bars
5 The fastest gun in Texas
6 Kill Dusty Fog!
7 The devil gun
8 The colt and the sabre
9 The rebel spy
10 The bloody border
11 Back to the bloody border

EDSON, J. T.
THE FLOATING OUTFIT
1 The Ysabel kid
2 .44 calibre man
3 A horse caled Mogollan
4 Goodnight's dream
5 From hide and horn
6 Set Texas back on its feet
7 The hide and tallow men
8 The hooded riders
9 Quiet town

10 Trail boss
11 Wagons to Backsight
12 Troubled range
13 Sidewinder
14 Rangeland Hercules
15 McGraw's inheritance
16 The half breed
17 The wildcats
18 The bad bunch
19 The fast gun
20 Chuchilo
21 A town called Yellowdog
22 Trigger fast
23 The making of a lawman
24 The trouble busters
25 Set a-foot
26 The law of the gun
27 The peacemakers
28 To arms! To arms! in Dixie
29 Hell in the Palo Duro
30 Go back to hell
31 The south will rise again
32 The quest for Bowie's blade
33 Beguinage
34 Beguinage is dead
35 The rushers
36 The fortune hunters
37 Rio guns
38 Gun wizard
39 The Texan
40 The Rio Hondo Kid
41 Waco's debt
42 The hard riders
43 The floating outfit
44 Apache rampage
45 The Rio Hondo war
46 The man from Texas
47 Gunsmoke thunder
48 The small Texan
49 The town tamers
50 Return to Backsight
51 Terror valley
52 Guns in the night

EDSON, J. T.
WACO
1 Sagebrush sleuth
2 Arizona ranger
3 Waco rides in
4 The drifter
5 Doc Leroy M.D.
6 Hound dog man

EDWARDS, J. C.
JACOB FLETCHER
1 Fletcher's fortune 1992
2 Fletcher's glorious 1st of June 1993

EDWARDS, M.
HARRY DEVLIN
1 All the lonely people 1991
2 Suspicious minds 1992
3 I remember you 1993
4 Yesterday's papers 1994

EDWARDS, R.
RICHARD III
1 Fortune's wheel 1978
2 Some touch of pity 1976

EDWARDS, R. D.
ROBERT AMISS
1 Corridors of death 1981
2 The St.Valentine's Day murders 1984
3 The School of English murder 1990
4 Clubbed to death 1992
5 Matricide at St.Martha's 1994

EGAN, L.
GLENDALE POLICE DEPT.
1 A case for appeal 1962
2 Scenes of crime 1976
3 A dream apart 1978
4 Random death 1982
5 Crime for Christmas 1984
6 Chain of violence 1985
These stories involve the whole police force, including Falkenstein and Varallo

EGAN, L.
VIC VARALLO
1 The borrowed alibi 1962
2 Run to evil 1963
3 Detective's due 1965
4 The nameless ones 1967
5 The wine of violence 1970
6 Malicious mischief 1972
7 The hunters and the hunted 1980
8 A choice of crimes 1981

EGAN, L. [E. LININGTON]
JESSE FALKENSTEIN
1 Against the evidence 1963
2 My name is death 1965
3 Some avenger,rise! 1967
4 A serious investigation 1969
5 In the death of a man 1970
6 Paper chase 1973
7 The blind search 1977
8 Look back on death 1979
9 Motive in shadow 1980
10 The miser 1982
11 Little boy lost 1984
12 The wine of life 1986

EGLETON, C.
1 A piece of resistance 1968
2 Last post for a partisan 1970
3 The Judas mandate 1972
About events during a possible Russian occupation of Britain

EGLETON, C.
CHARLES WINTER
1 The Winter touch 1981
2 The Russian enigma 1983

EGLETON, C.
PETER ASHTON
1 Hostile intent 1993
2 A killing in Moscow 1994
3 Death throes 1994

EHLE, J.
WRIGHT FAMILY
1 The land breakers 1964
2 The road 1967
3 Time of drums 1970
A pioneer family in North Carolina

EHRENBERG, I.
1 Childhood and youth 1891-1917 1961
2 First years of revolution 1918-1921 1961
3 Truce 1921-1933 1963
4 Eve of war 1933-1941 1963
5 The war 1914-1945 1963
6 The post-war years 1945-1954 1964
N.F. Autobiography

EICHER, A.
MARTIN AMES
1 Death at the mike 1954
2 Death of an artist 1955

ELAND, C.
MARK RANDALL
1 Dossier closed 1970
2 The desperate search 1971
3 The gold hijack 1973

ELDER, M.
PHILIP STEVENSON
1 Mindslip 1976
2 Mindquest 1977

ELDER, M.
THE BARCLAYS
1 Nowhere on earth 1972
2 The perfumed planet 1973
3 Down to earth 1975
4 The seeds of frenzy 1976
Science fiction

ELGIN, S. H.
NATIVE TONGUE
1 Native tongue
2 The Judas rose
Paperback science fiction

ELIAS, E.
1 On Sunday we wore white 1978
2 Straw hats and serge bloomers 1979
N.F. Autobiography

ELKINS, A.
GIDEON OLIVER
1 Murder in the Queen's Armes 1990
2 Icy clutches 1991
3 Make no bones 1992

ELLIOTT, J.
WILSON FAMILY
1 A state of peace 1970
2 Private life 1972
3 Heaven on earth 1974

ELLIS, A. T.
1 The clothes in the wardrobe 1987
2 The skeleton in the cupboard 1988
3 The fly in the ointment 1989
Not true sequels. The same story is told from the viewpoint of different characters.

ELLIS, H. F.
1 A.J.Wentworth,BA 1980
2 The swansong of A.J.Wentworth 1982

ELMAN, R. M.
THE YAGODAH FAMILY
1 The 28th day of Elul 1967
2 Lilo's diary 1968
3 The reckoning 1969

ELSNA, H.
1 A house called Pleasance 1962
2 To well beloved 1964
3 The undying past 1964

EMECHETA, B.
1 Second class citizen 1974
2 In the ditch 1979
Novels about a Nigerian woman in Britain

EMERSON, D.
1 The surgeon of Sedbridge 1955
2 The warden of Greys 1957

EMERSON, D.
PARSON CARNABY
1 The pride of Parson Carnaby 1953
2 The trouble at Shaplinck 1959

EMERSON, R.
THE TALE OF NEDAO
1 To the haunted mountains
2 In the caves of exile
3 On the seas of destiny
Paperback fantasy

EMERSON, S.
1 Second sight 1980
2 The listeners 1983

EMPIRES TRILOGY
1 Horselords, by David Cook
2 Dragonwell, by Troy Denning
3 Crusade, by James Lowden
Paperback fantasy

ENEFER, D.
DALE SHAND
1 The painted death 1966
2 The long hot night 1967
3 The girl chase 1968
4 Girl in arms 1968
5 The gilded kiss 1969
6 The deadline dolly 1970
7 The screaming orchid 1971
8 Pacific Northwest 1975
9 Seven nights at the resort 1976
10 Ice in the sun 1977
11 The goodbye blonde 1978

ENEFER, D.
SAM BAWTRY
1 Pierhead 627 1968
2 13 steps to Lime Street 1969
3 Riverside 90 1970
4 Girl in a million 1972
5 A long way to Pitt Street 1972
6 Girl on the M6 1973
7 Lakeside zero 1973
8 The jade green judy 1974
9 Last train to Rock Ferry 1975
10 The sixth raid 1979
11 The deadly streak 1982
12 The last leap 1983

ENGEL, H.
BENNY COOPERMAN
1 The ransom game 1982
2 Murder on location 1983
3 The suicide murders 1984
4 Murder sees the light 1985
5 A city called July 1987
6 A victim must be found 1988

ERDRICH, L.
1 Love medicine 1984
2 The beet queen 1987
3 Tracks 1988
*Related novels about present-day
American Indians*

ERSKINE, M.
SEPTIMUS FINCH
1 Give up the ghost 1948
2 I knew MacBean 1949
3 Whispering house 1950
4 Dead by now 1951
5 And being dead 1953
6 The disappearing bridegroom 1954
7 Fatal relations 1955
8 The voice of murder 1956
9 Death of our dear one 1957
10 Sleep no more 1958
11 The house of the enchantress 1959
12 The women at Belguardo 1961
13 The house at Belmont Square 1963
14 Take a dark journey 1965
15 The case with three husbands 1966
16 The ewe lamb 1968
17 The case of Mary Fielding 1970
18 The brood of folly 1971
19 Besides the wench is dead 1973
20 Harriet, farewell 1975

ERSKINE, R.
1 The passion flower hotel 1962
2 Passion flowers in Italy 1963
3 Passion flowers in business 1965

ESMONDE, J. & LARBEY, B.
1 The Good life 1976
2 More of the Good life 1977
Based on the TV series

ESTES, R.
GREYHAWK ADVENTURES
1 Master Wolf
2 The price of power
3 The demon hand
Paperback fantasy

ESTES, R.
THE HUNTER
1 The hunter
2 The hunter on Arena
3 The hunter victorious
Paperback fantasy

ESTLEMAN, L. D.
AMOS WALKER
1 Motor City blues 1981
2 Angel eyes 1982
3 The midnight man 1983

4 The glass highway 1984
5 Sugartown 1986
6 Every brilliant eye 1986
7 Lady yesterday 1987
8 Downriver 1988
9 General murders 1989
10 Silent thunder 1989
11 Sweet women lie 1990

ETTINGER, E.
1 Kindergarten 1988
2 Quicksand 1989

EVANS, A.
COMMANDER SMITH
1 Thunder at dawn 1979
2 Ship of force 1979
3 Dauntless 1980
4 Seek out and destroy 1982

EVANS, A.
CRAGG & FRAYNE
1 The end of the running 1965
2 Mantrap 1967

EVANS, C.
1 Love from Belinda 1961
2 Lalage in love 1962

EVANS, G. E.
1 Ask the fellows who cut the hay
   1962
2 The horse in the furrow 1963
3 The pattern under the plough 1966
   N.F. About farming life

EVANS, GERALDINE
INSPECTOR RAFFERTY
1 Dead before morning 1993
2 Down among the dead men 1994

EVANS, J.
HABBAKUK PARTON
1 The Portobello virgin 1986
2 The Mexico novice 1987
3 The Alamo design 1989

EVANS, M.
1 Autobiograph
2 Ray of darkness 1978
   N.F. Autobiography

EVANS, S.
WINDMILL HILL
1 Centres of ritual 1978
2 Occupational debris 1979
3 Temporary hearths 1982
4 Houses on the site 1984
5 Seasonal tribal feasts 1987

EVANS, T.
LONGARM
1 Longarm
2 Longarm on the border
3 Longarm and the avenging angels
4 Longarm and the Wendigo
5 Longarm in the Indian Nation
6 Longarm and the logger
7 longarm and the high graders
8 Longarm and the nesters
9 Longarm and the hatchetmen
10 Longarm and the Molly Maguires
11 Longarm and the Texas Rangers
12 Longarm in Lincoln County
   Paperback Westerns

EXLEY, F.
1 A fan's notes
2 Last notes from home 1990

EYRE, E.
SIGISMONDO
1 Death of a Duchess 1991
2 Curtains for the Cardinal 1992
3 Poison for the Prince 1993
4 Bravo for the bride 1994
   Detective stories set in 15th century
   Italy. The authors also write under
   their real names, Staynes and Storey.

FAIR, A. A. [E. S. GARDNER]
BERTHA COOL & DONALD LAM
1 Lam to the slaughter
2 Turn on the heat
3 Gold comes in bricks
4 Spill the jackpot
5 Axe to grind
6 Crows can't count
7 Owls don't blink
8 Cats prowl at night
9 Bats fly at dusk
10 Double or quits
11 Fools die on Friday 1955
12 Bedrooms have windows
13 Top of the heap 1957
14 Some women won't wait 1957
15 Beware of the curves 1958
16 You can die laughing 1958
17 Some slips don't show 1959
18 The count of nine 1959
19 Pass the gravy 1959
20 Kept women can't quit 1960
21 Bachelors get lonely 1961
22 Stop at the red 1962
23 Try anything once 1963
24 Fish or cut bait 1963
25 Up for grabs 1965
26 Cut thin to win 1966
27 Widows wear weeds 1966

28 Traps need fresh bait 1968
29 All grass isn't green 1969

FAIRBROTHER, N.
1 Children in the house 1954
2 The cheerful day 1960
N.F. Autobiography

FAIRLIE, G.
CARYLL
1 Scissors cut paper
2 The man who laughed
3 Stone blunts scissors

FAIRLIE, G.
JOHN MACALL
1 Winner take all 1954
2 No sleep for Macall 1955
3 Deadline for Macall 1956
4 Double for bluff 1957
5 Macall gets curious 1959
6 Murder most discreet 1960
7 Please kill my cousin 1961

FAIRLIE, G.
MR.MALCOLM
1 A shot in the dark 1950
2 Mr.Malcolm presents 1951
3 Men for counters 1952

FALKIRK, R.
1 Blackstone 1972
2 Blackstone's fancy
3 Beau Blackstone 1973
4 Blackstone and the scourge of
  Europe 1974
5 Blackstone underground 1976
6 Blackstone on Broadway 1977
About a Bow Street Runner

FALLON, M.
PAUL CHAVASSE
1 The testament of Caspar Schultz
  1963
2 The year of the tiger 1964
3 The keys of hell 1965
4 Midnight never comes 1966
5 The dark side of the street 1967
6 A fine night for dying 1969
Later reprinted under the name of
JACK HIGGINS

FAMILY AT WAR
1 A family at war, by K.Baker 1970
2 To the turn of the tide, by J.Powell
  1971
3 Towards victory, by R.Russell 1972
Adapted from the TV series

FANTE, J.
ARTURO BANDINI
1 Wait until Spring, Bandini 1938
2 Ask the dust 1939
3 Dreams from Bunker Hill 1982

FANTONI, M.
MIKE DIME
1 Mike Dime 1981
2 Stickman 1982

FARAH, N.
VARIATIONS ON THE THEME OF
AFRICAN DICTATORSHIP
1 Sweet and sour milk 1979
2 Sardines 1981
3 Close Sesame 1983

FARALLA, D.
1 The magnificent barb 1947
2 Black renegade 1954

FARELY, A.
PLANTAGENETS
1 Crown of splendour 1966
2 Devils royal 1968
3 The lion and the wolf 1968
4 The last roar of the lion 1970
5 Leopard from Anjou 1974
6 King Wolf 1974
7 Kingdom under tyranny 1975
8 Last howl of the wolf 1975

FAREWELL, N.
1 The unfair sex 1953
2 Someone to love 1958

FARMER, B. J.
SERGEANT WIGAN
1 Death at the cascades 1955
2 Death of a bookseller 1956
3 Once and then the funeral 1957
4 Murder next year 1959

FARMER, P. J.
AN EXORCISM
1 Blown
2 The image of the beast

FARMER, P. J.
DAYWORLD
1 Dayworld 1987
2 Dayworld rebel 1988
3 Dayworld break-up 1992

FARMER, P. J.
DOC CALIBAN
1 Lord of the trees 1981
2 Keepers of secrets 1985

FARMER, P. J.
OPAR
1 Hadon of Ancient Opar
2 Flight to Opar

FARMER, P. J.
RIVERWORLD SAGA
1 To your scattered bodies go
2 The fabulous riverboat
3 The dark design 1987
4 The magic labyrinth
5 Gods of Riverworld 1987
Fantasy, mainly paperback. Dates are for hardback.

FARMER, P. J.
WORLD OF THE TIERS
1 Makers of Universes
2 Private Cosmos
3 The gates of Creation
4 Behind the walls of Terra
5 The lavalite world
Paperback science fiction

FARRAN, R.
1 Winged dagger 1955
2 Operation Tombola 1960
N.F. Wartime experiences with the SAS

FARRAR, S.
1 The snake on 99 1962
2 Zero in the gate 1963
3 Death in the wrong bed 1964

FARRE, R.
1 Seal morning 1957
2 A time from the world 1962
3 The beckoning land 1969
N.F. Autobiography

FARRELL, J. G.
1 The siege of Krishnapur 1974
2 The hill station 1981
2 was unfinished at the author's death

FARRIMOND, J.
1 Dust in my throat 1963
2 Dust is forever 1969
Novels about coal mining

FARRINGTON, R.
HENRY MORANE
1 The killing of Richard the Third 1972
2 Tudor agent 1974
3 The traitors of Bosworth 1978

FARSON, N.
1 The way of a transgressor 1936
2 A mirror for Narcissus 1956
N.F. Autobiogrphy

FAST, H.
LAVETTE FAMILY
1 The immigrants 1977
2 Second generation 1979
3 The establishment 1980
4 The legacy 1981
5 The immigrant
A family saga about Jewish immigrants in America

FAULCON, R.
NIGHTHUNTER
1 The stalking
2 The talisman
3 The ghost dance
4 The shrine
5 The labyrinth
6 The hexing
Paperback horror stories

FAULKNER, W.
1 Sartoris 1929
2 The sound and the fury 1929
3 As I lay dying 1930
4 Sanctuary 1932
5 Light in August 1932
6 Absolom! Absolom! 1936
7 The hamlet 1948
8 Requiem for a nun 1951
9 The town 1957
10 The mansion 1959

FAULKNOR, C.
1 The white calf 1966
2 The white peril 1968

FAWCETT, Q.
MADAME VERNET
1 Napoleon must die
2 Death wears a crown
Paperback detective stories

FEARON, D.
MISS ARABELLA FRANT
1 Death before breakfast 1959
2 Murder-on-Thames 1960

FECHER, C.
RALEGH FAMILY
1 Queen's delight 1964
2 Traitor's son 1967
3 King's legacy 1968
4 Player Queen 1968

FEIST, R. E.
1 Prince of the blood 1991
2 The King's buccaneer 1992

FEIST, R. E.
RIFTWAR
1 Magician 1983
2 Silverthorn 1985
3 A darkness at Sethanon 1986
4 Prince of the blood 1989
Fantasy

FEIST, R. E. & WURTS, J.
EMPIRE
1 Daughter of the Empire 1989
2 Servant of the Empire 1990
3 Mistress of the Empire 1992

FELICITY, SISTER
1 Barefoot journey 1961
2 Spring comes barefoot 1965
N.F. Autobiography

FEN, E.
1 A Russian childhood 1961
2 A girl grew up in Russia 1970
3 Remember Russia 1973
N.F. Autobiography

FENNELLY, T.
MATTY SINCLAIR
1 The glory hole murders 1986
2 The closet hanging 1987

FENTON, S.
1 All the beasts in the field 1984
2 Creature comforts 1985
N.F. Rural life

FERGUSON, F.
DET.SERGEANT JANE PERRY
1 Missing person 1993
2 No fixed abode 1994

FERGUSSON, H.
FOLLOWERS OF THE SUN
1 Wolf song
2 In those days 1954
3 Blood of the conquerors

FERMOR, P. L.
1 Between the woods and the water 1986
2 A time of gifts 1977
N.F. Autobiography

FERMOR, P. L.
GREECE
1 Mani 1963

2 Roumeli 1965
N.F. Travel

FERRARI, I.
RYEMINSTER HOSPITAL
1 Doctor at Ryeminster 1964
2 Nurse at Ryeminster 1964
3 Sister at Ryeminster 1965
4 Almoner at Ryeminster 1965

FERRARS, E.
ANDREW BASNETT
1 Something wicked 1983
2 Root of all evil 1984
3 The crime and the crystal 1985
4 The other devil's name 1986
5 A murder too many 1988
6 Smoke without fire 1990
7 A hobby of murder 1994

FERRARS, E.
FELIX FREER
1 I met murder 1985
2 Last will and testament 1979
3 Frog in the throat 1980
4 Thinner than water 1981
5 Death of a minor character 1983
6 Woman slaughter 1989
7 Sleep of the unjust 1990
8 Beware of the dog 1992

FERRIS, C.
1 The darkness is light enough 1986
2 Out of the darkness 1988
3 The badgers of Ashcroft woods 1990
N.F. An account of the author's study of badgers, and her efforts to protect them from poachers.

FIELD, P.
POWDER VALLEY
1 Lawman of Powder Valley
2 Trail south from Powder Valley
3 Fight for Powder Valley
4 Death rides the night
5 Smoking iron
6 Gund from Powder Valley
7 Powder Valley vengeance
8 Canyon hideout
9 Road to Laramie
10 End of the trail
11 Powder Valley showdown
12 Ravaged range
13 Sherrif wanted
14 Gamblers' gold
15 Trail from Needle Rock
16 Outlaw valley
17 Sherrif on the spot

18 Return to Powder Valley
19 Blacksnake trail
20 Powder Valley ambush
21 Back trail to danger 1951
22 Three guns from Colorado
23 Guns in the saddle 1952
24 Powder Valley holdup 1952
25 Mustang mesa 1952
26 Outlaw of Eagle's nest 1952
27 Riders of the outlaw trail 1953
28 Powder Valley stampede 1953
29 Powder Valley deadlock 1954
30 War in the painted buttes 1954
31 Outlaw ofCattle Canyon 1955
32 Breakneck Pass 1955
33 Rawhide rider 1955

FIELDING, G.
JOHN BLAYDON
1 Brotherly love 1947
2 In the time of the greenbloom 1956
3 Pretty doll houses 1979
4 The women of Guinea Lane 1986

FIELDING, H.
1 Tom Jones
'The later adventures of Tom Jones', by B. Coleman (1986) is a sequel.

FINCH, J.
1 The spoils of war
2 The promised land
Paperback novels based on the TV series

FINCH, M.
1 Dentist in the chair 1955
2 Teething troubles 1956
3 The beauty bazaar 1965

FINCH, M.
DICK LANGHAM
1 Five are the symbols 1964
2 Jones is a rainbow 1965
3 The succubus 1967

FINCH, S.
1 The golden voyager 1978
2 Pagan voyager 1979
3 Voyager in bondage 1981
Novels about a galley slave in Rome

FINLAY, D. G.
BAYLESS FAMILY
1 Watchman 1984
2 The grey regard 1985
3 Deadly relations 1986

4 Graven image 1987

FINN, R. L.
1 Time remembered 1963
2 Spring in Aldgate 1968
N.F. A Jewish boyhood in London's East End. 2 was reprinted as 'Grief Forgotten' in 1985

FINN, T.
1 Knapworth at war 1982
2 Knapworth fights on 1989

FINNEGAN, R.
DAN BANNION
1 The lying ladies
2 The bandaged nude 1954
3 Many a monster

FINNEY, P.
LUGH THE HARPER
1 Shadow of gulls 1977
2 The crow goddess 1978

FIRBANK, T.
1 I bought a mountain 1940
2 I bought a star 1949
3 Country of memorable honour 1953
4 Log hut 1954
5 I am a traveller 1956
N.F. Autobiography

FISH, R. L.
CAPTAIN JOSE DA SILVA
1 The fugitive 1962
2 Isle of the snakes 1963
3 The shrunken head 1964
4 The diamond bubble 1965
5 Brazilian sleigh ride 1966
6 Always kiss a stranger
7 The bridge that went nowhere
8 The Xavier affair
9 The green hell treasure
10 Trouble in Paradise

FISH, R. L.
MURDER LEAGUE
1 The murder league
2 Tricks of the trade
3 Rub a dub dub
4 A gross carriage of justice

FISH, R. L.
SCHLOCK HOLMES
1 The incredible Schlock Holmes
2 The memoirs of Schlock Holmes

FISHER, D. E.
1 The man you sleep with 1982
2 Variation on a theme 1982
Linked novels, giving two views of a murder

FISHER, E.
WILLIAM SHAKESPEARE
1 Shakespeare and son 1963
2 Love's labour won 1965
3 The best house in Stratford 1966

FISHER, J. A.
FEAR GOD AND DREADNOUGHT
1 The making of an admiral 1952
2 Years of power 1956
3 Restoration,abdication and last years 1958
N.F. Autobiography

FISHER, N.
NIGEL MORRISON
1 Walk at a steady pace 1970
2 Rise at dawn 1971
3 The last assignment 1972

FITT, M.
SUPT.MALLETT
1 Expected death 1937
2 Sky rocket 1938
3 Death at dancing stones 1939
4 Murder of a mouse 1939
5 Death starts a rumour 1942
6 Death and Mary Dazill 1943
7 Death on Heron's Mere 1945
8 Requiem for Robert 1946
9 Death and the pleasant voices 1947
10 Clues re Christabel 1947
11 Death and the bright day 1950
12 The banquet ceases 1951
13 Death and the shortest day 1952
14 An ill wind 1953
15 The man who shot birds 1955
16 Love from Elizabeth 1957
17 Mizmaze 1959

FITZGERALD, J. D.
1 Papa married a Mormon 1956
2 Mamma's boarding house 1958
3 Uncle Will and the Fitzgerald curse 1962
N.F. Autobiography

FITZGERALD, JULIA
1 Desert queen 1986
2 Taboo 1985

FITZGERALD, N.
SUPT.DUFFY
1 Midsummer malice 1952
2 The rosy pastor 1953
3 The house is falling 1955
4 Imagine a man 1956
5 The candles are all out 1957
6 The student body 1958
7 This won't hurt 1958
8 Suffer a witch 1958
9 Ghost in the making 1960
10 Black welcome 1961
11 Day of the adder 1963
12 Affairs of death 1967

FITZGERALD, P.
1 BellaDonna
2 Jenny Bell
3 75 Brooke Street

FITZGIBBON, T.
1 With love 1982
2 Love lies at a loss 1982
N.F. Autobiography

FITZROY, R.
MALLAMSHIRE SERIES
1 The Manor of Braye 1979
2 The widow's might 1980
3 The American Duchess 1980
4 Ill fares the land 1987
5 Barnaby's Charity 1988
6 The Rockport rubies 1989

FITZWILLIAM, J.
1 Anyway, this particular Sunday 1976
2 How many years was it now? 1978

FLANDERS, P.
1 Doctor,doctor 1986
2 Mercenary doctor 1987
N.F. Autobiography

FLEETWOOD, F.
1 Concordia 1971
2 Concordia errant 1973

FLEISCHER, L.
1 Saturday night fever 1980
2 Staying alive 1983
Novels based on the films of the same name

FLEMING, G. H.
1 Rosetti and the Pre-Raphaelite Brotherhood 1961

2 That ne'er shall meet again 1971
N.F.

FLEMING, I
JAMES BOND
1 Casino Royale 1953
2 Live and let die 1954
3 Moonraker 1955
4 Diamonds are forever 1956
5 From Russia with love 1957
6 Dr. No 1958
7 Goldfinger 1959
8 For your eyes only 1960
9 Thunderball 1961
10 The spy who loved me 1961
11 On Her Majesty's Secret Service 1963
12 You only live twice 1964
13 The man with the golden gun 1965
14 Octopussy and The living daylights 1966
15 Dr. Sun, by R.Markham,i.e.K.Amis 1975
16 Licence renewed, by J. Gardner 1981
17 For special services, by J.Gardner 1982
18 Role of honour,by J. Gardner 1984
19 Icebreaker, by J.Gardner 1983
20 Nobody lives forever,by J.Gardner 1986
21 No deals, Mr.Bond, by J.Gardner 1987
22 Scorpius, by J.Gardner 1988
23 Brokenclaw, by J.Gardner 1990
24 Win lose or die,by J.Gardner 1990
25 The man from Barbarossa, by J.Gardner 1991
26 Death is forever, by J.Gardner 1992
27 Never send flowers, by J.Gardner 1993
28 Seafire, by J.Gardner 1994
3 and 10 were revised and rewritten for the films by Christopher Wood in 1979 and 1973. J. N. Chance has also written about a character called James Bond, but these do not carry on in the Fleming tradition, as do those by John Gardner.

FLEMING, J.
NURI BEY
1 When I grow rich 1964
2 Nothing is the number when you die 1965

FLETCHER, A.
OUTBACK SAGA
1 Outback 1978
2 Outback station 1991
3 Walkabout 1992
4 Wallaby track 1994

FLETCHER, B.
1 The wood burners 1992
2 The iron mouth 1994

FLETCHER, D.
RAINBOW
1 Rainbow in hell 1983
2 Rainbows end in tears 1984

FLETCHER, D.
ROBERT LUMAN
1 The accident of Robert Luman 1988
2 A wagon-load of monkeys 1988

FLETCHER, G. N.
1 In my father's house 1957
2 Preacher's kids 1959
3 I was born tomorrow 1962
N.F. Autobiography

FLETCHER, I.
HISTORY OF VIRGINIA
1 Roanoke hundred (Elizabethan) 1948
2 Bennett's welcome (Cromwellian) 1950
3 Men of Albemarle (1710-12) 1945
4 Cormorant's brood (1712-18) 1959
5 Lusty wind for Carolina (1718-25) 1944
6 Raleigh's Eden (1765-82) 1940
7 The wind in the forest (1771) 1957
8 Toil of the brave (1779-80) 1946
9 Queen's gift (1788) 1952
Listed in the suggested order of reading

FLINT, E.
1 Hot bread and chips 1963
2 Kipper stew 1964
N.F. Autobiography

FLINT, K. C.
THE SIDHE LEGENDS
1 The hound of Culain
2 Riders of the Sidhe
3 Champions of the Sidhe
4 Master of the Sidhe
5 The challenge of the Clans
6 Storm shield

7 The dark druid
Paperback fantasy

FLOWER, P.
INSPECTOR SWINTON
1 Goodbye sweet William 1953
2 Wax flowers for Gloria 1957
3 A wreath of water Lilies 1959
4 One rose less 1960
5 Hell for Heather 1963

FLYNN, B.
ANTHONY BATHURST
1 The billiard room mystery 1928
2 The case of the black twenty-two 1928
3 The mystery of the peacock's eye 1928
4 The murders near Mapleton 1928
5 Invisible death 1929
6 The five red fingers 1929
7 The creeping Jenny mystery 1930
8 Murder en route 1930
9 The orange axe 1931
10 The triple bit 1931
11 The padded door 1932
12 The edge of terror 1932
13 The spiked lion 1932
14 The League of Matttias 1933
15 The horn 1934
16 The case of the purple calf 1934
17 The Sussex cuckoo 1935
18 The Fortescue candle 1936
19 Fear and trembling 1936
20 Cold evil 1938
21 Tread softly 1937
22 The ebony stag 19387
23 Black edged 1939
24 The case of the faithful heart 1939
25 The case of the painted ladies 1940
26 They never came back 1940
27 Such bright disguises 1941
28 Glittering prizes 1942
29 Reverse the charge 1943
30 The grim maiden 1944
31 The case of Elymas the sorcerer 1945
32 Conspiracy at Angel 1946
33 The sharp quillet 1947
34 Exit Sir John 1948
35 The swinging death 1948
36 Men for pieces 1949
37 Black Agent 1950
38 Where there was smoke 1951
39 And cauldron bubble 1951
40 The ring of innocent 1952
41 The seventh sign 1952
42 The running nun 1952
43 Out of the dusk 1953

44 The feet of death 1954
45 The doll's done dancing 1954
46 The shaking spear 1955
47 The dice are dark 1955
48 The toy lamb 1956
49 The murder collection 1956
50 The wife who disappeared 1956
51 The hands of justice 1956
52 The nine cuts 1957
53 The saints are sinister 1958

FLYNN, K.
1 A Liverpool lass 1993
2 The Mersey girls 1994

FOLEY, R.
HIRAM POTTER
1 Dangerous to me 1960
2 The deadly noose 1962
3 It's murder, Mr.Potter 1963
4 Back door to death 1964
5 Fatal lady 1964
6 Call it accident 1966
7 A calculated risk 1968

FOLEY, W.
1 A child in the forest 1974
2 No pipe dreams for father 1978
3 Back to the forest 1981
4 In and out of the forest 1984
N.F. Autobiography

FOLLETT, J.
EARTHSEARCH
1 Earthsearch 1981
2 Deathship 1982

FOLLETT, K.
PIERS ROPER
1 The shake out 1975
2 The bear raid 1976

FORBES, C.
TWEED & NEWMAN
1 Cover story 1985
2 The Janus man 1987
3 Deadlock 1987
4 The Greek key 1988
5 Terminal 1984
6 Shockwave 1989
7 Whirlpool 1990
8 Cross of fire 1991
9 By stealth 1992
10 The power 1993

FORD, D.
GWYNETH
1 The following seasons
2 The catch of time 1960

3 No further elegy 1961

FORD, E.
MAPLECHESTER
1 The empty heart 1960
2 The cottage at Tumble 1961
3 Heron's nest 1962
4 A week by the sea 1963
5 A holiday engagement 1963
6 No room for Joanna 1964

FORD, H.
1 Felix walking 1968
2 Felix running 1969

FORD, J. A.
1 The brave white flag 1961
2 Season of escape 1964

FORD, R.
FARADAWN
1 Quest for Faradawn 1982
2 Melvaig's vision 1984
3 Children of Ashgaroth 1986
Fantasy

FORDE, N.
MARK URGENT
1 Urgent enquiry 1973
2 Urgent action 1974
3 Urgent delivery 1975
4 Urgent trip 1977
5 Urgent wedding 1979
6 Urgent honeymoon 1981

FORESTER, C. S.
HORNBLOWER
1 Mr.Midshipman Hornblower 1950
2 Lieutenant Hornblower 1952
3 Hornblower and the Atropos 1956
4 Hornblower and the Hotspur 1962
5 The happy return 1937
6 Ship of the line 1937
7 Flying colours 1938
8 The Commodore 1945
9 Lord Hornblower 1946
10 Hornblower in the West Indies 1958
11 Hornblower and the crisis 1967
Listed in chronological order of events

FORREST, A.
CAPTAIN JUSTICE
1 Captain Justice 1981
2 The Pandora secret 1982
3 A balance of dangers 1984

FORREST, K. V.
KATE DELAFIELD
1 Amateur city 1987
2 Murder at the Nightwood Bar 1987
3 Beverly Malibu 1990
4 Murder by tradition 1993
Feminist 'Private Eye' stories.

FORREST, R.
LYON WENTWORTH
1 Death through the looking glass 1978
2 The wizard of death 1979
3 A child's garland of death 1979
4 Death in the willows 1980
5 Death at Yew Corner 1981

FORRESTER, H.
1 Twopence to cross the Mersey 1974
2 Minerva's step-child 1979
3 By the waters of Liverpool 1981
4 Lime Street at two 1985
N.F.Autobiography of a Liverpool childhood

FORSTER, P.
ALEX SMITH & TONY BROWN
1 Play the ball 1967
2 Play the man 1970
3 The disinherited 1973

FORSYTE, C.
DET. INSPECTOR LEFT
1 Diplomatic death 1961
2 Diving death 1962
3 Double death 1964

FORTESCUE, LADY WINIFRED
1 Perfume from Provence 1950
2 Sunset house 1949
3 There's rosemary,there's rue 1950
4 Trampled ,lilies 1949
5 Mountain madness 1951
6 Beauty for ashes 1948
7 Laughter in Provence 1951
N.F. Autobiogrpahy

FORTSCHER, W.
THE LOST REGIMENT
1 Rally cry
2 Union forever
3 Terrible swift sword
Paperback s. f.

FORWARD, R.
THE OWL
1 The owl

2 Scarlet serenade
Paperback horror stories

FOSTER, A. D.
ALIEN
1 Alien 1986
2 Aliens 1990
3 Alien 3 1992
4 Earth hive, by S.Perry 1994
5 Nightmare asylum,by S.Perry (Aliens 2) 1994
6 The female war, by S.Perry 1994
7 Genocide, by S.Perry 1994
8 Predator prey, by S. and S. Perry 1994
Based on the films.

FOSTER, A. D.
FLINX AND PIP
1 The Tar Aiym Krang 1972
2 Nor crystal tears 1983
3 Flix in flux 1989
4 The end of the matter 1991
5 For love of mother-not 1992
Fantasy

FOSTER, A. D.
ICERIGGER TRILOGY
1 Ice rigger 1978
2 Mission to Moulokin 1979
3 The deluge drivers 1990

FOSTER, A. D.
SPELLSINGER
1 Spellsinger 1986
2 The hour of the gate 1986
3 The day of the dissonance
4 The moment of the magician
5 The paths of the Perambulator 1986
6 The time of the transference 1988
7 Son of Spellsinger 1993

FOSTER, A. D.
THE DAMNED
1 A call to arms
2 The great escape
3 The spoils of war

FOUNTAINE, M.
1 Love among the butterflies 1980
2 Butterflies and late loves 1986
N.F. Biography

FOX, A.
1 Slightly foxed 1986
2 Completely foxed 1989
N.F. Autobiography of the theatrical family

FOXALL, P. A.
CATFORD POLICE STATION
1 A dishonest way to die 1977
2 Act of terror 1979
3 Sequel to yesterday's crime 1979
4 To kill call girl 1980
5 The silent informer 1981

FOXALL, P. A.
DET. SERGEANT SCAMP
1 Vultures in the smoke 1972
2 The big time 1973
3 Confessions of a convict 1974
4 Scamp's law 1975
5 No life for a loser 1977
6 Taming the furies 1978
7 Hostage of the damned 1979

FOXALL, P. A.
INSPECTOR DERBEN
1 The murder machine 1976
2 Inspector Derben's war 1976
3 Inspector Derben and the widow maker 1977
4 The Hell's Angel kidnapping 1978

FOXALL, R.
HARRY ADKINS
1 The little ferret 1970
2 Brandy for the parson 1971
3 The dark forest 1972
4 The silver goblet 1974
5 The last Jacobite 1980
Detective stories set in the early 19th century

FOXELL, N.
EMMA HAMILTON
1 Loving Emma 1986
2 Emma expects 1987

FRALEY, O.
1 The untouchables 1967
2 Four against the mob 1968
3 The last of the untouchables 1970

FRAME, J.
1 to the Is-land 1983
2 An angel at my table 1984
3 The envoy from Mirror City 1985
N.F. Autobiography of a New Zealand author

FRANCIS, D.
KIT FIELDING
1 Break-in 1985
2 Bolt 1986

FRANCIS, D.
SID HALLEY
1 Odds against 1965
2 Whip hand 1980

FRANKAU, P.
CLOTHES FOR A KING'S SON
1 Sing for your supper 1963
2 Slaves of the lamp 1965
3 Over the mountains 1966

FRANKEN, R.
CLAUDIA
1 Claudia 1939
2 Claudia and David 1943
3 Another Claudia 1943
4 Young Claudia 1945
5 The marriage of Claudia 1947
6 From Claudia to David 1950
7 The fragile years 1953
8 The return of Claudia 1955

FRANKLIN, C.
GRANT GARFIELD
1 Exit without permit 1946
2 Cocktails with a stranger 1947
3 Rope of sand 1948
4 Storm in an inkpot 1949
5 The mask of Kane 1949
6 She'll love you dead 1950
7 One night to kill 1950
8 Maid for murder 1951
9 Escape to death 1951
10 No other victim 1952
11 Gallows for a fool 1952
12 The stranger came back 1953
13 Stop that man 1954
14 Girl in shadow 1955
15 Out of time 1956
16 Death on my shoulder 1958
17 Gentle you must be 1959
18 Breathe no more 1959
19 Handful of sinners 1959
20 Fear runs softly 1961

FRANKLIN, C.
JIM BURGESS
1 Guilt for innocence 1960
2 Kill me and live 1961
3 The bath of acid 1962
4 Murder before dinner 1963

FRANKLIN, C.
MRS.MAXINE DANGERFIELD
1 The dangerous ones 1964
2 On the day of the shooting 1965
3 Death in the east 1966
4 Escape 1967

FRANKLIN, M.
STARSKY & HUTCH
1 Starsky and Hutch
2 Death ride
3 Kill Huggy Bear
4 The bounty hunter
5 The psychic
6 Watcher on the docks
7 The set up
8 Murder on Playboy Island
Paperbacks based on the TV series

FRASER, A. S.
1 The hills of home 1973
2 In memory long 1977
3 Roses in December 1979
N.F. Autobiography

FRASER, ANTHEA
CHIEF INSPECTOR WEBB
1 A shroud for Delilah 1984
2 A necessary end 1985
3 Pretty maids all in a row 1986
4 Death speaks softly 1987
5 The nine bright shiners 1987
6 Six proud walkers 1988
7 The April rainers 1989
8 Symbols at your door 1990
9 The lily-white boys 1991
10 Three, three, the rivals 1992
11 The gospel makers 1994

FRASER, ANTONIA
JEMIMA SHORE
1 Quiet as a nun 1977
2 The wild island 1978
3 A splash of red 1981
4 Cool repentance 1982
5 Oxford blood 1985
6 Jemima Shore's first case and
other stories 1986
7 Your Royal Hostage 1987
8 The Cavalier case 1990
9 Jemima Shore at the sunny grave
1991
10 Political death 1994
Jemima also appears in a short story,
the Parr children 9 contains four
Jemima Shore short stories, and
several others.

FRASER, C. M.
1 Blue above the chimneys 1980
2 Roses round the door 1986
3 Green are my mountains 1990
N.F. Autobiography of the author of
'Rhanna'.

FRASER, C. M.
RHANNA
1 Rhanna 1978
2 Rhanna at war 1979
3 Children of Rhanna 1984
4 Return to Rhanna 1984
5 A song of Rhanna 1985
6 Storm over Rhanna 1988
7 Stranger on Rhanna 1992
   Novels about a Hebridean island

FRASER, C. M.
THE GRANTS OF ROTHIEDRUM
1 King's Croft 1986
2 King's Acre 1987
3 King's exile 1989
4 King's Close 1991
5 King's farewell 1993

FRASER, D.
THE HARDROW CHRONICLES
1 Adam Hardrow 1991
2 Codename Mercury 1992
3 Adam in the breach 1993
4 The pain of winning 1994

FRASER, D.
TREASON IN ARMS
1 A kiss for the enemy 1985
2 The killing times 1986
3 The dragon's teeth 1987
4 The seizure 1987
5 A candle for Judas 1989

FRASER, G. M.
1 The general danced at dawn 1973
2 McAuslan in the rough 1974
3 The Sheikh and the dustbin 1988

FRASER, G. M.
FLASHMAN
1 Flashman in the great game (1836-8) 1975
2 Flashman (1839-42) 1969
3 Royal Flash (1842-3) 1970
4 Flashman's lady (1842-5) 1977
5 Flash for freedom (1848-9) 1971
6 Flashman at the charge (1854-5) 1972
7 Flashman and the dragon (1860) 1985
8 Flashman and the Redskins (1849 & 1875/6) 1982
9 Flashman and the mountain of light 1990
10 Flashman and the angel of the lord 1994
   The later adventures of the bully in Tom Brown's Schooldays

FRASER, J.
DET. INSPECTOR BILL AVEYARD
1 The evergreen death 1968
2 A cockpit of roses 1969
3 Deadly nightshade 1970
4 Death in a pheasant's eye 1971
5 Blood on a widow's cross 1972
6 The five leafed clover 1974
7 A wreath of lords and ladies 1974
8 Who steals my name 1976
9 Hearts ease in death 1977

FRASER, M.
THE VILLAGE
1 The first summer 1979
2 The long winter 1980
3 Time of change 1981

FRASER, R.
1 A visit to Venus 1957
2 Jupiter in the chair 1958
3 Trout's testament 1959
4 City of the sun 1961

FRASER, S.
GRAINNE MCDERMOTT
1 The bitter dawning 1989
2 The harsh noontide 1990
3 The healing might fall 1992

FRASER, S. [R. CLEWS]
EDWARDIAN SERIES
1 The summer of the fancy man 1993
2 The sisterhood 1994

FRASER, S. [R. CLEWS]
TILDY CRAWFORD
1 Tildy 1985
2 Poorhouse woman 1986
3 Nursing woman 1987
4 Pointing woman 1988
5 Radical woman 1989
6 Gang woman 1989
7 Widow woman 1991
8 Invincible woman 1991

FRAZER, R. C.
MARK KILBY
1 Secret syndicate 1963
2 The Hollywood hoax 1964
3 The Miami mob 1965

FREDMAN, J.
CHARLES DEXTER
1 The fourth agency 1968
2 The false Joanna 1970

FREDMAN, M.
WILLIE HALLIDAY
1 You can always blame the rain
1977
2 Kisses leave no fingerprints 1979

FREE, C.
POLLITT FAMILY
1 Vinegar Hill
2 Bay of shadows 1980
3 Brannan 1981

FREELING, N.
ARLETTE VAN DER VALK
1 The widow 1979
2 One damn thing after another
1981
3 Sand castle 1989
Novels about Van der Valk's widow

FREELING, N.
HENRI CASTANG
1 Dressing of diamond 1974
2 What are the bugles blowing for
1975
3 Lake Isle 1976
4 Night lords 1978
5 Castang's city 1980
6 Wolfnight 1982
7 Back of the north wind 1983
8 No part in your death 1984
9 Cold iron 1986
10 Lady Macbeth 1988
11 Not as far as Velma 1989
12 Those in peril 1990
13 The pretty how town 1992
14 You who know 1993
15 The sea coast of Bohemia 1994
Arlette Van der Valk appears in 10.

FREELING, N.
VAN DER VALK
1 Love in Amsterdam 1962
2 Because of the cats 1963
3 Gun before butter 1963
4 Double-barrel 1964
5 Criminal conversations 1965
6 The king of the rainy country 1966
7 The Dresden green 1966
8 Strike out where not applicable
1967
9 Tsing-boum 1969
10 Over the high side 1971
11 A long silence 1972

FREEMANTLE, B.
CHARLIE MUFFIN
1 Charlie Muffin 1977

2 Clap hands,here comes Charlie
1978
3 The inscrutable Charlie Muffin
1979
4 Charlie Muffin's Uncle Sam 1980
5 Madrigal for Charlie Muffin 1981
6 Charlie Muffin and Russian Rose
1985
7 Charlie Muffin San 1987
8 The run around 1988
9 Comrade Charlie 1989
10 Charlie's apprentice 1993

FREEMANTLE, B.
DIMITRI DANILOV
1 The button man 1993
2 No time for heroes 1994

FRENCH, H.
1 I swore I never would 1970
2 I thought I never could 1973
N.F. Autobiography

FRERE, R.
1 Maxwell's ghost 1976
2 Beyond the Highland line 1984
N.F. Autobiography of a climber

FREZZA, R.
1 A small colonial war
2 Fire in a faraway place
Paperback s. f.

FRIEDMAN, M.
GEORGINA LEE MAXWELL
1 Deadly reflections 1989
2 Temporary ghost 1990

FRIEDMAN, R.
1 A loving mistress 1983
2 A second wife 1985

FRIEDMAN, R.
SHELTON FAMILY
1 Proofs of affection 1982
2 Rose of Jericho 1984
3 To live in peace 1988

FRIESNER, E.
1 Here be demons
2 Demon blues
3 Hooray for Hellywood
Paperback fantasy

FROST, G. R.
1 Recon
2 Recon strike
Paperback war stories

FULLER, E.
THE TROUBLESHOOTERS
1 The troubleshooters
2 The savage west
3 Violence in the Black Hills
4 The big killing Paperback
Westerns

FULLER, K.
RIVERVIEW
1 Bitter legacy 1988
2 The lion's share 1988
3 Pride of place 1989

FULLER, R.
1 Souvenirs 1981
2 Vamp until ready 1982
3 Home and dry 1984
N.F. Autobiography

FULLERTON, . A.
BOB COWAN
1 Bloody sunset 1991
2 Look to the wolves 1992

FULLERTON, A.
NICK EVERARD
1 Sixty minutes for St.George 1975
2 The blooding of the guns 1976
3 Patrol to the Golden Horn 1978
4 Storm force to Narvik 1979
5 Last lift from Crete 1980
6 All the drowning seas 1981
7 A share of honour 1982
8 The torch bearers 1983
9 The gate-crashers 1984

FULLERTON, A.
SBS
1 Special deliverance 1986
2 Special dynamic 1987
3 Special deception 1988
*Adventure stories about the Special
Boat Service*

FURST, R.
ROGER LEVIN
1 The Paris drop 1982
2 The Caribbean account 1983

FUSSEY, J.
1 Milk my ewes and weep 1974
2 Cows in the corn 1978
3 Calf love 1984
4 Cats in the coffee 1986
*N.F. Family life on a remote Yorkshire
farm*

FYFIELD, F.
HELEN WEST
1 A question of guilt 1988
2 Trial by fire 1990
3 Deep sleep 1991
4 Shadow play 1993
5 A clear conscience 1994

FYFIELD, F.
SARAH FORTUNE
1 Shadows on the mirror 1989
2 Perfectly pure and good 1994

GAAN, M.
OPIUM WAR TRILOGY
1 Red barbarian 1984
2 White poppy 1986
3 Blue mountain 1987

GAGE, N.
1 Eleni 1983
2 A place for us 1990
N.F. Autobiography

GAGNON, M.
DEIRDRE O'HARA
1 The inner ring 1985
2 A dark night offshore 1986
3 Doubtful motives 1987

GAINHAM, S.
VIENNESE TRILOGY
1 Night falls on the city 1967
2 A place in the country 1969
3 Private worlds 1971

GALLACHER, T.
BILL THOMPSON
1 Apprentice 1983
2 Journeyman 1984
3 Survivor 1985

GALLAGHER, J.
THE ARCHERS
1 To the victors the spoils 1987
2 Return to Ambridge 1987
3 Borchester echoes 1987
A trilogy based on the radio series

GALLAGHER, P.
1 Castles in the air
2 No greater love
Paperback

GALLICO, P.
ALEXANDER HERO
1 Too many ghosts 1961
2 The hand of Mary Constable 1964

GALLICO, P.
HIRAM HOLLIDAY
1 Adventures of Hiram Holliday
2 The secret front

GALLICO, P.
MRS.HARRIS
1 Flowers for Mrs.Harris 1958
2 Mrs.Harris goes to New York 1960
3 Mrs.Harris goes to Paris 1958
4 Mrs.Harris, M.P. 1965
5 Mrs.Harris goes to Moscow 1974

GALLICO, P.
POSEIDON
1 The Poseidon adventure 1969
2 Beyond the Poseidon adventure 1978

GALLISON, K.
1 Unbalanced accounts 1986
2 The death tape 1987

GALSWORTHY, J.
THE FORSYTE SAGA
The Forsytes, by S. Dawson 1994
continues the story after the death of
Jolyon.

GALWAY, R. C.
JAMES PACKARD
1 Assignment New York 1961
2 Assignment London 1963
3 Assignment Andalucia 1964
4 Assignment gaolbreak 1966
5 Assignment Argentina 1967
6 Assignment Fenland 1969
7 Assignment seabed 1969
8 Assignment Sydney 1970
9 Assignment deathsquad 1970

GANDOLFI, S.
GOLDEN GIRL
1 Golden girl 1992
2 Golden web 1993
3 Golden vengeance 1994
Based on story outlines by Alistair
Maclean

GANN, E. K.
1 The triumph 1986
2 The antagonists 1971

GARDNER, A.
DAVIS TROY
1 The escalator 1963
2 Assignment Tahiti 1964
3 Six day week 1965
4 The man who was too much 1967

GARDNER, C. S.
1 A difficulty with dwarves
2 A disagreement with death
3 An excess of enchantments
4 A malady of magicks
5 A multitude of monsters
6 A night in the Netherhells
Paperback fantasy

GARDNER, C. S.
ARABIAN NIGHTS TRILOGY
1 The other Sinbad
2 A bad day for Ali Baba
3 Scheherazade's night out

GARDNER, C. S.
CINEVERSE CYCLE
1 Bride of the slime monster
2 Slaves of the volcano god
3 Revenge of the fluffy bunnies

GARDNER, E. S.
DISTRICT ATTORNEY
1 The D.A. calls it murder 1937
2 The D.A. draws a circle 1940
3 The D.A. holds a candle 1941
4 The D.A. goes to trial 1941
5 The D.A. cooks a goose 1943
6 The D.A. calls a turn 1947
7 The D.A. breaks a seal 1950
8 The D.A. takes a chance 1956
9 The D.A. breaks an egg 1957

GARDNER, E. S.
PERRY MASON
1 The case of the velvet claw 1933
2 The case of the sulky girl 1933
3 The case of the lucky legs 1934
4 The case of the howling dog 1934
5 Thecase of the curious bride 1934
6 The case of the counterfeit eye 1935
7 The case of the caretaker's cat 1935
8 The case of the sleepwalker's niece 1938
9 The case of the dangerous dowager 1939
10 The case of the lame canary 1939
11 The case of the substitute face 1939
12 The case of the perjured parrot 1939
13 The case of the silent partner 1940
14 The case of the empty tin 1940
15 The case of the stuttering bishop 1940
16 The case of the rolling bones 1940

17 The case of the shoplifter's shoe 1941
18 The case of the baited hook 1941
19 The case of the haunted husband 1942
20 The case of the turning tide 1942
21 The case of the drowning duck 1944
22 The case of the careless kitten 1945
23 The case of the smoking chimney 1945
24 The case of the gold-digger's purse 1945
25 The case of the half-wakened wife 1945
26 Thecase of the buried clock 1946
27 The case of the drowsy mosquito 1946
28 The case of the crooked candle 1947
29 The case of the black eyed blonde 1948
30 The case of the borrowed brunette 1951
31 The case of the fan-dancer's horse 1952
32 The case of the vagabond virgin 1953
33 The case of the lonely heiress 1953
34 The case of the lazy lover 1954
35 The case of the dubious bridegroom 1954
36 The case of the backward mule 1955
37 The case of the cautious coquette 1955
38 The case of the negligent nymph 1956
39 The case of the one-eyed witness 1956
40 Thecase of the musical cow 1956
41 The case of the angry mourner 1957
42 The case of the fiery fingers 1957
43 The case of the grinning gorilla 1958
44 The case of the moth-eaten mink 1958
45 The case of the green eyed sister 1959
46 The case of the hesitant hostess 1959
47 The case of the fugitive nurse 1959
48 The case of the runaway corpse 1960
49 The case of the restless redhead 1960
50 Thecase of the glamorous ghost 1960

51 The case of the sunbather's diary 1961
52 The case of the nervous accomplice 1961
53 The case of the terrified typist 1961
54 The case of the gilded lily 1962
55 The case of the demure defendant 1962
56 The case of the lucky loser 1962
57 The case of the screaming woman 1963
58 The case of the daring decoy 1963
59 The case of the long legged models 1963
60 The case of the footloose doll 1964
61 The case of the calendar girl 1964
62 The case of the deadly toy 1964
63 The case of the mythical monkeys 1965
64 Thecase of the singing skirt 1965
65 The case of the waylaid wolf 1965
66 The case of the duplicate daughter 1966
67 The case of the shapely shadow 1966
68 The case of the spurious spinster 1966
69 The case of the bigamous spouse 1967
70 The case of the reluctant model 1967
71 The case of the blonde bonanza 1967
72 The case of the ice-cold hands 1968
73 The case of the mischievous doll 1968
74 The case of the step-daughter's secret 1968
75 The case of the amorous aunt 1969
76 The case of the daring divorcee 1969
77 The case of the phantom fortune 1970
78 The case of the horrified heirs 1971
79 The case of the troubled trustee 1971
80 The case of the beautiful beggar 1972
81 The case of the worried waitress 1972
82 The case of the careless Cupid 1973
83 The case of the queenly contestant 1973
84 The case of the fabulous fake 1974

85 The case of the crying swallow 1974
86 The case of the crimson kiss 1975
87 The case of the irate witness 1975
88 The case of the fenced-in woman 1976
89 The case of the postponed murder 1977

GARDNER, J.
DIPSPRING
1 Gunman
2 Dilemma at Dipspring 1976
3 The underhand mail 1976
4 The oldtimers 1979
5 Confession at Dipspring 1982
6 The jayhawk legacy 1983

GARDNER, JOHN
1 The secret generations 1987
2 The secret houses 1988
3 The secret families 1989

GARDNER, JOHN
BOYSIE OAKES
1 The liquidator 1964
2 The understrike 1965
3 Amber nine 1967
4 Madrigal 1967
5 Founder member 1969
6 Traitor's exit 1970
7 The airline pirates 1970
8 The champagne communist 1971
9 A killer for a song 1974

GARDNER, JOHN
DEREK TORRY
1 A complete state of death 1969
2 The corner men 1974

GARDNER, JOHN
HERBIE KRUGER
1 The Nostradamus traitor 1978
2 The garden of weapons 1980
3 The quiet dogs 1982
4 Maestro 1993

GARDNER, JOHN
MORIARTY
1 The return of Moriarty 1974
2 The revenge of Moriarty 1975
*Based on the character created by
A. C. Doyle*

GARFIELD, B.
PAUL BENJAMIN
1 Death wish 1974
2 Death sentence 1975
3 Recoil 1977

GARLOCK, D.
WABASH RIVER TRILOGY
1 Dream river 1990
2 Lonesome river 1990
3 River of tomorrow 1991

GARNER, W.
JOHN MORPURGO
1 Think big, think dirty 1983
2 Rats alley 1984

GARNER, W.
MIKE JAGGER
1 Overkill 1966
2 The deep, deep freeze 1967
3 The us or them war 1968
4 A big enough wreath 1974

GARNETT, W.
1 Farmer Gribbins and Farmer Green
2 Wrangledale Chase 1989

GARRETT, C. G.
GUNSLINGER
1 The massacre trail
2 The golden gun
3 White Apache
4 Fifty calibre kill
5 Arizona bloodline
6 Rebel vengeance
7 Death canyon
8 Peace maker!
9 The Russian lode

GARRETT, R.
ALAN BRETT
1 Run down 1970
2 Spiral 1971

GASH, J.
LOVEJOY
1 The Judas pair 1978
2 Gold from Gemini 1979
3 The Grail tree 1979
4 The spend game 1980
5 The Vatican rip 1981
6 The firefly gadroon 1982
7 The sleepers of Erin 1983
8 The gondola scam 1984
9 Pearlhanger 1985
10 The Tartan ringers 1986
11 Moonspender 1986
12 Jade woman 1988
13 The very last gambado 1989
14 The great California game 1990
15 The lies of fair ladies 1991
16 Paid and loving eyes 1993
17 The sin within her smile 1993

GASH, N.
1 Mr.Secretary Peel 1961
2 Sir Robert Peel 1972
N.F. Biography

GASKELL, E.
CRANFORD
*Cranford revisited, by J. R. Townsend
1989*

GASKELL, J.
1 The serpent 1963
2 Atlan 1965
3 The city 1966
4 Some summer lands 1977

GASTON, B.
LT.JASON WINTER
1 Winter and the 'Wild Cat' 1980
2 Winter and the 'White Witch' 1981
3 Winter and the 'Wild Rover' 1982
4 Winter and the widowmakers 1984
5 Winter and the 'Wanderer' 1986
*Novels about a Customs Revenue
cutter in the 18thC*

GATES, T.
1 Scipio 1969
2 Ancora Scipio 1970

GAULLE, C. DE.
1 The call to honour 1955
2 Unity 1959
3 Salvation 1960
4 Memoirs of hope 1971
N.F. Autobiography

GAUNT, R.
BORGIAS
1 Blood for Borgia 1965
2 Vendetta 1968
3 Lucrezia Borgia's lover 1971

GAUNT, R.
ENGLISH CIVIL WAR
1 Brother enemy 1969
2 The iron girdle 1969

GAVIN, C.
1 A light woman 1986
2 The glory road 1987

GAVIN, C.
RESISTANCE TRILOGY
1 Traitor
2 None dare call it treason 1979
3 How sleep the brave 1980
France under de Gaulle in WW2

GAVIN, C.
SECOND EMPIRE
1 The fortress (Finland 1855) 1950
2 The moon into blood (Italy 1859) 1952
3 The cactus and the crown (Mexico 1866) 1954
4 Madeleine (France 1870) 1957 rev.1971

GAVIN, C.
STRATHCLYDE
1 Clyde valley 1938
2 The hostile shore 1940

GAVIN, C.
WORLD WAR I
1 The devil in the harbour 1968
2 The house of war 1970
3 Give me the daggers 1972
4 The snow mountain 1973

GAYE, C.
JANE SCOTT
1 Jane Scott 1963
2 Jane Scott again 1964
3 Jane Scott meets the doctor 1965
4 Jane Scott married 1965
5 Jane Scott meets the pops 1966
6 Jane Scott, crime reporter 1967

GEAR, W. M. & K. O.
PREHISTORIC AMERICA
1 People of the wolf
2 People of the fire
3 People of the earth
4 People of the river
Paperback historical novels

GEDDES, P.
VENNIKER
1 The high game 1968
2 A November wind 1970
3 The Ottawa allegation 1973
4 A state of corruption 1985

GEE, M.
1 Plumb 1979
2 Meg 1981
3 Sole survivor 1983

GELLIS, R.
ROSELYNDE CHRONICLES
1 Roselynde 1978
2 Alinor 1979
3 Joanna 1979
4 Gilliane 1980
5 Rhiannon 1984
6 Sybelle 1984

GEMMELL, D.
1 Lion of Macedon 1991
2 Dark Prince 1991
3 Bloodstone 1994

GEMMELL, D.
SIPSTRASSI TALES
1 Wolf in shadow 1987
2 Ghost king 1988
3 Last sword of power 1988
4 The last guardian 1989
5 Knights of dark renown 1990
6 Morningstar 1992

GEMMELL, D.
THE DRENAI SAGA
1 Legend 1984
2 The King beyond the gate 1985
3 Waylander 1986
4 Quest for lost heroes 1990
5 In the realm of the wolf
  (Waylander II) 1992
6 The first chronicles of Druss the
  Legend 1993
Fantasy

GEMS, P.
MRS.FRAMPTON
1 Mrs.Frampton 1988
2 Bon voyage, Mrs.Frampton 1990

GENTLE, M.
1 Golden witchbreed 1983
2 Ancient light 1987
Fantasy

GENTLE, M.
WHITE CROW
1 Rats and gargoyles 1990
2 The architecture of desire 1991
3 Left to his own devices 1994

GEORGE, E.
DET.CHIEF INSPECTOR LYNLEY
1 A great deliverance 1989
2 Payment in blood 1989
3 A suitable vengeance 1991
4 Well-schooled in murder 1990
5 For the sake of Elena 1991
6 Missing Joseph 1993
7 Playing for the ashes 1994
Listed in chronological order

GEORGESON, V.
SHADOW OF THE ELEPHANT
1 Seeds of love 1986
2 Whispering roots 1987
3 The haunted tree 1989
4 The garden 1992

GERROLD, D.
WAR AGAINST THE CHTORR
1 A matter for men
2 A day for damnation
Paperback science fiction

GERSON, J.
INSPECTOR LOHMANN
1 Deaths head Berlin 1987
2 Death squad London 1989

GETHIN, D.
HALLORAN
1 Jack Lane's Browning 1985
2 Dane's testament 1986

GETHIN, D.
WYATT
1 Wyatt 1982
2 Wyatt and the Moresby legacy
  1983
3 Wyatt's orphan 1985

GHOSE, Z.
1 The incredible Brazilian
2 The beautiful Empire 1975
3 A different world 1978

GIBB, L.
1 The Joneses: how to keep up with
  them 1959
2 The higher Jones 1960
N.F. Humour

GIBBON, L. G.
A SCOTS QUAIR
1 Sunset song 1950
2 Cloud Howe 1952
3 Grey granite 1955

GIBBONS, S.
1 Cold Comfort Farm 1932
2 Christmas at Cold Comfort Farm
  1940
3 Conference at Cold Comfort Farm
  1949

GIBBS, H.
1 The splendour and the dust 1955
2 The winds of time 1956
3 Thunder at dawn 1957
4 The tumult and the shouting 1959
*Novels about the history of South
Africa*

GIBBS-SMITH, C.
PAUL HARVARD
1 Operation Caroline 1955
2 Escape and be secret 1957

GIBSON, M.
1 One man's medicine 1983
2 Doctor in the west 1984
N.F. Autobiography

GIBSON, W.
CYBERSPACE
1 Neuromancer 1984
2 Count Zero 1986
3 Mona Lisa overdrive 1988
Science fiction

GIELGUD, V.
PRINVEST
1 The goggle-box affair 1965
2 Prinvest - London 1966
3 Conduct of a member 1967
4 A necessary end 1969
5 The candle holders 1970
6 The Black Sambo affair 1972
7 In such a night 1974

GIFFORD, B.
1 Wild at heart 1990
2 59 and raining 1992

GILBERT, A.
ARTHUR CROOK
1 Murder by experts
2 The man who wasn't there
3 Murder has no tongue
4 Treason in my breast
5 The clock in the hat box
6 The bell of death
7 Dear dead women
8 The vanishing corpse
9 The woman in red
10 Something nasty in the woodshed
11 The case of the aunt's tea-cosy
12 The mouse who wouldn't play ball
13 He came by night
14 The scarlet button
15 Don't open the door
16 The black stage 1956
17 The spinster's secret
18 Death in the wrong room
19 Spy for Mr.Crook
20 Die in the dark
21 Lift up the lid
22 Death knocks three times
23 Murder comes home
24 A nice cup of tea
25 Lady killer
26 Miss Pinnegar disappears
27 Footsteps behind me
28 Snake in the grass
29 Give death a name 1957
30 Death against the clock 1959

31 Third time lucky 1959
32 Death takes a wife 1959
33 Out for the kill 1960
34 She shall die 1961
35 Uncertain death 1962
36 Ring for a noose 1963
37 Knock knock who's there? 1964
38 Passenger to nowhere 1965
39 The fingerprint 1966
40 The looking glass murder 1966
41 The visitor 1967
42 Night encounter 1968
43 Missing from her home 1969
44 Death wears a mask 1970
45 Tenant for the tomb 1971
46 Murder's a waiting game 1972
47 A nice little killing 1974

GILBERT, A.
SCOTT EGERTON
1 The tragedy at Freyne
2 The murder of Mrs.Davenport
3 Death at Four Corners
4 Mystery of the open window
5 The night of the fog
6 The body on the beam
7 The long shadow
8 The musical comedy crime
9 An old lady dies
10 The man who was too clever

GILBERT, M.
CALDER AND BEHRENS
1 Game without rules 1965
2 Mr.Calder and Mr.Behrens 1982

GILBERT, M.
CHIEF INSPECTOR HAZELRIGG
1 Close quarters 1947
2 They never looked inside 1948
3 The doors open 1949
4 Smallbone deceased 1950
5 Death has deep roots 1951
6 Fear to tread 1953

GILBERT, M.
PETRELLA
1 Young Petrella 1988
2 Petrella at Q 1977
3 Roller-coaster 1993

GILCHRIST, R.
DRAGONARD
1 Dragonard 1975
2 Master of Dragonard Hill 1976
3 Dragonard blood 1977
4 Dragonard rising 1978
5 The siege of Dragonard Hill 1979
6 Guns of Dragonard 1980

GILCHRIST, R.
SLAVES WITHOUT MASTERS
1 A girl called Friday Night 1983
2 The house at 3 o'clock 1982
3 The wrong side of town 1985

GILES, J. H.
FOWLER FAMILY
1 Hannah Fowler 1956
2 The believers 1957
3 Johnny Osage 1960
4 Voyage to Santa Fe 1962
5 Savanna 1961
6 The great adventure 1966
7 Shadygrove 1968
8 Six horse hitch 1969

GILES, J. H.
KENTUCKY
1 The enduring hills 1950
2 Miss Willie 1951
3 Tara's healing 1954

GILES, K.
INSPECTOR JAMES & SGT.HONEYBODY
1 Some beasts no more 1964
2 The big greed 1965
3 A provenance of death 1966
4 Death in diamonds 1966
5 Death and Mr.Prettyman 1967
6 Death among the stars 1968
7 Death cracks a bottle 1969
8 A death in the church 1970
9 Murder pluperfect 1971
10 A file on death 1973

GILES, R.
SABREHILL
1 Sabrehill
2 Slaves of Sabrehill
3 Rebels of Sabrehill
4 Storm over Sabrehill
5 Hell cat of Sabrehill
Papberback plantation novels

GILL, A.
EGYPTIAN MYSTERIES
1 City of the horizon 1991
2 City of dreams 1993

GILL, B.
CHIEF INSPECTOR MCGARR
1 McGarr and the Sienese
conspiracy 1978
2 McGarr and the politician's wife
1979
3 McGarr on the Cliffs of Moher
1980

4 McGarr at the Dublin Horse Show
1981
5 McGarr and the Prime Minister of
Belgrave Square
6 McGarr and the method of
Descartes 1985
7 McGarr and the legacy of a
woman scorned 1987
8 The death of a Joyce scholar 1989
9 The death of love 1992
10 Death on a cold, wild river 1993

GILL, B. M.
DET.CHIEF INSPECTOR MAYBRIDGE
1 Seminar for murder 1985
2 The fifth Rapunzel 1991

GILLESPIE, S.
LONGDEN-LORRISTONE FAMILY
1 The martyr 1955
2 The grandson 1957
3 The visitors 1959
4 The neighbour 1960
5 The summer at home 1961
6 The green blade 1963

GILLULY, S.
1 Greenbriar Queen 1989
2 The crystal keep 1989
3 Ritmyin's daughter 1989
Fantasy

GILLULY, S.
PAINTER
1 The boy from the Burren 1991
2 The giant of Inishkerry 1992
3 The Emperor of Earth-Above 1993

GILMAN, D.
MRS.POLLIFAX
1 The unexpected Mrs.Pollifax 1966
2 The amazing Mrs.Pollifax 1970
3 The elusive Mrs.Pollifax 1973
4 A palm for Mrs.Pollifax 1974
5 Mrs.Pollifax on the China Station
1985
6 Mrs.Pollifax and the Hong
KongBuddha 1986
7 Mrs.Pollifax and the golden
triangle 1989

GILMAN, G. G.
ADAM STEELE
1 The violent peace
2 Bounty hunter
3 Hell's junction
4 Valley of blood
5 Gun run
6 The killing art

7 Crossfire
8 Comanche carnage
9 Badge in the dust
10 The losers
11 Lynch town
12 Death trail
13 Bloody border
14 Delta duel
15 River of death
16 Nightmare at noon
17 Satan's daughter
18 The hard way
19 The tarnished star
20 Wanted for murder
21 Wagons East
22 The big game
23 Fort Despair
24 Manhunt
25 Steele's war: the woman
26 Steele's war:the preacher
27 Steele's war:the storekeeper
28 Steele's war:the stranger
29 The big prize
30 The killer mountains
31 The cheaters
32 The wrong man
33 The valley of the shadow
34 The runaway
35 Stranger in a strange town
36 The hellraisers
37 Canyon of death
38 High stakes
39 Rough justice
40 The sunset ride
41 The killing strain
42 The big gunfight
43 The hunted
44 Code of the West
45 The outcasts
46 Trouble in Paradise
47
48 Going back

GILMAN, G. G.
EDGE MEETS STEELE
1 Two of a kind
2 Matching pair
3 Double action

GILMAN, G. G.
EDGE THE LONER
1 The loner
2 $10,000 American
3 Apache death
4 Killer's breed
5 Blood on silver
6 The blue,the grey and the red
7 California killing
8 Seven out of hell

9 Bloody summer
10 Vengeance is black
11 Sioux uprising
12 The biggest bounty
13 A town called hate
14 The big gold
15 Blood run
16 The final shot
17 Vengeance valley
18 Ten tombstones to Texas
19 Ashes and dust
20 Sullivan's law
21 Rhapsody in red
22 Slaughter road
23 Echoes of war
24 The day democracy died
25 Violence trail
26 Savage dawn
27 Death drive
28 Eve of evil
29 The living,the dying and the dead
30 Waiting for a train
31 The guilty ones
32 The frightened gun
33 The hated
34 A ride in the sun
35 Death deal
36 Town on trial
37 Vengeance at Ventura
38 Massacre mission
39 The prisoners
40 Montana melodrama
41 The killing claim
42 Bloody sunrise
43 Arapaho revenge
44 The blind side
45 House on the range
46 The godforsaken
47 The moving cage
48 School for slaughter
49 Revenge ride
50 Shadow of the gallows
51 A time for killing
52 Brutal border
53 Hitting paydirt
54 Backshot
55 Uneasy riders
56 Doom town
57 Dying is forever
58 The desperadoes
59 Terror town
60 The breed woman

GILMAN, G. G.
THE UNDERTAKER
1 Black as death
2 Destined to die
3 Funeral by the sea
4 Three graves to a showdown

5 Back from the dead
6 Death in the desert
Paperback Westerns

GILRUTH, S.
INSPECTOR HUGH GORDON
1 Dawn her remembrance 1961
2 The snake is living yet 1963

GIOVENE, A.
1 The book of Guiliam Sansevero 1970
2 The dilemma of love 1973
3 The dice of war 1975

GITTINGS, R.
1 Young Thomas Hardy 1975
2 The older Hardy 1975

GLANFIELD, J.
1 Hotel Quadriga 1987
2 Viktoria 1989
Novels set in Vienna at the turn of the century

GLASKIN, G. M.
1 Windows of the mind 1974
2 Worlds within 1976
3 A door to eternity 1979
N.F. About the Christos experience

GLASSER, R.
1 Growing up in the Gorbals 1986
2 Gorbals boy at Oxford 1988
3 Gorbals voices, siren songs 1990
N.F. Autobiography

GLAZEBROOK, P.
1 Captain Vinegar's commission 1988
2 The gate at the end of the world 1989

GLOAG, J.
1 Caesar of the narrow seas 1970
2 The eagles depart 1973
3 Artorius Rex 1977

GLOVER, J.
FLYNN FAMILY
1 The stallion man 1982
2 Sisters and brothers 1984
3 To everything a season 1986
4 Birds in a gilded cage 1987

GLUBB, SIR J.
1 A soldier with the Arabs 1957
2 War in the desert 1960
N.F. Autobiography

GLUBB, SIR J.
HISTORY OF ARABIA
1 The grat Arab conquests 630-680 1961
2 The empire of the Arabs 680-860 1963
3 The curse of the empire 860-1150 1964

GLYN, C.
1 Don't knock the corners off 1964
2 Love and joy in the Mabillon 1985

GLYN, C.
THE STORY OF FULLIE
1 The unicorn girl 1965
2 Heights and depths 1967
3 The tree 1969

GOBINEAU, M.
STEPHANIE
1 The passions of spring 1974
2 The snows of Sebastopol 1975
3 The Emperor's agent 1976
4 All for my love 1976
5 The savage land 1976
6 The price of freedom 1977

GODDEN, R.
1 A time to dance, a time to weep 1987
2 A house with four rooms 1989
N.F. Autobiography of the novelist.

GODFREY, E.
JANE TREGAR
1 Murder behind locked doors 1989
2 Georgia disappeared 1992

GODWIN, E.
CAPTAIN JOHN HUNTER
1 Mission to Samarkand 1964
2 The towers of pain 1965

GOLD, H.
1 Fathers 1970
2 My last two thousand years 1973

GOLDING, W.
EDMUND TALBOT
1 Rites of passage 1980
2 Close quarters 1987
3 Fire down below 1989
Published in one vol. 'To the ends of the earth' in 1991.

GOLDMAN, W.
1 Marathon man 1974
2 Brothers 1986

GOLDREICH, G.
LEAH
1 Leah's journey 1983
2 Leah's children 1985

GOLDSBOROUGH, R.
NERO WOLFE
1 Murder in E minor 1986
2 Death on deadline 1989
3 The bloodied ivy 1989
4 The last coincidence 1991
A continuation of the series by Rex Stout.

GOLLANCZ, V.
1 My dear Timothy 1952
2 More for Timothy 1953
3 The last words for Timothy 1954
N.F. Autobiographical letters to a godson

GOLLIN, J.
1 The Verona Passamezzo 1987
2 Eliza's galiardo 1988
Thrillers with a musical background

GOLON, S.
ANGELIQUE
1 Angelique 1958
2 Angelique and the King 1960
3 Angelique and the Sultan 1961
4 Angelique in revolt 1962
5 Angelique in love 1963
6 The Countess Angelique 1965
7 The temptation of Angelique 1969
8 Angelique and the demon 1973
9 Angelique and the ghosts 1977

GOODCHILD, G.
MACLEAN
1 Maclean of Scotland Yard
2 Maclean investigates
3 Maclean at the Golden Owl
4 How now,Maclean
5 Chief Inspector Maclean
6 The triumph of Maclean
7 Yes, Inspector Maclean
8 Death on the centre court
9 Lead on, Maclean
10 Maclean remembers
11 Maclean finds a way
12 Maclean takes charge
13 Call Maclean
14 Maclean plays a hand
15 Maclean prevails
16 Maclean knows best
17 Maclean sees it through
18 Again Maclean
19 Up Maclean
20 Maclean intervenes
21 Maclean excels
22 Having no hearts
23 Maclean incomparable
24 Maclean deduces
25 Maclean the magnificent
26 Maclean non-stop
27 Maclean keeps going
28 Maclean takes a holiday
29 Uncle Oscar's niece
30 Hail Maclean
31 Companion to Sirius
32 Inspector Maclean's casebook
33 The Efford triangle
34 Maclean carries on
35 Maclean predominant
36 Maclean to the dark tower came
37 Maclean steps in
38 The last redoubt
39 Well caught Maclean
40 Double acrostic
41 Trust Maclean
42 Find the lady
43 Watch Maclean 1955
44 Maclean solves it 1956
45 Next of kin 1957
46 Forever Maclean 1957
47 Maclean disposes 1958
48 Tiger tiger 1959
49 Maclean scores again 1959
50 Follow Maclean 1960
51 Savage encounter 1962
52 Maclean invincible 1962
53 Laurels for Maclean 1963
54 Maclean takes over 1964
55 Maclean knows the answers 1967

GOODMAN, P.
EMPIRE CITY
1 The state of nature 1946
2 The dead of spring 1950
3 The holy terror 1959
4 Grand piano 1942

GOODWIN, S.
1 Winter spring 1978
2 Winter sisters 1980

GOOLDEN, B.
CONSETT TRILOGY
1 Goodbye to yesterday 1975
2 In the melting pot 1976
3 Unborn tomorrow 1977

GORDON, D.
1 Blackblocks baby doctor 1956
2 Doctor down under 1957
N.F. Autobiography

GORDON, G.
1 Better to arrive 1968
2 The old warriors 1970
N.F. Autobiography

GORDON, GILES
1 About a marriage 1972
2 Scenes from married life 1976

GORDON, K.
PEACOCKS
1 Emerald peacock 1978
2 Peacock in flight 1979
3 In the shadow of the peacock 1980
4 The peacock ring 1981
5 Peacock in jeopardy 1982
A family chronicle set in 19th century India

GORDON, N.
ROB COLE
1 The physician 1990
2 Shaman 1992

GORDON, R.
1 The facemaker 1967
2 Surgeon at arms 1968
The story of a plastic surgeon

GORDON, R.
DOCTOR
1 Doctor in the house 1952
2 Doctor at sea 1954
3 Doctor at large 1955
4 Doctor in love 1957
5 Doctor and son 1958
6 Doctor in clover 1960
7 Doctor on toast 1961
8 Doctor in the swim 1962
9 The summer of Sir Lancelot 1963
10 Love and Sir Lancelot 1965
11 Doctor on the boil 1970
12 Doctor on the brain 1972
13 Doctor in the nude 1973
14 Doctor on the job 1976
15 Doctor in the nest 1979
16 Doctor on the ball 1985
17 Doctor in the soup 1986

GORDON, S.
1 One eye 1974
2 Two eyes 1975
3 Three eyes 1976
Science fiction

GORDON, S.
THE WATCHERS
1 The watchers
2 The hidden world

3 The mask
Paperback fantasy

GORDONS, THE
1 Undercover cat 1965
2 Undercover cat prowls again 1967
3 Cat napped 1973

GORDONS, THE
FRANK & GAIL MITCHELL
1 The night before the wedding 1978
2 The night after the wedding 1980

GORES, J.
THE DKA FILE
1 Dead skip 1973
2 Final notice 1974

GOSLING, P.
LT. JACK STRYKER
1 Monkey puzzle 1988
2 Backlash 1989

GOSLING, P.
LUKE ABBOTT
1 The Wychford murders 1986
2 Death penalties 1991

GOSLING, P.
SHERIFF MATT GABRIEL
1 The body in Blackwater Bay 1992
2 A few dying words 1993
Lt. Jack Stryker appears in 1.

GOUDGE, E.
ELIOT FAMILY
1 Bird in the tree 1940
2 The herb of grace 1948
3 The heart of the family 1953
Published in one vol as 'The Eliots of Damerosehay' in 1957

GOUGH, L.
WILLOWS & PARKER
1 The goldfish bowl 1987
2 Death on a No.8 hook 1988
3 Hot shots 1989
4 Serious crimes 1990
5 Accidental deaths 1991
6 Killers 1993

GOULD, J.
1 The Texas years 1989
2 Lovemakers 1985

GOWER, I.
1 The copper cloud 1976
2 Return to Tip Row 1977
Novels about copper smelting in

South Wales. They are the fore-
runners of her series about Swansea
Published in an omnibus edition in
1987 as 'The Loves of Catrin'.

GOWER, I.
CORDWAINERS
1 The shoemaker's daughter 1991
2 The oyster catchers 1992
3 Honey's farm 1993
4 Arian 1994

GOWER, I.
SWEYNESEYE
1 Copper kingdom 1983
2 Proud Mary 1984
3 Spinners Wharf 1985
4 Morgan's woman 1986
5 Fiddler's ferry 1987
6 Black gold 1988
A series of novels about Swansea from
the late 19thC to the Second World
War. The same characters
appear, with varying degrees of
importance

GRADY, J.
1 Six days of the Condor 1975
2 Shadow of the Condor 1976

GRAEME, B.
BLACKSHIRT
1 Blackshirt 1925
2 The return of Blackshirt 1927
3 Blackshirt again 1929
4 Alias Blackshirt 1932
5 Blackshirt the audacious 1936
6 Blackshirt the adventurer 1936
7 Blackshirt takes a hand 1937
8 Blackshirt - counterspy 1938
9 Blackshirt interferes 1939
10 Blackshirt strikes back 1940
11 Son of Blackshirt 1942
12 Lord Blackshirt 1942
13 Calling Lord Blackshirt 1944
14 Concerning Blackshirt 1947
15 Blackshirt wins the trick 1948
16 Blackshirt passes by 1950
17 Salute to Blackshirt 1952
18 Amazing, Mr.Blackshirt 1955
19 Blackshirt meets the lady 1956
20 Paging Blackshirt 1957
21 Blackshirt helps himself 1957
22 Double for Blackshirt 1958
23 Blackshirt sets the pace 1959
24 Blackshirt sees it through 1959
25 Blackshirt finds trouble 1961
26 Blackshirt takes the trail 1962
27 Call for Blackshirt 1962

28 Blackshirt on the spot 1963
29 Blackshirt saves the day 1964
30 Danger for Blackshirt 1965
31 Blackshirt atlarge 1966
32 Blackshirt in peril 1967
33 Blackshirt stirs things up 1968
13-33 are by Roderick Graeme, Bruce
Graeme's son

GRAEME, BRUCE
DET.SERGEANT MATHER
1 The quiet ones 1970
2 Two and two make five 1973
3 The D notice 1974
4 The snatch 1976
5 Two faced 1977
6 Double trouble 1978
7 Mather again 1979
8 Invitation to Mather 1980
9 Mather investigates 1980

GRAEME, BRUCE
HENRY MAXWELL
1 Blind date for a private eye 1969
2 The D notice 1974

GRAFF, P.
JOSE DUST
1 Dust and the curious boy 1958
2 Daughter fair 1958
3 The Sapphire conference 1959

GRAFTON, S.
KINSEY MILLHONE
1 A is for alibi 1985
2 B is for burglar 1986
3 C is for corpse 1987
4 D is for deadbeat 1987
5 E is for evidence 1988
6 F is for fugitive 1989
7 G is for gumshoe 1990
8 H is for homicide 1991
9 I is for innocent 1992
10 J is for judgment 1993
11 K is for killer 1994

GRAHAM, B.
MICHAEL EVANS
1 The spy trap 1971
2 Spy or die 1972

GRAHAM, C.
INSPECTOR TOM BARNABY
1 The killings at Badger's Drift 1987
2 Death of a hollow man 1989
3 Death in disguise 1992
4 Written in blood 1994

GRAHAM, H.
AMERICAN CIVIL WAR
1 One wore blue 1992
2 And one wore gray 1993
3 And one rode west 1994

GRAHAM, N.
SOLO MALCOLM
1 Murder makes a date 1955
2 Play it solo 1956
3 Say it with murder '1957
4 You can't call it murder 1957
5 Hit me hard 1958
6 Salute to murder 1958
7 Murder rings the bell 1959
8 Killers are on velvet 1960
9 Murder is my weakness 1961
10 Murder on the Duchess 1962
11 Make minemurder 1962
12 Murder makes it certain 1962
13 Graft town 1963
14 Label it murder 1963
15 Murder made easy 1964
16 Murder of a black cat 1964
17 Murdr on my hands 1965
18 Murder's always final 1965
19 Money for murder 1966
20 Murder on demand 1966
21 Murder makes the news 1967
22 Murder has been done 1967
23 Pay off 1968
24 Candidate for a coffin 1968
25 Death of a canary 1969
26 Murder lies in waiting 1969
27 Blood on the pavement 1970
28 One for the book 1970
29 A matter of murder 1971
30 Murder double murder 1971
31 Frame-up 1972
32 Cop in a tight frame 1973
33 Murder in a dark room 1973
34 Assignment murder 1974
35 Murder on the list 1975
36 Search for a missing lady 1976

GRAHAM, N.
SUPT. SANDYMAN
1 Passport to murder
2 Murder walks on tiptoe
3 The quest of Mr.Sandyman
4 Again Mr.Sandyman
5 The amazing Mr.Sandyman
6 Salute Mr.Sandyman

GRAHAM, WINSTON
POLDARK
1 Ross Poldark (1783-87) 1945
2 Demelza (1788-90) 1946
3 Jeremy Poldark (1790-91) 1950

4 Warleggan (1792-93) 1953
5 The black moon (1794-95) 1973
6 The four swans (1795-97) 1976
7 The angry tide (1798-99) 1977
8 The stranger from the sea (1810-11) 1981
9 The miller's dance (1812-13) 1982
10 The loving cup (1813-15) 1984
11 Twisted sword 1990
A family saga set in Cornwall

GRAHAME, K.
1 The wind in the willows 1908
2 A fresh wind in the willows, by D.Scott 1983
3 The willows in winter, by W.Horwood 1993

GRANGE, P.
L'EREE FAMILY
1 King Creole 1967
2 Devil's emissary 1968
3 Tumult at the gate 1970
4 The golden goddess 1973

GRANGER, A.
MITCHELL & MARKBY
1 Say it with murder 1990
2 A season for murder 1991
3 Cold in the earth 1992
4 Murder among us 1992
5 Where old bones lie 1993
6 A fine place for death 1994
7 Flowers for his funeral 1994

GRANGER, B.
THE NOVEMBER MAN
1 The November man 1980
2 Schism 1982
3 The shattered eye 1984
4 The British Cross 1985
5 The Zurich numbers 1985
6 Hemingway's notebook 1986
7 There are no spies 1992
8 The infant of Prague 1988
9 Henry McGee is not dead 1989
10 League of terror 1991
11 The man who heard too much 1993

GRANT, JAMES
MACE
1 Mace 1984
2 Mace's luck 1985

GRANT, JANE
1 Come hither, nurse 1964
2 Come again, nurse 1965
3 Sister under their skins 1966

4 Round-the-clock nurse 1968
N.F. Autobiography

GRANT, JOAN
1 The owl on the teapot 1991
2 The cuckoo on the kettle 1993
N.F. The author runs a hospital for wild birds

GRANT, JOHN
1 Albion 1991
2 The world 1992

GRANT, JONATHAN
SEALANDINGS
1 Shores of Sealandings 1991
2 Storms at Sealandings 1992
3 Mehala: lady of Sealandings 1993

GRANT-ADAMSON, L.
JIM RUSH
1 A life of adventure 1993
2 Dangerous games 1994

GRANT-ADAMSON, L.
RAIN MORGAN
1 Patterns in the dust 1984
2 Faces of death 1985
3 Guilty knowledge 1987
4 Wild justice 1987
5 Curse the darkness 1990

GRASS, G.
THE DANZIG TRILOGY
1 The tin drum 1959
2 Cat and mouse 1966
3 Dog years 1965
Published as one volume in 1987. The books are linked by background and period rather than characters.

GRAVE, S.
MIAMI VICE
1 China white
2 Hellhole
3 Probing by fire
4 The razor's edge
Paperbacks, based on the TV series

GRAY, B.
NORMAN CONQUEST
1 Mr.Mortimer gets the jitters
2 Vultures, Ltd.
3 Miss Dynamite
4 Conquest marches on
5 Leave it to Conquest
6 Conquest takes all
7 Meet the Don
8 Six to kill
9 Convict 1066
10 Thank you Mr.Conquest
11 Six feet of dynamite
12 Blonde for danger
13 The gay desderado
14 Cavalier Conquest
15 Alias Norman Conquest
16 Mr.Ball of fire
17 Killer Conquest
18 The Conquest touch
19 The spot marked X
20 Duel murder
21 Dare devil Conquest
22 Operation Conquest
23 Seven dawns to death
24 Conquest in Scotland
25 The lady is poison
26 The half-open door
27 Target for Conquest
28 Follow the lady
29 Conquest goes west
30 Turn left for danger
31 House of the lost 1956
32 Conquest at midnight 1957
33 Conquest goes home 1957
34 Conquest in command 1958
35 Conquest in California 1958
36 Death on the hit-parade 1958
37 The big brain 1959
38 Conquest on the run 1960
39 Get ready to die 1960
40 Call Conquest for danger 1961
41 Conquest in the underworld 1962
42 Count down for Conquest 1963
43 Conquest overboard 1964
44 Calamity Conquest 1965
45 Conquest likes it hot 1965
46 Curtains for Conquest 1966
47 Conquest calls the tune 1969
48 Conquest in Ireland 1969

GRAY, CAROLINE
HELIER L'EREE
1 Spawn of the devil 1993
2 Sword of the devil 1994
3 Death of the devil 1994

GRAY, E.
1 No survivors 1975
2 Action Atlantic 1976
3 Tokyo torpedo 1977
Novels about German U-boats

GRAY, S.
1 Unnatural pursuit 1985
2 How's that for telling 'em, fat lady? 1988
N.F. Autobiography of the playwright

GRAYLAND, V. M.
HOANI MATA
1 Nightof the reaper 1963
2 The grave-digger's apprentice 1964

GRAYSON, RICHARD
INSPECTOR GAUTIER
1 The murders at the Impasse
  Louvain 1979
2 The Monterant affair 1980
3 The death of Abbe Didier 1981
4 The Montmartre murders 1982
5 Crime without passion 1983
6 Death en voyage 1986
7 Death on the cards 1988
8 Death off stage 1991
9 Death au gratin 1994
  Set in Paris at the turn of the century

GRAYSON, RUPERT
1 Voyage not completed 1969
2 Stand fast the Holy Ghost 1973
  N.F. Autobiography

GREATOREX, W.
AIRLINE
1 Take-off 1981
2 Ruskin's Berlin 1982

GREAVES, J.
JACKIE GROVES
1 The final 1979
2 The ball game 1980
  About a professional footballer

GREAVES, J.
STEVE WALKER
1 The boss 1980
2 The second half 1981
  About a football club manager

GREELEY, A. M.
FATHER 'BLACKIE' RYAN
1 Happy are the meek 1986
2 Happy are the clean of heart 1987
3 Rite of spring 1988
4 Happy are those who thirst for
  justice 1988
5 Love song 1990
6 St.Valentine's night 1990
7 Happy are the merciful 1993
8 Happy are the peacemakers 1994

GREELEY, A. M.
THE PASSOVER TRILOGY
1 Thy brother's wife 1982
2 Ascent into Hell 1983
3 Lord of the dance 1988

GREELEY, A. M.
TIME BETWEEN THE STARS
1 Virgin and martyr 1985
2 Angels of September 1986
3 Patience of a Saint 1988

GREEN, CHRISTINE
KATE KINSELLA
1 Deadly errand 1991
2 Deadly admirer 1992
3 Deadly practice 1994

GREEN, E.
1 Adam's empire 1990
2 Kalinda 1991
  Historical novels set in Australia

GREEN, H.
TRIPLE S AGENTS
1 A woman called Omega 1984
2 The Fidelio affair 1985

GREEN, M.
1 The boy who shot down an
  airship 1988
2 Nobody lost in small earthquake
  1990
  N.F. Autobiography

GREEN, S.
1 The warrior within
2 The warrior enchained
  Paperback fantasy

GREEN, S. R.
HAWK & FISHER
1 No haven for the guilty
2 Devil take the hindmost
3 The God killer
4 Vengeance for a lonely man
5 Guard against dishonour
6 Two kings in haven
  Paperback thrillers set in the space age

GREEN, S. R.
TWILIGHT OF EMPIRE
1 Mistworld
2 Blue moon rising
3 Blood and honour
4 Ghostworld
  Paperback fantasy

GREENE, B.
1 Summer of the German soldier
  1974
2 Morning is a long time coming
  1978

GREENLEAF, S.
JOHN TANNER,P.I.
1 Grave error 1981
2 Death bed 1982
3 State's evidence 1984
4 Fatal obsession 1985
5 Beyond blame 1987

GREENWOOD, D. M.
DEACONESS THEODORA
BRAITHWAITE
1 Clerical errors 1990
2 Unholy ghosts 1991
3 Idol bones 1993
4 Holy terrors 1994
   *Detective stories with a clerical
   setting*

GREENWOOD, J.
DET.INSPECTOR MOSLEY
1 Murder,Mr.Mosley 1983
2 Mosley by moonlight 1984
3 Mosley went to mow 1985
4 Mists over Mosley 1986
5 The mind of Mr.Mosley 1987
6 What, me, Mr.Mosley? 1987
   *Detective stories set in the Yorkshire
   Dales See also entries under the
   author's real name, J. B. Hilton.*

GREENWOOD, R.
MR.BUNTING
1 Mr. Bunting 1940
2 Mr. Bunting at war 1941
3 Mr. Bunting in the promised land
1949

GREENWOOD, R.
ROSIE DAWES
1 Good angel slept 1952
2 O mistress mine 1955

GREENWOOD, W.
TRELOOE
1 So brief the spring 1952
2 What everybody wants 1953
3 Down by the sea 1956

GREGG, C. F.
INSPECTOR HIGGINS
1 The murdered manservant
2 The three daggers
3 The murder on the bus
4 The brazen confession
5 The Rutland mystery
6 The double solution
7 Inspector Higgins hurries
8 The body behind the bar
9 The duke's last trick

10 Inspector Higgins sees it through
11 The execution of Diamond
   Deutsch
12 The ten black pearls
13 Danger at Cliff House
14 Tragedy at Wembley
15 The wrong house
16 Mystery at Moor Street
17 Who dialled 999?
18 Danger in the dark
19 The fatal error
20 Justice!
21 The Vandor mystery
22 Two died at three
23 Melander's millions
24 The old manor
25 Exit Harlequin
26 Murder at midnight
27 The man with the monocle
28 The ugly customer
29 From information received
30 Inspector Higgins goes fishing
31 Accidental murder
32 Sufficient rope
33 Night flight to Zurich
34 The Chief Constable
35 Dead on time 1955
36 The obvious solution 1958
37 Professional jealousy 1959

GREGORIAN, J. B.
THE TREDANA TRILOGY
1 The broken citadel
2 Castle-down
3 The great wheel
   Paperback fantasy

GREGORY, P.
1 Wideacre 1987
2 The favoured child 1989
3 Meridon 1990

GREGSON, J. M.
SUPT.JOHN LAMBERT
1 Murder on the 19th 1989
2 For sale,with corpse 1990
3 Bring forth your dead 1991
4 Dead on course 1991
5 The fox in the forest 1992
6 Stranglehold 1993
7 Watermarked 1994

GRENFELL, J.
1 Joyce Grenfell requests the
   pleasure 1977
2 In pleasant places 1979
3 Joyce 1980
4 An invisible friendship 1981
   N.F. Autobiography

GREY, ROMER ZANE
BUCK DUANE
1 Rider of distant trails 1969
2 High valley river 1970
3 King of the range 1970
4 Rustlers of the cattle range 1970
5 Three deaths for Buck Duane 1971
6 Track the man down 1971

GREY, ROMER ZANE
LARAMIE NELSON
1 Last stand at Indigo Flats 1970
2 The other side of the river 1970
This character first appeared in

GRIBBIN, J. & CHOWN, M.
1 Double planet 1988
2 Reunion 1991

GRIBBLE, L. R.
ANTHONY SLADE
1 Gillespie suicide murder 1929
2 The Grand Modena murder 1930
3 The stolen Home Secretary 1932
4 Is this revenge? 1931
5 The secret of Tangles 1933
6 The riddle of the ravens 1934
7 Riley of the Special Branch 1936
8 The case of the Malverne
   diamonds 1936
9 The casebook of Anthony Slade
   1937
10 Tragedy in E flat 1938
11 The Arsenal Stadium mystery 1939
12 Atomic murder 1947
13 Hangman's moon 1949
14 They kidnapped Stanley Matthews
   1950
15 The frightened chameleon 1951
16 Murder out of season 1952
17 Death pays the piper 1956
18 Superintendent Slade investigates
   1957
19 Stand in for murder 1957
20 Don't argue with death 1958
21 Wantons die hard 1961
22 Heads you die 1964
23 The violent dark1965
24 Strip tease macabre 1967
25 A diplomat dies 1969
26 Alias the victim 1971
27 Programmed for death 1973
28 Midsummer slay ride 1976
29 You can't die tomorrow 1978
30 Dead end in Mayfair 1981
31 The dead don't scream 1984
32 Violent midnight 1986

GRIEG, D.
1 Daisy 1978
2 Daisy reminisces 1979
N.F. Autobiography

GRIERSON, F. D.
SUPT.ASH
1 The blind frog 1955
2 The sign of the nine 1956
3 Green evil 1958
4 The red cobra 1960

GRIERSON, F. D.
SUPT.MUIR
1 The mad hatter murder
2 Thrice Judas
3 Entertaining murder
4 Out of the ashes
5 He had it coming to him

GRIFFIN, J.
RICHARD RAVEN
1 The Midas operation 1972
2 Standing into danger 1973
3 Circle of darkness 1974
4 Seeds of destruction 1975
5 Anarchist's moon 1976
6 The ring of Kerry 1977
7 St. Catherine's wheel 1978
8 The Antarctic convergance 1979
9 The Florentine Madonna 1980
10 The Camelot conundrum 1981
11 The flame of Persepolis 1982

GRIFFIN, W. E. B.
BADGE OF HONOR
1 Men in blue 1982
2 Special operations 1984
3 The victim 1986

GRIFFIN, W. E. B.
BROTHERHOOD OF WAR
1 The Lieutenants 1988
2 The Captains 1988
3 The Majors 1989
4 The Colonels 1989
5 The Berets 1989
6 The Generals 1990
7 The new breed 1990
8 Aviators 1990
About the US Army in Vietnam

GRIFFIN, W. E. B.
CORPS
1 Semper fi 1992
2 Call to arms 1993
3 Counterattack 1993
4 Battleground 1994

5 Line of fire 1994
Novels about the US Marine Corps

GRIFFITHS, E.
RUDOLF & KARSTEN NILSEN
1 Murder on Page 3 1985
2 The water widow 1986

GRIMES, M.
CHIEF INSPECTOR RICHARD JURY
1 The man with a load of mischief 1981
2 The old fox deceiv'd 1982
3 The anodyne necklace 1984
4 The Dirty Duck 1986
5 I am the only Running Footman 1987
6 Jerusalem Inn 1987
7 The Five Bells and Bladebone 1988
8 The Deer Leap 1988
9 Help the poor struggler 1989
10 The Old Silent 1990
11 The Old Contemptibles 1991
12 The horse you came in on 1993

GROSS, J.
1 The lives of Rachel 1985
2 The books of Rachel 1980

GROSSMAN, A.
1 Marie beginning 1965
2 The do-gooders 1968

GROSSMITH, G.
1 Diary of a nobody 1892
2 Mrs.Pooter's diary, by K.Waterhouse 1983
3 Collected letters of a nobody,by K.Waterhouse 1986

GUARESCHI, G.
DON CAMILLO
1 The little world of Don Camillo 1953
2 Don Camillo and the prodigal son 1955
3 Don Camillo's dilemma 1957
4 Don Camillo and the devil 1959
5 Comrade Don Camillo 1960
6 Don Camillo meets Hell's Angels 1970

GUILD, N.
1 The Assyrian 1988
2 The blood star 1989

GUNN, V.
CHIEF INSPECTOR BILL CROMWELL
1 Footsteps of death

2 Ironsides of the Yard
3 Ironsides smashes through
4 Ironsides' lone hand
5 DEath's doorway
6 Mad Hatter's rock
7 Ironsides sees red
8 The dead man laughs
9 Nice day for a murder
10 Ironsides smells blood
11 Death in shivering sand
12 Three dates with death
13 Ironsides on the spot 1948
14 Road to murder 1949
15 Dead man's morning 1949
16 Alias the hangman 1950
17 Murder on ice 1951
18 The Borgia head mystery 1951
19 The body vanishes 1952
20 Death comes laughing 1952
21 The whistling key 1953
22 The crooked staircase 1953
23 The crippled canary 1954
24 The laughing grave 1954
25 Castle dangerous 1955
26 The 64thousand murder 1956
27 The painted dog 1956
28 Dead men's bells 1957
29 The treble chance murder 1958
30 Dead in a ditch 1959
31 Death on Bodmin Moor 1960
32 Devil in the maze 1960
33 Death at Traitor's Gate 1960
34 Sweet smelling death 1961
35 All change for murder 1962
36 The body in the boot 1962
37 Murder with a kiss 1963
38 The black cap murder 1965
39 Murder on Whispering Sands 1965
40 The Petticoat Lane murders 1966

GUNNARSON, T.
STARWOLVES
1 Starwolves
2 Battle of the ring
3 Tactical error
4 Dreadnought
Paperback s. f.

GUTHRIE, A. B.
1 The big sky 1947
2 The way west 1956
3 These thousand hills 1957
4 Arfive 1972

GUTTERIDGE, L.
MATTHEW DILKE
1 Cold war in a country garden 1971
2 Killer pine 1973
3 Fratricide is a gas 1975

GUY, R.
1 The friends 1974
2 Edith Jackson 1979
3 Ruby 1981

GYGAX, G.
DANGEROUS JOURNEYS
1 The Anubis murders
2 The Samarkand solution
3 Death in Delhi
Paperback thrillers, in which the detective is an ancient Egyptian priest.

HAAS, B.
CHANDLER FAMILY
1 The Chandler heritage 1972
2 Daisy Canfield 1973

HACKFORTH-JONES, G.
EARL OF MILLINGTON
1 Submarine flotilla
2 Rough passage
3 The price was high
4 The questing hound
5 Sixteen bells

HACKFORTH-JONES, G.
JOE GARTON
1 Danger below 1962
2 I am the captain 1963

HACKFORTH-JONES, G.
PAUL DEXTER
1 Chinese poison 1968
2 All stations Malta 1970
3 An explosive situation 1973
4 Shadow of the Rock 1973
5 Second-in-Command 1974
6 The redoubtable Dexter 1975
7 Dexter at war 1976

HACKNEY, A.
1 I'm all right, Jack 1960
2 Whatever turns you on, Jack 1972

HACKNEY, A.
NATIONAL SERVICE
1 Private's progress 1955
2 Private life 1957

HADDAD, C. A.
BECKY BELSKI
1 Caught in the shadows 1993
2 Root canal 1994

HAEDRICH, M.
BELLE
1 Belle de Paris 1970

2 Belle in diamonds 1971

HAGAN, P.
COLTRANE FAMILY
1 Love and war 1990
2 Raging hearts 1990

HAGGARD, W.
COL.CHARLES RUSSELL
1 The high wire 1963
2 The antagonists 1964
3 The powder barrel 1965
4 The hard sell 1965
5 The power house 1966
6 The conspirators 1967
7 A cool day for killing 1968
8 The hardliners 1970
9 The bitter harvest 1971
10 The old masters 1973
11 The poison people 1977
12 Scorpion's tail 1976
13 The median line 1978
14 The money men 1981
15 Visa to limbo 1978
16 The mischief maker 1982
17 The heirloom 1983
18 The need to know 1984
19 The meritocrats 1985
20 The doubtful disciples 1969
21 Slow burner 1958
22 Venetian blind 1959
23 The arena 1961
24 The unquiet sleep 1962
25 The vendettists 1990

HAGGARD, W.
PAUL MARTINY
1 The protectors 1972
2 The kinsmen 1974

HAIG, A.
ALEC HAIG
1 Sign on for Tokyo 1971
2 Flight from Montego Bay 1972
3 Peruvian printout 1973

HALDEMAN, C.
1 The sun's attendant 1963
2 The snowman 1965

HALDEMAN, J.
WORLDS TRILOGY
1 Worlds
2 Worlds apart
3 Worlds enough and time 1992
Science fiction

HALEY, A.
1 Roots 1977

2 Queen 1993
1 was published as non-fiction. 2 is fiction.

HALL, A. [E. TREVOR]
QUILLER
1 The Berlin memorandum 1965
2 The striker portfolio 1969
3 The Warsaw document 1971
4 The Tango briefing 1973
5 The Mandarin cipher 1975
6 The Kobra manifesto 1976
7 The Sinkiang executive 1978
8 The scorpion signal 1980
9 The Pekin target 1981
10 Northlight 1985
11 Quiller's run 1988
12 The ninth directive 1966
13 Quiller KGB 1989
14 Quiller Baracuda 1991
15 Quiller bamboo 1992
16 Quiller solitaire 1992
17 Quiller meridian 1993
18 Quiller Salamander 1994
Paperback science fiction

HALL, P.
1 The India man 1968
2 Sun and grey shadow 1974

HALL, PATRICIA
INSPECTOR THACKERAY
1 The coldness of killers 1992
2 Death by election 1993
3 Dying fall 1994

HALLIDAY, B.
MICHAEL SHAYNE
1 Divided on death
2 The private practice of Michael Shayne
3 The uncomplaining corpse
4 Tickets for death
5 Michael Shayne investigates
6 Michael Shayne takes a hand
7 Michael Shayne's long chance
8 Murder is my business
9 Murder and the married virgin
10 Marked for murder
11 Blood on Biscayne Bay
12 Counterfeit wife
13 Murder is a habit
14 Call for Michael Shayne
15 A taste for violence
16 This is it, Michael Shayne
17 Framed in blood
18 When Dorinda dances
19 What really happened
20 Lady came by night

21 She woke to darkness 1955
22 Death has three lives 1955
23 Stranger in town 1956
24 The blonde cried murder 1956
25 Weep for a blonde 1956
26 Shot the works 1957
27 Murder of the wanton bride 1957
28 Death of a stranger 1957
29 Missing from home 1958
30 Fit to kill 1959
31 Date with a dead man 1960
32 Target:Mike Shayne 1960
33 Die like a dog 1961

HALLIDAY, D.
JOHNSON AND 'DOLLY'
1 'Dolly' and the singing bird 1968
2 'Dolly' and the cookie bird 1970
3 'Dolly' and the doctor bird 1971
4 'Dolly' and the starry bird 1973
5 'Dolly' and the nanny bird 1977
6 'Dolly' and the bird of paradise 1983
For new editions and change of title, see under DUNNETT, D.

HAMBLE, B.
DARWATH TRILOGY
1 The time of the dark
2 The walls of air
3 The armies of daylight
Paperback fantasy

HAMBLY, B.
1 The rainbow abyss 1991
2 Time like infinity 1991
3 Magicians of the night 1992

HAMBLY, B.
SUN WOLF
1 The ladies of Mandrigyu 1984
2 The witches of Wenshar 1987
3 Dark hand of magic 1990

HAMER, M.
CHRIS LUDLOW
1 Sudden death 1991
2 A deadly lie 1992
3 Death trap 1993
4 Shadows on the green 1994
Thrillers about golf.

HAMILTON, A.
NEFERTITI
1 The beautiful one 1978
2 Lady of grace 1979
3 The devious being 1980

HAMILTON, D.
MATT HELM
1 The removers
2 Murderer's row
3 The ambushers
4 The shadowers
5 The ravagers
6 The devastators
7 The silencers
8 Wrecking crew
9 Death of a citizen
10 The betrayers 1968
11 The menacers 1969
1-9 published in paperback

HAMILTON, E.
1 The river full of stars 1954
2 An Irish childhood 1963
N.F. Autobiography

HAMILTON, H.
JOHN & SALLY HELDAR
1 The two hundred ghost 1956
2 Death at one blow 1957
3 At night to die 1958
4 Answer in the negative 1959

HAMILTON, I.
PETE HEYSEN
1 The persecutor 1965
2 The man with the brown paper face 1967
3 The thrill machine 1968

HAMILTON, J.
THE HABSBURGS
1 Changeling Queen 1977
2 The Emperor's daughter 1977
3 Pearl of the Habsburgs 1978
4 The Snow Queen 1979
5 The Habsburg inheritance 1980

HAMILTON, M.
MONTY
1 Monty:the making of a general,1887-1942 1981
2 Monty:master of the battlefield,1942-44 1983
3 Monty the Field Marshal,1944-46 1986
N.F. Biography of Field-Marshal Montgomery of Alamein.

HAMMOND, G.
BEAU PEPYS
1 Fred in situ 1965
2 The loose screw 1966
3 Mud in his eye 1967

HAMMOND, G.
JOHN CUNNINGHAM
1 Dog in the dark 1989
2 Doghouse 1989
3 Whose dog are you? 1990
4 Give a dog a bad name 1992
5 The curse of the cockers 1993
6 Sting in the tale 1994
Thrillers about a gundog trainer

HAMMOND, G.
KEITH CALDER
1 Dead game 1979
2 The reward game 1980
3 The revenge game 1981
4 Fair game 1982
5 The game 1982
6 Sauce for the pigeon 1984
7 Cousin once removed 1984
8 Pursuit of arms 1985
9 Silver city scandal 1986
10 The executor 1986
11 The worried widow 1987
12 Adverse report 1987
13 Stray shot 1988
14 A brace of skeet 1989
15 Let us prey 1990
16 Home to roost 1990
17 Snatch crop 1991
18 Thin air 1993
19 Hook or crook 1994
Thrillers set in the Scottish Borders, whose hero is a gunsmith. From 14, Deborah, Keith Calder's daughter, plays a leading role. In 19, the main character is Wallace James, Calder's brother-in-law.

HAMNER, E.
THE WALTONS
1 Spencer's mountain 1966
2 The homecoming 1970

HAN SUYIN
1 The crippled tree 1964
2 A mortal flower 1966
3 Birdless summer 1968
4 My house has two doors 1975

HANCOCK, N.
CIRCLE OF LIGHT
1 Greyfax Grimwald
2 Faragon Fairingay
3 Calix stay
4 Squaring the circle
Paperback fantasies

HANCOCK, N.
THE WILDERNESS OF FOUR
1 Across the far mountain
2 The plains of sea
3 On the boundaries of darkness
4 The road to the Middle Islands
Paperback fantasies

HAND, E.
1 Winterlong
2 Aestival tide
Paperback fantasy

HANDKE, P.
1 The long way round 1979
2 The lesson of Monte-Sainte-
Victoire 1980
3 A child's story 1981
*Published in one vol. 'Slow home
coming' 1986*

HANDL, I.
1 The Sioux 1970
2 The gold tipped Pfitzer 1973

HANFF, H.

1 84 Charing Cross Road 1973
2 The Duchess of Bloomsbury Street
1974
3 Q's legacy 1985
N.F. Autobiography

HANLEY, J.
THE FURIES CHRONICLE
1 The furies 1935
2 The secret journey 1936
3 Our time is gone 1938
4 Winter song 1939
5 An end and a beginning 1958

HANRAHAN, B.
1 The scent of eucalyptus 1973
2 Kewpie doll 1984

HANSEN, J.
DAVE BRANDSTETTER
1 Fadeout 1972
2 Death claims 1973
3 The troublemaker 1975
4 The man everybody was afraid of
1978
5 Skinflick 1980
6 Gravedigger 1982
7 A smile in a lifetime 1983
8 Nightwork 1984

HANSON, V. J.
AMOS
1 Amos lives! 1990
2 Shroud for Amos 1990
3 Legend of Amos 1991
Westerns

HARDING, I.
ASSAULT TROOP
1 Blood beach 1983
2 Death in the forest 1983
3 Clash on the Rhine 1984
4 End run 1984

HARDING, P.
BROTHER ATHELSTAN
1 The nightingale gallery 1991
2 The house of the red slayer 1992
3 Murder most holy 1992
4 The anger of God 1993
5 By murder's bright light 1994
*Mystery stories set in a medieval
nonastery.*

HARDWICK, MICHAEL
RACKSTRAW
1 Regency rake 1979
2 Regency revenge 1980
3 Regency revels 1982

HARDWICK, MICHAEL
THE CEDAR TREE
1 The cedar tree 1976
2 Autumn of an age 1977
3 The bough breaks 1978

HARDWICK, MOLLIE
ATKINSON FAMILY
1 The Atkinson inheritance 1978
2 Sisters in love 1979
3 The Atkinson century 1980

HARDWICK, MOLLIE
DORAN FAIRWEATHER CHELMARSH
1 Malice domestic 1986
2 Parson's pleasure 1987
3 Uneaseful death 1988
4 The bandersnatch 1989
5 Perish in July 1989
6 The dreaming Damozel 1990

HARDWICK, MOLLIE
JULIET BRAVO
1 New arrivals 1981
2 Calling Juliet Bravo 1981

HARDWICK, MOLLIE
THE DUCHESS OF DUKE STREET
1 The way up 1976

2 The golden years 1976
3 The world keeps turning 1977

HARDY, A.
GEORGE ABERCROMBIE FOX
1 The Press Gang 1973
2 Prize money 1973
3 Siege 1974
4 Treasure 1974

HARDY, ADAM
STRIKE FORCE FALKLANDS
1 Operation Exocet 1983
2 Raiders dawn 1984
3 Red alert
4 Recce patrol
5 Covert op
6 Ware mines!
4-6 are only in paperback

HARE, C.
SUPT.MALLETT & MR.PETTIGREW
1 Tenant for death 1937
2 Death is no sportsman 1938
3 Tragedy at law 1942
4 With a bare bodkin 1946
5 When the wind blows 1949
6 The yew tree's shade 1954
7 He should have died hereafter
1958

HARKNETT, T.
STEPHEN WAYNE
1 The benevolent blackmailer 1962
2 Scratch on the surface 1962
3 Invitation to a funeral 1962
4 Dead little rich girl 1963
5 Evil money 1964
6 The man who did not die 1964
7 Death of an aunt 1966
8 Two way frame 1967
9 The soft cover kill 1971

HARPERS
1 The parched sea, by T.Denning
2 Elfshadow, by E.Cunningham
3 Red magic, by J.Rabe
4 The night parade,by S.Ciencin
5 The ring of winter,by J.Lowder
6 Crypt of the shadowking, by
M.Anthony
7 Crown of fire, by E.Greenwood
*Paperback fantasy, linked by the series
title.*

HARRELL, A.
SAM SHANK
1 The twin bridges murder 1982
2 Trailersnatch 1983

3 Rivermist 1983
4 Kickback 1984
5 A touch of jade 1985

HARRER, H.
1 Seven years in Tibet
2 Tibet is my country 1960
3 Return to Tibet 1984

HARRINGTON, J.
FRANK X KERRIGAN
1 Last known address 1966
2 Blind spot 1967
3 Last doorbell 1968

HARRIS, D. T.
THE MAGES OF GARILLON
1 The burning stone
2 The gauntlet of malice
Paperback fantasy

HARRIS, E.
LARGE LEE
1 Largely luck 1984
2 Largely trouble 1986

HARRIS, J.
IRA PENALUNA
1 The mustering of the hawks 1971
2 The mercenaries 1968
3 The Courtney entry 1970

HARRIS, MARION
1 Soldiers' wives 1987
2 Officers' ladies 1987

HARRIS, MARION
HEART OF THE DRAGON
1 Nesta 1988
2 Amelda 1990

HARRIS, MOLLIE
1 A kind of magic 1969
2 Another kind of magic 1972
N.F. Country life

HARRIS, R. E.
PURCELL SISTERS
1 The silent shore 1986
2 The beckoning hills 1987
3

HARRIS, W.
1 Carnival 1985
2 Infinite rehearsal
3 Four banks of the river of space
1990

HARRIS, W.
GUIANA QUARTET
1 The palace of the peacock 1960
2 The far journey of Oudin 1961
3 The whole armour 1962
4 The secret ladder 1962

HARRISON, C.
1 Arctic rose 1985
2 Wild flower 1986

HARRISON, CAREY
TO LISKEARD
1 Richard's feet 1990
2 Cley 1991
3 Egon 1993

HARRISON, H.
BILL THE GALACTIC HERO
1 Bill.....on the planet of robot slaves 1989
2 Bill.....on the planet of bottled brains 1990
3 Bill.....on the planet of tasteless pleasure 1991
4 Bill.....on the planet of zombie vampires 1992
5 Bill....on the planet of hippies from hell 1992
6 Bill.....the final incoherent adventure! 1993
Galactic Dreams, 1994, has short stories linked to Bill.

HARRISON, H.
STAINLESS STEEL RAT
1 The stainless steel rat is born 1985
2 The stainless steel rat 1961
3 The stainless steel rat's revenge 1971
4 The stainless steel rat saves the world 1973
5 The stainless steel rat wants you 1975
6 The stainless steel rat for President 1983
7 The stainless steel rat gets drafted 1987
8 Stainless steel visions 1993
9 The stainless steel rat sings the blues 1994
Science fiction detective stories

HARRISON, H.
TO THE STARS
1 Wheelworld
2 Epic to the stars
3 Starworld 1988

4 Homeworld
Paperback science fiction

HARRISON, H.
WEST OF EDEN
1 West of Eden 1986
2 Winter in Eden 1987
3 Return to Eden 1988

HARRISON, M. J.
1 In Viriconium 1981
2 Viriconium nights 1985
Science fiction

HARRISON, RAY.
SGT. BRAGG & P.C. MORTON
1 French ordinary murder 1983
2 Death of an Honourable member 1984
3 Death watch 1985
4 Death of a dancing lady 1985
5 Counterfeit of murder 1987
6 A season for death 1987
7 Tincture of death 1989
8 Sphere of death 1990
9 Patently murder 1991
10 Akin to murder 1992
11 Murder in Petticoat Square 1993
Detective stories set in Victorian London

HARRISON, ROSINA
1 Rose:my life in service 1975
2 Gentlemen's gentlemen:my friends in service 1976
N.F. Reminiscences of life in domestic service

HARRISON, S.
1 Hot breath 1988
2 Cold feet 1989
3 Foreign parts 1992

HARRISON, SUE
1 Mother Earth, Father Sky 1991
2 My sister the moon 1992
Set in the Aleutian Islands in pre-historic times.

HARROD-EAGLES, C.
DET.INSPECTOR BILL SLIDER
1 Orchestrated death 1991
2 Death watch 1992
3 Necrochip 1993
4 Dead end 1994

HARROD-EAGLES, C.
KIROV SAGA
1 Anna 1990

2 Fleur 1991
3 Emily 1992

HARROD-EAGLES, C.
MORLAND DYNASTY
1 The foundling 1980
2 Dark rose 1981
3 The princeling 1981
4 The oak apple 1982
5 The black pearl 1982
6 The long shadow 1983
7 The Chevalier 1984
8 The maiden 1985
9 The flood-tide 1986
10 The tangled thread 1987
11 The Emperor 1988
12 The victory 1989
13 The Regency 1990
14 Campaigners 1991
15 The reckoning 1992
16 The devil's horse 1993
17 The poison tree 1994
A family saga set in Yorkshire from the 15thC to WW2.

HART, J.
CARL PEDERSON
1 Some die young 1990
2 A decent killer 1991

HART, R.
DET. SUPT. ROPER
1 Seascape with dead figures 1987
2 A pretty place for a murder 1987
3 A fox in the night 1988
4 Remains to be seen 1989
5 Robbed blind 1990
6 Breach of promise 1990
7 Blood kin 1991
8 Final appointment 1993
9 A deadly schedule 1993

HART, SUSANNE
1 Too short a day 1967
2 Life with Daktari 1969
3 Listen to the wild 1972
N.F. Work with animals in Africa

HARTLAND, M.
DAVID NAIRN
1 Down among the dead men 1983
2 The third betrayal 1986

HARTMAN, D.
DIRTY HARRY
1 Duel for cannons
2 Death on the docks
3 The long death

126

4 The Mexico kill
Paperback thrillers

HARTON, R.
1 Under the hammer 1992
2 An auctioneer's lot 1992
N.F. Autobiography of an auctioneer

HARVESTER, S.
BLUNDEN
1 A breastplate for Aaron
2 Sheep may safely graze
3 Obols for Charon

HARVESTER, S.
DORIAN SILK
1 Unsung road 1960
2 Silk road 1962
3 Red road 1963
4 Assassin's road 1965
5 Treacherous road 1966
6 Battle road 1967
7 Zion road 1968
8 Nameless road 1969
9 Moscow road 1970
10 Sahara road 1972
11 Forgotten road 1974
12 Siberian road 1975

HARVESTER, S.
HERON MARMORIN
1 The Chinese hammer 1959
2 Troika 1962

HARVESTER, S.
MALCOLM KENTON
1 The bamboo screen 1955
2 Dragon road 1955

HARVEY, A.
1 Burning houses
2 The web 1987

HARVEY, J. B.
HART THE REGULATOR
1 Cherokee outlet
2 Blood trail
3 Tago
4 The silver lie
5 Blood on the border
6 Ride the wide country
7 Arkansas breakout
8 John Wesley Hardin
9 California bloodlines
10 The skinning place
Paperback Westerns. 6 also in hardback

HARVEY, JOHN
DET.INSPECTOR CHARLIE RESNICK
1 Lonely hearts 1989
2 Rough treatment 1990
3 Cutting edge 1991
4 Off minor 1992
5 Wasted years 1993
6 Cold light 1994

HARVEY, M.
1 The dark horseman 1978
2 The proud hunter 1980
3 Foxgate 1982

HASEK, J.
1 The good soldier Schweik
2 Adventures of good comrade
  Schweik,byH.Putz 1969
3 The red commissar 1981

HASTINGS, M.
MONTAGUE CORK
1 Cork on the water 1953
2 Cork in bottle 1954
3 Cork and the serpent 1955
4 Cork in the doghouse 1957
5 Cork on the telly 1966

HASTINGS, P.
LONDON QUARTET
1 The candles of night 1977
2 The feast of the peacock 1978
3 Running Thursday 1980
4 Blackberry summer 1984

HATTERSLEY, R.
1 The maker's mark 1990
2 In that quiet earth 1991
3 Skylark's song 1993
  *Novels based on the author's family
  history.*

HAWKE, S.
TIME WARS
1 The Ivanhoe gambit
2 The time-keeper conspiracy
3 The Pimpernel plot
4 The Zenda vendetta
5 The Nautilus sanction
6 The Khyber connection
7 The argonaut affair
8 The dracula caper
  (*Paperback fantasy*)

HAWKE, S.
TRIBE OF ONE
1 The outcast
2 The seeker
3 The nomad

HAWKE, S.
WIZARD SERIES
1 Wizard of 4th Street
2 Wizard of Whitechapel
3 Wizard of Sunset Strip
4 Wizard of the Rue Morgue
5 Reluctant sorcerer
6 Wizard of Camelot
  Paperback fantasy

HAWKES, J.
1 The blood oranges 1971
2 Death,sleep and the traveller 1975
3 Travesty 1976

HAWKEY, R.
PRESIDENTIAL TRILOGY
1 Wild card 1974
2 Side effect 1979
3 End stage 1983

HAWKINS, J.
CHOPPER
1 Blood trails
2 Tunnel warriors
3 Jungle sweep
4
5 Renegade MIAs
  Paperback war stories

HAWORTH, E.
HOWTON
1 Mistress of Howton 1978
2 The Farrers of Howton 1979
3 The Howton inheritance 1980

HAY, HEATHER
THE MONTFORD SAGA
1 Heritage 1990
2 Honour 1990
3 Heroes 1991

HAYMON, S. T.
1 Opposite the Cross Keys 1989
2 The quivering tree 1990
  N.F. Autobiography

HAYMON, S. T.
DET.INSPECTOR BEN JURNET
1 Death of a pregnant virgin 1980
2 Ritual murder 1982
3 Stately homicide 1985
4 Death of a god 1987
5 A very particular murder 1989
6 Death of a warrior queen 1991
7 Beautiful death 1993

HAYNES, C.
PROFESSOR HARRY BISHOP
1 Bishop's gambit,declined 1990
2 Perpetual check
3 Sacrifice play 1990

HAYTHORNE, J.
OLIVER MANDRAKE
1 The Streslan dimension 1981
2 Mandrake in Granada 1984
3 Mandrake in the monastery 1985

HAYTON, S.
DARK AGE TRILOGY
1 Hidden daughters 1992
2 The governors 1992
3 The last flight 1993

HAYWOOD, G. A.
AARON GUNNER
1 Fear of the dark 1988
2 Not long for this world 1991

HAZEL, P.
FINNBRANCH SAGA
1 Yearwood
2 Undersea
3 Winterking
Paperback fantasy. Also published in one vol.

HEADLEY, V.
1 Yardie 1992
2 Excess 1993
3 Yush! 1994
Novels about crack dealing

HEALD, T.
SIMON BOGNOR
1 Unbecoming habits 1973
2 Blue blood will out 1974
3 Deadline 1975
4 Let sleeping dogs lie 1976
5 Just desserts 1977
6 Murder at Moose Jaw 1981
7 Masterstroke 1982
8 Red herrings 1985
9 Brought to book 1988
10 Business unusual 1989

HEALEY, B.
HAVOC
1 Havoc 1978
2 Havoc in the Indies 1979

HEALEY, B.
PAUL HEDLEY
1 Waiting for a tiger 1966
2 Millstone men 1967

3 Death in three masks 1967
4 Murder without crime 1968
5 The trouble with Penelope 1972
6 Last ferry from the Lido 1980

HEALY, J.
J.F.CUDDY
1 Blunt darts 1986
2 The tethered goat 1986
3 So like sleep 1987
4 Swan dive 1988
5 Yesterday's news 1989
6 Right to die 1991

HEATH, R.
1 From the heat of the day 1978
2 One generation 1980
3 Genetha 1981
Family life in Georgetown, Guyana

HEATH-MILLER, M.
HARDWICK FAMILY
1 The wrong side of the park 1975
2 Storm above the Park 1976
3 A time for silence 1977
4 The day before yesterday 1978

HEATH-MILLER, M.
THE RAYNES OF RAYLEIGH
1 Never go back 1968
2 No exit 1969
3 Give me tomorrow 1970
4 The bitter herb 1973
5 The narrow stair 1974

HEAVEN, C.
1 House of Kuragin 1972
2 The Astrov inheritance 1973
3 Heir to Kuragin 1978

HEAVEN, C.
AYLSHAM FAMILY
1 Lord of Ravensley 1980
2 The Ravensley touch 1982
3 The raging fire 1987
4 The fire still burns 1989

HEBDEN, M.
COLONEL MOSTYN
1 Mask of violence 1971
2 A pride of dolphins 1974

HEBDEN, M.
INSPECTOR PEL
1 Death set to music 1978
2 Pel and the faceless corpse 1979
3 Pel under pressure 1980
4 Pel is puzzled 1981
5 Pel and the staghound 1982

6 Pel and the bombers 1983
7 Pel and the predators 1984
8 Pel and the pirates 1984
9 Pel and the prowler 1985
10 Pel and the Paris mob 1986
11 Pel among the pueblos 1987
12 Pel and the touch of pitch 1987
13 Pel and the picture of innocence 1988
14 Pel and the party spirit 1989
15 Pel and the missing persons 1990
16 Pel and the promised land 1991
17 Pel and the sepulchre job 1992
18 Pel picks up the pieces 1993
19 Pel and the perfect partner 1994
Mark Hebden (i. e. John Harris) died in 1992. The series has been continued by his daughter, Juliet.

HEENAN, J. C., CARDINAL
1 Not the whole truth 1971
2 A crown of thorns 1974
N.F. Autobiography

HEIMLER, E.
1 Night of the mist 1959
2 A link in the chain 1962
N.F. Autobiography

HEINLEIN, R.
FUTURE HISTORY
1 Universe
2 Common sense
3 Methusaleh's children 1941
4 The man who sold the moon 1950
5 The green hills of Earth 1951
6 Revolt in 2100 1953
7 Time enough for love 1973
8 Number of the beast 1979
9 The cat who walks through walls 1985
10 To sail beyond the sunset
A loosely linked series, much of which is in the form of short stories. 1 & 2 were published together as 'Orphans of the Sky' in 1963. Many of the stories were collected together in 'The Past Through Tomorrow' 1967

HEINRICH, D. J.
PENHALIGON TRILOGY
1 The tainted sword
2 The dragon's tomb
3 The fall of magic
Paperback fantasy based on 'Dungeons and Dragons'

HELLER, J.
1 Catch 22 1961

2 Closing time 1994

HELLER, K.
GEORGE MAN
1 Man's illegal life 1984
2 Man's storm 1985
3 Man's loving family 1986
Detective stories about the 18thC Parish Watch

HELLMAN, L.
1 An unfinished life 1969
2 Pentimento 1974
3 Scoundrel time 1978
N.F. Autobiography

HELM, E.
VIETNAM GROUND ZERO
1 Strike
2 The raid
3 Incident at Plei Soi
4 Tet
5 Red dust
Paperback war stories

HENDERSON, C.
LONE RIDER
1 Lone rider
2 Lone rider's guns
3 Lone rider's justice 1955
4 Lone rider's trail 1955
5 Lone rider's range 1957
6 Lone rider's quest 1957
7 Lone rider's war 1958

HENDERSON, Z.
1 Pilgrimage 1965
2 The people: no different flesh 1966
Science fiction

HENNEKER, P.
SUSAN CAMPBELL & PAUL ROSS
1 And one must die 1965
2 Don't be afraid of the dark 1967
3 Too late for tears 1969

HENNESSEY, M.
1 The bright blue sky 1982
2 The challenging heights 1983
3 Once more the hawks 1984
A trilogy about the RFC in WW1

HENNESSEY, M.
CAVALRY TRILOGY
1 Soldier of the Queen 1980
2 Regimental lance 1981
3 The iron stallions 1982

HENNESSEY, M.
KELLY MAGUIRE
1 The lion at sea 1977
2 Thedangerous years 1978
3 Back to battle 1979

HENREY, MRS. R.
1 Paloma 1951
2 Madeleine's journal 1953
3 A month in Paris 1954
4 Mistress of myself 1959
5 Bloomsbury Fair
6 Milou's daughter 1955
7 London 1949
8 The virgin of Aldermanbury 1958
9 Spring in a Soho street 1962
10 Winter wild 1966
N.F. Fringe books to the main sequence of auto- biography, listed below. The author's own order of reading.

HENREY, MRS. R.
MADELEINE
1 The little Madeleine 1951
2 An exile in Soho 1952
3 Julia 1971
4 A girl at twenty 1974
5 Madeleine grown up 1952
6 Madeleine young wife 1960
7 London under fire, 1940-45 1960
8 Her April days 1963
9 Wednesday at four 1964
10 Green leaves 1976
11 She who pays 1969
N.F. Autobiography. Listed in chronological order

HENRY, M.
BOB & HILARY DEAN
1 Unlucky dip 1963
2 The householders 1964

HEPPENSTALL, R.
1 The connecting door 1962
2 The woodshed 1962

HERBERT, F.
DUNE
1 Dune 1967
2 Dune Messiah 1971
3 Children of Dune 1976
4 God Emperor of Dune 1981
5 Heretics of Dune 1984
6 Chapterhouse Dune 1985
'The road to Dune', a short story is in 'Eye' 1986

HERBERT, F.
JORJ AND MCKIE
1 Whipping star 1979
2 The Dosadi experiment 1978
The characters also appear in 'Eye' 1986.

HERBERT, F. & RANSON, B.
1 The Jesus incident 1982
2 The Lazarus effect 1983

HERBERT, J.
1 The rats 1977
2 Lair 1979
3 Domain 1984
Horror stories

HERBERT, K.
1 Queen of the lightning 1984
2 Ghost in the sunlight 1986
3 Bride of the spear 1988
Historical novels set in England in the Dark Ages

HERBERT, M. H.
DARK HORSE
1 Valorian
2 Dark horse
3 Lightning's daughter
4 City of the sorcerers
Paperback fantasy

HERLEY, R.
THE PAGANS
1 The flint lord 1981
2 The stone arrow 1979
3 The earth goddess 1984

HERMAN, R.
MATT PONTOWSKI
1 Warbirds 1989
2 Force of eagles 1990
3 Dark wing 1994

HERON, J.
JASON TRASK
1 Trask the avenger 1982
2 Trask and the fighting Irishman 1983

HERRING, C.
1 The Waterloo legacy 1979
2 Waterloo's ward 1980

HERRIOT, J.
1 If only they could talk 1964
2 It shouldn't happen to a vet 1971
3 Let sleeping vets lie 1973
4 Vet in harness 1974

5 Vets might fly 1976
6 Vet in a spin 1977
7 The Lord God made them all 1981
8 Every living thing 1992
   N.F. Autobiography

HERRON, S.
1 Miro 1970
2 The Miro papers 1972
3 Through the dark and hairy wood 1973

HERVEY, E.
MISS UNWIN
1 The governess 1984
2 The man of gold 1985
3 Into the valley of death 1986
   Detective stories set in Victorian
   London A pseudonym of
   H. R. F. Keating.

HESKY, O.
SHIMONI & BARZILAI
1 The serpent's smile 1966
2 Time for treason 1967
3 The sequin syndicate 1968
4 The different night 1970

HEWITT, A.
1 Piccolo 1961
2 Piccolo and Maria 1962

HIGGINS, G. V.
JERRY KENNEDY
1 Kennedy for the defense 1980
2 Penance for Jerry Kennedy 1985
3 Defending Billy Ryan 1993

HIGGINS, J.
LIAM DEVLIN
1 The eagle has landed 1975
2 Touch the devil 1983
3 Confessional 1985
4 The eagle has flown 1991

HIGHSMITH, D.
1 Leonora 1992
2 Lukan 1993

HIGHSMITH, DOMINI
1 Frankie 1990
2 Mammy's boy 1991

HILL, D.
APOTHEOSIS TRILOGY
1 The lightless dome 1993
2 The leafless forest 1994

HILL, PAMELA
1 Fenfallow 1987
2 The Sutburys 1988

HILL, PORTER
CAPT.ADAM HORNE
1 The Bombay Marines 1985
2 The war chest 1986
3 China flyer 1987
   Naval adventure in the 19th century

HILL, R.
DALZIEL AND PASCOE
1 A clubbable woman 1971
2 Fell of dark 1971
3 An advancement of learning 1971
4 A fairly dangerous thing 1972
5 Ruling passion 1974
6 An April shroud 1976
7 A pinch of snuff 1978
8 Pascoe's ghost and other stories 1979
9 A killing kindness 1980
10 Deadheads 1983
11 Exit lines 1984
12 Child's play 1986
13 Under world 1988
14 Bones and silence 1990
15 One small step 1990
16 Recalled to life 1992
17 Pictures of perfection 1994
   15 is a novella, in which Dalziel
   solves a murder committed in space.

HILL, R.
JOE SIXSMITH
1 Blood sympathy 1993
2 Born guilty 1994
   Private eye stories set in Luton

HILLERMAN, T.
JIM CHEE
1 People of darkness 1982
2 The dark wind 1983
3 The ghostway 1985
4 Skinwalkers 1988
   Detective stories set among American
   Indians. Sgt. Chee is a Navajo.

HILLERMAN, T.
LEAPHORN AND CHEE
1 A thief of time 1989
2 Talking God 1990
3 Coyote waits 1991
4 Sacred clowns 1994

HILLERMAN, T.
LIEUT.JOE LEAPHORN
1 The blessing way 1970

2 The fly on the wall 1971
3 Dance hall of the dead 1973
4 Listening women 1979
5 Skinwalkers 1988
Jim Chee also appears in 5 1 and 3
published in 1 vol as 'The Lephorn
Mysteries' 1991

HILLIARD, N.
1 Maori girl 1960
2 Power of joy 1965
3 Maori woman 1974
4 Glory and the dream 1975

HILTON, J. B.
SGT. BRUNT
1 The quiet stranger 1985
2 Gamekeeper's gallows 1973
3 Rescue from the Rose 1975
4 Dead nettle 1977
5 Mr.Fred 1983
6 Slickensides 1987

HILTON, J. B.
SUPT.SIMON KENWORTHY
1 Death of an Alderman 1968
2 Death in midwinter 1969
3 Hangman's tide 1972
4 No birds sang 1975
5 Some run crooked 1977
6 The anathema stone 1979
7 Playground of death 1980
8 Surrender value 1981
9 The green frontier 1982
10 The sunset law 1982
11 The asking price 1983
12 Corridors of guilt 1984
13 The Hobbema prospect 1984
14 Passion in the Peak 1985
15 Moondrop to murder 1986
16 The innocents at home 1986
17 Displaced person 1987

HIMES, C.
GRAVE DIGGER JONES & COFFIN ED
JOHNSON
1 Cotton comes to Harlem 1965
2 The heat's on 1966
3 Run man run 1967
4 Blind man with a pistol 1968
5 All shot up 1969
6 The real cool killers 1970

HIMMEL, R.
JOHNNY MAGUIRE
1 The Chinese keyhole
2 I have Gloria Kirby
3 The cry of the flesh 1958
4 The rich and the damned 1958

5 The name's Maguire 1963
6 It's murder Maguire 1963
7 Two deaths must die 1964

HINXMAN, M.
DET.INSPECTOR RALPH BRAND
1 One way cemetery 1977
2 Death of a good woman 1981
3 The telephone never tells 1983
4 The sound of murder 1986

HIRSCHFIELD, B.
DALLAS
1 The Ewings of Dallas 1980
2 The women of Dallas 1981
3 The men of Dallas 1982

HIRSCHFIELD, B.
FIRE ISLAND
1 Fire Island
2 Fire in the embers
3 Cindy on Fire
4 Return to Fire Island
Paperbacks

HISLOP, J.
1 Far from a gentleman 1963
2 Anything but a soldier 1965

HOBSON, H.
BRAD FORD
1 The gallant affair 1957
2 Death makes a claim 1958
3 The big twist 1959
4 Mission House murder 1959
5 Beyond tolerance 1960

HOBSON, R. B.
1 Grass beyond the mountains
2 Nothing too good for a cowboy
3 The rancher takes a wife
N.F. Autobiography

HOCKE, M.
1 The ancient solitary reign 1989
2 The lost domain 1993

HOCKEN, E.
1 Emma and I 1977
2 Emma VIP 1980
3 Emma and Co. 1983
4 After Emma 1988
N.F. About the author's guide dog

HOCKING, A.
DET.CHIEF SUPT.WILLIAM AUSTEN
1 Poison in Paradise 1955
2 Murder at midday 1956
3 Relative murder 1957

4 Epitaph for a nurse 1958
5 To cease upon the midnight 1959
6 Poisoned chalice 1959
7 The thin-spun life 1960
8 Candidate for murder 1961
9 He had to die 1962
10 Spies have no friends 1962
11 Murder cries out 1963

HOCKING, M.
1 A time of war 1968
2 The hopeful travellers 1970

HOCKING, M.
FAIRLEYS
1 Good daughters 1984
2 Indifferent heroes 1985
3 Welcome strangers 1986

HODGE, J. A.
LISTENBURG
1 Last act 1979
2 First night 1989
3 Leading lady 1990

HODGE, J. A.
PURCHIS FAMILY
1 Judas flowering 1979
2 Wide is the water 1981
3 Savannah Purchase 1971
4 Runaway bride 1977

HOFF, B. J.
EMERALD BALLAD
1 Song of the silent harp 1991
2 Heart of the lonely exile 1992
3 Land of a thousand dreams 1993
4 Sons of an ancient glory 1993
A sequence about Irish immigrants in America.

HOGAN, J. P.
GIANTS
1 Inherit the stars
2 The gentle giants of Ganymede
3 Giants' star

HOGGART, R.
1 A local habitation (1918-40) 1988
2 A sort of clowning (1940-59) 1990
3 An imagined life 1992
N.F. Autobiography N.F. Autobiography

HOLBROOK, D.
PAUL GRIMMER
1 Flesh wounds 1966
2 A play of passion 1978
3 Nothing larger than life 1987

4 A little Athens 1990
5 The gold in father's heart 1992

HOLDEN, M.
SQUADRON
1 Sons of the morning 1978
2 The sun climbs slowly 1978
3 Scramble Dieppe 1979
4 Desert Spitfire 1980
5 Whirlwind at Arromanches 1981
6 Massacre at Falaise 1981

HOLDEN, U.
1 Tin toys 1986
2 The unicorn sisters 1988

HOLDSTOCK, R.
MYTHAGO
1 Mythago Wood 1985
2 Lavondyss 1988
3 The bore forest (novella) 1991
4 The hollowing 1993
5 Merlin's Wood 1994
Fantasy

HOLGATE, J.
1 Make a cow laugh
2 On a pig's back
3 A sheep's eye view
N.F. Autobiography of a farmer

HOLLAND, I.
ST.ANSELM'S
1 Death at St.Anselm's 1985
2 Bump in the night 1989
3 Thief 1989
4 A fatal Advent 1991
5 The long search 1991
Detective stories set in an urban parish.

HOLLAND, V.
1 Son of Oscar Wilde 1954
2 Time remembered after Pere Lachaise 1966
N.F. Autobiography

HOLME, T.
INSPECTOR ACHILLE PERONI
1 The Neapolitan streak 1980
2 A funeral of gondolas 1981
3 The devil and the dolce vita 1982
4 The Assisi murders 1985
5 At the lake of sudden death 1987

HOLROYD, M.
GEORGE BERNARD SHAW
1 The search for love 1988
2 The pusuit of power 1988

3 The lure of fantasy 1991
4 The last laugh 1992
N.F. Biography.

HOLT, H.
SHEILA MALLORY
1 Gone away 1990
2 The cruellest month 1991
3 The shortest journey 1992
4 Uncertain death 1993
5 Murder on campus 1994

HOLT, T.
THE WALLED ORCHARD
1 Goatsong 1989
2 The walled orchard 1990

HOLZER, H.
AMITYVILLE
1 Murder in Amityville 1980
2 The Amityville curse 1981
3 The secret of Amityville 1985

HOOD, E.
1 A stranger in the town 1985
2 Silver bells, white linen 1988
Novels set in Paisley in the 18th century

HOOKER, R.
MASH
1 MASH
2 MASH goes to Maine
3 MASH goes to Hollywood
4 MASH goes to New Orleans
5 MASH goes to Vienna
6 MASH goes to Paris
7 MASH goes to Texas
8 MASH goes to San Francisco
9 MASH goes to Miami
10 MASH goes to Morocco
11 MASH goes to Montreal
12 MASH goes to Moscow
13 MASH mania
Paperbacks, loosely based on the TV series

HOOVER, H.
1 The gift of the deer
2 A place in the woods 1970
3 The years of the forest 1973
N.F. Autobiography

HOPKINS, K.
DR.BLOW & PROFESSOR MANCIPLE
1 She died because 1958
2 Dead against my principles 1959
3 Body blow 1961

HOPKINS, K.
JERRY LEE
1 The girl who dies
2 The forty-first passenger
3 Pierce with a pin
4 Camper's corpse

HORANSKY, R.
NIKKI TRAKOS
1 Dead ahead 1992
2 Dead centre 1993

HORGAN, P.
1 Maine line west
2 A lamp on the plain

HORGAN, P.
RICHARD
1 Things as they are 1965
2 Everything to live for 1969
3 The thin mountain air 1978

HORNIG, D.
LOREN SWIFT
1 Hardball 1986
2 The dark side 1987

HORST, K.
1 Sink the Ark Royal 1981
2 Caribbean pirate 1982
Novels about the German Navy in WW2.

HORWOOD, W.
DUNCTON CHRONICLES
1 Duncton Wood 1980
2 Duncton quest 1988
3 Duncton found 1989
4 Duncton tales 1991
5 Duncton rising 1992
6 Duncton stone 1993

HOSSENT, H.
MAX HEALD
1 Spies die at dawn 1960
2 No end to fear 1961
3 Memory of treason 1962
4 Spies have no friends 1963
5 Run for your death 1965
6 The fear business 1966

HOUGH, R.
1 Angels one-five 1978
2 Fight of the Few 1979
3 Fight to the finish 1980

HOUGH, R.
BULLER
1 Buller's guns 1981

2 Buller's dreadnought 1982
3 Buller's victory 1984

HOUGH, S. B.
INSPECTOR BRENTFORD
1 Dear daughter dead 1966
2 Sweet sister seduced 1968

HOUGRON, J.
M.LASTIN
1 Blaze of the sun 1957
2 Reap the whirlwind 1958

HOUSEHOLD, G.
1 Rogue male 1939
2 Rogue justice 1982

HOUSEHOLD, G.
ROGER TAINE
1 Rough shoot 1951
2 Time to kill 1952

HOUSEMAN, J.
1 Run-through 1973
2 Front and centre 1979
3 Final dress 1983
   *N.F. Autobiography of the film
   director. Published in one vol. as
   'Unfinished Business' in 1986*

HOWARD, A.
CHAPMAN FAMILY
1 The mallow years 1990
2 Shining threads 1991

HOWARD, A.
OSBORNE FAMILY
1 Ambitions 1986
2 All the dear faces 1992
3 There is no parting 1993

HOWARD, E. J.
CAZALET CHRONICLES
1 Light years 1990
2 Marking time 1991
3 Confusion 1993

HOWARD, H.
GLENN BOWMAN
1 Last appointment
2 Last deception
3 Last vanity
4 Death of Cecilia
5 The other side of the door
6 Bowman strikes again
7 Bowman on Broadway
8 Bowman at a venture
9 No target for Bowman
10 Sleep for the wicked 1955

11 A hearse for Cinderella 1956
12 The Bowman touch 1956
13 Key to the morgue 1957
14 Sleep my pretty one 1957
15 The long night 1957
16 The big snatch 1958
17 The Armitage secret 1958
18 Deadline 1959
19 Extortion 1960
20 Time bomb 1960
21 Fall guy 1960
22 I'm no hero 1961
23 Countdown 1962
24 Out of the fire 1965
25 Portrait of a beautiful harlot 1966
26 Routine investigations 1967
27 The secret of Simon Cornell 1969
28 Cry on my shoulder 1970
29 Room 37 1970
30 Million dollar snapshot 1971
31 Murder one 1971
32 Epitaph for Joanna 1972
33 Nice day for a funeral 1973
34 Highway to murder 1973
35 Dead drunk 1974
36 Treble cross 1975
37 Pay off 1977
38 One way ticket 1978
39 The sealed envelope 1979

HOWARD, H.
PHILIP SCOTT:DEPARTMENT K
1 Department K 1966
2 The eye of the hurricane 1968

HOWARD, L.
FYTTON OF GAWSWORTH
1 Elizabeth Fytton of Gawsworth
   Hall 1985
2 The master of Littlecote Manor
   1986
3 The squire of Holdenby 1986
4 Isabel the girl 1989
5 Isabel the woman 1990

HOWARD, R. E.
CONAN
1 Conan
2 Conan the usurper,by L.Sprague
   de Camp
3 Conan the wanderer, by L.Sprague
   de Camp
4 Conan the conqueror
5 Conan the adventurer
6 Conan the avenger
7 Conan of the Isles, by L.Sprague
   de Camp
8 Conan the warrior

9 Conan the buccaneer, by
L.Sprague de Camp
10 Conan of Cimmeria, by L.Sprague
de Camp
11 Conan the freebooter
12 Conan of Aquilonia, by L.Sprague
de camp
13 Conan the swordsman, by
L.Sprague de Camp
14 Conan the liberator, by A.J.Offut
15 Conan the mercenary, by A.J.Offut
16 The sword of Skelos, by A.J.Offut
17 The road of kings, by K.E.Wagner
18 Conan and the spider god, by
L.Sprague de Camp
19 Conan the rebel, by P.Anderson
20 Conan the invincible, by R.Jordan
21 Conan the defender, by R.Jordan
22 Conan the unconquered,by
R.Jordan
23 Conan the triumphant, by
R.Jordan
24 Conan the barbarian, by R.Jordan
25 Conan the magnificent, by
R.Jordan
26 Conan the victorious, by R.Jordan
27 Conan the valorous, by
J.M.Roberts
28 Conan the champion, by
J.M.Roberts
29 Conan the fearless, by S.Perry
Science fiction, mainly in paperback

HOWATCH, S.
1 The rich are different 1978
2 Sins of the fathers 1980

HOWATCH, SUSAN
CHURCH OF ENGLAND SERIES
1 Glittering images 1987
2 Glamorous powers 1988
3 Ultimate prizes 1989
4 Scandalous risks 1990
5 Absolute truths 1994

HOWELLS, B.
MAY & OTLEY
1 Wuthering depths 1990
2 Silver riding 1991
3 Dandelion days 1991
Humorous novels set in Yorkshire.

HOYLE, F. & ELLIOT, J.
1 A for Andromeda 1963
2 Andromeda breakthrough 1964

HOYT, R.
JOHN DENSON
1 Decoy

136

2 30 for a Harry 1982
3 Fish story 1987

HUBBARD, L. R.
MISSION EARTH
1 The invaders plan 1986
2 Black genesis 1986
3 The enemy within 1987
4 An alien affair 1987
5 Fortune of fear 1987
6 Death quest 1987
7 Voyage of vengeance 1988
8 Disaster 1988
9 Villainy victorious 1988
10 The doomed planet 1988
Science fiction

HUDSON, J. F.
1 Rabshakeh 1993
2 Zoheleth 1994
Set in Israel, in Old Testament times

HUGHART, B.
MASTER LI
1 Bridge of birds 1989
2 The story of the stone 1989
3 Eight skilled gentlemen 1991

HUGHES, G.
GEORGE WILLIS
1 Split on red 1980
2 Cover zero 1981
3 The French deal 1982

HUGHES, GLYN
1 The hawthorn goddess 1986
2 The rape of the rose 1987

HUGHES, M. V.
1 London child of the seventies 1978
2 London girl of the eighties 1979
3 London home in the nineties 1980
N.F. Family life in London, 1870-1900

HUGHES, R. D.
PELMAN THE POWERSHAPER
1 The prophet of Lamath
2 The wizard in waiting
Paperback fantasy

HUGHES, RICHARD
THE HUMAN PREDICAMENT
1 The fox in the attic 1961
2 The wooden shepherdess 1973

HUGHESDON, B.
1 Roses have thorns 1993
2 Silver fountains 1994

HULME, A.
1 The flying man 1988
2 Whisper in the wind 1989

HUMMER, G. B.
WHITMORE FAMILY
1 Red branch 1993
2 West of the sun 1994

HUMPHREYS, E.
1 Flesh and blood 1974
2 The best of friends 1978
3 Salt of the earth 1985
4 An absolute hero 1986
5 Open secrets 1988
6 Bonds of attachment 1991
Follows the lives and careers of two girls in Wales in the 1920s and 30s.

HUNT, J., LORD
1 The ascent of Everest 1953
2 Our Everest adventure 1954
N.F. Mountaineering

HUNT, R.
DET.CHIEF INSPECTOR SYDNEY WALSH
1 Death in ruins 1991
2 Death sounds grand 1991
3 Death of a merry widow 1992
4 Deadlocked 1994

HUNTER, A.
SUPT.GEORGE GENTLY
1 Gently does it 1955
2 Gently by the shore 1956
3 Gently down the stream 1957
4 Landed Gently 1958
5 Gently through the mill 1958
6 Gently in the sun 1959
7 Gently with the painters 1960
8 Gently to the summit 1960
9 Gently go man 1961
10 Gently where the roads go 1962
11 Gently floating 1963
12 Gently Sahib 1964
13 Gently with the ladies 1965
14 Gently northwest 1966
15 Gently continental 1968
16 Gently coloured 1969
17 Gently with the innocents 1970
18 Gently at a gallop 1971
19 Vivienne:Gently where she lay 1972
20 Gently French 1973
21 Gently in trees 1974
22 Gently with love 1975
23 Gently where the birds are 1976
24 Gently instrumental 1977

25 Gently to a sleep 1978
26 The Honfleur decision 1980
27 Gabrielle's way 1981
28 Fields of heather 1981
29 Gent
30 Amorous Leander 1983
31 The unhung man 1983
32 Once a prostitute... 1984
33 The Chelsea ghost 1985
34 Goodnight, sweet prince 1986
35 Strangling man 1987
36 Traitor's end 1988
37 Gently with the millions 1989
38 Gently scandalous 1990
39 Gently to a kill 1991
40 Gently tragic 1992
41 Gently in the glens 1993
42 Bomber's moon 1994

HUNTER, C.
1 Island of stone 1982
2 Fiercely the tempest 1984
Novels set in Portland, Dorset

HUNTER, E.
1 Last summer 1971
2 Come winter 1973

HUNTER, J. D.
BRUNO STACHEL
1 The blue Max 1965
2 Blood order 1980
3 The tin cravat 1981

HUNTER, N.
BODIE THE STALKER
1 Trackdown
2 Bloody bounty
3 High hell
4 The killing trail
5 Hangtown
6 Day of the savage
Paperback Westerns

HUNTER, R.
SIMON QUARRY
1 The fourth angel 1986
2 Quarry's contract 1987

HURD, D. & OSMOND, A.
1 Send him victorious 1967
2 The smile on the face of the tiger 1969
3 Scotch on the rocks 1971

HURT, F. M.
INSPECTOR BROOM
1 The body at Bowman's Hollow 1959

2 Death by request 1960
3 Sweet death 1961
4 Acquainted with murder 1962

HUTSON, S.
1 Slugs 1984
2 Breeding ground 1985
Horror stories

HUTSON, S.
SGT. ROLF KESSLER
1 No survivors 1985
2 Sledgehammer 1981
3 Kessler's raid 1982
4 Convoy of steel 1982
5 Slaughterhouse 1983
6 Men of blood 1984
7 Taken by force 1987

HUXLEY, E.
1 The flame trees of Thika 1959
2 The mottled lizard 1962
3 Love among the daughters 1968
4 Out in the midday sun 1985
N.F. Autobiography and travel in Kenya

IBARGUENGOITIA, J.
1 Two dead girls 1983
2 Two crimes 1984
Set in Mexico

INCHBALD, P.
INSPECTOR FRANCO CORTI
1 Tondo for Short 1981
2 The sweet short grass 1982
3 Short break in Venice 1983
4 Or the bambino dies 1985

INCHBALD, R.
COLONEL PATERNOSTER
1 Colonel Paternoster 1953
2 The five inns 1954
3 Spetember story 1955

INCHFAWN, F.
1 Those remembered days 1962
2 Something more to say 1965
3 Not the final word 1969
N.F. Autobiography

INFANTE, A.
MICKEY DOUGLAS
1 Death on a hot summer night 1989
2 Death among the dunes 1990
3 Deathwater 1991
4 Death in green 1992
5 Death launch 1993
Thrillers set in Australia

INGATE, M.
1 The sound of the weir 1974
2 This water laps gently 1977

INNES, B.
1 The Red Baron lives 1982
2 The red Red Baron 1983

INNES, H.
IAIN WARD & PETER KETTIL
1 Isvik 1991
2 Target Antarctica 1993

INNES, M.
HONEYBATH
1 The mysterious commission 1974
2 Honeybath's haven 1977
3 Lord Mullion's secret 1981
4 Appleby and Honeybath 1983

INNES, M.
SIR JOHN APPLEBY
1 Death at the President's lodging 1936
2 Hamlet,revenge! 1937
3 Lament for a maker 1938
4 Stop press 1939
5 There came both mist and snow 1940
6 The secret vanguard 1940
7 Appleby on Ararat 1941
8 The daffodilaffair 1942
9 The weight of the evidence 1944
10 Appleby's end 1945
11 From London far 1946
12 What happened at Hazelwood 1947
13 A night of errors 1948
14 Operation Pax 1951
15 A private view 1952
16 Appleby talking 1954
17 Appleby talks again 1956
18 Appleby plays chicken 1956
19 The long farewell 1958
20 Hare sitting up 1959
21 Silence observed 1961
22 A connoisseur's case 1962
23 Money from Holme 1964
24 The bloody wood 1966
25 A change of heir 1966
26 Appleby at Allington 1968
27 A family affair 1969
28 Death at the chase 1970
29 An awkward lie 1971
30 The open house 1972
31 Appleby's answer 1973
32 Appleby's other story 1974
33 The Appleby file 1975
34 The gay phoenix 1976

35 The Ampersand papers 1978
36 Sheiks and adders 1982
37 Appleby and Honeybath 1983
38 Carson's conspiracy 1984
39 Appleby and the Ospreys 1986

INSIGHT, J.
1 I turned my collar round 1955
2 I am the vicar 1956
3 Country parson 1961
4 I am a guinea pig 1964
N.F. Autobiography

IRISH, L.
COLONIAL TRILOGY
1 And the wild birds sing 1984
2 The place of the swan 1986
3 The house of O'Shea 1990

IRVINE, L.
1 Runaway 1986
2 Castaway 1983
N.F. Autobiography

IRVING, L.
1 Henry Irving 1968
2 The successors 1969
3 The precarious crust 1971
*N.F. The author's family's
involvement with the theatre from
Victorian times*

IRWIN, G.
1 Least of all saints 1957
2 Andrew Connington 1958

IRWIN, M.
ELIZABETH I
1 Young Bess 1945
2 Elizabeth, captive princess 1948
3 Elizabeth and the Prince of Spain
1960

ISON, G.
DET.CHIEF SUPT.JOHN GAFFNEY
1 Cold light of dawn 1988
2 Confirm or deny 1989
3 A damned serious business 1990

ISON, G.
DET. CHIEF SUPT. TOMMY FOX
1 The Home Secretary will see you
now 1989
2 Lead me to the slaughter 1990
3 Tomfoolery 1992
4 The taming of Tango Harris 1993
5 Underneath the arches 1994

ISRAEL, P.
B. F. CAGE
1 Hush money 1975
2 The French kiss 1977
3 The stiff upper lip 1979

JACK, D.
THE JOURNALS OF BARTHOLOMEW
DANDY
1 Three cheers for me 1973
2 That's me in the middle 1974
3 It's me again
4 Me Dandy, you Cissie
5 Me too 1984

JACKMAN, S.
1 The Davidson affair 1973
2 Slingshot 1974

JACKSON, A.
1 Tales from a country practice 1986
2 More tales from a country practice
1987
N.F. Memoirs of a Suffolk G. P.

JACKSON, B
AIR DETECTIVE
1 Crooked flight 1985
2 Spy's flight 1986
3 Terror flight 1988

JACKSON, G.
1 Soledad brother 1968
2 Blood in my eye 1972
N.F. Autobiography

JACKSON, R.
1 Before the storm 1972
2 Storm from the skies 1974
*N.F. A history of the WW2 air
offensive against Germany*

JACKSON, R.
HURRICANE SQUADRON
1 Yeoman goes to war 1978
2 Squadron scramble 1978
3 Target Tobruk 1979
4 Malta victory 1980
5 Mosquito squadron 1981
6 Operation diver 1981
7 Tempest squadron 1981
8 The last battle 1982
9 Operation Firedog 1982
10 Korean combat 1983
11 Venom squadron 1983
12 Hunter squadron 1984

JACKSON, R.
SAS
1 Desert Commando 1986
2 Partisan! 1987
3 Attack at night 1988
4 Wind of death 1990
5 The last secret 1991

JACKSON, S.
1 Life among the savages 1953
2 Raising demons 1956
N.F. Autobiography

JACOBS, A.
1 Salem Street 1994
2 High Street 1994
Set in the Lancashire milltowns

JACOBS, T. C. H.
TEMPLE FORTUNE
1 The red eyes of Kali 1955
2 Good night sailor 1956
3 Death in the mews 1957
4 Final payment 1962
5 Sweet poison 1966
6 Ashes in the cellar 1966
7 Death of a scoundrel 1967
8 Wild weekend 1967
9 House of horror 1969
10 The black devil 1969

JAFFE, R.
1 Class reunion
2 After the reunion 1985

JAGGER, B.
BARFORTH FAMILY
1 The clouded hills 1980
2 Flint and roses 1981
3 The sleeping sword 1982

JAKES, J.
1 North and South 1983
2 Love and war 1985
3 Heaven and hell 1987
*A family chronicle set in the
American Civil War*

JAKES, J.
BRAK THE BARBARIAN
1 Brak the barbarian
2 The sorcerers
3 The mark of the demons
Paperback fantasy

JAKES, J.
KENT FAMILY CHRONICLES
1 The bastard
2 The rebels

3 The seekers
4 The warriors
5 The titans 1990
6 The furies 1990
7 Lawless 1990
8 Americans 1990
1-4 published in paperback

JAMES, B.
DET. CHIEF SUPT. COLIN HARPUR
1 You'd better believe it 1985
2 The Lolita man 1986
3 Halo parade 1987
4 Protection 1988
5 Come clean 1989
6 Take 1990
7 Club 1991
8 Astride a grave 1991
9 Gospel 1992
10 Roses, roses 1993
11 In good hands 1994

JAMES, E.
1 Life class 1990
2 Life lines 1991
3 Lovers and friends 1991

JAMES, J.
PHOTINUS THE GREEK
1 Votan 1966
2 Not for all the gold in Ireland
1968

JAMES, L. D.
RED KINGS OF WYNNAMYR
1 Sorcerer's stone
2 Kingslayer
3 Book of stones
Paperback fantasy

JAMES, M.
LAWRENCE FAMILY
1 A touch of earth 1988
2 Fortune's favourite child 1989
3 The treasures of existence 1989

JAMES, P. D.
CORDELIA GRAY
1 An unsuitable job for a woman
1972
2 The skull beneath the skin 1982

JAMES, P. D.
SUPT.ADAM DALGLEISH
1 Cover her face 1962
2 A mind to murder 1963
3 Unnatural causes 1967
4 Shroud for a nightingale 1971
5 The black tower 1975

6 Death of an expert witness 1977
7 A taste for death 1985
8 Devices and desires 1989
9 Original sin 1994

JAMES, PETER
MAX FLYNN
1 Dead letter drop 1981
2 Atom bomb angel 1982

JAMES, W.
SUNFALL TRILOGY
1 The earth is the Lord's
2 The other side of heaven 1992
3 Before the sun falls 1993

JAMES, W. M.
APACHE
1 The first death
2 Knife in the nightr
3 Duel to the death
4 Death train
5 Fort Treachery
6 Sonora slaughter
7 Blood line
8 Blood on the trail
9 The naked and the savage
10 All blood is red
11 The cruel trail

JAMESON, D.
1 Touched by angels 1989
2 Last of the hot metal men 1990
N.F. Autobiography

JANCE, J. A.
DET.J.P.BEAUMONT
1 Until proven guilty
2 Injustice for all
3 Trial by fury
4 Taking the fifth
5 Improbable cause 1988
6 A more perfect union 1992
7 Dismissed with prejudice 1993

JANES, J. R.
JEAN-LOUIS ST. CYR & HERMANN
KOHLER
1 Mayhem 1991
2 Carousel 1992
3 Kaleidoscope 1993
4 Salamander 1994
5 Mannequin 1994
Detective stories set in Paris in WW2.

JANES, P.
GALAXY GAME
1 Galaxy game 1993

2 Fission impossible 1993
Humorous s. f.

JANSEN, S.
1 Mary Maddison 1991
2 Della Dolan 1993
*Family sagas set in North East
England.*

JARDINE, Q.
ASST.CHIEF CONSTABLE ROBERT
SKINNER
1 Skinner's rules 1993
2 Skinner's festival 1994

JARMAN, R. H.
1 We speak no treason 1970
2 The King's grey mare 1972
3 The courts of illusion 1983
*Novels about Richard III and the
Wars of the Roses*

JEFFREY, E.
CHISWELL FAMILY
1 Stranger's Hall 1988
2 Gin and gingerbread 1989
*A family saga set in Essex and the
oyster trade*

JEFFRIES, I.
1 Thirteen days 1959
2 Dignity and purity 1960
3 It wasn't me 1961

JEFFRIES, M.
LOREMASTERS OF ELUNDIUM
1 The road to Underfall 1987
2 Palace of kings 1988
3 Shadowlight
Fantasy. No. 3 in paperback only

JEFFRIES, M.
THE HEIRS TO GNARLSMYRE
1 Glitterspike Hall
2 Hall of whispers

JEFFRIES, R.
INSPECTOR ALVAREZ
1 Mistakenly in Mallorca 1973
2 Two-faced death 1975
3 Troubled deaths 1977
4 Murder begets murder 1979
5 Just desserts 1980
6 Unseemly end 1981
7 Deadly petard 1983
8 Three and one make five 1984
9 Layers of deceit 1985
10 Almost murder 1986
11 Relatively dangerous 1987

12 Death trick 1988
13 Dead clever 1989
14 Too clever by half 1990
15 Murder's long memory 1991
16 A fatal fleece 1992
17 Murder confounded 1993
18 Death takes time 1994

JENKINS, G.
COMMANDER GEOFFREY PEACE
1 A twist of sand 1966
2 Hunter-killer 1967

JEPSON, S.
EVE GILL
1 Man running 1948
2 The golden dart 1949
3 The hungry spider 1950
4 Man dead 1951
5 The black Italian 1954
6 The laughing fish 1960

JETER, K. W.
1 Dr.Adder
2 The glass hammer
3 Death arms 1987

JEVONS, M.
PROFESSOR HENRY SPEARMAN
1 Murder at the margin 1978
2 The fatal equilibrium 1985

JEWELL, D.
1 Come in, number one, your time
   is up 1972
2 Sellout 1973

JOHN, O.
HAGGAI GODIN
1 Thirty days hath September 1966
2 The disinformer 1967
3 A beam of black light 1968
4 Dead on time 1969

JOHNSON, B. F.
1 Delta blood
2 Homeward winds the river
3 The heirs of love
   *A paperback saga set in the Deep
   South*

JOHNSON, D. MCINTOSH
1 A doctor regrets 1948
2 Bars and barricades 1952
3 A doctor returns 1956
4 A doctor in Parliament 1958
5 A Cassandra in Westminster 1967
6 A doctor reflects 1975
   N.F. Autobiography

JOHNSON, P. H.
1 The good listener 1975
2 The good husband 1978

JOHNSON, P. H.
HELENA
1 Too dear for possessing 1940
2 Avenue of stone 1947
3 A summer to decide 1952

JOHNSTON, B.
1 It's been a lot of fun 1976
2 It's a funny game 1976
3 It's been a piece of cake 1989
   *N.F. Cricket and broadcasting
   reminiscences*

JOHNSTON, G.
SILBER
1 The claws of the scorpion
2 The two kings

JOHNSTON, GEORGE
DAVID MEREDITH
1 My brother Jack 1967
2 Clean straw for nothing 1969
3 A cartload of clay 1971

JOHNSTON, R.
JAMES BRUCE
1 Disaster at Dungeness 1965
2 The angry ocean 1967

JOLLEY, E.
1 My father's moon 1989
2 Cabin fever 1991

JON, M.
STEVEN KALE
1 The Wallington case 1981
2 A question of law 1981

JONES, B.
CLAUDE RAVEL
1 The Hamlet ;problem 1961
2 The crooked phoenix 1962
3 Tiger from the shadows 1963
4 Death on a pale horse 1963
5 Private vendetta 1965
6 The embers of hate 1966
7 Testament of evil 1967
8 A den of savage men 1967
9 The deadly trade 1968

JONES, ELWYN
CHIEF INSPECTOR BARLOW
1 Barlow 1972
2 Barlow in charge 1973
3 Barlow comes to judgment 1974

4 The Barlow casebook 1975
5 Barlow exposed 1976
6 Barlow down under 1978

JONES, G.
1 Lord of misrule 1983
2 Noble savage 1985

JONES, H. W.
EMMA SHAW
1 Death and the trumpets of
   Tuscany 1988
2 Shot on location 1990

JONES, I. H.
1 Sister 1987
2 Senior sister 1988
   Novels about hospital life

JONES, JACK
1 Unfinished journey 1937
2 Me and mine 1946
3 Give me back my heart 1950
   N.F. Autobiography

JONES, JENNY
FLIGHT OVER FIRE
1 Fly by night 1990
2 The edge of vengeance 1991
3 Lies and flames 1992
   Fantasy

JONES, JOANNA
1 Nurse is a neighbour 1956
2 Nurse on the district 1958
   N.F. Autobiography

JONES, R.
1 The age of wonder 1967
2 The tower rise 1971

JONES, R. W.
INSPECTOR EVANS & SGT.BEDDOES
1 Saving Grace 1986
2 Cop out 1987
3 The green reapers 1988

JONES, T.
1 A steady trade 1982
2 Heart of oak 1984
3 The incredible voyage 1977
4 Ice 1979
5 Saga of a wayward sailor 1980
6 Adrift 1981
7 A star to steer her by 1985
8 The improbable voyage 1986
   N.F. Autobiography of a yachtsman

JONG, E.
ISADORA WING
1 Fear of flying 1975
2 How to save your own life 1977
3 Parachutes and kisses 1985

JORDAN, J.
THE VAUGHANS
1 A good weekend for murder 1987
2 Murder under the mistletoe 1988

JORDAN, M.
TYLER BROTHERS
1 Brigham's way 1976
2 Jacob's road 1976

JORDAN, R.
THE WHEEL OF TIME
1 Eye of the world 1990
2 The great hunt 1991
3 The dragon reborn 1992
4 The shadow rising 1992
5 The fires of heaven 1993
6 Lord of chaos 1994
   Fantasy

JOSEPH, M.
DAISY PENNY
1 A better world than this 1987
2 A world apart 1988

JOYCE, C.
GREG ALLARD
1 Errant witness 1981
2 Errant target 1982
3 Errant sleuth 1983

JOYCE, C.
INSPECTOR PAT STOCKTON
1 Run a golden mile 1978
2 Sentence suspended 1979
3 A hitch in time 1980
4 Death of a left-handed woman
   1980
5 Calculated risk 1981
6 A bullet for Betty 1981
7 From the grave to the cradle 1982
8 Murder is a pendulum 1983

JOYCE, J.
1 Ulysses 1922
2 Leopold, by P.Costello 1981

JOYNSON, C.
1 In spite of Henry 1960
2 In search of Henry 1962
3 Yes, Henry 1964
   N.F. Autobiography

JUDD, B.
FORREST EVERS
1 Formula one 1989
2 Indy 1990
3 Monza 1991
4 Phoenix 1992
5 Silverstone 1993
Thrillers about motor racing.

JUDGE DREDD
1 The savage amusement,by
  D.Bishop
2 Death masques, by D.Stone
3 Dreddlocked, by S.Marley
4 Cursed earth asylum, by D.Bishop
5 The Medusa seed, by D.Stone
6 Dredd dominion, by S.Marley
7 The hundredfold problem, by
  J.Grant
  Paperback novels based on the comic
  book character

KAHN, J.
NEW WORLD TRILOGY
1 World enough and time
2 Time's dark laughter
  Paperback science fiction

KAKONIS, T.
WAVERLEY
1 Michigan role 1991
2 Double down 1992

KALLEN, L.
C.B.GREENFIELD
1 Introducing C.B. Greenfield 1979
2 C.B.Greenfield and the
  tanglewood murder 1980
3 C.B.Greenfield:lady in the house
  1982
4 C.B.Greenfield:the piano bird 1984
5 A little madness 1986

KALMAN, Y.
MORGAN AND RENNIE FAMILIES
1 Mists of heaven 1988
2 After the rainbow 1989

KALMAN, Y.
YARDLEY FAMILY
1 Greenstone land 1982
2 Juliette's daughter 1983
3 Riversong 1985
  A family saga set in New Zealand

KAMADA, A.
1 A love so bold 1980
2 Richer than a crown 1981
  Novels set in 11thC England

KAMINSKY, S. M.
INSPECTOR PORFIRY ROSTNIKOV
1 Rostnikov's corpse 1981
2 Black Knight in Red Square 1988
3 Cold red sunrise 1990
4 The man who walked like a bear
  1991

KAMINSKY, S. M.
TOBY PETERS
1 The Howard Hughes affair 1980
2 Bullet for a star 1981
3 Murder on the Yellow Brick Road
  1981
4 High midnight 1982
5 Buried Caesars 1990
6 The devil met a lady 1993

KANE, H.
MARLA TRENT
1 Killer's kiss
2 Devil to pay 1966

KANE, H.
PETER CHAMBERS
1 A halo for nobody
2 Armchair in hell
3 Hang by your neck
4 Report for a corpse
5 A corpse for Christmas
6 Trinity in violence
7 Trilogy in jeopardy
8 Death on the double
9 The narrowing lust
10 Sweet Charlie
11 Triple terror
12 The dangling dean
13 Nirvana can also mean death
14 Death of a flack
15 Death of a hooker
16 Death of a dastard
17 Killer's kiss
18 Dead in bed
19 Snatch an eye
20 Nobody loves a loser
21 Murder for the millions
22 Devil to pay 1966

KAPP, C.
CAGEWORLD
1 Search for the sun
2 The lost world of Cronos
3 The tyrant of Hades
4 Star search
  Paperback science fiction

KAPP, Y.
ELEANOR MARX
1 Family life (1855-83) 1972

2 The crowded years 1976
N.F. Biography

KARTUN, D.
ALFRED BAUM
1 Beaver to fox 1983
2 Flittermouse 1984
3 Megiddo 1987
4 Safe house 1989

KAUFMAN, P.
1 Shield of three lions 1986
2 Banners of gold 1987
Historical novels set in the reign of Richard I

KAVANAGH, D.
DUFFY
1 Duffy 1980
2 Fiddle City 1981
3 Putting the boot in 1985
4 Going to the dogs 1987

KAVANAGH, P. J.
1 Perfect stranger 1966
2 Finding connections 1990
N.F. Autobiography of a poet

KAY, G. G.
THE FIONAVAR TAPESTRY
1 The summer tree 1985
2 The wandering fire 1986
3 The darkest road 1987
Fantasy

KAZAN, E.
1 America,America 1969
2 The Anatolian 1983

KEAST, F.
DARRYL KRUSTOV
1 Sunburst
2 Cloudburst 1986

KEATING, H. R. F.
INSPECTOR GHOTE
1 The perfect murder 1964
2 Inspector Ghote's good crusade 1966
3 Inspector Ghote caught in meshes 1967
4 Inspector Ghote hunts the peacock 1968
5 Inspector Ghote plays a joker 1969
6 Inspector Ghote breaks an egg 1970
7 Inspector Ghote goes by train 1971
8 Inspector Ghote trusts the heart 1972

9 Bats fly up for Inspector Ghote 1974
10 Filmi,filmi Inspector Ghote 1976
11 Inspector Ghote draws a line 1979
12 Go West, Inspector Ghote 1981
13 The Sherriff of Bombay 1984
14 Under a monsoon cloud 1986
15 The body in the billiard room 1987
16 Dead on time 1988
17 The iciest sin 1990
18 Cheating death 1992
19 Doing wrong 1994

KEE, R.
SIMON BROADSTROP
1 Sign of the times 1955
2 Private eyeful 1958

KEENAN, W.
NO.1 AREA CRIME SQUAD
1 Lonely beat 1968
2 Mosaic of death 1969
3 Murder in melancholy 1970

KEILLOR, G.
LAKE WOBEGONE
1 Lake Woebegone days 1986
2 Leaving home 1988
Humorous short stories set in an imaginary Mid- Western town

KEITH, W. H.
INVADERS OF CHARON
1 The genesis web
2 Nomads of the sky
3 Warlords of Jupiter

KELLERMAN, F.
SGT.PETE DECKER
1 Ritual bath 1987
2 Sacred and profane 1989
3 The quality of mercy 1989
4 Day of atonement 1991
5 False prophet 1992
6 Grievous sin 1993
7 Sanctuary 1994

KELLERMAN, J.
ALEX DELAWARE
1 Shrunken heads 1985
2 Blood test 1985
3 The butcher's theatre 1988
4 Silent partner 1989
5 Time bomb 1990
6 Private eyes 1991
7 Devil's waltz 1992
8 Bad love 1993
9 Self defence 1994

KELLEY, L. P.
LUKE SUTTON
1 Outlaw 1981
2 Gunfighter 1982
3 Indian fighter 1983
4 Avenger 1984
5 Outrider 1986
6 Bounty hunter 1991
7 Hired gun 1991
8 Lawman 1992
9 Mustanger 1992

**KELLOGG, M. B. &
ROSSOW, W. B.**
LEAR'S DAUGHTERS
1 The wave and the flame 1987
2 Reign of fire 1988
Fantasy

KELLS, S.
LAZENDER FAMILY
1 A crowning mercy 1983
2 The fallen angels 1984

KELLY, MARY
DET.INSPECTOR NIGHTINGALE
1 A cold coming 1956
2 Deadman's riddle 1957
3 The Christmas egg 1958

KELLY, N.
GILLIAN ADAMS
1 In the shadow of King's 1990
2 My sister's keeper 1992
3 Bad chemistry 1993

KELLY, S.
FEENEY FAMILY
1 A long way from heaven 1985
2 For my brother's sins 1986
3 Erin's child 1987
4 Dickie 1989

KELLY, SUSAN
DET.INSPECTOR NICK TREVELYAN
1 Hope against hope 1989
2 Time of hope 1990
3 Hope will answer 1992

KELLY, T.
1 FEPOW 1985
2 The Genki boys 1967
*N.F. Experiences of POWs in
Japanese prison camps. Listed in
chronological order.*

KEMAL, Y.
SLIM MEHMED
1 Mehmed, my hawk 1971

146

2 They burn the thistles 1973

KEMELMAN, H.
RABBI DAVID SMALL
1 Friday the rabbi slept late 1966
2 Saturday the Rabbi went hungry
1967
3 Sunday the Rabbi stayed home
1969
4 Monday the Rabbi took off 1972
5 Tuesday the Rabbi saw red 1974
6 Wednesday the Rabbi got wet
1976
7 Thursday the Rabbi walked out
1979
8 Some day the Rabbi will leave
1985
9 One fine day the Rabbi bought a
cross 1988
10 The day the Rabbi resigned 1992

KEMP, P.
1 Mine were of trouble 1958
2 No colours or crest 1960
3 Alms for oblivion 1961
N.F. Autobiography

KEMP, S.
DR. TINA MAY
1 No escape 1985
2 The lure of sweet death 1986
3 What dread hand? 1987

KENDRICK, B.
DUNCAN MACLAIN
1 Blind man's bluff
2 Death knell
3 Out of control
4 You die today
5 Reservations for death
6 Clear and present danger 1958
7 The whistling hangman 1959

KENNEALY, P.
THE KELTIAD
1 The copper crown
2 The throne of Scone
3 The hawk's grey feather
4 The oak above the kings
Paperback fantasy

KENNEDY, A.
BRADSHAW TRILOGY
1 No place to cry 1986
2 The fires of summer 1987
3 Alldreams denied 1988

KENNEDY, A.
KINCAID TRILOGY
1 Passion never knows 1990
2 Dancing in the shadows 1991
3 Love, come no more 1992

KENNEDY, W.
ALBANY CYCLE
1 Legs 1975
2 Billy Phelan's greatest game 1978
3 Ironweed 1983
4 Quinn's book 1988
5 Very old bones 1992

KENNELLY, A.
1 The peacable kingdom 1949
2 Up home Houghton 1955

KENNETH, C.
1 The love riddle 1963
2 May in Manhattan 1963

KENT, A.
RICHARD BOLITHO
1 With all despatch (1792) 1988
2 Richard Bolitho -
   Midshipman(1772)
3 Midshipman Bolitho and the
   'Avenger'(1773) 1971
4 Stand into danger (1774) 1980
5 In gallant company (1777) 1977
6 Sloop of war (1778) 1972
7 To glory we steer (1782) 1967
8 Command a King's ship (1789)
   1973
9 Passage to mutiny (1789) 1976
10 Form line of battle (1793) 1969
11 Enemy in sight (1794) 1970
12 The flag captain (1795) 1971
13 Signal - close action (1798) 1974
14 Inshore squadron (1800) 1978
15 A tradition of victory (1801) 1981
16 Success to the brave (1802) 1983
17 Colours aloft (1803) 1986
18 Honour this day (1804-5) 1987
19 The only victor (1806) 1990
20 Beyond the reef (1808) 1992
21 The darkening sea (1809-10) 1993
   *The author's chronological order of
   reading*

KENWORTHY, C.
MATTHEW AND SON
1 In the dark of the moon 1981
2 Ride a dark tide 1982
3 A storm in the dark 1983
4 Against a dark shore 1985
   Sea stories set in the 19thC

KENYON, F. W.
1 Eugenie 1964
2 Imperial courtesan 1967

KENYON, F. W.
JOHN CHURCHILL,DUKE OF
MARLBOROUGH
1 The seeds of time 1961
2 Glory o' the dream 1963

KENYON, M.
HARRY PECKOVER
1 The rapist 1979
2 Zigzag 1981
3 The God squad bod 1982
4 A free range wife 1983
5 A healthy way to die 1986
6 Peckover holds the baby 1988
7 Kill the butler 1991
8 Peckover joins the choir 1992
9 Peckover and the bog man 1994

KEROUAC, J.
JACK DULOUZ
1 On the road 1957
2 The Dharma bums 1958
3 The subterraneans 1958
4 The lonesome traveller 1960
5 Big Sur 1962

KERR, K.
DEVERRY
1 Daggerspell 1987
2 Darkspell 1988
3 Dawnspell;the bristling wood 1989
4 Dragonspell;the Southern sea 1990
   Fantasy

KERR, K.
DEVERRY-WESTLANDS CYCLE
1 A time of exile 1991
2 A time of omens 1992
3 A time of war:days of blood and
   fire 1993
4 A time of justice:days of air and
   darkness 1994

KERR, P.
1 The pale criminal 1990
2 A German requiem 1991
3 A philosophical investigation 1992

KERR, R.
JAMIE STUART
1 The Stuart legacy 1973
2 The black pearls 1975
3 The dark lady 1975

KERRIGAN, J.
SBS
1 Fireball 1983
2 Bluebeard 1984
3 Watchdog 1984

KERSH, C.
1 The aggravations of Minnie Ash 1975
2 Minnie Ash at war 1979

KERSHAW, H.
CORONATION STREET
1 Early days 1975
2 Trouble at 'The Rovers' 1976
3 Elsie Tanner strikes back 1977

KERSHAW, V.
MITCH MITCHELL
1 Murder is too expensive 1993
2 Funny money 1994

KESSLER, L.
COSSACKS
1 Black Cossacks
2 Sabres of the Reich
3 The mountain of skulls
4 Breakthrough

KESSLER, L.
OTTO STAHL
1 Otto's phoney war 1981
2 Otto's blitzkrieg 1982
3 Otto and the Reds 1982
4 Otto and the Yanks 1983
5 Otto and the SS 1984
6 Otto and the Himmler loveletters 1984

KESSLER, L.
REBEL
1 Cannon fodder 1986
2 The die-hards 1987
3 Death match 1987
4 Breakout 1988

KESSLER, L.
ROMMEL
1 Ghost division 1981
2 Massacre

KESSLER, L.
SEA WOLVES
1 Sink the Scharnhorst 1982
2 Death to the Deutschland 1982

KESSLER, L.
SS WOTAN
1 Assault on Baghdad 1992

2 Flight from Moscow 1992
3 Fire over Serbia 1993
4 Operation longjump 1993
5 SS attacks! 1994

KESSLER, L.
STORM TROOP
1 Storm troop 1983
2 Blood mountain 1983
3 Valley of the assassins 1984
4 Red assault
5 Himmler's gold
6 Fire over Kabul 1982
7 Wave of terror 1983
8 Fire over Africa 1984

KESSLER, L.
STUKA SQUADRON
1 The black knights 1983
2 The hawks of death 1983
3 The tank busters 1984
4 Blood mission 1984

KESSLER, L.
SUBMARINE
1 The wolf pack 1985
2 Operation deathwatch 1985
3 Convoy to catastrophe 1986
4 Fire in the west 1986
5 Flight to the Reich 1987

KESSLER, L.
WOTAN/PANZER DIVISION
1 SS Panzer Battalion 1975
2 Death's head 1978
3 Claws of steel 1978
4 Guns at Cassino 1978
5 The march on Warsaw 1988
6 Hammer of the Gods 1979
7 Forced march 1979
8 Blood and ice 1977
9 Sand panthers 1977
10 Counter attack 1979
11 Hell fire 1978
12 Panzer hunt 1979
13 Slaughter ground 1980
14 Flash point 1980
15 Cauldron of blood 1981
16 Schirmer's head hunters 1981
17 Whores of war 1982
18 Schirmer's death legions 1983
19 Slaughter at Salerno 1985
20 Death ride
21 The Hess assault 1987
22 March or die
All the Kessler series were originally published in paperback. Dates given are for hardback eds.

KETTLE, J.
1 The Athelsons 1973
2 A gift of onyx 1974

KHANNA, B.
1 Nation of fools 1984
2 Sweet chilies 1991

KIENZLE, W. X.
FATHER KOESLER
1 The rosary murders 1978
2 Death wears a red hat 1980
3 Mind over murder 1981
4 Shadow of death 1984
5 Sudden death 1986
6 Masquerade 1992
7 Eminence 1992

KIJEWSKI, K.
KAT COLORADO
1 Kat walk
2 Katapult
3 Kat's cradle 1994
4 Copy Kat 1994

KILLILEA, M.
1 Karen 1963
2 With love from Karen 1964
   N.F. Autobiography

KILWORTH, G. D.
ANGEL
1 Angel 1993
2 Archangel 1994

KIM, R. E.
1 The martyred 1967
2 The innocent 1969

KING, A.
1 Mine enemy grows older 1958
2 May this house be safe from tigers 1960
3 I should have kissed her more 1961
4 Is there a life after birth 1962
   N.F. Autobiography

KING, B.
MASTERFUL INVENTION
1 The destroying angel
2 The time-fighters
3 Skyfire

KING, B.
NORDIC TRILOGY
1 Starkadder 1985
2 Vargr moon 1986
   Fantasy

KING, BETTY
THE BEAUFORT FAMILY
1 Lady Margaret 1961
2 Captive James 1966
3 Lord Jasper 1967
4 The King's mother 1969

KING, F.
THE DORMOUSE
1 Enter the Dormouse
2 The Dormouse- undertaker
3 The Dormouse has nine lives
4 The Dormouse - peacemaker
5 Dough for the Dormouse
6 This doll is dangerous
7 They vanished at night
8 What price doubloons
9 Crook's cross
10 Gestapo Dormouse
11 Sinister light
12 Catastrophe club
13 Operation halter
14 Operation honeymoon
15 Big blackmail
16 Crook's caravan 1955
17 The case of the strange beauties
18 That charming crook 1958
19 The two who talked 1958
20 The case of the frightened brother 1959

KING, S.
THE DARK TOWER
1 The gunslinger 1988
2 The drawing of the three 1989
3 The wastelands 1992

KINGSTON, B.
EASTER EMPIRE
1 Tuppeny times 1988
2 Fourpenny flier 1989
3 Sixpenny stalls 1990

KINGSTON, G.
1 A wing and a prayer
2 Main force
3 The boys of Coastal
   Paperback novels about the RAF in WW2

KIPLING, R.
1 Kim
2 The Imperial agent, by T.N.Murari 1987
3 The last victory, by T.N.Murari 1988
   Continues the story of Kim as a man

KIRKUP, J.
1 The only child 1957
2 Sorrows, passions and alarms 1959
3 I, of all people 1988
N.F. Autobiography

KIRKWOOD, G.
FAIRLYDEN
1 Fairlyden 1990
2 Mistress of Fairlyden 1991
3 The family at Fairlyden 1992
4 Fairlyden at war 1993

KIRST, H. H.
MUNICH TRILOGY
1 A time for scandal 1972
2 A time for truth 1974
3 A time for payment 1966

KIRST, H. H.
ZERO EIGHT-FIFTEEN
1 The strange mutiny of Gunner Asch 1955
2 Gunner Asch goes to war 1956
3 The return of Gunner Asch 1958
4 What became of Gunner Asch 1964

KIRSTEIN, R.
1 The steerswoman
2 The outskirter's secret
Paperback fantasy

KIRSTEN, A.
RALPH WHITGIFT
1 Young Lucifer 1984
2 Satan's child 1985

KITCHEN, P.
1 Lying-in 1968
2 A fleshly school 1970
3 Linsey-Woolsey 1971
4 Paradise 1972

KLEIN, N.
1 Sunshine 1983
2 The sunshine years 1984

KNAAK, R.
DRAGONREALM
1 Firedrake
2 Ice dragon

KNEALE, N.
1 The Quatermass experiment
2 Quatermass II
3 Quatermass 1979

KNEF, H.
1 The gift horse 1974
2 The verdict 1976
N.F. Autobiography

KNIGHT, A.
INSPECTOR JEREMY FARO
1 Enter second murderer 1988
2 Blood line 1989
3 Deadly beloved 1989
4 Killing cousins 1990
5 A quiet death 1991
6 To kill a queen 1992
7 The evil that men do 1993
8 The missing Duchess 1994
Detective stories set in 19th
C. Edinburgh

KNOWLES, A.
1 Single in the field 1984
2 An ark on the flood 1985
Novels about a woman vet in the
Cotswolds

KNOWLES, A.
MATTHEW RATTON
1 Matthew Ratton 1979
2 The raven tree 1981

KNOX, B.
THANE AND MOSS
1 Deadline for a dream 1957
2 Death department 1958
3 Leave it to the hangman 1959
4 Little drops of blood 1960
5 Sanctuary Isle 1961
6 The man in the bottle 1962
7 Taste of proof 1965
8 Deep fall 1966
9 Justice on the rocks 1967
10 The tallyman 1969
11 Children of the mist 1970
12 To kill a witch 1971
13 Draw batons 1973
14 Rally to kill 1975
15 Pilot error 1976
16 Live bait 1978
17 A killing in antiques 1981
18 The hanging tree 1983
19 The crossfire killings 1986
20 The interface man 1989

KNOX, B.
WEBB CARRICK, FISHERY PROTECTION
1 The scavengers 1964
2 Devilweed 1965
3 Blacklight 1966
4 The Klondyker 1968

5 Blueback 1969
6 Seafire 1970
7 Stormtide 1972
8 Whitewater 1974
9 Hellspout 1976
10 Witchrock 1977
11 Bombship 1979
12 Bloodtide 1982
13 Wavecrest 1985
14 Dead man's mooring 1987
15 The drowning nets 1991

KNOX-MAWER, J.
1 The sultans came to tea 1961
2 A gift of islands 1984
N.F. Life in the South Seas

KOESTLER, A.
1 Arrow in the blue 1969
2 The invisible writing 1954
3 Stranger in the square 1984
N.F. Autobiography

KONRAD, K.
RUSSIAN SERIES
1 First blood 1981
2 March on Moscow 1981
3 Front swine 1982

KONSALIK, H.
LOVE ON THE DON
1 Deep waters 1979
2 Against the tide 1980

KOSTOV, K. N.
PUNISHMENT BATTALION
1 Baptism of blood
2 The Gulag rats
3 Blood on the Baltic
4 The Steppe wolves
Paperback war stories

KRANTZ, J.
SCRUPLES
1 Scruples 1978
2 Scruples two 1993

KRASNEY, S. A.
LIEUT. ABE LASEN
1 Death dies in the street 1957
2 Homicide West 1962
3 Homicide call 1963

KRUGER, P.
PHIL KRAMER
1 Weep for Willow Green 1966
2 Weave a wicked web 1967
3 If a shroud fits 1969

KRUK, Z.
1 Taste of fear
2 Taste of hope
N.F. Autobiography

KURTZ, K.
DERYNI CHRONICLES
1 Deryni rising
2 Deryni checkmate
3 High Deryni 1986
4 Deryni archives
Fantasies, mainly paperback

KURTZ, K.
THE HISTORIES OF KING KELSON
1 The Bishop's heir
2 The King's justice 1986
3 The quest for Saint Camber 1987
Fantasy. No. 1 in paperback only

KURTZ, K.
THE LEGENDS OF CAMBER OF CULDI
1 Camber of Culdi 1986
2 Saint Camber
3 Camber the heretic
Paperback fantasies. No. 1 now in hardback

KURTZ, K. & HARRIS, D.
ADEPT
1 The adept 1992
2 The lodge of the lynx 1993
3 The Templar treasure 1994

L'AMOUR, L.
SACKETT
1 Sackett's land 1964
2 To the far blue mountains 1975
3 The warrior's path 1975
4 Jubal Sackett 1986
5 Ride the river
6 The daybreakers
7 Sackett
8 Lando
9 Mojave crossing
10 The Sackett brand
11 The lonely men
12 Treasure mountain
13 Mustang men
14 Galloway
15 The sky-liners
16 The man from Broken Hills
17 Ride the dark trail
18 Lonely on the mountain

L'AMOUR, L.
THE CHANTRY FAMILY
1 Fair blows the wind 1985
2 Over on the dry side 1988

LA PLANTE, L.
DET.INSPECTOR JANE TENNISON
1 Prime suspect 1992
2 Prime suspect 2 1992
3 Prime suspect 3 1993
Based on the television series.

LA PLANTE, R.
TEGNE
1 Warlord of Zendow
2 The killing blow

LACEY, E.
TOUSSAINT MOLORE
1 Room to swing 1964
2 Moment of untruth 1965

LACEY, P.
'MAUDIE'MORGAN
1 The limit 1988
2 The bagman 1989

LACEY, S.
LEAH HUNTER
1 File under:deceased 1992
2 File under:missing 1993
3 File under:arson 1994

LACKEY, M.
BARDIC VOICES
1 The lark and the wren 1993
2 The robin and the kestrel 1994

LACKEY, M.
SERRATED EDGE
1 Born to run
2 Wheels of fire
3 When the bough breaks
Paperback fantasy

LACKEY, M.
THE LAST HERALD-MAGE
1 Magic's pawn
2 Magic's promise
3 Magic's price

LADD, J.
ABILENE
1 The peacemaker 1989
2 The sharpshooter
3 The prizefighter 1993
4 The night riders 1989
5 The half-breed 1990

LAGERKVIST, P.
TOBIAS TRILOGY
1 Death of Ahasuerus 1963
2 Pilgrim at sea 1964
3 The Holyland 1965

LAINE, A.
THE EARL OF MORISTON
1 The reluctant heiress 1980
2 The melancholy virgin 1981

LAKER, R.
EASTHAMPTON
1 Warwyck's wife 1978
2 Claudine's daughter 1979
3 The Warwycks of Easthampton 1980

LAMB, C.
BARBARY WHARF
1 Besieged 1992
2 Battle for possession 1992
3 Too close for comfort 1992
4 Playing hard to get 1992
5 A sweet addiction 1992
6 Surrender 1992

LAMB, L.
1 Death of a dissenter 1968
2 Worse than death 1971
3 Picture frame 1972
4 Man in a mist 1974

LAMBERT, E.
1 The 20,000 thieves
2 The veterans
N.F.The Australian army in WW2

LAMONT, M.
1 Nine moons wasted 1977
2 Horns of the moon 1979

LAMPITT, D.
SUTTON PLACE
1 Sutton Place 1983
2 The silver swan 1984
3 Fortune's soldier 1985
4 Zachary 1990

LANCASTER, O.
1 All done from memory 1965
2 With an eye to the future 1967
N.F. Autobiography

LANCING, G.
TZU HSI,EMPRESS OF CHINA
1 Imperial motherhood
2 The mating of the dragon
3 Dragon in chains
4 Phoenix triumphant

LANDSBOROUGH, G.
DESERT COMMANDOS
1 The glasshouse gang 1976
2 Desert marauders 1976

3 The Benghazi breakout 1977
4 Dead commando 1977

LANE, J.
CHARLES I
1 The young and lonely king 1969
2 The questing beast 1970
3 A call of trumpets 1971

LANE, K.
1 Diary of a medical nobody 1982
2 West country doctor 1984
N.F. Autobiography

LANE, MARGARET
1 A night at sea 1963
2 A smell of burning 1965

LANE, MAXIE
1 Running 1977
2 Sea running 1978
N.F. Autobiography

LANG, F.
GILLONNE DE BEAUREGARD
1 The well wisher 1966
2 The duke's daughter 1967
3 The malcontent 1968

LANG, M.
PUCK BURE & CHRISTOPHER WICK
1 Wreath for the bride 1965
2 No more murders 1966
3 Death awaits thee 1967

LANG-SIMS, L.
1 A time to be born 1973
2 Flower in a teacup 1974
N.F. Autobiography

LANGSFORD, A. E.
1 HMS Marathon 1989
2 HMS Crusader 1990
3 HMS Inflexible 1991

LANGTON, J.
HOMER KELLY
1 Emily Dickinson is dead 1989
2 The Memorial Hall murder 1990
3 The Dante game 1991

LAPIERRE, J.
MEG HALLORAN
1 Unquiet grave 1988
2 Children's games 1990
3 The cruel mother 1991

LARSON, C.
NILS BLIXEN
1 Matthew's hand 1977
2 Muir's blood 1978

LARTEGUY, J.
1 The centurions 1962
2 The praetorians 1963

LASGARN, H.
1 A vet for all seasons 1986
2 Vet in a storm 1987
3 Vet in a storm 1987
4 Vet in the village 1988
N.F. Experiences of a vet

LASH, J. C.
1 Eleanor and Franklin 1971
2 Eleanor: the years alone 1972
N.F. Biography of Eleanor Roosevelt

LATHEN, E.
JOHN PUTNAM THATCHER
1 Banking on death 1962
2 A place for murder 1963
3 Accounting for murder 1965
4 Murder makes the wheels go round 1966
5 Death shall overcome 1967
6 Murder against the grain 1967
7 A stitch in time 1968
8 When in Greece 1969
9 Come to dust 1970
10 Murder to go 1970
11 Pick up sticks 1971
12 Ashes to ashes 1971
13 The longer the thread 1972
14 Murder without icing 1973
15 Sweet and low 1974
16 By hook or by crook 1975
17 Double, double, oil and trouble 1979
18 Going for gold 1981
19 Green grow the dollars 1982
20 Something in the air 1988
21 East is east 1991
22 Right on the money 1993
Thrillers set in the world of finance.

LAUBEN, P.
HOMER CLAY
1 A nice sound alibi 1981
2 A surfeit of alibis 1982
3 A sort of tragedy 1985

LAUMER, K.
LAFAYETTE O'LEARY
1 The tune bender 1975
2 The world bender 1973

3 The shape changer 1977

LAUMER, K.
MR.CURLON
1 Worlds of the Imperium 1968
2 The other side of time 1969
3 Assignment in nowhere 1971

LAUMER, K.
RETIEF
1 Envoy to new worlds 1963
2 Retief and the Warlords
3 Retief's war 1965
4 Retief's ransome 1971
5 Retief of the CDT 1971
Science fiction

LAUNAY, D.
ADAM FLUTE
1 She modelled her coffin 1961
2 New shining white murder 1962
3 Corpse in camera 1963
4 Death and still life 1964
5 Two-way mirror 1965
6 The scream 1966

LAURENCE, J.
DARINA LISLE
1 A deepe coffyne 1989
2 A tasty way to die 1990
3 Hotel morgue 1991
4 Recipe for death 1992
5 Death and the epicure 1993
6 Death at the table 1994

LAW, J.
ANNA PETERS
1 The big payoff 1978
2 The Gemini trip 1979
3 Under Orion 1980
4 The shadow of the palms 1981
5 Death under par 1983

LAWHEAD, S.
DRAGON KING SAGA
1 In the hall of the Dragon King
2 The warlords of Nin
3 The sword and the flame

LAWHEAD, S.
EMPYRION
1 Search for Fierra
2 The siege of Dome

LAWHEAD, S.
SONG OF ALBION
1 The paradise war 1991
2 The silver hand 1992
3 The endless knot 1993

LAWHEAD, S.
THE PENDRAGON CYCLE
1 Taliesin
2 Merlin
3 Arthur
4 Pendragon 1994
Paperback fantasies

LAWRENCE, H.
MARK EAST
1 Blood upon the snow
2 Death of a doll
3 A time to die

LAYBERRY, L. G. J.
OAKLEIGH FARM
1 Hayseed 1980
2 Gleanings 1981
3 To be a farmer's girl 1982
4 A pocket full of rye 1984
5 Tangled harvest 1984
6 The last mophrey 1987
7 As long as the fields are green 1987
8 A new earth 1988
Novels about a farming family in Derbyshire. The last three titles in the series were published later, and by a different publisher.

LE BRETON, A.
1 Rififi 1947
2 Rififi in New York 1970

LE CARRE, J.
GEORGE SMILEY
1 A murder of quality 1962
2 Call for the dead 1961
3 The spy who came in from the cold 1963
4 The looking glass war 1965
5 Tinker, tailor, soldier, spy 1974
6 The honourable schoolboy 1977
7 Smiley's people 1980
8 The secret pilgrim 1990
'The quest for Carla' (1982) contains 5, 6, &7

LEACH, B.
VANESSA CARTER
1 I'm a vegetarian 1992
2 Summer without Mum 1993
3 Vanessa 1994

LEAHY, S.
1 Family ties 1983
2 Family truths 1985

LEAHY, S.
CHRISTINE BENNETT
1 The Good Friday murder 1993
2 The atonement murder 1994
3 The St. Patrick's Day murder

LEASOR, J.
ARISTO MOTORS
1 They don't make them like that any more 1969
2 Never had a spanner on her 1970
3 Host of extras 1973
3 also features Jason Love.

LEASOR, J.
CHINA SERIES
1 Follow the drum 1972
2 Mandarin gold 1973
3 The Chinese widow 1975
4 Jade gate 1976

LEASOR, J.
DR. JASON LOVE
1 Passport to oblivion (Where the spies are) 1965
2 Passport to peril (Spylight) 1966
3 The Yang meridian 1967
4 Passport in suspense 1967
5 Passport for a pilgrim 1968
6 A week for Love 1969
7 Love-all 1971
8 Love and the land beyond 1979
9 Frozen assets 1989
10 Love down under 1992

LEATHER, E.
RUPERT CONWAY
1 The Vienna elephant 1977
2 The Mozart score 1979
3 The Duveen collection 1980

LEDUC, V.
1 La batarde 1960
2 Mad in pursuit 1971
N.F. Autobiography

LEDWITH, F.
1 The best of all possible worlds 1987
2 Ships that go bump in the night 1974
3 Ships afloat in the city 1977
N.F. Autobiography. Listed in chronological order

LEE, A.
MISS HOGG
1 Sheep's clothing
2 Call in Miss Hogg

3 Miss Hogg and the Bronte murders 1956
4 Miss Hogg and the squash club murder 1957
5 Miss Hogg and the dead dean 1957
6 Miss Hogg flies high 1958
7 Miss Hogg and the Covent Garden murders 1960
8 Miss Hogg and the missing sisters 1961
9 Miss Hogg's last case 1963

LEE, J.
1 The unicorn quest 1987
2 The unicorn dilemma 1989

LEE, L.
1 Cider with Rosie 1959
2 As I walked out one midsummer morning 1969
3 A moment of war 1991
4 I can't stay longer 1976
N.F. Autobiography

LEE, M.
HEARTS OF FIRE
1 Seduction and sacrifice 1994
2 Desire and deception 1994
3 Passion and the past 1994
4 Fantasies and the future 1994
5 Scandals and secrets 1994
6 Marriage and miracles 1994

LEE, S.
OWEN LIGHTBRINGER
1 The quest for the sword of infinity
2 The land where the serpents rule
3 The path through the circle of time
Paperback fantasy

LEE, T.
BIRTHGRAVE
1 Birthgrave
2 The storm cloud
3 Shadow fire
4 Quest for the white witch

LEE, T.
BLOOD OPERA
1 Dark dance 1992
2 Personal darkness 1993
3 Darkness, I 1994

LEE, T.
THE SECRET BOOKS OF PARADYS
1 The book of the damned 1988

2 The book of the beast 1988
Fantasy

LEES, D.
CONSTABLE CRAIG
1 Our man in Morton Episcopi 1979
2 Mayhem in Morton Episcopi 1980

LEES, D.
JEFF PLUMMER
1 The rainbow conspiracy 1971
2 Zodiac 1972
3 Rape of a quiet town 1973
4 Elizabeth, R.I.P. 1974

LEES-MILNE, J.
1 Ancestral voices 1975
2 Prophesying peace 1977
3 Caves of ice 1983
4 Midway on the waves 1985
N.F. Autobiography

LEGAT, M.
1 The silk maker 1985
2 The cast iron man 1987

LEHMANN, J.
1 The whispering gallery 1955
2 I am my brother 1959
3 The ample proposition 1966
N.F. Autobiography

LEIBER, F.
SWORDS
1 Swords and deviltry
2 Swords against death
3 Swords in the mist
4 Swords against wizardry
5 Swords of Lankhmar
6 Swords and ice magic
7 The Knight and Knave of Swords
Paperback fantasy

LEIGH, H.
THE VINTAGE YEARS
1 The grapes of Paradise
2 Wild vines
3 Kingdoms of the vine
Paperback novels about a family vineyard

LEIGH, P.
1 Garnet 1978
2 Coral 1979
3 Rosewood 1979

LEIGH, R.
SAM CARROLL
1 The cheap dream 1982

2 The girl with the bright head 1982

LEITCH, D.
1 God stand up for bastards 1973
2 Family secrets 1984
N.F. The author

LEITH, A. [A. BURGH]
TALES FROM SARSON MAGNA
1 Molly's flashings 1991
2 Hector's hobbies 1994

LEJEUNE, A.
1 Professor in peril 1987
2 Key without a door 1988

LEMARCHAND, E.
DET. SUPT. TOM POLLARD
1 Death of an old girl 1967
2 The Affacombe affair 1968
3 Alibi for a corpse 1969
4 Death on doomsday 1970
5 Cyanide with compliments 1972
6 Let or hindrance 1973
7 Buried in the past 1974
8 A step in the dark 1976
9 Unhappy returns 1977
10 Suddenly, while gardening 1978
11 Change for the worse 1980
12 Nothing to do with the case 1981
13 Troubled waters 1982
14 The wheel turns 1983
15 Light through glass 1984
16 Who goes home? 1986
17 The Glade Manor murder 1988

LEON, D.
COMMISSARIO GUIDO BRUNETTI
1 Death in La Fenice 1992
2 Death in a strange country 1993
3 The anonymous Venetian 1994

LEONARD, H.
1 Home before night 1979
2 Out after dark 1982

LEROUX, E.
THE WELGEVONDEN TRILOGY
1 Seven days at the Silbersteins 1968
2 One for the devil 1969
3 The third eye 1970

LESLIE, A.
1 The gilt and the gingerbread 1981
2 A story half told 1983
N.F. Autobiography

LESLIE, C.
HOUSE OF GODWIN
1 a farrago of foxes 1975
2 Feud royal 1977

LESLIE, D. S.
1 Snap, crackle, pop 1970
2 Bad medicine 1971

LESLIE, P.
1 The Melbourne virus 1991
2 The catapult ultimatum 1990
3 No deal in diamonds 1992

LESLIE, R.
HERACLES TRILOGY
1 Trouble in the wind 1984
2 The fateful dawn 1984
3 Under a shrieking sky 1984

LESLIE, R.
VICTORY TRILOGY
1 Dawn readiness 1984
2 The raging skies 1985
3 The hunters 1986

LESSING, D.
CANOPUS IN ARGOS
1 Shikasta 1979
2 The marriages between Zones 3,4
 & 5 1980
3 The Sirian experiments 1981
4 The making of the representative
 for Planet 8 1983
5 Documents relating to the
 sentimental agents in
 the Volyen Empire 1983
 Science fiction

LESSING, D.
CHILDREN OF VIOLENCE
1 Martha Quest 1952
2 A proper marriage 1956
3 A ripple from the storm 1958
4 Landlocked 1965
5 The four-gated city 1966

LESTER, F.
GEOFFREY SLADE
1 The corpse wore rubies 1958
2 Death and the south wind 1958
3 The golden murder 1959

LEVENE, P.
AMBROSE WEST
1 Ambrose in London 1959
2 Ambrose in Paris 1960

LEVI, P.
BEN JONSON
1 Grave witness 1985
2 Knit one, drop one 1987

LEWIN, M. Z.
ALBERT SAMSON & DET. LT. POWDER
1 Ask the right question 1972
2 The enemies within 1973
3 The way we die now 1974
4 The silent salesman 1976
5 Missing woman 1982
6 Out of time 1984
7 Night cover 1976
8 Hard line 1983
9 Late payments 1986
10 Child proof 1988
11 Called by a Panther 1991
12 Called by a partner 1992

LEWIS, C.
HOWARD HAYES
1 The golden grin
2 Acid test
3 Hot rain

LEWIS, H.
MARY OF ENGLAND
1 Rose of England 1977
2 Heart of a rose 1978

LEWIS, H.
MARY TUDOR
1 I am Mary Tudor 1971
2 Mary the Queen 1973
3 Bloody Mary 1974

LEWIS, O.
SANCHEZ FAMILY
1 The children of Sanchez 1968
2 A death in the Sanchez gamily
 1970

LEWIS, R.
ARNOLD LANDON
1 A gathering of ghosts 1983
2 Most cunning workmen 1984
3 A trout in the milk 1986
4 Men of subtle craft 1987
5 The devil is dead 1989
6 A wisp of smoke 1991
7 A secret dying 1992
8 Bloodeagle 1993
9 Cross bearer 1994

LEWIS, R.
ERIC WARD
1 A certain blindness 1980
2 Dwell in danger 1982

3 A limited vision 1983
4 Once dying,twice dead 1984
5 A blurred reality 1985
6 Premium on death 1986
7 The salamander chill 1988
8 A necessary dealing 1989
9 A kind of transaction 1991

LEWIS, R.
INSPECTOR CROW
1 A lover too many 1967
2 Wolf by the ears 1970
3 Error of judgment 1971
4 A secret singing 1972
5 Blood money 1973
6 A part of virtue 1976
7 A question of degree 1976
8 Nothing but foxes 1977
9 A relative distance 1981

LEWIS, R. H.
MATTHEW COLL
1 A cracking of spines 1980
2 The manuscript murders 1981
3 A pension for death 1983
4 Where agents fear to tread 1984
5 Death in Verona 1989
Thrillers about an antiquarian bookseller

LEWIS, T.
JACK CARTER
1 Jack's return home 1971
2 Jack Carter's law 1974
3 Jack Carter and the Mafia pigeon 1977

LEY, A. C.
EVERSLEY FAMILY
1 The clandestine betrothal
2 The toast of the town

LEY, A. C.
JUSTIN & ANTHEA RUTHERFORD
1 A fatal assignation 1987
2 Masquerade of vengeance 1989
Romantic thrillers set in the Regency period

LIDDELL, R.
1 Kind relations 1939
2 Stepsons 1969
3 The last enchantments 1991

LIDDELL, R.
CHARLES HARBORD
1 Unreal city 1952
2 The rivers of Babylon 1959
3 An object for a walk 1966

LIDE, M.
ANN OF CAMBRAY
1 Ann of Cambray
2 Gifts of the Queen
3 Hawks of Sedgemont
Paperback historical romance

LIMB, S.
1 Dulcie Domum's manual of bad housekeeping 1991
2 More bad housekeeping 1992
3 Dulcie dishes the dirt 1994

LIND, J.
1 Counting my steps 1970
2 Numbers 1972
N.F. Autobiography

LINDBERGH, A. M.
1 Bring me a unicorn 1972
2 Hour of gold, hour of lead 1973
3 Locked rooms and open doors 1974
N.F. Autobiography

LINDHOLM, M.
1 The reindeer people 1987
2 Wolf's brother 1989

LINDOP, A. E.
1 The singer not the song 1954
2 The Judas figures 1956

LINDSAY, JOAN
1 Time without clocks
2 Facts soft and hard
N.F. Autobiography

LINDSAY, JOAN
HANGING ROCK
1 Picnic at Hanging Rock 1968
2 The secret of Hanging Rock 1987

LINDSAY, K.
1 Enchantress of the Nile 1964
2 Queen of the mirage 1966

LINDSAY, P.
SUSSEX SERIES
1 The devil comes to Winchelsea 1956
2 The bells of Rye 1957
3 Sister of Rye 1959

LINDSEY, D. L.
1 Cold mind 1984
2 Heat from another sun 1985
3 Spiral 1987

LINDSEY, R.
1 The falcon and the snowman 1980
2 The flight of the falcon 1985
   N.F. Exploits of a spy

LING, P.
JUDGE FAMILY
1 High water 1991
2 Flood water 1992
3 Storm water 1993

LINKLATER, E.
1 The man on my back 1941
2 A year of space 1953
3 Fanfare for a tin hat 1970
   N.F. Autobiography

LINSCOTT, G.
BIRDY AND NIMUE HAWTHORN
1 A healthy body 1984
2 Murder makes tracks 1985
3 A whiff of sulphur 1987

LINSCOTT, G.
NELL BRAY
1 Sister beneath the sheet 1991
2 Hanging on the wire 1992
3 Stage fright 1993
4 Widow's peak 1994

LINZEE, D.
INQUIRIES INC.
1 Discretion 1981
2 Belgravia 1982

LISTER, S.
SAINTE MONIQUE
1 Mistral Hotel
2 Sunset of France
3 Peace comes to Sainte Monique
4 Marise
5 Miss Sainte Monique
6 Delorme in deep water
7 Sainte Monique roundabout 1967
8 Sainte Monique unlimited 1968
9 Broom 1969
10 The empty valley 1971
11 Hungarian roulette 1972
12 Tycoon in Eden 1973
13 A smell of brimstone 1974
14 The dog that never was 1975
15 Becky 1976
16 The abominable goat 1977

LITCHFIELD, M.
DET. SUPT. FERGUS MCQUEEN
1 See how they run 1984
2 Murder circus 1985

LITVINOFF, E.
FACES OF TERROR
1 A death out of season 1973
2 Blood on the snow 1975
3 The force of terror 1978

LIVINGS, H.
RAVENSGILL
1 Pennine tales 1983
2 Flying eggs and things 1986
   *Humorous short stories set in the
   Pennines*

LIVINGSTON, J.
JOE BINNEY
1 A piece of the silence 1983
2 Die again,Macready 1984
3 The nightmare file 1987

LIVINGSTON, N.
MCKIE FAMILY
1 The far side of the hill 1987
2 The land of our dreams 1989

LIVINGSTON, N.
MR. PRINGLE
1 The trouble at Aquitaine 1985
2 Fatality at Bath and Wells 1986
3 Incident at Parga 1987
4 Death in a distant land 1988
5 Death in close-up 1989
6 Mayhem in Parva 1990
7 Unwillingly to Vegas 1991
8 A quiet murder 1992

LLEWELLYN, R.
1 How green was my valley 1939
2 Up,into the singing mountain 1963
3 Down where the moon is small
   1966
4 Green green my valley now 1975

LLEWELLYN, R.
EDMUND TROTHE
1 The end of the rug 1969
2 But we didn't get the fox 1970
3 White horse to Banbury Cross
   1972
4 The night is a child 1974

LLEWELLYN, S.
CHARLIE AGUTTER
1 Dead reckoning 1987
2 Blood orange 1988
   *Thrillers set in the world of yacht
   racing*

LLEWELLYN, S.
GURNEY
1 Gurney's revenge 1977
2 Gurney's reward 1978
3 Gurney's release 1979

LLOYD, A. R.
THE KINE SAGA
1 Marshworld (Kine) 1982
2 Witchwood 1989
3 Dragonpond 1990

LLOYD, J.
GREGORY DANGERFIELD
1 The further adventures of
  Capt.G.Dangerfield 1975
2 The continuing adventures of
  G.Dangerfield 1979

LLOYD-JONES, B.
1 The animals came in one by one
  1966
2 Come into my world 1972
  N.F. Autobiography of a vet

LLYWELYN, M.
THE ODYSSEY OF THE IRISH
1 Lion of Ireland 1980
2 The horse goddess 1983
3 Bard 1985

LOCHTE, D.
SERENDIPITY DALHQUIST
1 Sleeping dog 1987
2 Laughing dog 1988

LOCKLEY, R. M.
1 Island days 1934
2 Inland farm 1943
3 The island farmers 1947
4 Golden year 1948
5 The island 1969
6 Orielton 1977
7 Myself when young 1980
  N.F. Autobiography

LOCKRIDGE, F. & R.
ASST.D.A. BERNIE SIMMONS
1 Squire of death 1966
2 A plate of red herrings 1969
3 Twice retired 1971
4 Something up a sleeve 1974

LOCKRIDGE, F. & R.
CAPTAIN HEIMRICH
1 I want to go home 1948
2 Spin your web, lady 1949
3 Foggy foggy death 1953
4 The client is cancelled 1955

5 Stand up and die 1955
6 Death by association 1957
7 Death and the gentle bull 1957
8 Burnt offering 1959
9 Let dead enough alone 1959
10 Practice to deceive 1959
11 Accent on murder 1960
12 Show red for danger 1961
13 No dignity in death 1962
14 First come first kill 1963
15 The distant clue 1964
16 Murder can't wait 1965
17 Murder roundabout 1967
18 With option to die 1968
19 A risky way to kill 1970
20 Inspector's holiday 1972
21 Not I said the sparrow 1974

LOCKRIDGE, F. & R.
MR. AND MRS. NORTH
1 Mr. and Mrs. North
2 The Norths meet murder 1940
3 Murder out of turn 1941
4 Hanged for a sheep 1943
5 Death takes a bow 1945
6 Killing the goose 1947
7 A pinch of poison 1948
8 Death on the aisle 1949
9 Death of a tall man 1949
10 Pay off for the banker 1949
11 Murder within murder 1950
12 Murder is served 1950
13 Dishonest murderer 1951
14 Murder in a hurry 1952
15 Untidy murder 1953
16 Murder comes first 1954
17 Death has a small voice 1955
18 Dead as a dinosaur 1956
19 Curtain for a jester 1956
20 Death of an angel 1957
21 Voyage into violence 1958
22 The long skeleton 1958
23 Murder is suggested 1961
24 The judge is reversed 1961
25 Murder has its points 1962
26 The ticking clock 1963
27 Murder by the book 1964

LOCKRIDGE, F. & R.
NATHAN SHAPIRO
1 Catch as catch can 1960
2 The innocent house 1961
3 Four hours to fear 1964
4 Murder for art's sake 1968
5 Die laughing 1970
6 Preach no more 1972
7 Write murder down 1974

8 The old die young 1981
After 1970 books were published
under the name of Richard Lockridge.

LODGE, D.
1 Changing places 1975
2 Small world 1984

LODI, M.
1 Charlotte Morel 1963
2 The dream 1968
3 The siege 1970

LOFTS, N.
1 Gad's Hall 1977
2 The haunted house 1978

LOFTS, N.
A HOUSE IN SUFFOLK
1 The town house 1959
2 The house at Old Vine 1961
3 The house at sunset 1963

LOFTS, N.
INDONESIAN SERIES
1 The silver nutmeg 1947
2 A scent of cloves 1957

LOFTS, N.
SUFFOLK TRILOGY
1 Knight's Acre 1974
2 The homecoming 1975
3 The lonely furrow 1976

LOGAN, M.
NICK MINETT
1 Tricoleur 1976
2 Guillotine 1976
3 Brumaire 1978

LOMER, M.
1 Robert of Normandy 1991
2 Fortune's knave 1992

LONES, L. S.
1 Daughters of Eve 1991
2 A woman's reach 1993

LONGMATE, N.
DET.SERGEANT RAYMOND
1 Death won't wash 1957
2 A head from death 1958
3 Strip death naked 1958
4 Vote for death 1960

LONGSTREET, S.
FIORE FAMILY
1 All or nothing 1984
2 Our father's house 1986

LONGSTREET, S.
PEDLOCK FAMILY
1 The Pedlocks 1967
2 Pedlock and sons 1969
3 Pedlock saint, Pedlock sinner 1970
4 The Pedlock inheritance 1971
5 The strange case of Sarah Pedlock 1977

LORAC, E. C. R.
INSPECTOR MACDONALD
1 Murder on the burrows 1931
2 The affair on Thor's head 1932
3 The Greenwell mystery 1932
4 Murder in St.John's Wood 1934
5 Murder in Chelsea 1934
6 The affair of Colonel Marchand 1935
7 Death on the Oxford Road 1935
8 The organ speaks 1936
9 Death of an author 1937
10 Crime counter crime 1937
11 Post after post mortem 1938
12 A pall for a painter 1938
13 Bats in the belfry 1939
14 The devil and the C.I.D. 1939
15 These names make clues 1942
16 Slippery staircase 1943
17 John Brown's body 1944
18 Black beadle 1945
19 Death at Dyke's Corner 1945
20 Tryst for a tragedy 1946
21 Case in the clinic 1946
22 Rope's end, rogue's end 1947
23 The sixteenth stair 1948
24 Death came softly 1948
25 Checkmate to murder 1949
26 Fell murder 1949
27 Murder by matchlight 1949
28 Fire in the thatch 1950
29 The theft of the iron dogs 1950
30 Relative to poison 1950
31 Death before dinner 1950
32 Part of a p;oisoner 1951
33 Still waters 1951
34 Policemen in the precinct 1951
35 Accident by design 1952
36 Murder of a martinet 1952
37 The dog it was that died 1953
38 Murder in the millrace 1953
39 Crook o'Lune 1953
40 Shroud of darkness 1954
41 Ask for a policeman 1955
42 Murder in Vienna 1956
43 Dangerous domicile 1957
44 Murder on a monument 1958
45 Death in triplicate 1959
46 Dishonour among thieves 1960

LORRIMER, C.
1 Mavreen 1977
2 Tamarisk 1978
3 Chantal 1980

LORRIMER, C.
ROCHFORD TRILOGY
1 The Chatelaine 1981
2 The wilderling 1982
3 Fool's curtain 1994

LOUVISH, S.
AVRAM BLOK
1 The therapy of Avram Blok 1985
2 City of Blok 1988
3 The last trump of Avram Blok
1990

LOVELL, M.
APPLETON PORTER
1 The spy game 1981
2 The spy with his head in the
clouds 1982

LOVESEY, P.
DETECTIVE MEMOIRS OF KING
EDWARD VII
1 Bertie and the tin man 1987
2 Bertie and the seven bodies 1990
3 Bertie and the crime of passion
1993

LOVESEY, P.
PETER DIAMOND
1 The last detective 1991
2 Diamond solitaire 1992

LOVESEY, P.
SERGEANT CRIBB & CONSTABLE
THACKERAY
1 Wobble to death 1969
2 The detective wore silk drawers
1971
3 Abracadaver 1972
4 Mad hatter's holiday 1973
5 Invitation to a dynamite party
1974
6 A case of spirits 1975
7 Swing, swing together 1976
8 Waxwork 1978

LOW, O.
ARVO LAURILA
1 To his just deserts 1986
2 Murky shallows 1987

LUDLUM, R.
BOURNE
1 The bourne identity 1980

2 The Bourne supremacy 1986
3 The Bourne ultimatum 1990

LUDLUM, R.
THE HAWK
1 The road to Gandolfo 1976
2 The road to Omaha 1992

LUMLEY, B.
NECROSCOPE
1 Necroscope
2 Wamphyri
3 The source
4 Deadspeak
5 Deadspawn
Paperback horror stories

LUMLEY, B.
TALES OF THE PRIMAL LAND
1 The house of Cthulu
2 Tarra Khash throssak
3 Sorcery in Shad

LUSTBADER, E.
CHINA MAROC
1 Jian 1985
2 Shan 1987

LUSTBADER, E.
NICHOLAS LINNEAR
1 The Ninja 1980
2 The Miko 1984
3 White Ninja 1990
4 The Kaisho 1993
5 Floating city 1994

LUSTBADER, E.
SUNSET WARRIOR
1 The sunset warrior 1979
2 Shallows of night 1980
3 Dai-San 1980
4 Beneath an opal moon 1981

LUTYENS, M.
RUSKIN,MILLAIS AND EFFIE GRAY
1 Effie in Venice 1965
2 Millais and the Ruskins 1967
3 The Ruskins and the Grays 1972
N.F. Based on contemporary letters

LUTZ, G.
NAZI PARATROOPER
1 Storm Belgium
2 Crete must fall
3 Cassino corpse factory

LUTZ, G.
PANZER PLATOON
1 Invade Russia

2 Blood and ice
3 Blitzkrieg
4 Support Rommel
5 Death ride
6 Attack Anzio

LUTZ, J.
FRED CARVER
1 Tropical heat 1986
2 Scorcher 1988
3 Kiss 1989
4 Flame 1990
5 Blood fire 1991

LYALL, F.
SUPT.MASON
1 A death in time 1987
2 Death and the remembrancer 1988
3 The croaking of the raven 1990
4 Death in the winter garden 1993

LYALL, G.
1 The wrong side of the sky 1961
2 The most dangerous game 1964

LYALL, G.
HARRY MAXIM
1 The secret servant 1980
2 The conduct of Major Maxim 1982
3 The crocus list 1985
4 Uncle Target 1988

LYNN, E. A.
CHRONICLES OF TORNOR
1 Watchtower
2 The dancers of Arun
3 The Northern girl
Paperback fantasy

LYONS, A.
JACOB ASCH
1 The dead are discreet 1977
2 All God's children 1977
3 The killing floor 1977
4 Dead ringer 1983
5 Castles burning 1983
6 Hard trade 1984
7 Three with a bullet 1987
8 Other people's money 1990
9 Fast fade 1990

LYONS, G.
1 Slievelea 1985
2 The green years 1987

LYTTLETON, H.
1 I play as I please 1954
2 Secord chorus 1958

3 Take it from the top 1975
N.F. Autobiography

MACAVOY, R. A.
DAMIANO TRILOGY
1 Damiano
2 Damiano's lute
3 Raphael
Paperback fantasy

MACAVOY, R. A.
NAZURHET OF SORDALING
1 Lens of the heart 1992
2 King of the dead 1992
3 Winter of the wolf 1993

MACCOLLUM, M,
1 Antares passage 1989
2 Antares dawn 1989

MACDONALD, D.
TOMMY BRIGGS
1 Briggs investigates 1968
2 No judge's rules 1969
3 The organiser 1970
4 The Ryan affair 1970
5 Two kinds of murder 1971
6 Two bullets for Briggs 1971

MACDONALD, F. J.
1 Crowdie and cream 1982
2 Crotal and white 1983
N.F. Autobiography

MACDONALD, M.
STEVENSON FAMILY
1 The world from rough stones 1975
2 The rich are with you always 1977
3 Sons of fortune 1978
4 Abigail 1979

MACDONALD, PETER
BEN HART
1 The hope of glory 1980
2 Wide horizons 1980
3 One way street 1981
4 Exit 1983
5 Dead end 1986
Novels about the British Army after WW2

MACDONALD, ROSS
LEW ARCHER
1 The moving target 1949
2 The three roads 1950
3 The way some people die 1953
4 The ivory grin 1953

5 The drowning pool 1955
6 Experience with evil 1955
7 Find a victim 1955
8 The barbarous coast 1957
9 The doomsters 1958
10 The Galton case 1960
11 The Ferguson affair 1961
12 The Wycherly woman 1962
13 The chill 1963
14 The zebra striped hearse 1963
15 The far side of the dollar 1964
16 Black money 1966
17 Instant enemy 1967
18 The goodbye look 1968
19 The undergrou
20 Sleeping beauty 1973
21 The blue hammer 1976

MACENROE, R. S.
FAR STARS AND FUTURE TIMES
1 The shattered stars
2 Flight of honour
3 Skinner
Paperback science fiction

MACGOWAN, R.
SHANE MACKENZIE
1 Monopoly to murder
2 Barracuda

MACGREGOR, A. A.
1 Auld Reekie 1943
2 Vanished waters 1942
3 The goat wife 1939
4 Turbulent years 1945
5 Go not, happy day 1956
6 The golden lamp 1964
7 Land of the mountain and the flood 1965
N.F. Autobiography

MACINNES, C.
LONDON SERIES
1 City of spades 1957
2 Absolute beginners 1958
3 Mr.Love and justice 1960

MACINNES, H.
ROBERT RENWICK
1 The hidden target 1981
2 The cloak of darkness 1982

MACINTYRE, L.
CHRONICLES OF INVERNEVIS
1 Cruel in the shadow 1979
2 The blind bend 1981

MACKAY, AMANDA
1 Death is academic 1976

2 Death on the river 1983

MACKEN, W.
MACMAHON FAMILY
1 Seek the fair land 1960
2 The silent people 1962
3 The scorching wind 1964

MACKENZIE, DONALD
RAVEN
1 Raven in flight 1976
2 Raven and the ratcatcher 1976
3 Raven and the Kamikaze 1977
4 Deep,dark and dead 1977
5 Raven settles a score 1978
6 Raven feathers his nest 1979
7 Raven and the paper-hangers 1980
8 Raven's revenge 1982
9 Raven's longest night 1984
10 Raven's shadow 1985
11 Nobody here by that name 1986
12 A savage state of grace 1988
13 By any illegal means 1990
14 Loose cannon 1991
15 The eyes of the goat 1992
16 The sixth deadly sin 1993

MACKENZIE, LEE
EMMERDALE FARM
1 The legacy
2 Prodigal's progress
3 All that a man has
4 Lover's meeting
5 A sad and happy summer
6 A sense of responsibility
7 Nothing stays the same
8 The couple at Demdyke Row
9 Whispers of scandal
10 Shadows from the past
11 Lucky for some
12 Face value
13 Good neighbours
14 Innocent victim
15 False witness
16 The homecoming
17 Old flames
18 New beginnings
19 Family feuds
20 Young passions
21 Another door opens 1986
22 A friend in need, by James Ferguson
23 Divided loyalties, by James Ferguson
24 Wives and lovers, by J.Ferguson
Based on the TV series. Farm

MACKENZIE, SIR C.
HIGHLAND SERIES
1 Monarch of the glen 1951
2 Keep the Home Guard turning 1945
3 Whisky galore 1947
4 Hunting for fairies 1949
5 The rival monster 1952
6 Ben Nevis goes east 1954
7 Rockets galore 1957
8 The stolen soprano 1965

MACKENZIE, SIR C.
OLIVER HUFFNAM
1 The red tapeworm 1958
2 Paper lives 1966

MACKINNON, C.
A SCOTTISH CHRONICLE
1 A house at war 1973
2 The years beyond 1974
3 To whom the glory 1975
4 The house remains 1977

MACKINTOSH, I.
TIM BLACKGROVE
1 A slaying in September 1970
2 The drug called power 1971
3 The brave cannot yield 1973

MACKINTOSH, I.
WARSHIP
1 Warship 1973
2 HMS Hero 1976
3 Holt,RN 1977

MACKINTOSH, J. T.
AMBROSE & DOMINIQUE
1 Take a pair of private eyes 1969
2 A coat of blackmail 1970

MACKINTOSH, M.
LAURIE GRANT
1 Appointment in Andalucia 1971
2 A king and two queens 1973
3 The Sicilian affair 1974

MACLAINE, SHIRLEY
1 Don't fall off the mountain 1972
2 You can get there from here 1975
3 Out on a limb 1983
4 Dancing in the light 1985
5 It's all in the playing 1987
6 Going within 1989
   N.F. *Autobiography and personal philosophy*

MACLAUGHLIN, W. R. D.
1 Antarctic raider 1961

2 So thin the line 1963
   N.F. *The whaling fleet during WW2*

MACLEAN, A.
1 The guns of Navarone 1957
2 Force ten from Navarone 1968

MACLEOD, A.
TOM VAUGHAN
1 The trusted servant 1966
2 No need of the sun 1969

MACLEOD, C.
PETER SHANDY
1 Rest you merry 1980
2 The luck runs out 1981
3 Wrack and rune 1982
4 Something the cat dragged in 1984
5 The corpse in Oozak's pond 1986
6 Vane pursuit 1989
7 An owl too many 1991
8 Something in the water 1994
   Thrillers set in an American agricultural college

MACLEOD, C.
SARAH KELLING
1 The family vault 1980
2 The withdrawing room 1981
3 The palace guard 1982
4 The Bilbao looking glass 1983
5 The convivial codfish 1984
6 The plain old man 1985
7 The recycled citizen 1987
8 The silver ghost 1987
9 The Gladstone bag 1989
10 The resurrection man 1992

MACLEOD, R.
ANDREW LAIRD
1 All other perils 1974
2 Dragonship 1976
3 Salvage job 1978
4 Cargo risk 1980
5 Mayday from Malaga 1983
6 A cut in diamonds 1985
7 Witchline 1988

MACLEOD, R.
JONATHAN GAUNT
1 A witch dance in Bavaria 1975
2 A pay-off in Switzerland 1977
3 Incident in Iceland 1979
4 A problem in Prague 1981
5 A property in Cyprus 1970
6 A killing in Malta 1972
7 A burial in Portugal 1973
8 A legacy from Tenerife 1984
9 The money mountain 1987

10 Spanish maze game 1990

MACLEOD, R.
TALOS CORD
1 Drum of power 1965
2 Cave of bats 1966
3 Lake of fury 1967
4 Isle of dragons 1968
5 Place of mists 1969
6 Path of ghosts 1970
7 Nest of vultures 1973

MACMILLAN, H.
1 The winds of change, 1914-1939 1966
2 The blast of war,1939-1945 1967
3 The tides of fortune, 1945-1955 1969
4 Riding the storm, 1955-1959 1970
5 Pointing the way, 1959-1961 1972
6 At the end of the day 1973
N.F. Autobiography

MACNAGHTEN, P.
1 The car that Jack built 1964
2 The right line 1966

MACVICAR, A.
1 Silver in my sporran 1980
2 Salt in my porridge 1972
3 Heather in my ears 1974
4 Rocks in my scotch 1976
5 Bees in my bonnet 1982
6 Golf in my gallowses 1983
7 Gremlins in my garden 1985
8 Capers in the Kirk 1987
N.F.Autobiography

MACVICAR, A.
BRUCE MCLINTOCK
1 The golden Venus affair 1972
2 The painted doll affair 1973

MAGUIRE, M.
SIMON DRAKE
1 Shot silk 1975
2 Slaughter horse 1975
3 Scratchproof 1976

MAHFOUZ, N.
CAIRO TRILOGY
1 Palace walk 1990
2 Palace of desire 1991
3 Sugar Street 1992

MAIMAN, J.
ROBIN MILLER
1 I left my heart
2 Crazy for love

3 Under my skin 1994
Feminist private eye stories.

MAINE, C. E.
MIKE DELANEY
1 The isotope man 1962
2 Subterfuge 1963
3 Never let up 1964

MAIR, G. B.
DAVID GRANT
1 Death's foot forward 1963
2 Miss Turquoise 1964
3 Live, love and cry 1965
4 Kisses from Satan 1966
5 The girl from Peking 1967
6 Black champagne 1968
7 Godesses never die 1969
8 A wreath of camellias 1970
9 Crimson jade 1971
10 Paradise spells danger 1972

MAISKY, I.
1 Before the storm 1944
2 Journey into the past 1960
3 Who helped Hitler? 1962
4 Spanish notebooks 1962
N.F. Autobiography

MALCOLM, A.
DAUGHTERS OF CAMERON
1 The taming 1982
2 Ride out the storm 1982

MALCOLM, J.
TIM SIMPSON
1 A back room in Somers Town 1983
2 The Godwin sideboard 1984
3 The Gwen John sculpture 1985
4 Whistler in the dark 1986
5 Gothic pursuit 1987
6 Mortal ruin 1987
7 The wrong impression 1989
8 Sheep,goats and soap 1991
9 A deceptive appearance 1992
10 The burning ground 1993
11 Hung over 1994

MALET, L.
NESTOR BURMA
1 120, Rue de la Gare
2 The rats of Montsouris
3 Sunrise behind the Louvre
4 Mayhem in the Marais
5 Fog on the Tolbiac Bridge
Originally published in France in the 1950s under the series title 'Les nouveaux mysteres de Paris'

MALING, A.
BROCK POTTER
1 Schroeder's game 1977
2 Lucky devil 1978
3 The Rheingold route 1979
4 The Koberg link 1980
5 A taste of treason 1983

MALLOCH, P.
DAVE NORTON
1 Blood on pale fingers 1969
2 The slugger 1971

MALLOY, L.
MARTIN MOON
1 JoJo and the private eye 1980
2 The happiest ghost in town 1981
3 Beware the yellow Packard 1982
4 So help me Hannah 1982
5 The bullet proof toga 1984

MALONE, M.
CUDDY MANGUM
1 Uncivil seasons 1983
2 Handling sin 1986
3 Time's witness 1989

MALPASS, E.
PENTECOST FAMKILY
1 Morning's at seven 1966
2 At the height of the moon 1967
3 Fortinbras has escaped 1970
4 Oh, my darling daughter 1973

MALPASS, E.
WILLIAM SHAKESPEARE
1 Sweet Will 1972
2 The Cleopatra boy 1974
3 House of women 1975

MANDLSTAM, N.
1 Hope against hope 1971
2 Hope abandoned 1973
N.F. Autobiography

MANN, J.
TAMARA HOYLAND
1 Funeral sites 1981
2 No man's island 1983
3 Grave goods 1984
4 A kind of healthy grave 1986
5 Death beyond the Nile 1988
6 Faith, hope and homicide 1991

MANN, P.
LAND FIT FOR HEROES
1 Escape to the wild wood 1993
2 Stand alone Stan 1994

MANN, P.
THE STORY OF THE GARDENER
1 Master of Paxwax 1986
2 The fall of the families 1987

MANNERS, A.
THE ISLAND
1 Echoing yesterday
2 Karran Kinrade 1986
3 The red bird 1987
No. 1 in paperback only

MANNING, O.
BALKAN TRILOGY
1 The great fortune 1960
2 The spoilt city 1962
3 Friends and heroes 1964

MANNING, O.
LEVANT TRILOGY
1 The danger tree 1977
2 The battle lost and won 1978
3 The sum of things 1980

MANNING, V.
1 Falcon Queen 1974
2 Fertility Queen 1975

MANTEL, H.
1 Every day is Mother's Day 1985
2 Vacant possession 1986

MANTELL, L.
STEVEN ARROW
1 Murder in fancy dress 1978
2 A murder or three 1980
3 Murder and chips 1981
4 Murder to burn 1983
5 Murder in vain 1984
Thrillers set in New Zealand

MARCUS, D.
1 A land not theirs 1986
2 A land in flames 1987
Novels about Ireland

MARCUS, J. [LUCILLA ANDREWS]
1 A few days in Endel 1979
2 Marsh blood 1980

MARLEY, S.
1 Spirit mirror
2 Dark mask
3 Shadow sisters 1993
Fantasies set in ancient China.

MARLOW, J.
WHITWORTH FAMILY
1 Kessie 1985

2 Sarah 1988
3 Anne 1989

MARLOWE, P.
FRANK DRURY
1 Loaded dice 1960
2 The double thirteen 1961
3 The dead don't scare 1963
4 The man in her death 1964
5 Promise to kill 1965
6 A knife in your heart 1966
7 Hire me a hearse 1968
8 Cash my chips, croupier 1969

MARLOWE, S.
CHESTER DRUM
1 The second longest night 1966
2 Trouble is my name 1967
3 Danger is my line 1968

MARON, M.
LT. SIGRID HAROLD
1 One coffee with 1988
2 Death of a butterfly 1988
3 Death in blue folders 1989

MARQUEZ, G. G.
1 One hundred years of solitude 1968
2 No one writes to the Colonel 1970

MARQUIS, M.
DET.INSPECTOR HARRY TIMBERLAKE
1 Vengeance 1992
2 Elimination 1993

MARQUIS, M.
GENERAL HOSPITAL
1 The caretakers 1976
2 A matter of life 1977

MARSH, J.
RAY FELTON
1 Murderer's maze 1957
2 Operation snatch 1958
3 City of fear 1958
4 Small and deadly 1960

MARSH, J.
SIMON LUCK
1 The relectant executioner 1959
2 Girl in the net 1962

MARSH, N.
INSPECTOR ALLEYN
1 A man lay dead 1934
2 Enter a murderer 1935
3 The Nursing Home murder 1936
4 Death in ecstasy 1937

5 Vintage murder 1937
6 Artists in crime 1938
7 Death kin a white tie 1938
8 Overture to death 1939
9 Death at the bar 1940
10 Death and the dancing footman 1942
11 Died in the wool 1945
12 Surfeit of lampreys 1941
13 Colour scheme 1943
14 Final curtain 1947
15 Swing brother swing 1948
16 Opening night 1951
17 Spinsters in jeopardy 1953
18 Scales of justice 1954
19 Off with his head 1957
20 Singing in the shrouds 1959
21 False scent 1960
22 Hand in glove 1962
23 Dead water 1964
24 Death at the Dolphin 1967
25 A cluster of Constables 1968
26 When in Rome 1970
27 Tied up in tinsel 1972
28 Black as he's painted 1974
29 Last ditch 1977
30 Grave mistake 1978
31 Photo finish 1980
32 Light thickens 1982

MARSHALL, A.
1 I can jump puddles
2 This is the grass
3 In mine own heart
N.F. *Autobiography*

MARSHALL, B.
1 The bishop 1970
2 Urban the Ninth 1972
3 Marx the First 1975
4 Peter the Second 1976

MARSHALL, L.
SUGAR KANE
1 Sugar for the lady 1955
2 Sugar on the target 1958
3 Sugar cuts the corners 1958
4 Sugar on the carpet 1959
5 Sugar on the cuff 1960
6 Sugar on the kill 1961
7 Sugar on the loose 1962
8 Sugar on the prowl 1963
9 Ladies can be dangerous 1964
10 Murder is the reason 1964
11 Death strikes in the darkness 1965
12 The dead are silent 1966
13 The dead are dangerous 1967
14 Murder of a lady 1968
15 Blood on the blotter 1968

16 Money means murder 1969
17 Death is for ever 1969
18 Murder's out of season 1970
19 Murder's just for cops 1971
20 Death casts a shadow 1972
21 Moment of murder 1973
22 Loose lady death 1973

MARSHALL, S.
1 A nest of magpies 1993
2 Sharp through the hawthorn 1994
Novels about village life in Norfolk.

MARSHALL, W. L.
1 The age of death 1968
2 The middle kingdom 1971

MARSHALL, W. L.
MANILA BAY MYSTERIES
1 Manila Bay 1896
2 Whisper 1988

MARSHALL, W. L.
YELLOWTHREAD STREET
1 Yellowthread Street 1975
2 The hatchet man 1976
3 Gelignite 1976
4 Thin air 1977
5 Skulduggery 1979
6 Sci Fi 1981
7 Perfect end 1981
8 War machines 1982
9 The faraway man 1984
10 Roadshow 1985
11 Head first 1986
12 Frogmouth 1987
13

MARSTON, E.
NICHOLAS BRACEWELL
1 The Queen's Head 1988
2 The merry devils 1989
3 The trip to Jerusalem 1990
4 The nine giants 1991
5 The mad courtesan 1992
Mysteries set in Elizabethan times

MARTIN, K.
1 Father figures, 1879-1931 1966
2 Editor, 1931-1945 1968
N.F. Autobiography

MARTIN, L.
DEB RALSTON
1 Too sane a murder 1987
2 A conspiracy of strangers 1988
3 Murder at the Blue Owl 1989

MARTIN, R.
1 Gallows wedding 1978
2 The unicorn summer 1984
*Not direct sequels, but two of the
same characters appear*

MARTIN, S.
PROFESSOR CHALLIS
1 Twelve girls in a garden 1957
2 The man made of tin 1958
3 The Saracen shadow 1957
4 The myth is murder 1959

MARVIN, J. W.
CROW
1 The red hills
2 Worse than death
3 Tears of blood
4 The black trail
5 Bodyguard
6 The sisters
7 One-eyed death
8 A good day
Paperback Westerns

MASON, F. VAN W.
AMERICAN CIVIL WAR
1 Proud new flags 1954
2 Blue hurricane 1956
3 To whom be glory 1957

MASON, F. VAN W.
COLONEL NORTH
1 The Vesper service murders
2 The branded spy murders
3 The yellow arrow murders
4 The Budapest parade murders
5 The seven seas murders
6 The Sulu sea murders
7 The Fort Terror murders
8 The Shanghai bund murders
9 The Washington Legation murders
10 The Hong Kong air base murders
11 The Singapore exile murders
12 The Cairo garter murders
13 The Bucharest ballerina murders
14 The forgotten fleet mystery
15 The Rio Casino intrigue
16 The Dardanelles derelict
17 The Saigon singer
18 The Himalayan assignment
19 Two tickets to Tangiers 1955
20 The gracious lily affair 1958
21 Secret mission to Bangkok 1960
22 Trouble in Burma 1961
23 The Zanzibar intrigue 1964
24 The Maracaibo mission 1966
25 The deadly orbit mission 1968

MASON, H.
SPENCER FAMILY
1 Fool's gold 1961
2 Our hills cry woe 1963

MASSIE, A.
1 The last peacock 1981
2 These enchanted woods 1993

MASSIE, A.
THE EMPERORS
1 Caesar 1993
2 Augustus 1986
3 Tiberius 1990

MASTERS, A.
MARIUS LARCHE
1 Murder is a long time coming 1991
2 Confessional 1993
3 Death's door 1994

MASTERS, A.
MINDER
1 Minder 1984
2 Minder - back again 1985
3 Minder - yet again 1986
Based on the TV series

MASTERS, J.
1 Bugles and a tiger 1959
2 The road past Mandalay 1961
3 Pilgrim son 1972
N.F. Autobiography

MASTERS, J.
LOSS OF EDEN
1 Now God be thanked 1979
2 Heart of war 1980
3 By the green of the spring 1981

MASTERS, J.
SAVAGE FAMILY
1 Coromandel(Jason Savage,1622-1640) 1955
2 The deceivers(William Savage,18th century) 1952
3 Nightrunners of Bengal(Rodney Savage 1,1857) 1951
4 The lotus and the wind(Robin Savage,1879-81) 1953
5 Far,far the mountain peak(PeterSavage,1902-21)1957
6 Bhowani Junction(Rodney Savage II,1945) 1954
7 To the coral strand(Rodney Savage II,1945-50)1962

MASTERTON, G.
1 The Manitou 1976
2 Revenge of the Manitou 1984

MASUR, H. Q.
SCOTT JORDAN
1 Suddenly a corpse 1950
2 You can't live forever 1951
3 So rich, so lovely and so dead 1953
4 The big money 1955
5 Tall, dark and deadly 1957
6 The last breath 1958
7 Send another hearse 1960
8 Bury me deep 1961
9 The name is Jordan 1962
10 Making a killing 1964
11 The legacy lenders 1967

MATHER, B.
ROBINSON FAMILY
1 Through the mill
2 Left foot forward

MATHER, BERKELEY
JAMES WAINWRIGHT & ISWAL REES
1 The pass beyond Kashmir 1964
2 The springers 1968
3 The break in the line 1970
4 The terminators 1971

MATHER, BERKELEY
STAFFORD FAMILY
1 The pagoda tree 1979
2 The midnight gun 1981
3 Hour of the dog 1982

MATHER, L.
JO HUGHES
1 Blood of an Aries 1993
2 Beware Taurus 1994

MATHESON, H.
GEOFFREY BRANSCOMBE
1 The third force 1960
2 The balance of fear 1961

MATHEW, D.
1 Mango on the mango tree 1950
2 In Valambrosa 1951
3 Prince of Wales' feathers 1953

MATTHEW, C.
SIMON CRISP
1 Diary of a somebody 1978
2 Loosely engaged 1980
3 The crisp report 1981
4 Family matters 1986

MATTHEWS, P.
CASEY FARRELL
1 Scent of fear 1992
2 Vision of death 1993
3 Taste of evil 1993

MAUGHAN, A. M.
1 Young Pitt 1976
2 The King's malady 1978

MAUPIN, A.
1 Tales of the city 1978
2 More of the city 1980
3 Further tales of the city 1982
4 Babycakes 1986
5 Significant others 1988
6 Sure of you 1990
First three published as an omnibus vol. in 1989

MAXWELL, G.
1 The house of Elrig (1914-30) 1965
2 Harpoon at a venture (1945-48) 1952
3 Ring of bright water (1948-59) 1960
4 A reed shaken by the wind (1956) 1957
5 The rocks remain (1960-61) 1963
6 Raven seek thy brother (1961-68) 1968
7 The white island, by J.L.Kaye (1968-69) 1972
N.F. Autobiography. 7 covers the last months of Maxwell's life.

MAY, J.
GALACTIC MILIEU
1 Jack the Bodiless 1992
2 Diamond mask 1994

MAY, J.
THE EXILES
1 The many coloured land
2 The golden torc
3 The non-born king
4 The adversary
Paperback fantasy

MAY, J.
TRILLIUM
1 Black trillium 1991
2 Blood trillium 1992

MAYNARD, K.
LIEUT. LAMB
1 Lieutenant Lamb 1984
2 First Lieutenant 1985
3 Lamb in command 1986

4 Lamb's mixed fortunes 1987
Novels about the Royal Navy in the 18thC

MAYNARD, N.
1 This is my street 1971
2 A crumb for every sparrow 1974

MAYNARD, N.
SCARLETT SISTERS
1 Wayward flesh 1974
2 A grief ago 1976

MAYO, J.
CHARLES HOOD
1 Hammerhead 1964
2 Let sleeping girls lie 1965
3 Shame, lady 1966
4 Once in a lifetime 1968
5 The man above suspicion 1969
6 Asking for it 1971

MAYO, J. K.
HARRY SEDDALL
1 The hunting season 1985
2 Wolf's head 1987
3 Cry havoc 1990
4 A shred of honour 1993

MAYOR, A.
JOE GUNTHER
1 Open season 1989
2 Borderline 1991
3 Scent of evil 1993
4 The skeleton's knee 1994

MAYS, S.
1 Reuben's corner 1969
2 Fall out the officers 1970
3 No more soldiering for me 1971
4 Last post 1973
5 The band rats 1976
6 Return to Anglia 1986
N.F. Autobiography

MAZZETTI, L.
1 The sky falls 1963
2 Rage 1964

MCBAIN, E.
MATTHEW HOPE
1 Goldilocks 1978
2 Rumpelstiltskin 1981
3 Beauty and the beast 1982
4 Jack and the beanstalk 1984
5 Snow white and rose red 1985
6 Cinderella 1986
7 Puss in Boots 1987
8 The house that Jack built 1988

9 Three blind mice 1991
10 Mary, Mary 1992
11 There was a little girl 1994

MCBAIN, E.
THE 87TH PRECINCT
1 Cop hater 1956
2 The mugger 1956
3 The pusher 1956
4 The con man 1957
5 Killer's choice 1958
6 Killer's payoff 1958
7 Lady killer 1958
8 Killer's wedge 1959
9 'Til death 1959
10 King's ransom 1959
11 Give the boys a great big hand 1960
12 The heckler 1961
13 See them die 1961
14 Lady,lady I did it 1961
15 The empty hou
16 Like love 1962
17 Ten plus one 1963
18 Axe 1964
19 He who hesitates 1964
20 Doll 1965
21 Eighty million eyes 1966
22 Fuzz 1968
23 Shotgun 1969
24 Jigsaw 1970
25 Hail,hail the gang's all here 1971
26 Sadie when she died 1972
27 Let's hear it for the deaf man 1972
28 Hail to the chief 1973
29 Bread 1974
30 Blood relatives 1975
31 So long as you both shall live 1976
32 Long time no see 1977
33 Calypso 1979
34 Ghosts 1980
35 Heat 1981
36 Ice 1983
37 Lightning 1984
38 Eight black horses 1985
39 Poison 1987
40 Tricks 1987
41 McBain's ladies:women of the 87th Precinct 1988
42 Lullaby 1989
43 McBain's ladies,too 1990
44 Vespers 1990
45 Widows 1991
46 Kiss 1992
47 Mischief 1993

MCCAFFREY, A.
CRYSTAL
1 Crystalsinger 1982

2 Killashandra 1986
3 Crystal line 1992

MCCAFFREY, A.
DINOSAUR PLANET
1 Dinosaur planet 1992
2 Survivors 1992

MCCAFFREY, A.
PERN
1 Dragonflight 1971
2 Dragonquest 1973
3 Dragonsong 1974
4 Dragonsinger 1977
5 The white dragon 1979
6 Dragondrums 1979
7 Moreta, dragonlady of Pern 1983
8 Dragonsdawn 1988
9 The renegades of Pern 1990
10 All the weyrs of Pern 1991
11 First fall 1993
12 The dolphins of Pern 1994

MCCAFFREY, A.
THE SHIP
1 The ship who sang (with M.Lackey) 1993
2 The ship who searched (with M.Lackey) 1994
3 Partnership (with M.Ball) 1994

MCCAFFREY, A.
THE TOWER AND HIVE
1 The rowan 1990
2 Damia 1992
3 Damia's children 1993
4 Lyon's pride 1994

MCCAFFREY, A. & MOON, E.
PLANET PIRATES
1 Sassinak 1991
2 The death of sleep 1991
3 Generation warriors 1992

MCCAFFREY, A. & NYE, J. L.
DOONA
1 Crisis on Doona 1993
2 Treaty planet 1994

MCCARRY, C.
PAUL CHRISTOPHER
1 The Miernik dossier 1974
2 Tears of autumn 1975
3 Secret lovers 1977
4 The better angels 1979
5 The last supper 1983
6 Second sight 1991

MCCARTHY, C.
BORDER TRILOGY
1 All the pretty horses 1993
2 The crossing 1994

MCCARTY, D.
THLASSA MEY
1 Flight to Thlassa Mey
2 Warriors of Thlassa Mey
3 Lords of Thlassa Mey
4 Across the Thlassa Mey

MCCAUGHREN, T.
1 Run with the wind 1983
2 Run to earth 1984

MCCLOY, H.
BASIL WILLING
1 Design for dying 1938
2 The man in the moonlight 1940
3 The deadly truth 1940
4 Who's calling 1942
5 Cue for murder 1942
6 The goblin market 1943
7 The one that got away 1956
8 Through a glass, darkly 1957
9 Alias Basil Willing
10 The long body 1957
11 Two thirds of a ghost 1957
12 Mr.Splitfoot 1969
13 Burn this 1980

MCCLURE, J.
LIEUT.KRAMER & SGT.ZONDI
1 The steam pig 1970
2 The caterpillar cop 1972
3 Four and twenty virgins 1973
4 The gooseberry fool 1974
5 Snake 1976
6 Killers 1976
7 The Sunday hangmen 1977
8 The blood of an Emglishman 1980
9 The artful egg 1984
10 The song dog 1992
*Thrillers about the South African
police force*

MCCRUMB, S.
ELIZABETH MCPHERSON
1 The Windsor knot 1990
2 Paying the piper 1991
3 Sick of shadows 1992
4 Highland laddie gone 1993
5 Lovely in her bones 1993
6 Missing Susan
7 McPherson's lament 1992
6 & 7 not published in UK

MCCULLOUGH, C.
1 First man in Rome 1990
2 The grass crown 1991
3 Fortune's favourites 1993

MCCUTCHAN, P.
CAMERON
1 Cameron, Ordinary Seaman 1979
2 Cameron comes through 1980
3 Cameron of the 'Castle Bay' 1981
4 Lt.Cameron, RNVR 1981
5 Cameron's convoy 1982
6 Cameron in the gap 1982
7 Orders for Cameron 1983
8 Cameron in command 1983
9 Cameron and the Kaiserhof 1984
10 Cameron's raid 1985
11 Cameron's chase 1986
12 Cameron's troop lift 1987
13 Cameron's commitment 1988
14 Cameron's crossing 1993

MCCUTCHAN, P.
COMMANDER SHAW
1 Gibraltar Road 1960
2 Redcap 1961
3 Bluebolt one 1961
4 The man from Moscow 1962
5 Warmaster 1963
6 The Moscow coach 1964
7 Deadline 1965
8 Skyprobe 1966
9 The screaming red balloons 1968
10 The bright red businessmen 1969
11 The all-purpose bodies 1969
12 Hartinger's mouse 1970
13 This Drakotny... 1971
14 Sunstrike 1979
15 Corpse 1980
16 Werewolf 1982
17 Rollerball 1984
18 Greenfly 1987
19 The boy who liked monsters 1989
20 The spatchcock plan 1990
21 Polecat Brennan 1994

MCCUTCHAN, P.
JOHN MASON KEMP
1 The convoy Commodore 1986
2 Convoy north 1987
3 Convoy south 1988
4 Convoy east 1989
5 Convoy of fear 1990
6 Convoy homeward 1992

MCCUTCHAN, P.
LIEUT. HALFHYDE
1 Beware,beware the Bight of Benin
1974

2 Halfhyde's island 1975
3 The guns of arrest 1976
4 Halfhyde to the narrows 1977
5 Halfhyde for the Queen 1978
6 Halfhyde ordered south 1979
7 Halfhyde and the Flag Captain 1980
8 Halfhyde on the Yangtze 1981
9 Halfhyde on Zanatu 1982
10 Halfhyde outward bound 1983
11 The Halfhyde line 1984
12 Halfhyde and the chain-gang 1985
13 Halfhyde goes to war 1986
14 Halfhyde on the Amazon 1987
15 Halfhyde and the Admiral 1990
16 Halfhyde and the Fleet Review 1991

MCCUTCHAN, P.
SIMON SHARD
1 Call for Simon Shard 1973
2 A very big bang 1975
3 Blood runs East 1976
4 The Eros affair 1977
5 Blackmail north 1979
6 Shard calls the tune 1980
7 The hoof 1983
8 Shard at bay 1985
9 The executioners 1986
10 Overnight express 1988
11 The Logan file 1991
12 The Abbot of Stockbridge 1992

MCCUTCHEON, H.
ANTONY HOWARD
1 The angel of light 1951
2 Cover her face 1955

MCCUTCHEON, H.
JIMMY CARROLL
1 Treasure of the sun 1964
2 Black attendant 1965
3 Scorpion's nest 1967
4 Hot wind from hell 1968
5 Something wicked 1970

MCCUTCHEON, H.
RICHARD LOGAN
1 To dusty death 1962
2 Suddenly in Vienna 1963

MCDERMID, V.
KATE BRANNIGAN
1 Dead beat 1992
2 Kick back 1993
3 Crack down 1994

MCDERMID, V.
LINDSAY GORDON
1 Report for murder 1987
2 Common murder 1989
3 Final edition 1991
4 Union Jack 1993

MCDONALD, GREGORY
FLETCH
1 Fletch,too 1987
2 Fletch won 1985
3 Fletch and the Widow Bradley 1981
4 Fletch 1975
5 Confess,Fletch 1977
6 Fletch's fortune 1979
7 Fletch's Moxie 1983
8 Fletch and the man who 1984
9 Fletch forever 1978
10 Carioca Fletch 1984
11 Son of Fletch 1994
   Listed in chronological order

MCDONALD, GREGORY
INSPECTOR FLYNN
1 Flynn 1976
2 Snatched 1980
3 The buck passes Flynn 1982
4 Flynn's Inn 1985
   Flynn also appears in some of the Fletch series

MCDONALD, J. D.
TRAVIS MCGEE
1 The deep blue goodbye 1965
2 Nightmare in pink 1966
3 A purple place for dying 1966
4 The quick red fox 1967
5 A deadly shade of gold 1967
6 Bright orange for the shroud 1967
7 Darker than amber 1968
8 One fearful yellow eye 1968
9 Pale grey for guilt 1969
10 The girl in the pale brown wrapper 1969
11 Dress her in indigo 1971
12 Flash of green 1972
13 The long lavender look 1972
14 A tan and sandy silence 1973
15 McGee 1974
16 The scarlet ruse 1975
17 The turquoise lament 1975
18 The dreadful lemon sky 1976
19 Dead low tide 1976
20 Murder for the bride 1977
21 You live once 1978
22 The empty copper sea 1979
23 The green ripper 1980
24 Free fall in crimson 1982

25 Cinnamon skin 1982
26 The lonely silver rain 1985

MCDONELL, J. E.
JIM BRADY
1 Jim Brady, leading seaman 1954
2 Commander Brady 1956
3 Subsmash 1960

MCDOWELL, C.
CONSTANCE CASTELFRANCO
1 A woman of style 1992
2 A woman of spirit 1993

MCGIRR, E.
PIRON
1 The funeral was in Spain 1966
2 Here lies my wife 1967
3 A hearse with horses 1967
4 The lead lined coffin 1968
5 An entry of death 1969
6 Death pays the wages 1970
7 No better fiend 1971
8 Bardel's murder 1973
9 A murderous journey 1974

MCGIRT, D.
JASON COSMO
1 Jason Cosmo
2 Royal chaos
3 Dirty work
Humorous fantasy

MCGOWN, J.
INSPECTOR LLOYD & SGT.HILL
1 A perfect match 1983
2 Redemption 1988
3 Death of a dancer 1989
4 The murders of Mrs.Austin and
  Mrs.Beale 1991
5 The other woman 1992
6 Murder...now and then 1993

MCGREGOR, B.
1 The Liffey runs black 1978
2 The uncertain trumpet 1980

MCHUGH, A.
1 A banner with a strange device
  1964
2 The seacoast of Bohemia 1965

MCILVANNEY, W.
LAIDLAW
1 Laidlaw 1980
2 The papers of Tony Veitch 1983
3 Strange loyalties 1991

MCINERNY, R.
FATHER DOWLING
1 Her death of cold 1977
2 The seventh station 1978
3 Bishop as pawn 1979
4 Lying there 1980
5 Second Vespers 1981
6 Thicker than water 1982
7 Getting a way with murder 1987
8 Sleight of body 1989
9 The Judas priest 1991
10 The basket case 1992
11 Getting away with murder 1992
12 Desert sinner 1994

MCINNES, G.
1 The road to Gundagai 1965
2 Humping my bluey 1966
3 Finding a father 1967
4 Goodbye Melbourne town 1968
  N.F. Autobiography

MCKEOWN, J.
1 Back crack boy
2 Liam at large
  *Paperback novels about Liverpool in
  the 1930s*

MCKIE, C.
STEWARTS OF BADENOCH
1 The wolf 1978
2 Mariota 1981
3 Blood of the wolf 1980

MCKILLIP, P. A.
CHRONICLES OF MORGAN,PRINCE OF
HED
1 Riddlemaster of Hed 1979
2 Heir of sea and fire 1979
3 Harpist in the wind 1979

MCKILLIP, P. A.
CYGNET
1 The sorceress and the cygnet
2 The cygnet and the firebird

MCKINLAY, M.
JOHN LEITH
1 Double entry 1991
2 Legacy 1992
3 The caring game 1993

MCKINNEY, J.
ROBOTECH
1 Genesis
2 Battle cry
3 Homecoming
4 Battlehymn
5 Force of arms

6 Doomsday
7 Southern cross
8 Metal fire
9 The final nightmare
10 Invid invasion
11 Metamorphosis
12 Symphony of light
Paperback s. f.

MCKINNEY, J.
SENTINELS
1 The devil's hand
2 Dark powers
3 Death dance
4 World killers
5 Rubicon
Paperback s. f.

MCKINNEY, J.
THE BLACK HOLE TRAVEL AGENCY
1 Event horizon
2 Artifact of the system
3 Free radicals
4 Hostile takeover
Paperback fantasy

MCLAGLEN, J.
HERNE THE HUNTER
1 White death
2 River of blood
3 Black widow
4 Shadow of the vulture
5 Apache squaw
6 Blood ties
7 Death rites
8 Cross draw
9 Massacre
10 Vigilante
11 Silver threads
12 Sundance
13 Billy the Kid
14 Death school
15 Till death
16 Geronimo
17 The hanging
18 Dying ways
19 Blood line
20 Hearts of gold
21 Pony Express
Paperback Westerns

MCLEAVE, H.
BRODIE AND SHANE
1 A borderline case 1979
2 Double exposure 1980
3 The Icarus threat 1984
4 Under the icefall 1987

MCLEAVE, H.
GREG MACLEAN
1 Second time around 1984
2 Death masque 1985

MCMASTER, T.
WHITE APACHE
1 Hangman's knot
2 Warpath
3 Warrior born
Paperback westerns.

MCMILLAN, J.
1 The way we were, 1900-1914 1978
2 The way it was, 1914-1934 1979
3 The way it happened,1935-1950 1980
N.F. Social history

MCMULLEN, J.
1 My small country living 1984
2 The wind in the ashtree 1988
3 A small country living goes ever on 1990
N.F. Autobiography of a smallholder in Wales

MCMURTRY, L.
1 The last picture show 1966
2 Texasville 1987

MCMURTRY, L.
AURORA GREENWAY
1 Terms of endearment 1977
2 The evening star 1992

MCMURTRY, L.
LONESOME DOVE
1 Lonesome dove 1986
2 Streets of Laredo 1993

MCMURTRY, LARRY
1 All my friends are going to be strangers
2 Some can whistle 1990

MCNAB, C.
CAROL ASHTON
1 The Shipley report 1990
2 Death down under 1991

MCNALLY, C.
GHOST HOUSE
1 The ghost house 1979
2 The ghost house revenge 1987
Horror stories

MCNAMARA, J. D.
1 The first directive

2 Fatal command 1988

MCNEIL, D.
JAMES OGILVIE
1 Drums along the Khyber 1968
2 Lieutenant of the line 1970
3 Sadhu of the mountain peak 1971
4 The gates of Kunarja 1972
5 The red Daniel 1973
6 Subaltern's choice 1974
7 By command of the Viceroy 1975
8 Mullah from Kashmir 1976
9 Wolf in the fold 1977
10 No charge of cowardice 1978
11 Restless frontier 1979
12 Cunningham's revenge 1980
13 The train at Bundabar 1981
14 A matter for the Regiment 1982

MCPHERSON, W.
1 Testing the current 1986
2 To the Sargasso Sea 1988
*Not strictly sequels, but some
characters appear in both books.*

MEACHAM, E. K.
CAPT.PERCIVAL MEREWETHER
1 The East Indiaman 1969
2 On the Company's service 1972
3 For King and Company 1977

MEADE, R.
JOHN ALLISON
1 Beyond the Danube 1967
2 One round high explosive 1969

MEADOWS, R.
1 The show must go on 1969
2 A bouquet of brides 1970
3 Pretty maids all in a row 1971
4 Slander most savage 1973

MECK, G. VON
1 As I remember them 1973
2 The alien years 1976
N.F. Autobiography

MEEK, M. R. D.
LENNOX KEMP
1 Hang the consequences 1983
2 The sitting ducks 1984
3 The split second 1985
4 In remembrance of Rose 1986
5 A worm of doubt 1987
6 A mouthful of sand 1988
7 A loose connection 1989
8 This blessed plot 1990
9 Touch and go 1992

MEHTA, V.
CONTINENTS OF EXILE
1 Daddiji 1977
2 Mamaji 1979
3 Vedi 1983
4 The ledge between the streams 1984
5 Sound shadows of the New World 1986
6 The stolen light 1989
7 Up at Oxford 1993
N.F. Autobiography of an Indian

MELLY, G.
1 Scouse mouse 1984
2 Rum,bum and concertina 1977
3 Owning up 1965
N.F. Autobiography, in chronological order

MELVILLE, A.
LORIMER SAGA
1 The Lorimer line 1977
2 Lorimer legacy 1979
3 Lorimers at war 1980
4 Lorimers in love 1981
5 The last of the Lorimers 1983
6 Lorimer loyalties 1984

MELVILLE, A.
THE HOUSE OF HARDIE
1 The House of Hardie 1987
2 Grace Hardie 1988
3 The Hardie inheritance 1990

MELVILLE, JAMES
SUPT.OTANI
1 The wages of Zen 1978
2 The chrysanthemum chain 1980
3 A sort of Samurai 1981
4 The ninth netsuke 1982
5 Sayonara.sweet Amaryllis 1983
6 Death of a Diamyo 1984
7 The death ceremony 1985
8 Go gently Gaijin 1986
9 Kimono for a corpse 1987
10 The reluctant ronin 1988
11 A Haiku for Hanae 1989
12 Bogus Buddha 1990
13 The body wore brocade 1992

MELVILLE, JENNIE
CHARMIAN DANIELS
1 Come home and be killed 1962
2 Burning is a substitute for loving 1963
3 Murderers' houses 1964
4 There lies your love 1965
5 Nell alone 1966

6 A different kind of summer 1967
7 A new kind of killer, an old kind of death 1970
8 Murder wears a pretty face 1981
9 Windsor red 1987
10 A cure for dying 1989
11 Witching murder 1990
12 Footsteps in the blood 1990
13 Dead set 1992
14 Whoever has the heart 1993
15 Baby drop 1994

MELVILLE-ROSS, A.
HARDING
1 Shadow 1984
2 Trigger 1983
3 Talon 1983
4 Command 1985
Novels about submarines in WW2.

MELVILLE-ROSS, A.
TRELAWNEY
1 Blindfold 1977
2 The two faces of Nemesis 1979
3 Tightrope 1981

MENZIES, SIR R.
1 Afternoon light 1967
2 Measure of the years 1970
N.F. Autobiography

MEREDITH, R. C.
TIMELINE TRILOGY
1 At the narrow passage
2 No brother, no friend
3 Vestiges of time
Paperback science fiction

METALIOUS, G.
PEYTON PLACE
1 Peyton Place
2 Return to Peyton Place
3 Again Peyton Place
4 Carnival at Peyton Place
5 Pleasures of Peyton Place

MEYNELL, L. W.
HOOKY HEFFERMAN
1 Death by arrangement 1972
2 The fatal flaw 1973
3 The thirteen trumpeters 1973
4 The fairly innocent little man 1974
5 Don't stop for Hooky Hefferman 1975
6 Hooky and the crock of gold 1975
7 The lost half-hour 1976
8 Hooky gets the wooden spoon 1977

9 Hooky and the villainous chauffeur 1979
10 Hooky and the prancing horse 1980
11 Hooky goes to blazes 1981
12 The open door 1984
13 The affair at Barwold 1985
14 Hooky catches a tartar 1986
15 Hooky on loan 1987
16 Hooky hooked 1988

MEYRICK, B.
PEMBROKESHIRE FAMILY
1 Behind the stream 1973
2 Behind the light 1975

MICHAEL, S.
CHARLES HOLROYD
1 The cut throat 1991
2 The long lie 1992

MICHAELS, B.
GREYHAVEN MANOR
1 Black rainbow 1982
2 Someone in the house 1981

MICHAELS, F.
SINS
1 Sins of the flesh 1993
2 Sins of omission 1994

MICHAELS, F.
TEXAS
1 Texas rich 1988
2 Texas heat 1989
3 Texas fury 1991
4 Texas sunrise 1993

MICHAELS, F.
THE CAPTIVE
1 Captive passions 1992
2 Captive embraces 1993
3 Captive slendours 1994
Bodice rippers.

MILES, K.
ALAN SAXON
1 Bullet hole 1986
2 Double eagle 1987
3 Green murder 1990
4 Flagstick 1991

MILES, R.
EDEN
1 Bitter legacy 1985
2 Return to Eden 1986

MILLAR, M.
TOM ARAGON
1 Ask for me tomorrow 1976
2 The murder of Miranda 1979
3 Mermaid 1982

MILLER, H.
MACBAIN FAMILY
1 The open city 1973
2 Kingpin 1974

MILLER, HUGH
DET.INSPECTOR MIKE FLETCHER
1 Echo of justice 1990
2 Skin deep 1991

MILLER, HUGH
DISTRICT NURSE
1 The District Nurse 1986
2 Snow on the wind 1987
Based on the TV series.

MILLER, HUGH
EASTENDERS
1 Home fires burning 1986
2 Swings and roundabouts 1986
3 Good intentions 1986
4 The flower of Albert Square 1986
5 Blind spots 1986
6 Hopes and horizons 1987
7 The baffled heart 1987
8 Growing wild 1987
9 A place in life 1988
10 A single man 1988
11 Taking chances 1988
12 Elbow room 1988
Novels about the early lives of
characters in the TV series.

MILLER, J.
CALLAGHAN BROTHERS
1 Gone to Texas 1984
2 War clouds 1984
3 Comanche trail 1988
4 Riding shotgun 1988

MILLHISER, M.
CHARLIE GREENE
1 Murder at Moot Point 1992
2 Death of the office witch 1993

MILLIGAN, S.
1 Adolf Hitler:my part in his
  downfall 1971
2 Rommel? Gunner who? 1973
3 Monty: his part in my victory 1976
4 Mussolini: his part in my downfall
  1978

5 Where have all the bullets gone
  1985
6 Goodbye soldier 1986
N.F. Humorous war memoirs

MILNE, C.
1 The enchanted places 1979
2 The path through the trees 1980
3 The hollow hill 1982
N.F. Autobiography of the original
Christopher Robin.

MILNE, J.
JIMMY JENNER
1 Dead birds 1986
2 Shadow play 1987
3 Daddy's girl 1988

MILNE, S.
DET.SERGEANT STEYTLER
1 The hammer of justice 1963
2 False witness 1964

MILSTED, D.
1 The chronicles of Craigfieth 1988
2 Market forces 1989

MINTON, M.
1 Yesterday's road 1986
2 The marriage bowl 1987
3 The weeping doves 1987
Novels about a Midlands family

MISHIMA, YUKIO
THE SEA OF FERTILITY
1 Spring snow 1971
2 Runaway horses 1973
3 The temple of dawn 1974
4 The decay of the angel 1975

MITCHELL, G.
DAME BEATRICE BRADLEY
1 Speedy death 1929
2 Mystery of a butcher's shop 1931
3 The longer bodies
4 The Saltmarsh murders
5 Death at the opera
6 The devil at Saxon Wall
7 Dead men's morris 1936
8 Come away death 1937
9 St. Peter's finger 1938
10 Printer's error 1939
11 Brazen tongue 1940
12 Hangman's curfew 1940
13 When last I died 1941
14 The greenstone griffins 1983
15 Laurels are poison 1942
16 The worsted viper 1942
17 Sunset over Soho 1943

18 My father sleeps 1944
19 The rising of the moon 1945
20 Here comes a chopper 1946
21 Death and the maiden 1947
22 The dancing druids 1948
23 Tom Brown's body 1949
24 Groaning spinney 1950
25 The devil's elbow 1951
26 The echoing strangers 1952
27 Merlin's furlong 1953
28 Faintley speaking 1954
29 Watson's choice 1955
30 Twelve horses and the hangman's noose 1956
31 The twentythird man 1957
32 Spotted hemlock 1958
33 The man who grew tomatoes 1959
34 Say it with flowers 1960
35 The nodding canaries 1961
36 My bones will keep 1962
37 Adders on the heath 1963
38 Death of a delft blue 1964
39 Pageant of murder 1965
40 The croaking raven 1966
41 Skeleton island 1966
42 Three quick and five dead 1968
43 Dance to your daddy 1969
44 Gory dew 1970
45 Lament for Leto 1971
46 A hearse on Mayday 1972
47 The murder of busy Lizzie 1973
48 A javelin for Jonah 1973
49 Winking at the brim 1974
50 Convent on Styx 1975
51 Late, late in the evening 1976
52 Fault in the structure 1977
53 Noonday and night 1977
54 Wraiths and changelings 1978
55 Mingled with venom 1978
56 Nest of vipers 1979
57 The mudflats of the dead 1979
58 Uncoffined clay 1980
59 The whispering knights 1980
60 The death-cap dancers 1981
61 Here lies Gloria Mundy 1982
62 Death of a burrowing mole 1982
63 Cold, lone and still 1983
64 The hangman's noose 1983
65 No winding sheet 1984
66 The Crozier pharaohs 1984 *Dame Beatrice is assisted by Laura Gavin after 14*

MITCHELL, J.
CALLAN
1 A magnum for Schneider 1969
2 Venus in plastic 1970
3 Red file for Callan 1971
4 Russian roulette 1973

5 Death and bright water 1974

MITCHELL, J.
JOE CAVE
1 Dead Ernest 1986
2 KGB kill 1987
3 Dying day 1988

MITCHELL, J.
RON HOGGET
1 Sometimes you could die 1985
2 Dead Ernest 1986

MITCHELL, J.
WHEN THE BOAT COMES IN
1 When the boat comes in 1976
2 The hungry years 1976
3 Upward and onward 1977

MITCHELL, JAMES
1 A woman to be loved 1990
2 An impossible woman 1992

MITCHELL, JOHN
MORRIS SIMPSON'S DIARIES
1 Class struggle
2 Chalked off
3 Absolutely chalked off
4 Chalk's away! 1993
Paperback humour

MITCHELL, K.
CHIEF INSPECTOR JOHN MORRISSEY
1 A lively form of death 1990
2 In stony places 1991
3 A strange desire 1993

MITCHELL, M.
1 Gone with the wind 1936
2 Scarlett, by Alexandra Ripley 1991

MITCHELL, S.
BROCK DEVLIN
1 Some dames play rough 1963
2 Sables spell trouble 1963
3 Deadly persuasion 1964
4 The lovely shroud 1965
5 Come sweet death 1965
6 Double bluff 1966
7 A knife-edged thing 1969
8 You'll never get to heaven 1971
9 Haven for the damned 1971
10 Rage in Babylon 1972
11 The girl in the wet look bikini 1973
12 Dead on arrival 1974
13 Nice guys don't win 1974
14 Over my dead body 1974
15 Death's busy crossroads 1975

16 Obsession 1976

MITCHISON, N.
1 Small talk 1973
2 All change here 1975
3 You may well ask 1981
N.F. Autobiography

MITTELHOLZER, E.
KAYWANA
1 Children of Kaywana 1953
2 Kaywana heritage 1956
3 Kaywana blood 1957
4 Kaywana stock 1958

MOBERG, V.
1 The emigrants 1955
2 Unto a good land 1959
3 The last letter home 1961

MOBERG, V.
THE EARTH IS OURS
1 Memory of youth
2 Sleepless nights
3 The earth is ours

MODESITT, L. E.
THE FOREVER HERO
1 Down from a distant earth
2 The silent warrior
3 The endless twilight

MODESSIT, L. E.
1 The magic of Recluse
2 The towers of the sunset
Paperback fantasy

MOFFAT, G.
1 Space below my feet 1961
2 On my home ground 1968
3 Survival count 1972
*N.F. Autobiography and
mountaineering*

MOFFAT, G.
JACK PHARAOH
1 Pit bull 1991
2 The outside edge 1993

MOFFAT, G.
MISS PINK
1 Lady with a cool eye 1973
2 Deviant death 1974
3 The corpse road 1975
4 Miss Pink at the edge of the world 1975
5 Hard option 1976
6 Over the sea to death 1976
7 A short time to live 1977

8 Persons unknown 1978
9 Die like a dog 1982
10 Last chance country 1983
11 Grizzly trail 1984
12 Snare 1987
13 The stone hawk 1989
14 Rage 1990
15 Raptor zone 1990
16 Veronica's sisters 1992

MOLE, W.
CASSON DUKER
1 The Hammersmith maggot 1955
2 Goodbye is not worthwhile 1956
3 Skin trap 1957

MOLL, L.
1 Seidman and son 1958
2 Mr.Seidman and the geisha 1963

MOLLOY, M.
THE GAZETTE MYSTERIES
1 Sweet sixteen 1992
2 Cat's paw 1993
3 Home before dark 1994

MONACO, R.
ARTHURIAN LEGEND
1 The Grail war
2 Parsifal
3 The final quest
Paperback

MONIG, C.
BRIAN BRETT
1 The burned man 1957
2 Abra-Cadaver 1958
3 Once upon a crime 1960
4 The lonely graves 1961

MONK, C.
1 A field of bright laughter 1990
2 Flame of courage 1992

MONSARRAT, N.
1 The tribe that lost its head 1956
2 Richer than all his tribe 1968

MONSARRAT, N.
LIFE IS A FOUR LETTER WORD
1 Breaking in 1966
2 Breaking out 1970
N.F. Autobiography

MONSARRAT, N.
THE MASTER MARINER
1 Running proud 1978
2 Darken ship 1980

MONTROSE, G.
ANGEL BROWN
1 Angel of no mercy
2 Angel of death 1964
3 Where Angels tread 1966
4 Angel abroad 1967
5 Angel of vengeance 1967
6 Angel in Paradise 1968
7 Send for Angel 1969
8 Ask for Angel 1970
9 Angel and the Nero 1971
10 Fanfare for Angel 1972
11 Angel at arms 1972
12 Angel and the red admiral 1973

MOODY, L.
TUDOR TRILOGY
1 The dark-eyed client 1974
2 The golden princess 1976
3 The greatest Tudor 1977

MOODY, S.
CASSIE SWANN
1 Takeout double 1993
2 Grand slam 1994

MOODY, S.
PENNY WANAWAKE
1 Penny black 1983
2 Penny dreadful 1984
3 Penny post 1985
4 Penny royal 1986
5 Penny wise 1988
6 Penny pinching 1989
7 Penny saving 1991

MOON, E.
THE DEAD OF PAKESNARRION
1 Sheepfarmer's daughter
2 Divided allegiance
3 Oath of gold
Published as 1 vol. under the series title 1993

MOORCOCK, M.
1 Byzantium endures 1981
2 Laughter at Carthage 1986

MOORCOCK, M.
CORUM
1 The Knight of the swords
2 The Queen of the swords
3 The King of the swords
4 The bull and the spear
5 The oak and the ram
6 The sword and the stallion

MOORCOCK, M.
DANCERS AT THE END OF TIME
1 Alien heat 1974
2 The hollow lands 1975
3 The end of all songs 1976
4 Legends from the end of time 1976
5 The transformation of Miss Mavis Ming 1977

MOORCOCK, M.
ELRIC
1 Elric of Melnibone 1972
2 Sailor on the seas of fate 1976
3 The weird of the white wolf
4 The vanishing tower
5 The bane of the black sword
6 Stormbringer
7 Elric at the end of time:short stories
8 The fortress of the pearl 1989
9 The revenge of the rose 1991

MOORCOCK, M.
HAWKMOON
1 The jewel in the skull 1973
2 The mad god
3 The sword of dawn 1973
4 The runestaff 1974
5 Count Brass
6 The champion of Garathorm
7 The quest for Tanelorn
The last three are in paperback

MOORCOCK, M.
JERRY CORNELIUS
1 The final programme 1969
2 A cure for cancer 1970
3 The English assassin 1972
4 The life and times of Jerry Cornelius 1975
5 The condition of Muzak 1976
6 The entropy tango 1981
Jerry Cornelius also appears in Una Persson and Catherine Cornelius in the 20th century

MOORCOCK, M.
JOHN DAKER, ETERNAL CHAMPION OF EREKOSE
1 The eternal champion
2 Phoenix in Obsidian
3 The dragon in the sword 1987

MOORCOCK, M.
KARL GLOGAUER
1 Behold the man 1970
2 Breakfast in the ruins 1972

MOORCOCK, M.
MICHAEL KANE
1 The city of the beast
2 The lord of the spiders
3 Masters of the pit

MOORCOCK, M.
OSWALD BASTABLE
1 War lord of the air 1973
2 The land leviathan 1974
3 The steel Tsar 1981

MOORCOCK, M.
PYAT
1 Byzantium endures 1981
2 Laughter at Carthage 1986
3 Jerusalem commands 1992

MOORCOCK, M.
VON BEK FAMILY
1 The war hound and the world's pain 1982
2 The city in the autumn stars 1986

MOORE, G.
1 Am I too loud? 1962
2 Farewell recital 1978
3 Furthermoore 1983
N.F. *Autobiography of the celebrated accompanist*

MOORE, M.
DET.INSPECTOR RICHARD BAXTER
1 Forests of the night 1988
2 Dangerous conceits 1989
3 Murder in good measure 1990
4 Fringe ending 1991

MOORE, R.
1 The French connection 1971
2 The fifth estate 1973
3 French connection II 1976
4 The terminal connection 1978
5 The New York connection 1979

MOORE, R.
PULSAR
1 The London connection 1980
2 The Italian connection 1981

MORAY, H.
1 The harvest burns 1972
2 Blood on the wind 1973

MORAY, H.
ALEXANDER THE GREAT
1 I,Roxana 1969
2 Roxana and Alexander 1970
3 A son for Roxana 1971

MORAY, H.
DEAN BROTHERS
1 Clear to sail 1974
2 The Ruby fleet 1976

MORAY, H.
HENRI,LADY RHONDA
1 Four winds 1983
2 Before the dawn 1984

MORAY, H.
VAN RIEBECK FAMILY
1 Untamed 1966
2 The savage earth 1968
3 Footsteps in the night 1975
4 To make a light 1977
5 Beacon of gold 1978

MORGAN, C.
LILY WALTERS
1 Lily of the valleys 1989
2 Lily among thorns 1990
3 Comfort me with apples 1991

MORGAN, D.
RALPH DE GIRET
1 The second son 1980
2 The Kingmaker's knight 1981
3 Sons and roses 1981

MORGAN, G.
1 A small piece of Paradise 1966
2 A touch of magic 1968
3 A window of sky 1969

MORGAN, R.
CODY WALLACE
1 Tall dead wives 1990
2 Low mean men 1992

MORICE, A.
TESSA CRICHTON
1 Death in the grand manor 1970
2 Murder in married life 1970
3 Death of a gay dog 1971
4 Murder on French leave 1972
5 Death and the dutiful daughter 1973
6 Death of a heavenly twin 1974
7 Killing with kindness 1974
8 Nursery tea and poison 1975
9 death of a wedding guest 1976
10 Murder in mimicry 1977
11 Scared to death 1977
12 Murder by proxy 1978
13 Murder in outline 1978
14 Death in the round 1980
15 The men in her death 1981
16 Hollow vengeance 1982

17 Sleep of death 1982
18 Murder post-dated 1983
19 Getting away with murder 1984
20 Dead on cue 1985
21 Publish and be killed 1986
22 Treble exposure 1987
23 Design for dying 1988
24 Fatal charm 1988
25 Planning for murder 1990
The main character is the wife of Chief Insp. Price

MORLAND, N.
ANDY MCMURDO
1 She didn't like dying 1948
2 No coupons for a shroud 1949
3 Two dead charwomen 1950
4 The corpse was no lady 1950
5 Blood on the stars 1951
6 He hanged his mother on Monday 1951
7 The moon was made for murder 1953

MORLAND, N.
MRS.PYM
1 The moon murders 1935
2 The phantom gunman 1935
3 Street of the leopard 1936
4 The clue of the bricklayer's aunt 1936
5 The clue in the mirror 1937
6 The case without a clue 1938
7 A rope for the hanging 1938
8 A knife for the killer 1938
9 A gun for a god 1940
10 The clue of the careless hangman 1940
11 A corpse on the flying trapeze 1941
12 A coffin for the body 1943
13 Dressed to kill 1947
14 The lady had a gun 1951
15 Call him early for the murder 1952
16 Sing a song of cyanide 1953
17 Look in any doorway 1957
18 Death and the golden boy 1958
19 A bullet for Midas 1958
20 So quiet a death 1960
21 The concrete maze 1960
22 The dear dead girls 1961
23 Mrs.Pym and other stories 1976

MORRELL, D.
ISRAEL SAUL GRISMAN
1 The Brotherhood of the Rose 1985
2 The Fraternity of the Stone 1986
3 The League of Night and Fog 1987

MORRELL, D.
RAMBO
1 First blood 1975
2 First blood II
3 Rambo III
2 and 3 based on the films which arose from 1

MORRELL, LADY O.
1 Ottoline 1963
2 Ottoline at Garsington 1974
N.F. Autobiography

MORRIS, E.
1 Flowers of Hiroshima 1962
2 Seeds of Hiroshima 1965

MORRIS, G. H.
THE BRIGHTSIDE TRILOGY
1 Doves and silk handkerchiefs 1986
2 Grandmother, grandmother, come and see 1989
3 The Brightside dinosaur 1991

MORRIS, I. J.
1 A kingdom for a song 1951
2 The witch's son 1954

MORRIS, J.
THE KERRION SAGA
1 Dream dancer
2 Cruiser dreams
Paperback fantasy

MORRIS, JAN
1 Heaven's command:an Imperial progress 1973
2 Pax Britannica 1972
3 Farewell the trumpets 1978
N.F. A history of the British Empire

MORRIS, JOHN
COMMISSIONER ROBIN MACKAY OF JAMAICA
1 Fever grass 1967
2 The Candywine development 1970

MORRIS, W.
SCANLON FAMILY
1 The field of vision 1966
2 Ceremony in Lone Tree 1960

MORTIMER, J.
RUMPOLE
1 Rumpole of the Bailey 1978
2 The trials of Rumpole 1979
3 Rumpole's return 1980
4 Regina v Rumpole 1981

5 Rumpole and the golden thread 1983
6 Rumpole's last case 1987
7 Rumpole and the age of miracles 1988
8 Rumpole a la carte 1990
9 Rumpole on trial 1992
10 The best of Rumpole 1993
1 & 2 published in hardback as 'Rumpole'

MORTIMER, J.
THE RAPSTONE CHRONICLES
1 Paradise postponed 1987
2 Titmuss regained 1990

MORTIMER, P.
1 About time 1979
2 About time,too 1993
N.F. Autobiography

MORWOOD, P.
ALDRIC TALVARIN
1 The horse lord 1984
2 The demon lord 1985
3 The dragon lord 1987
4 The warlord's domain 1989
Fantasy

MORWOOD, P.
CLAN WARS
1 Greylady 1993
2 Widowmaker 1994

MORWOOD, P.
PRINCE IVAN
1 Prince Ivan 1990
2 Firebird 1992
3 The golden horde 1993

MOSCO, M.
1 Almonds and raisins 1979
2 Scattered seed 1980
3 Children's children 1981
4 Out of the ashes 1989
5 New beginnings 1991
Novels about a Jewish family in Manchester

MOSCO, M.
ALISON PLANTAINE
1 Between two worlds 1983
2 A sense of place 1984
3 The price of fame 1985

MOSCO, M. .
1 The waiting game 1987
2 After the dream 1988

MOSLEY, N.
1 Catastrophe practice 1979
2 Imago bird 1980
3 Serpent 1981
4 Judith 1986
5 Hopeful monsters 1990

MOSLEY, W.
EASY RAWLINS
1 Devil in a blue dress 1992
2 A red death 1993
3 Black Betty 1994

MOTION, A.
FRANCIS MAYNE
1 The pale companion 1989
2 Famous for the creatures 1991

MOTLEY, M.
1 Devils in waiting 1959
2 Morning glory 1961
3 Home to Nurmidia 1963
N.F. Autobiography

MOTTRAM, R. H.
LIFE OBSERVED
1 The window seat 1954
2 Another window seat 1956
N.F. Autobiography

MOYES, P.
CHIEF INSPECTOR HENRY TIBBETT
1 Dead men don't ski 1960
2 The sunken sailor 1961
3 Death on the agenda 1962
4 Murder a la mode 1963
5 Falling star 1964
6 Johnny underground 1965
7 Murder fantastical 1967
8 Death and the Dutch uncle 1968
9 Who saw him die? 1970
10 Season of snows and sins 1971
11 The black widower 1975
12 To kill a coconut 1976
13 Who is Simon Warwick? 1978
14 Angel death 1980
15 A six-letter word for death 1983
16 Night ferry to death 1985
17 Black girl, white girl 1990
18 Twice in a blue moon 1993

MUGGERIDGE, M.
CHRONICLES OF WASTED TIME
1 The green stick 1972
2 The infernal grove 1973
N.F. Autobiography

MUIR, J. A.
BREED
1 Lonely hunt
2 Silent kill
3 Cry for vengeance
4 Death stage
5 Gallows tree
6 Judas goat
7 Time of the wolf
8 Blood debt
9 Bloodstock
10 Outlaws road
11 The dying and the damned
12 Killer's moon
13 Bounty hunter
14 Spanish gold
15 Slaughter time
16 Bad habits
17 The day of the gun
18 The colour of death
19 Blood valley
20 Gundown
Paperback Westerns

MUIR, T.
ROGER CRAMMOND
1 Death in reserve 1948
2 Death in the trooper 1949
3 Death in the lock 1949
4 Death without question 1951
5 Death below zero 1951
6 Death under Virgo 1952
7 Death on the agenda 1953
8 Death in Soundings 1955

MULLALLY, F.
BOB SULLIVAN
1 Danse macabre 1967
2 The Munich involvement 1968
3 The Malta conspiracy 1971

MULLER, M.
ANNA & JOHANN DE VILLIERS
1 Green peaches ripen 1969
2 Cloud across the moon 1970
3 Stones of Africa 1972

MULLER, M.
SHARON MCCONE
1 Edwin of the iron shoes 1981
2 Ask the cards a question 1983
3 The Cheshire Cat's eye 1984
4 Games to keep the dark away 1985
5 Trophies and dead things 1990
6 Where echoes live 1991
7 There's something in a Sunday 1992
8 The shape of dread 1992

9 Pennies on a dead woman's eyes 1993
10 Wolf in the shadows 1994

MUNNINGS, SIR A.
1 An artist's life 1950
2 Second burst 1951
3 The finish 1953
N.F. Autobiography

MUNRO, H.
CLUTHA
1 Who told Clutha? 1958
2 Clutha plays a hunch 1959
3 A clue for Clutha 1960
4 Clutha and the lady 1966
5 Get Clutha 1974
6 Evil innocence 1976
7 The brain robbers 1977

MUNRO, J.
JOHN CRAIG
1 The man who sold death 1964
2 Die rich, die happy 1965
3 The money that money can't buy 1967
4 The innocent bystanders 1968

MURARI, T. N.
KIM
1 The Imperial agent 1987
2 The last victory 1988
Sequels to Kipling's 'Kim'

MURDOCH, M. S.
THE MARTIAN WARS
1 Rebellion 2456
2 Hammer of Mars
3 Armageddon off Vesta
Paperback science fiction

MURPHY, E.
1 The land is bright 1989
2 To give and to take 1990
3 There is a season 1991

MURPHY, H.
REUBEN FROST
1 Murder for lunch 1986
2 Murder takes a partner 1987
3 Murders and acquisitions 1988
4 Murder keeps a secret 1989
5 Murder times two 1990
6 Murder saves face 1991
7 A very Venetian murder 1994

MURPHY-GIBB, D.
CORMAC
1 The seers 1992

2 The king making 1993

MURRAY, MARY
1 Escape 1965
2 Hunted 1967
N.F. Autobiography and wartime experiences

MURRAY, S.
DET. INSPECTOR ALEC STAINTON
1 A cool killing 1988
2 The noose of time 1989
3 Salty waters 1989
4 Fetch out no shroud 1990
5 Fatal opinions 1991
6 Offences against the person 1993
7 Death and transfiguration 1994

MURRAY, W. H.
JOHN TAUNT
1 Five frontiers 1959
2 The spurs of Troodos 1960

MUSIL, R.
A MAN WITHOUT QUALITIES
1 A sort of introduction 1953
2 The like of it now happens 1954
3 Into the millennium 1960

MYERS, A.
AUGUSTE DIDIER
1 Murder in Pug's Parlour 1986
2 Murder in the limelight 1987
3 Murder at Plum's 1989
4 Murder at the masque 1991
5 Murder makes an entree 1992
6 Murder under the kissing bough 1992
7 Murder in the smoke house 1994

MYERS, P.
MARK HOLLAND
1 Deadly variations 1985
2 Deadly cadenza 1986
3 Deadly aria 1987
4 Deadly sonata 1987
5 Deadly score 1988
6 Deadly crescendo 1989
Thrillers about a musician

MYKLE, A.
1 Lasso round the moon 1959
2 The song of the red ruby 1961

MYRIVILLIS, S.
1 The mermaid madonna
2 The schoolmistress with the golden eyes

NABB, M.
MARSHAL GUARNACCIA
1 Death of an Englishman 1981
2 Death of a Dutchman 1982
3 Death in Springtime 1983
4 Death in Autumn 1984
5 The Marshal and the murderer 1987
6 The Marshal and the madwoman 1988
7 The Marshal's own case 1990
8 The Marshal makes his report 1991
9 The Marshal at the Villa Torrini 1993
Detective stories set in Florence

NAJAFI, M.
1 Persia is my heart 1956
2 Reveille for a Persian village 1959
3 A wall and three willows 1961
N.F. Autobiography

NAPIER, P.
1 The sword dance 1970
2 A difficult country 1972
3 Revolution and the Napier brothers 1973
N.F. Family history

NARAYAN, R. K.
MALGUDI
1 Waiting for the Mahatma 1955
2 The financial expert 1952
3 Mr.Sampath 1949
4 The English teacher 1945
5 The dark room 1938
6 Swami and friends 1935
7 The guide 1958
8 The man-eater of Malgudi 1961
9 The sweet vendor 1967
10 A horse and two goats 1970
11 Malgudi days 1982
12 The tiger of Malgudi 1983
13 Under the banyan tree 1985
14 The talkative man 1986
15 The world of Nagaraj 1990

NASH, P.
GRASS
1 Grass 1982
2 Grass's fancy 1982
3 Coup de Grass 1983
4 Grass in idleness 1983
5 Wayward seeds of Grass 1983
6 Grass and supergrass 1984
7 Grass makes hay 1985
8 Sheep grass 1986
Thrillers about a police informer

NASH, S.
INSPECTOR MONTERO & ADAM
LUDLOW
1 Dead of a counterplot 1961
2 Killed by scandal 1962
3 Death over deep water 1962
4 Dead woman's ditch 1964
5 Unhallowed murder 1965

NATHANSON, E. M.
1 The dirty dozen 1966
2 A dirty distant war 1988

NAUGHTON, B.
1 On the pig's back 1987
2 Saintly Billy 1988
  N.F. Autobiography

NAUGHTON, B.
ALFIE
1 Alfie 1968
2 Alfie darling 1970

NAYLOR, G.
RED DWARF
1 Red Dwarf 1989
2 Better than life 1990
  Based on the TV series

NEAME, A.
1 The adventures of Maud Noakes
  1963
2 Maud Noakes, guerrilla 1965

NEAVE, A.
1 They have their exits 1964
2 Saturday at M19 1969
  N.F. Wartime experiences

NEEL, J.
DET. CHIEF INSPECTOR JOHN
MCLEISH
1 Death's bright angel 1988
2 Death on site 1989
3 Death of a partner 1991
4 Death among the dons 1993

NEILL, R.
SIR HARRY BURNABY
1 Crown and mitre 1971
2 The golden days 1972
3 Lillibulero 1975

NEUMAN, F.
CAPT. REDDER,PSYCHIATRIST
1 The seclusion room 1982
2 Manoeuvres 1984

NEVILLE, M.
INSPECTOR GROGAN
1 Murder and gardenias 1946
2 Murder in Rockwater 1949
3 Murder of a nymph 1949
4 Murder in a blue moon 1949
5 Murder before marriage 1951
6 Come thick night 1951
7 The seagull said murder 1952
8 Murder of the well-beloved 1953
9 Murder of Olympia 1958
10 Murder to welcome her 1959
11 Sweet night to murder her 1959
12 Confession of murder 1960
13 Murder beyond the pale 1961
14 My bad boy 1964
15 Ladies in the dark 1965
16 Head on the sill 1966

NEW AVENGERS
1 House of cards, by P.Cave
2 Eagle's nest, by J.Carter
3 Fighting men,by J.Cartwright
4 To catch a rat, by W.Harris
5 The last of the Cybernauts, by
  P.Cave
6 Hostage, by P.Cave

NEWBY, P. H.
1 A picnic at Sakkara 1955
2 Revolution and roses 1957
3 A guest and his going 1959

NEWMAN, A.
1 A bouquet of barbed wire 1969
2 Another bouquet... 1984

NEWMAN, A.
FELIX CRAMER
1 A sense of guilt 1985
2 A gift of poison 1991

NEWMAN, G. F.
1 Sir, you bastard 1971
2 You nice bastard 1972
3 You flash bastard 1977

NEWMAN, G. F.
JACK BENTHAM
1 Set a thief 1985
2 The testing ground 1987

NEWMAN, G. F.
LAW AND ORDER
1 A prisoner's tale 1981
2 A detective's tale 1981
3 A villain's tale 1981

NEWMAN, S.
ARTHURIAN SERIES
1 Guinevere 1985
2 The chessboard queen 1985
3 Guinevere evermore 1986
Fantasies, based on Arthurian legend

NEWTON, W.
JOEY BINNS
1 Someone has to take the fall 1979
2 The smell of money 1980
3 The set-up 1981
4 The Rio contract 1982

NICHOLLS, D.
LEANDER HAWKSWORTH
1 With magic in her eyes 1990
2 Heirs to adventure 1991

NICHOLS, B.
1 25 1926
2 All I could never be 1949
3 Down the garden path 1932
4 Thatched roof 1933
5 Village in a valley 1934
6 Merry Hall 1951
7 Laughter on the stairs 1953
8 Sunlight on the lawn 1956
9 The unforgiving minute 1978
N.F. Autobiography

NICHOLS, B.
MR.GREEN
1 No man's street 1954
2 Moonflower 1955
3 Death to slow music 1956
4 The rich die hard 1958
5 Murder by request 1959

NICOL, J.
1 Hotel Regina 1967
2 Home is the hotel 1976
3 Bertioni's Hotel 1984

NICOLE, C.
AMYOT FAMILY
1 Amyot's Cay 1963
2 Blood Amyot 1964
3 The Amyot crime 1965

NICOLE, C.
ANDERSON LINE
1 The seas of fortune 1984
2 The rivals 1985

NICOLE, C.
BLACK MAJESTY
1 Seeds of rebellion 1984

2 Wild harvest 1985
Novels about Henri Christophe and Haiti

NICOLE, C.
CHINA TRILOGY
1 The crimson pagoda 1984
2 The scarlet princess 1985
3 Red dawn 1985

NICOLE, C.
DAWSON FAMILY
1 Days of wine and roses 1991
2 The Titans 1992

NICOLE, C.
HAGGARD
1 Haggard 1980
2 Haggard's inheritance 1981
3 The young Haggards 1982

NICOLE, C.
HILTON FAMILY
1 Caribee 1974
2 The devil's own 1975
3 Mistress of darkness 1976
4 Black dawn 1977
5 Sunset 1978

NICOLE, C.
JAPANESE TRILOGY
1 The sun rises 1985
2 The sun and the dragon 1986
3 The sun on fire 1987

NICOLE, C.
KENYAN TRILOGY
1 The high country 1988
2 The happy valley 1989

NICOLE, C.
MCGANN FAMILY
1 Old Glory 1986
2 The sea and the sand 1986
3 Iron ships, iron men 1987
4 Wind of destiny 1987
5 Raging sea, searing sky 1988
6 The passion and the glory 1988

NICOLE, C.
RICHARD BRYANT
1 Sword of fortune 1990
2 Sword of Empire 1991

NICOLE, C.
ROYAL WESTERN DRAGOON GUARDS
1 The Regiment 1988
2 The Command 1989
3 The triumph 1989

NICOLE, C.
SINGAPORE
1 Pearl of the Orient 1988
2 Dragon's blood 1989
3 Dark sun 1990

NICOLSON, R.
MRS.ROSS
1 Mrs.Ross 1965
2 A flight of steps 1966

NIELSON, H.
SIMON DRAKE
1 After midnight 1967
2 A killer in the street 1967
3 Darkest hour 1969
4 Thesevered key 1973
5 The brink of murder 1976

NILES, D.
THE DRUIDHOLME TRILOGY
1 Prophet of Moonshae
2 The coral kingdom
3 The druid queen

NILES, D.
THE MAZTICA TRILOGY
1 Ironhelm
2 Viperhand
3 Feathered dragon

NILES, D.
THE MOONSHAE TRILOGY
(FORGOTTEN REALMS)
1 Darkwalker on Moonshae
2 Black wizards
3 Darkwell
Paperback fantasy

NIN, A.
CITIES OF THE INTERIOR
1 Ladders to fire 1946
2 Children of the albatross 1947
3 The four chambered heart 1959
4 Spy in the house of love 1954
5 Seduction of the minotaur 1961

NIVEN, D.
1 The moon's a balloon 1971
2 Bring on the empty horses 1975
N.F. Autobiography

NIVEN, L.
1 The integral trees 1984
2 The smoke ring 1987
Science fiction

NIVEN, L.
RINGWORLD
1 Ringworld 1971
2 Ringworld engineers 1980

NIVEN, L. & BARNES, S.
DREAM PARK
1 The Barsoom project 1990
2 The voodoo game 1991

NIVEN, L. & POURNELLE, J.
1 The mote in God's eye 1980
2 The moat around Murcheson's eye 1993

NIXON, A.
LARRY MAVER
1 Item 7 1970
2 The attack on Vienna 1971

NOBBS, D.
1 A bit of a 'do' 1989
2 Fair do's 1990

NOBBS, D.
HENRY PRATT
1 Second from last in the sack race 1983
2 Pratt of the Argus 1988
3 The cucumber man 1994
Tragi-comic novels about a young journalist

NOBBS, D.
REGINALD PERRIN
1 The death of Reginald Perrin 1975
2 The return of Reginald Perrin 1977
3 The better world of Reginald Perrin 1978

NOLAN, F.
A CALL TO ARMS
1 A promise of glory 1983
2 Blind duty 1984
Novels about the American Civil War

NOLAN, F.
LIEUT.PETROSINO
1 No place to be a cop 1974
2 Kill Petrosino! 1975

NOLAN, F.
THE GARRETT DOSSIER
1 Sweet sister death 1989
2 Alert state black 1990
3 Designated assassin 1990
4 Rat run 1991

NOLAN, W. F.
1 Logan's run
2 Logan's world
3 Logan's search
Science fiction

NORMAN, D.
HENRY II
1 The morning gift 1985
2 Fitzempress' law 1980
3 King of the last days 1981
Listed in order of reading

NORMAN, F.
1 Bang to rights 1957
2 Stand on me 1960
3 The Guntz 1962
4 Banana boy 1964
N.F. Autobiography

NORMAN, F.
ED NELSON
1 The dead butler caper 1978
2 Too many crooks spoil the caper 1979
3 The Baskerville caper 1982

NORMAN, J.
GOR
1 Tarnsman of Gor
2 Outlaw of Gor
3 Priest kings of Gor
4 Nomads of Gor
5 Assassin of Gor
6 Raiders of Gor
7 Captive of Gor
8 Hunters of Gor
9 Marauders of Gor
10 Tribesmen of Gor
11 Slave girl of Gor
12 Beasts of Gor
13 Explorers of Gor
14 Fighting slave of Gor
15 Rogue of Gor
16 Guardsman of Gor
17 Savages of Gor
18 Bloodbrothers of Gor
19 Kajira of Gor
20 Players of Gor
21 Dancer of Gor
22 Mercenaries of Gor
23 Renegades of Gor
24 Vagabonds of Gor
Paperback fantasy

NORTH, G.
SERGEANT CLUFF
1 Sergeant Cluff stands firm 1960

2 The methods of Sergeant Cluff 1961
3 Sergeant Cluff goes fishing 1962
4 More deaths for Sergeant Cluff 1963
5 Sergeant Cluff and the madmen 1964
6 Sergeant Cluff and the price of pity 1965
7 The confounding of Sergeant Cluff 1966
8 Sergeant Cluff and the day of reckoning 1967
9 The procrastination of Sergeant Cluff 1969
10 No choice for Sergeant Cluff 1971
11 Sergeant Cluff rings true 1972

NORTON, A.
JANUS
1 Judgment on Janus
2 Victory on Janus
Paperback science fiction

NORTON, A.
ROSS MURDOCK
1 The tune traders 1979
2 Galactic derelict 1979
3 The defiant agents 1979
4 Key out of tune 1979

NORTON, A.
WITCHWORLD
1 Witch world
2 Web of Witch World
3 Three against Witch World
4 Warlock of WitchWorld
5 Sorceress of Witch World
6 Year of the unicorn
7 Spell of Witch World
8 Trey of Swords
9 Ware Hawk
Paperback fantasy

NOVAK, K. & GRUBB, J.
THE FINDER'S STONE TRILOGY
1 Azure bonds
2 The wyvern's spur
3 Song of the saurials
Paperback fantasy

O'BRIAN, P.
JACK AUBREY
1 Master and Commander 1969
2 Post Captain 1972
3 HMS Surprise 1973
4 The Mauritius command 1977
5 Desolation Island 1978
6 Fortune of war 1979

7 The surgeon's mate 1980
8 The Ionian mission 1982
9 Treason's harbour 1983
10 The far side of the world 1985
11 The reverse of the medal 1986
12 The letter of Marque 1988
13 The thirteen gun salute 1989
14 Nutmeg of consolation 1990
15 Clarissa Oakes 1992
16 The wine-dark sea 1993
17 The Commodore 1994
Novels about the British navy in Napoleonic times

O'BRIEN, E.
1 The country girls 1962
2 The lonely girl 1963
3 Girls in their married bliss 1964

O'BRIEN, MEG
JESSICA JAMES
1 The Daphne decisions 1993
2 Salmon in the soup 1993
3 Hare today,gone tomorrow 1993
4 Eagles die too 1993

O'BRINE, P. M.
MICHAEL O'KELLY
1 Dodos don't duck 1950
2 Killers must eat 1951
3 Corpse to Cairo 1952
4 Deadly interlude 1954
5 Passport to treason 1955
6 The hungry killer 1956
7 Dagger before me 1957

O'BRINE, P. M.
MILLS,SECRET AGENT
1 Mills 1973
2 No earth for foxes 1974

O'CASEY, S.
1 I knock at the door 1939
2 Pictures in the hallway 1945
3 Drums under the window 1947
4 Inishfallen fare thee well 1950
5 Rose and crown 1952
6 Sunset and evening star 1954
7 The green crow 1957
N.F.Autobiography

O'CONNOR, E.
1 Steak for breakfast 1968
2 Second helping 1969
N.F. Autobiography

O'CONNOR, F.
1 An only child 1961

2 My father's son 1963
F. Autobiography

O'CONNOR, P.
1 Down the Bath rocks 1973
2 In a marmalade saloon 1974

O'DONNELL, L.
MICI ANHALT
1 Leisure dying
2 Falling star 1981
3 Wicked designs 1983

O'DONNELL, L.
NORAH MULCAHANEY
1 The phone calls 1972
2 Don't wear your wedding ring 1973
3 Dial 577 R.A.P.E. 1975
4 Aftershock 1977
5 No business being a cop 1980
6 The children's zoo 1982
7 A private crime 1991

O'DONNELL, PETER
MODESTY BLAISE
1 Modesty Blaise 1965
2 Modesty Blaise and Sabre Tooth 1966
3 I,Lucifer 1967
4 A taste for death 1969
5 The impossible virgin 1971
6 The silver mistress 1973
7 Last day in Limbo 1976
8 The dragon's claw 1978
9 The Xanadu talisman 1981
10 The night of Morningstar 1982
11 Dead man's handle 1985

O'HARA, K.
CHICO BRETT
1 The customer's always wrong 1951
2 Exit and curtain 1952
3 Sing, clubman, sing 1952
4 Always tell the sleuth 1954
5 Keep your fingers crossed 1955
6 If anything should happen 1956
7 It leaves tham cold 1956
8 Women like to know 1957
9 Danger, women at work 1958
10 And here is the noose 1959
11 Well, I'll be hanged 1960
12 Take life easy 1961
13 Don't tell the police 1963
14 Don't neglect the body 1966
15 It's your funeral 1966

O'NEILL, D.
BRIAN SAGA
1 Crucible 1986
2 Of Gods and men 1987
3 Sons of death 1988

O'NEILL, F.
GIOVANNI STEARS
1 Agents of sympathy 1986
2 Roman circus 1990

O'SULLIVAN, J. B.
STEVE SILK
1 I die possessed 1953
2 Nerve beat 1953
3 Don't hang me too high 1954
4 The stuffed man 1955
5 Someone walked over my grave 1958
6 Gale fever 1959
7 The long spoon 1960
8 Number proof 1961

OAKES, P.
1 From middle England 1980
2 Dwellers all in time and space 1981
3 At the Jazz Band Ball 1983
N.F. Autobiography

OATES, J. C.
1 A garden of earthly delights 1968
2 Them 1971

OELLRICHS, I.
MATT WINTER
1 Kettel Mill mystery 1940
2 Death of a white witch 1953
3 And die she did 1953
4 Murder comes at night 1955
5 Murder makes us gay 1956
6 Death in a chilly corner 1964

OLBRICH, F.
INSPECTOR DESOUZA
1 Desouza pays the price 1978
2 Sweet and deadly 1979
3 Desouza in stardust 1980
Thrillers about the Bombay CID

OLDENBOURG, Z.
1 The world is not enough 1948
2 The cornerstone 1955

OLDENBOURG, Z.
PARIS
1 The awakened 1957
2 Chains of love 1959

OLDFIELD, P.
FOXEARTH TRILOGY
1 Green harvest 1983
2 Summer song 1984
3 Golden tally 1985
Novels about a family of hop-growers, 1900-1930

OLDFIELD, P.
THE HERON SAGA
1 The rich earth 1982
2 This ravished land 1982
3 After the storm 1982
4 White water 1983
Set in 16thC Devon and Kent

OLINTO, A.
1 The water house 1985
2 The King of Ketu 1987

OLIVER, A.
1 The Pew Group 1980
2 Property of a lady 1983
3 The Ehlberg collection 1985
4 Cover-up 1987
Thrillers set in the world of antiques

OMEN
1 The Omen,by David Deltzer
2 Damien, by Joseph Howard
3 The final conflict, by Gordon McGill
4 Armageddon 2000, by Gordon McGill
5 The abomination, by Gordon McGill
Based on the horror films 'Omen' and 'Omen 2'

OMMANEY, F. D.
1 The house in the park 1964
2 The river bank 1966
N.F. Autobiography

ONSTOTT, K.
FALCONHURST
1 Mandingo 1960
2 Drum 1963
3 Master of Falconhurst 1964
4 Falconhurst fancy 1966
5 The mustee 1968
6 Heir to Falconhurst 1968
7 Flight to Falconhurst 1970
8 Mistress of Falconhurst 1973
9 Taproots of Falconhurst 1979
10 Scandal of Falconhurst 1980
11 Rogue of Falconhurst 1983
12 Miz Lucretia of Falconhurst 1985

13 Falconhurst fugitive 1988
*Novels about a slave estate in
Louisiana. 5-10 are written by Lance
Horner, and 11-13 by Ashley Carter*

ORAM, N.
THE WARP
1 The storms howling through Tiflis
2 Lemmings on the edge
3 The balustrade paradox
Paperback fantasy

ORDE, A. J.
JASON LYNX
1 A little neighbourhood murder
1989
2 Death and the dogwalker 1990
3 Death for old time's akes 1992
4 Dead on Sunday 1993

ORDE, L.
DANIEL KERR
1 The lion's way 1985
2 The lion's progress 1987

ORDE, L.
TIGER'S HEART
1 The tiger's heart 1987
2 The tiger's claw 1988

ORLOVITZ, G.
1 Milkbottle H. 1969
2 Ice never F. 1970

ORMEROD, R.
MALLIN & COE
1 A time to kill 1974
2 The silence of the night 1974
3 Full fury 1975
4 A spoonful of Luger 1975
5 Sealed with a loving kill 1976
6 The colour of fear 1976
7 A glimpse of death 1976
8 Too late for the funeral 1977
9 This murder came to mind 1977
10 A dip into murder 1978
11 The weight of evidence 1978
12 The bright face of danger 1979
13 The amnesia trap 1979
14 Cart before the hearse 1980
15 More dead than alive 1980
16 Double take 1980
17 One deathless hour 1981
18 Face value 1983

ORMEROD, R.
PHILIPA LOWE
1 Hung in the balance 1990
2 Bury him darkly 1991

3 A shot at nothing 1993

ORUM, P.
INSPECTOR MORCK
1 The whipping boy 1975
2 Nothing but the truth 1976

OSBORNE, G.
JAMES DINGLE & GLYN JONES
1 The power bug 1968
2 Balance of fear 1968
3 Traitor's gait 1969
4 Checkmate for China 1969
5 Death's no antidote 1971

OSBORNE, H.
1 White poppy 1977
2 The joker 1978

OSBOURNE, I.
1 The mango season 1985
2 Prodigal 1987

OWEN, A.
1 Gentlemen of the West 1984
2 Like birds in the wilderness 1987

OWEN, H.
JOURNEY FROM OBSCURITY
1 Childhood 1962
2 Youth 1964
3 War 1965
*N.F. Family history, mainly about
Wilfred Owen*

OWEN, J.
HAGGAI GODIN
1 Thirty days hath September 1965
2 The disinformer 1967

OWEN, R.
1 Green heart of heaven 1954
2 Worse than wanton 1956

OWENS, V.
1 At Point Blank 1991
2 Congregation 1992
3 A multitude of sins 1994

PACKER, J.
1 Pack and follow 1945
2 Grey mistress 1949
3 Apes and ivory 1953
4 Home from sea 1963
N.F. Autobiography of a naval wife

PADFIELD, P.
GUY GREVILLA
1 The lion's claw 1978

2 The unquiet gods 1980
3 Gold chains of Empire 1982

PAGE, E.
DET.CHIEF INSPECTOR KELSEY
1 Every second Thursday 1981
2 Last walk home 1982
3 Cold light of day 1983
4 Scent of death 1985
5 Final moments 1986
6 A violent end 1988
7 Deadlock 1991
8 In the event of my death 1994

PAIGE, F.
MACKINTOSH FAMILY
1 Glasgow girls 1994
2 The painted ladies 1994

PAIGE, F.
MCGRATH FAMILY
1 The Sholtie burn 1986
2 Maeve's daughter 1987
3 The distaff side 1988
4 Men who march away 1989
5 Sholtie flyer 1990

PAKENHAM, F. A., EARL OF LONGFORD
1 Born to believe 1953
2 Five lives 1964
3 A grain of wheat 1974
4 N.F. Autobiography
   N.F. Autobiography

PALEY, G.
1 The little disturbances of men 1959
2 Enormous changes at the last minute 1974
3 Later the same day 1985
   Volumes of short stories, in which the same characters appear.

PALMER, F.
DET.INSPECTOR 'JACKO' JACKSON
1 Testimony 1992
2 Unfit to plead 1992
3 Bent grasses 1993
4 Blood brother 1993
5 Nightwatch 1994
6 China hand 1994

PALMER, J.
GUY PLANT & FREYA MATTHEWS
1 Above and below 1966
2 So much for Gennaro 1968

PALMER, M.
LOVELL FAMILY
1 The white boar 1971
2 The wrong Plantagenet 1972

PARETSKY, S.
V.I.WARSHAWSKI
1 Indemnity only 1982
2 Deadlock 1984
3 Killing orders 1986
4 Bitter medicine 1987
5 Toxic shock 1988
6 Burn marks 1990
7 Guardian angel 1992
8 Tunnel vision 1994

PARGETER, E.
1 The eighth champion of Christendom 1945
2 Reluctant odyssey 1946
3 Warfare accomplished 1947
   Reprinted in paperback in 1992

PARGETER, E.
BROTHERS OF GWYNEDD
1 Sunrise in the west 1974
2 Dragon at noonday 1975
3 Hounds at sunset 1976
4 Afterglow and nightfall 1977

PARGETER, E.
WELSH TRILOGY
1 The heaven tree 1961
2 The green branch 1962
3 The scarlet seed 1963

PARK, R.
1 Missus 1985
2 The harp in the south 1948
3 Poor man's orange 1949
   Although 1 was written last, it precedes the others

PARKER, F. M.
1 Coldiron
2 Shadow of the wolf
   Paperback Westerns

PARKER, J.
1 The village cricket match 1978
2 Test time at Tillingfold 1979
3 Tillingfold's tour 1986

PARKER, R. B.
SPENSER
1 The Godwolf manuscript 1973
2 God save the child 1975
3 Mortal stakes 1976
4 Promised land 1977

5 The Judas goat 1982
6 Looking for Rachel Wallace 1982
7 A savage place 1982
8 Ceremony 1983
9 A Catskill eagle 1986
10 Valediction 1986
11 Taming a seahorse 1987
12 Early autumn 1987
13 Pale kings and princes 1988
14 Crimson joy 1989
15 Playmates 1990
16 The widening gyre 1991
17 Double deuce 1992
18 Paper doll 1993

PARKES, R.
DET.INSPECTOR TAFF ROBERTS
1 Riot 1987
2 An abuse of justice 1988
3 Gamelord 1990

PARKIN, R.
1 Out of the smoke 1960
2 Into the smother 1961
3 The sword and the blossom 1968
N.F. The story of a prisoner of war of the Japs

PARKINSON, C. N.
RICHARD DELANCEY
1 The Guernseyman 1982
2 Devil to pay 1973
3 Fireship 1974
4 Touch and go 1977
5 Dead reckoning 1978
6 So near,so far 1981

PARKINSON, R.
1 Peace for our time 1970
2 Blood, toil, tears and sweat 1972
3 A day's march nearer home 1974
N.F. History of WW2

PARKS, J.
1 Runs in the sun 1963
2 Time to hit out 1967
N.F. Autobiography and cricketing memoirs

PARLAND, O.
RIKI
1 The year of the bull 1991
2 The enchanted way 1991

PARRISH, F.
DAN MALLETT
1 Fire in the barley 1977
2 Sting of the honeybee 1978
3 Snare in the dark 1982

4 Bait on the hook 1983
5 Face at the window 1984
6 Fly in the cobweb 1986
7 Caught in the birdlime 1987
8 Voices from the dark 1993

PARTRIDGE, F.
1 A pacifist's war 1978
2 Everything to lose 1985
N.F. Autobiography

PASSMORE, R.
1 Blenheim boy 1981
2 Moving tent 1982
N.F. The author's experiences in World War II

PASTERNAK, B.
1 Doctor Zhivago
2 Lara's child, by A.Mollin 1994

PATON, A.
1 Towards the mountain 1980
2 Journey continued 1988
N.F. Autobiography of the South African novelist

PATTERSON, H.
NICK MILLER
1 The graveyard shift 1964
2 Brought in dead 1967

PATTINSON, J.
HARVEY LANDON
1 Contact Mr.Delgado 1960
2 The liberators 1961
3 The last stronghold 1962
4 The sinister stars 1964

PAUL, B.
MARION LARCH
1 You have the right to remain silent 1992
2 The apostrophe thief 1994

PAUL, E.
GEORGE BARCLAY
1 Jewels in jeopardy 1966
2 The Konespi affair 1967
3 Curtains for Konespi 1968
4 The golden fleece 1969
5 The silent murder 1970
6 The reluctant cloak and dagger man 1971

PAUL, L.
1 Living hedge 1946
2 Angry young man 1951

3 The boy down Kitchener Street
1957
N.F. Autobiography

PAUL, W.
DET.CHIEF INSPECTOR DAVID FYFE
1 Dance of death 1991
2 Sleeping dogs 1994

PAUSTOVSKY, K.
1 Childhood and schooldays 1964
2 Slow approach of thunder 1965
3 In that dawn 1967
4 Years of hope 1968
5 Southern adventure 1969
6 The restless years 1974
N.F. Autobiography

PAXSON, D. L.
WESTRIA
1 Lady of light,lady of darkness
2 Silverhair the warrior
3 The earthstone
4 The sea star
5 The wind crystal
6 The jewel of fire
Paperback fantasy

PAYNE, L.
DET.INSPECTOR SAM BIRKETT
1 The nose on my face 1961
2 Too small for his shoes 1962
3 Deep and crisp and even 1963

PAYNE, L.
JOHN TIBBETT
1 Spy for sale 1969
2 Even my foot's asleep 1971

PAYNE, L.
MARK SAVAGE
1 Take the money and run 1982
2 Malice in camera 1983
3 Vienna blood 1985
4 Dead for a ducat 1985
5 Late knight 1987

PEAKE, M.
1 Titus Groan 1946
2 Gormenghast 1950
3 Titus alone 1964

PEARCE, M.
THE MAMUR ZAPT
1 The Mamur Zapt and the return
of the carpet 1988
2 The Mamur Zapt and the night of
the dog 1989

3 The Mamur Zapt and the donkey-
vous 1990
4 The Mamur Zapt and the men
behind 1991
5 The Mamur Zapt and the girl in
the Nile 1992
6 The Mamur Zapt and the spoils of
Egypt 1992
7 The Mamur Zapt and the camel of
destruction 1993
*Detective stories set in Egypt in the
early 20thC*

PEARCE, M. E.
APPLETREE SAGA
1 Apple tree lean down 1975
2 Jack Mercybright 1976
3 The sorrowing wind 1977
4 The land endures 1979
5 Seedtime and harvest 1980

PEARS, I.
JONATHAN ARGYLL
1 The Raphael affair 1990
2 The Titian committee 1991
3 The Bernini bust 1992
4 The last judgement 1993
5 Giotto's hand 1994

PEARSALL, R.
OAKWOOD SAGA
1 Tides of war 1977
2 The iron sleep 1979

PEARSON, D.
1 The marigold field 1969
2 Sarah Whitman 1971

PEGRAM, L.
1 Blood and fire 1978
2 A day among many 1955
3 A long way from home 1986

PELL, S.
LOUIS XIV
1 Shadow of the sun 1978
2 The sun princess 1979

PELLA, J. & PHILLIPS, M.
JOURNALS OF CORRIE BELLE
HOLLISTER
1 My father's world
2 Daughters of grace
3 On the trail of the truth
4 A place in the sun
5 Sea to shining sea
6 Into the long dark night
7 Land of the brave and the free

PELLA, J. & PHILLIPS, M.
THE RUSSIANS
1 The crown and the crucible 1991
2 A house divided 1992
3 Travail and triumph 1992

PELLA, J. & PHILLIPS, M.
THE STONEWYCKE TRILOGY
1 The heather hills of Stonewycke
2 Shadows over Stonewycke
3 Treasure of Stonewycke

PELLOW, J.
1 Pastor's green 1980
2 Parson's progress 1981
3 Parson's princess 1983
Novels about a village parson

PEMBERTON, V.
1 Our family 1991
2 Our street 1993
3 Our Rose 1994

PENN, J.
DET. CHIEF INSPECTOR TANSEY
1 Outrageous exposures 1988
2 A feast of death 1989
3 A killing to hide 1990
4 A legacy of death 1992
5 A haven of danger 1993
6 Widow's end 1993
7 The guilty party 1994

PENN, J.
INSPECTOR THORNE AND SGT. ABBOT
1 Notice of death 1982
2 Deceitful death 1983
3 Will to kill 1983
4 Mortal term 1984
5 A deadly sickness 1985
6 Unto the grave 1986
7 Barren revenge 1986
8 Accident prone 1987

PENTECOST, H.
JOHN JERICHO
1 Hide her from every eye 1966
2 Sniper 1967
3 The creeping hours 1968
4 Dead woman of the year 1969
5 The girl with six fingers 1970
6 A plague of violence 1971

PENTECOST, H.
JULIAN QUIST
1 Don't drop dead tomorrow 1972
2 The champagne killer 1974
3 The beautiful dead 1975
4 The Judas freak 1976

5 Honeymoon with death 1977
6 Die after dark 1978
7 The steel palace 1978
8 Deadly trap 1979
9 The homicidal horse 1980
10 Death mask 1981
11 Sow death,reap death 1982
12 Past,present and murder 1983
13 Murder out of wedlock 1985
14 The substitute victim 1986
15 The party killer 1987
16 Kill and kill again 1988

PENTECOST, H.
PIERRE CHAMBRUN
1 The cannibal who over-ate 1963
2 The shape of fear 1964
3 The evil that men do 1966
4 The golden trap 1967
5 The gilded nightmare 1969
6 Girl watcher's funeral 1970
7 The deadly joke 1971
8 Birthday,deathday 1975
9 Walking dead man 1975
10 Bargain with death 1976
11 Time of terror 1977
12 The 14 dilemma 1978
13 Death after breakfast 1979
14 Random killer 1980
15 Beware young lovers 1981
16 Murder in luxury 1981
17 With intent to kill 1983
18 Murder in high places1983
19 Remember to kill me 1985
20 Nightmare time 1987
21 Murder goes round and round 1989

PENTECOST, H.
UNCLE GEORGE
1 The price of silence 1981
2 The copycat killers 1984
3 Death by fire 1991
4 Murder sweet and sour 1991
5 Pattern for terror 1991

PERHAM, M.
1 Lugard, the years of adventure 1959
2 Lugard, the years of authority 1960
N.F. Biography

PEROWNE, S.
1 The life and times of Herod the Great 1956
2 The later Herods 1958
N.F. History

PERRY, A.
THOMAS AND CHARLOTTE PITT
1 Silence in Hanover Close 1989
2 Cardington Crescent 1990
3 Death in the Devil's Acre 1991
4 Bethlehem Road 1991
5 Bluegate Fields 1992
6 Highgate Rise 1992
7 Belgrave Square 1993
8 Farrier's Lane 1994
Detective stories set in Victorian London

PERRY, A.
WILLIAM MONK
1 A sudden fearful death 1993
2 The face of a stranger 1994
3 A dangerous mourning 1994
4 Sins of the wolf 1994

PERRY, R.
PHILIS
1 The fall guy 1971
2 The nowhere man 1972
3 Ticket to ride 1973
4 Holiday with vengeance 1974
5 One good death deserves another 1976
6 Dead end 1977
7 Dutch courage 1978
8 Bishop's pawn 1979
9 Grand slam 1980
10 Fool's mate 1981
11 Foul up 1985
12 Kolwezi 1986

PERRY, S.
THE MATADOR TRILOGY
1 The man who never missed
2 Matadora
3 The Machiavelli interface

PERRY, T.
1 The butcher's boy 1992
2 Sleeping dogs 1992

PETERS, ELIZABETH
AMELIA PEABODY
1 Crocodile on the sandbank 1976
2 The curse of the Pharaohs 1982
3 The mummy case 1986
4 Lion in the valley 1987
5 The deeds of the disturber 1989
6 The last camel died at noon 1991
7 The snake, the crocodile and the dog 1993
Thrillers featuring a 19thC lady archaeologist

PETERS, ELIZABETH
JACQUELINE KIRBY
1 The murders of Richard III 1989 (1974 in US)
2 Naked once more 1990

PETERS, ELIZABETH
VICKY BLISS
1 Silhouette in scarlet 1984
2 Street of the Five Moons 1988
3 Borrower of the night 1974
4 Trojan gold 1987
Listed in chronological order

PETERS, ELLIS
BROTHER CADFAEL
1 A morbid taste for bones 1977
2 One corpse too many 1979
3 Monk's wood 1980
4 Saint Peter's Fair 1981
5 The leper of St. Giles 1981
6 The virgin in the ice 1982
7 The sanctuary sparrow 1983
8 The devil's novice 1983
9 Dead man's ransom 1984
10 The pilgrim of hate 1985
11 An excellent mystery 1985
12 The raven in the foregate 1986
13 The rose rent 1986
14 The hermit of Eyton Forest 1987
15 The confession of Brother Haluin 1988
16 The heretic's apprentice 1989
17 The Potters Field 1989
18 The summer of the Danes 1991
19 The holy thief 1992
20 Brother Cadfael's penance 1994
Detective stories whose hero is an 13thC monk 'A rare Benedictine' (1988) was an illustrated gift book, about the early life of Brother Cadfael

PETERS, ELLIS
CHIEF INSPECTOR GEORGE FELSE
1 Flight of a witch 1964
2 A nice derangement of epitaphs 1965
3 Piper on the mountain 1966
4 Black is the colour of my true love's heart 1966
5 Grass widow's tale 1967
6 The house of green turf 1967
7 Mourning raga 1969
8 The knocker on death's door 1970
9 Death to thelandlords 1972

PETERS, G.
INSPECTOR TREVOR NICHOLLS & SGT.
TOM BUXTON
1 The claw of the cat 1963
2 The eye of a serpent 1964
3 The whirl of a bird 1965
4 The twist of a stick 1966
5 The flick of a fin 1967
6 The mark of a buoy 1967
7 The chill of a corpse 1968

PETERS, L.
IAN FIRTH
1 Two sets to murder 1963
2 Out by the river 1964
3 Two after Malic 1966
4 Riot 71 1967

PETERS, M.
1 The vinegar seed 1986
2 The vinegar blossom 1986
3 The vinegar tree 1987

PETERS, M.
MALONE FAMILY
1 Tansy 1975
2 Kate Alanna 1975
3 A child called Freedom 1976

PETRIE, G.
MYCROFT HOLMES
1 The Dorking Gap affair 1989
2 The monstrous regiment 1991
*The adventures of Sherlock Holmes's
brother*

PETRIE, R.
INSPECTOR MACLURG
1 Death in Deakin's Wood 1963
2 Murder by precedent 1964
3 Running deep 1965
4 Dead loss 1966
5 Maclurg goes west 1968

PETRIE, R.
NASSIM PRIDE
1 Foreign bodies 1967
2 Despatch of a dove 1968

PETROCELLI, O. R.
1 The pact 1974
2 Olympia's inheritance 1975

PHELPS, H.
1 Just across the fields 1976
2 Just over yonder 1977
3 Just where we belong 1978
N.F. Autobiography

PHILBIN, T.
PRECINCT SIBERIA
1 Precinct Siberia
2 Under cover
3 Cop killer
Paperback thrillers

PHILIPS, J.
PETER STYLES
1 The laughter trap 1963
2 The black glass city 1964
3 The twisted people 1965
4 The wings of madness 1967
5 Thursday's folly 1967
6 Hot summer's killing 1968
7 Nightmare at dawn 1971
8 Escape a killer 1972
9 The vanishing senator 1973
10 The larkspur conspiracy 1974
11 The power killers 1975
12 Walk a crooked mile 1976
13 Backlash 1977
14 Five roads to death 1978
15 A murder arranged 1979
16 Why murder 1980
17 Death is a dirty trick 1981
18 A target for tragedy 1983

PHILLIPS, S.
MATTHEW FURNIVAL
1 Down to earth 1967
2 Hidden wrath 1968
3 Death in Arcady 1969
4 Death makes the scene 1970
5 Death in sheep's clothing 1971

PICKARD, N.
JENNY CAIN
1 Dead crazy
2 Generous death
3 Marriage is murder
4 No body
5 Say no to murder
6 Crossbones 1990
7 I.O.U. 1991
8 But I wouldn't want to die there
1993
9 Confession 1994
1-5 published in US

PIERCE, D. M.
VIC DANIEL
1 Down in the valley
2 Hear the wind blow,dear
3 Roses love sunshine
4 Angels in heaven
5 Write me a letter 1992

PIERCE, M. A.
DARKANGEL TRILOGY
1 The darkangel 1983
2 A gathering of gargoyles 1984
3 The pearl of the soul of the world
   1990

PIERCE, M. A.
FIREBRINGER TRILOGY
1 Birth of the firebringer 1985
2 Dark moon 1992

PIKE, C.
FINAL FRIENDS
1 The party 1991
2 The dance 1991
3 The graduation 1991
   Horror stories

PIKE, C. R.
JUBAL CADE
1 The killing trail
2 Double cross
3 The hungry gun
4 Killer silver
5 Vengeance hunt
6 The burning man
7 The golden dead
8 Death wears grey
9 Days of blood
10 The killing ground
11 Brand of vengeance
12 Bounty road
13 Ashes and blood
14 The death pit
15 Angel of death
16 Mourning is red
17 Bloody Christmas
18 Time of the damned
19 The waiting game
20 Spoils of war
21 The violent land
22 Gallows bait
   *Paperback Westerns, some of which
   are also published in large print*

PIKE, R. L.
THE 52ND PRECINCT
1 Mute witness 1965
2 The quarry 1964
3 Police blotter 1966

PILCHER, R.
1 The shell seekers 1988
2 September 1990

PILKINGTON, R.
1 Small boat through Belgium 1960
2 Small boat through Holland 1960
3 Small boat to the Skagerrak 1961
4 Small boat through Sweden 1961
5 Small boat to Alsace 1962
6 Small boat through France 1963
7 Small boat through Germany 1963
8 Small boat through Southern
   France 1964
9 Small boat on the Meuse 1964
10 Small boat to Luxembourg 1965
11 Small boat on the Moselle 1965
12 Small boat on theThames 1966
13 Small boat to Elsinore 1969
14 Small boat to Northern Germany
   1970
15 Small boat on the Upper Rhine
   1971
16 Small boat on the Lower Rhine
   1971
   N.F. Travel

PIRINCCI, A.
FELIDAE
1 Felidae 1993
2 Felidae on the road 1994

PIRSIG, R.
1 Zen and the art of motorcycle
   maintenance 1974
2 Lila 1991

PLAGEMANN, B.
WALLACE FAMILY
1 Father to the man 1964
2 The best is yet to be 1966
3 A world of difference 1969

PLAIDY, J.
CATHERINE DE MEDICI
1 Madame SErpent 1951
2 The Italian woman 1952
3 Queen Jezebel 1953

PLAIDY, J.
CATHERINE OF ARAGON
1 Catherine the virgin widow 1961
2 The shadow of the pomegranate
   1962
3 The King's secret matter 1962

PLAIDY, J.
CHARLES II
1 The wandering prince 1956
2 A health unto His Majesty 1956
3 Here lies our sovereign lord 1956

PLAIDY, J.
GEORGIAN SAGA
1 Princes of Celle 1967
2 Queen in waiting 1967

3 Caroline the Queen 1968
4 The Prince and the Quakeress 1968
5 The third George 1969
6 Perdita's prince 1969
7 Sweet lass of Richmond Hill 1970
8 Indiscretions of the Queen 1970
9 The Regent's daughter 1971
10 Goddess of the green room 1971
11 Victoria in the wings 1972

PLAIDY, J.
ISABELLA AND FERDINAND
1 Castile for Isabella 1960
2 Spain for the Sovereigns 1960
3 Daughters of Spain 1961

PLAIDY, J.
LOUIS XV
1 Louis the well beloved 1959
2 The road to Compiegne 1959

PLAIDY, J.
LUCREZIA BORGIA
1 Madonna of the Seven Hills 1958
2 Light on Lucrezia 1958

PLAIDY, J.
MARY QUEEN OF SCOTS
1 The royal road to Fotheringhay 1966
2 The captive Queen ofScots 1969

PLAIDY, J.
NORMAN TRILOGY
1 The bastard King 1975
2 The lion of justice 1975
3 The passionate enemies 1976

PLAIDY, J.
PLANTAGENET SAGA
1 Plantagenet prelude 1976
2 Revolt of the eaglets 1977
3 Heart of the lion 1977
4 Prince of darkness 1978
5 The battle of the Queens 1978
6 The Queen from Provence 1979
7 Edward Longshanks 1979
8 The follies of the King 1980
9 The vow on the heron 1980
10 Passage to Pontefract 1981
11 The star of Lancaster 1981
12 Epitaph for three women 1981
13 Red rose of Anjou 1982
14 The sun in splendour 1982

PLAIDY, J.
QUEEN VICTORIA
1 The captive of Kensington Palace 1972
2 The Queen and Lord M. 1973
3 The Queen's husband 1973
4 The widow of Windsor 1974

PLAIDY, J.
QUEENS OF ENGLAND
1 Myself my enemy (Henrietta Maria) 1983
2 Queen of this realm (Elizabeth I) 1984
3 Victoria victorious 1985
4 Lady in the Tower (Anne Boleyn) 1986
5 The courts of love (Eleanor of Aquitaine) 1987
6 In the shadow of the crown (Mary Tudor) 1988
7 The Queen's secret (Catherine de Valois) 1989
8 Reluctant Queen (Anne Neville) 1990
9 The pleasures of love (catherine de Braganza)1991
10 William's wife (Anne) 1992
11 Rose without a thorn (Catherine Howard) 1993

PLAIDY, J.
SPANISH INQUISITION
1 The rise of the Spanish Inquisition 1959
2 The growth of the Spanish Inquisition 1960
3 The end of the Spanish Inquisition 1962
N.F. History

PLAIDY, J.
WILLIAM AND MARY
1 The three crowns 1965
2 The haunted sisters 1966
3 The Queen's favourites 1966

PLAIN, B.
1 Evergreen 1984
2 The golden cup 1986
3 Tapestry 1988

PLANTE, D.
FRANCOEUR FAMILY
1 The family 1978
2 The country 1981
3 The woods 1982

4 The native 1987
Published in one vol. 'The Francoeur Family' 1984

PLATER, A.
1 The Beiderbecke affair 1985
2 The Beiderbecke tapes 1986
3 The Beiderbecke connection

PLOWDEN, A.
ELIZABETH I
1 The young Elizabeth 1972
2 Danger to Elizabeth 1973
3 Marriage with my kingdom 1976
4 Elizabeth Regina 1980
N.F. History

PLOWMAN, S.
HAMILTON FAMILY
1 Three lives for the Czar 1969
2 My kingdom for a grave 1970

PLUMB, J. H.
SIR ROBERT WALPOLE
1 Themaking of a statesman 1956
2 The King's minister 1960
N.F. Biography

PLUMMER, T. A.
FRAMPTON
1 Shadowed by the C.I.D.
2 Shot at night 1934
3 Frampton of the Yard 1935
4 Dumb witness 1936
5 Was the Mayor murdered? 1936
6 Death symbol 1937
7 The man they put away 1938
8 Five were murdered 1938
9 The man they feared 1939
10 Two men from the East 1939
11 The Muse Theatre murder 1939
12 Melody of death 1940
13 The black ribbon murders 1940
14 Crime at 'Crooked Gables' 1941
15 Fool of the Yard 1942
16 The devil's tea party 1942
17 The man who changed his face 1943
18 Murder limps by 1943
19 Murder by an idiot 1944
20 Simon takes the rap 1944
21 Murder in the village 1945
22 The strangler 1945
23 The man with the crooked arm 1945
24 The J for Jennie murders 1945
25 The Barush mystery 1946
26 The pierced ear murders 1947
27 Who fired the factory? 1947

28 The silent four 1947
29 Hunted! 1948
30 Strychnine for one 1949
31 Death haunts the repertory 1950
32 The yellow disc murders 1950
33 The murder of Doctor Gray 1950
34 Murder through Room 45 1952
35 Frampton sees red 1953
36 Murder at Marlington 1953
37 The Westlade murders 1953
38 Murder in Windy Coppice 1954
39 A scream at midnight 1954
40 The black rat 1955
41 Where was Fruit murdered? 1955
42 Murder in the surgery 1955
43 Pagan Joe 1956
44 Condemned to live 1956
45 Murder at Lantern Corner 1958
46 The elusive killer 1958
47 The hospital thief 1959
48 The vestry murder 1959
49 The spider man 1960
50 Murder at Brownhill 1962

PODHAJSKY, A.
1 The white stallions of Vienna 1963
2 My dancing white horses 1964
N.F. The story of the Spanish Riding School in Vienna.

POE, E. A.
1 Fall of the House of Usher
2 Usher's passing by Robert McCammon 1989

POHL, F.
HEECHEE
1 Gateway 1978
2 Beyond the Blue Event horizon 1980
3 Heechee rendezvous 1984
4 The annals of Heechee 1987
Science fiction

POHL, F.
SPACE MERCHANTS
1 Space merchants 1985
2 The merchants' war 1985
Science fiction

POHL, F. & WILIAMSON, J.
JACK EDEN
1 Undersea quest 1964
2 Undersea fleet 1968
3 Undersea city 1969

POHL, F. & WILLIAMSON, J.
1 The reefs of space 1964

2 Starchild 1966
Science fiction

POLLACK, R.
1 Unquenchable fire 1988
2 Temporary agency 1994
S. F.

PONSONBY, D. A.
JASPARD FAMILY
1 The general 1958
2 The fortunate adventure 1959
3 The Bristol cousins 1961

POOK, P.
POOK
1 Banking on form 1961
2 Pook in boots 1962
3 Pook in business 1963
4 Pook Sahib 1964
5 Bwana Pook 1965
6 ProfessorPook 1966
7 Banker Pook confesses 1966
8 Pookat college 1968
9 Pook's tender years 1969
10 Pook and partners 1969
11 Playboy Pook 1970
12 Pook's class war 1971
13 Pook's tale of woo 1972
14 Pook's Eastern promise 1972
15 Beau Pook proposes 1973
16 Pook's tours 1974
17 The teacher's hand Pook 1975
18 Gigolo Pook 1976
19 Pook's lovenest 1976
20 Pook's china doll 1977
21 Pook's curiosity shop 1977
22 Marine Pook, Esq. 1978
23 Pook's Viking virgins 1979

POPE, D.
EDWARD YORKE
1 Convoy 1979
2 Decoy 1983

POPE, D.
NED YORKE
1 Buccaneer 1981
2 Admiral 1982
3 Galleon 1986
4 Corsair 1987
Set in the Caribbean in the days of the pirates Ned Yorke is an ancestor of Edward Yorke

POPE, D.
RAMAGE
1 Ramage 1966
2 Ramage and the drum beat 1967

3 Ramage and the free-booters 1969
4 Governor Ramage,RN 1972
5 Ramage's prize 1974
6 Ramage and the guillotine 1975
7 Ramage's diamond 1976
8 Ramage's mutiny 1977
9 Ramage and the rebels 1978
10 The Ramage touch 1979
11 Ramage's signal 1980
12 Ramage and the renegades 1981
13 Ramage's devil 1982
14 Ramage's trial 1984
15 Ramage's challenge 1985
16 Ramage at Trafalgar (1805) 1986
17 Ramage and the Saracens 1988
18 Ramage and the Dido 1989
Novels set in the Napoleonic Wars

POPE, R.
1 Strosa light 1965
2 Salvage from Strosa 1967

PORTER, D. C.
WHITE INDIAN
1 White Indian 1992
2 The renegade 1993
3 War chief 1994

PORTER, H.
1 The watcher on the cast-iron balcony 1963
2 The paper chase 1965
N.F. Autobiography

PORTER, J.
DET. CHIEF INSPECTOR DOVER
1 Dover one 1964
2 Dover two 1965
3 Dover three 1965
4 Dover and the unkindest cut of all 1966
5 Dover goes to Pott 1968
6 Dover strikes again 1970
7 It's murder with Dover 1973
8 Dover and the claret tappers 1977
9 Dead easy for Dover 1978
10 Dover beats the band 1980

PORTER, J.
EDDIE BROWN
1 Sour cream with everything 1968
2 The chinks in the curtain 1969
3 Neither a candle nor a pitchfork 1970
4 Only with a bargepole 1971

PORTER, J.
HON.CONSTANCE MORRISON BURKE
1 Rather a common sort of crime 1970
2 The meddler and her murder 1972
3 The package included murder 1975
4 Who the heck is Sylvia? 1977
5 The cart before the crime 1979

POSEY, C. A.
STEVEN BORG
1 Kiev footprint 1983
2 Prospero drill 1984

POTOK, C.
REUVEN & DANNY
1 The chosen 1968
2 The promise 1970

POTTER, J.
INSPECTOR HISCOCK
1 Death in office 1965
2 Foul play 1967
3 Dance of death 1968
4 Trail of blood 1970

POTTER, J. H.
PILGRIM
1 Call me Pilgrim 1981
2 Pilgrim's trail 1981
3 Young Joe Pilgrim 1982
4 Pilgrim's blood 1982
5 Bounty for Pilgrim 1983
6 Requiem for Pilgrim 1983
7 The Pilgrim raid 1983
8 A coffin for Pilgrim 1984
9 The Pilgrim kill 1984
10 Pilgrim's revenge 1990
Westerns

POURNELLE, J.
FALKENBERG'S LEGION
1 Prince of mercenaries
2 Go tell the Spartans
3 Falkenberg's legion
4 Birth of fire
5 High justice
6 King David's spaceship
7 Prince of Sparta
Paperback s. f.

POURNELLE, J.
JANISSARIES
1 Janissaries
2 Clan and crown
3 Storms of victory
Paperback science fiction

POWE, R.
1 Possessed 1990
2 Possessed II 1991

POWELL, A.
THE MUSIC OF TIME
1 A question of upbringing 1951
2 A buyer's market 1952
3 The acceptance world 1955
4 At Lady Molly's 1957
5 Casanova's Chinese restaurant 1960
6 The kindly ones 1963
7 The valley of bones 1964
8 The soldier's art 1966
9 The military philosophers 1968
10 Books do furnish a room 1971
11 Temporary kings 1973
12 Hearing secret harmonies 1975

POWELL, A.
TO KEEP THE BALL ROLLING
1 Infants of the spring 1976
2 Messengers of the day 1978
3 Faces in my time 1980
4 The strangers all are gone 1982
N.F. Autobiography

POWELL, D.
HOLLIS CARPENTER
1 Bayou city secrets 1992
2 Houston town 1992

POWELL, M.
1 Below stairs 1968
2 Climbing the stairs 1969
3 The treasure upstairs 1970
4 The London season 1971
5 My mother and I 1972
6 Margaret Powell in America 1973
7 Albert, my consort 1975
8 My children and I 1977
N.F. Autobiography

POWER, M. S.
CHILDREN OF THE NORTH
1 The killing of yesterday's children 1985
2 Lonely the man without heroes 1986
3 Darkness in the eye 1987
Novels set in contemporary Northern Ireland

POYER, J.
A TIME OF WAR
1 The transgressors 1984
2 Come evil days 1985

PRATCHETT, T.
DISCWORLD
1 The colour of magic
2 The light fantastic
3 Equal rites 1986
4 Mort 1987
5 Sorcery 1988
6 Wyrd sisters 1988
7 Pyramids 1989
8 Guards! Guards! 1989
9 Eric 1990
10 Moving pictures 1990
11 Reaper man 1991
12 Witches abroad 1991
13 Small gods 1992
14 Lords and ladies 1992
15 Men at arms 1993
16 Soul music 1994
17 Interesting times 1994
Fantasy. The Streets of Ankh Morpork (1993) is a map of the Discworld capital, and The Discworld Companion (1994) is a guide to the series.

PRATHER, R. S.
SHELL SCOTT
1 Kill the clown 1967
2 The vanishing beauty 1968

PRENTIS, E.
1 A nurse in time 1978
2 Nurse in action 1979
3 Nurse in parts 1980
4 A nurse nearby 1981
5 A turn for the nurse 1982
N.F. Autobiography

PRESCOT, J.
CASEBOOKS
1 Both sides of the case 1958
2 The case continued 1959
3 The case proceeding 1960
4 Case for theaccused 1961
5 Case for trial 1962
6 Case for hearing 1963
7 Case for court 1964
8 The case re-opened 1965
9 Case counterfeit 1967

PRESCOTT, H. F. M.
PILGRIMAGES OF FRIAR FELIX FABIO
1 Jerusalem journey 1955
2 Once to Sinai 1957

PREUSSLER, O.
1 Robber Hotzenplotz 1970
2 Further adventures of Robber Hotzenplotz 1973

PRICE, A.
DR.DAVID AUDLEY
1 44 vintage 1977
2 A new kind of war 1987
3 Alamut ambush 1971
4 Colonel Butler's wolf 1972
5 October men 1973
6 Other paths to glory 1974
7 Our man in Camelot 1975
8 War game 1976
9 Tomorrow's ghost 1979
10 The Old Vengeful 1982
11 Gunner Kelly 1983
12 Sion Crossing 1984
13 Here be monsters 1985
14 For the good of the state 1986
15 The labyrinth makers 1970
16 A prospect of vengeance 1988

PRICE, E.
1 Savannah 1986
2 To see your face again 1987
3 Before the darkness falls 1988

PRICE, E.
ST.SIMONS TRILOGY
1 The lighthouse 1972
2 New moon rising 1973
3 The beloved invader 1974

PRICE, R.
MUSTIAN FAMILY
1 A long and happy life 1962
2 A generous man 1967

PRIESTLEY, J. B.
1 Midnight on the desert 1937
2 Rain upon Godshill 1939
3 Margin released 1962
4 *N.F. Autobiography*

PRIESTLEY, J. B.
THE IMAGE MEN
1 Out of town 1968
2 London end 1968

PRIOR, A.
1 The sky cage 1967
2 Mirror image 1969

PRISONER
1 The prisoner, by T.L.Disch
2 A day in the life, by H.Stine
3 Who is No.2, by H.Stine
Paperbacks based on the TV series

PRITCHETT, V. S.
1 A cab at the door 1968

2 Midnight oil 1971
N.F. Autobiography

PRITT, D. N.
1 From right to left,1887-1941 1965
2 Brasshats and bureaucrats,1941-1950 1966
3 The defence accuses 1966
N.F. Autobiography

PROCTER, M.
CHIEF INSPECTOR MARTINEAU
1 No proud chivalry 1946
2 Each man's destiny 1947
3 The end of the street 1948
4 Hurry the darkness 1952
5 Rich is the treasure 1952
6 Hell is a city 1953
7 I will speak daggers 1956
8 Man in ambush 1957
9 The midnight plumber 1957
10 Killer at large 1958
11 Three at the Angel 1958
12 The pub crawler 1958
13 Devil's due 1960
14 The devil was handsome 1961
15 The spearhead death 1961
16 A body to spare 1962
17 The devil in moonlight 1962
18 The moonlight flitting 1963
19 Two men in twenty 1964
20 Death has a shadow 1964
21 The graveyard rolls 1964
22 His weight in gold 1965
23 Rogue running 1967
24 Exercise hoodwink 1967
25 Hideaway 1968
26 The dog man 1969

PROFESSIONALS
1 Where the jungle ends
2 Long shot
3 stake-out
4 Hunter hunted
5 Blind run
6 Fall girl
7 Hiding to nothing
8 Dead reckoning
9 no stone
10 Cry wolf
11 Spy probe
12 Fox hole
13 The untouchables
14 Operation Susie
15 You'll be all right
Paperbacks based on the TV series

PROLE, L.
TUDOR TRILOGY
1 The ghost that haunted a King 1963
2 The ten day Queen 1973
3 Consort to the Queen 1975

PRONZINI, B.
THE NAMELESS DETECTIVE
1 The snatch 1974
2 The vanished 1975
3 Undercurrent 1975
4 Blowback 1978
5 Two spot 1980
6 Labyrinth 1981
7 Hoodwink 1981
8 Scattershot 1982
9 Dragonfire 1983
10 Casefile 1983
11 Bindlestaff 1984
12 Quicksilver 1984
13 Nightshades 1986
14 Jackpot 1991
15 Breakdown 1991
16 Quarry 1992

PUCKETT, A.
TOM JONES,D.H.S.S.
1 Bloodstains 1987
2 Bed of nails 1989
3 Terminus 1990
4 Bloodhound 1991

PUGH, D.
IRIS THORNE
1 Cold call 1993
2 Slow squeeze 1994

PUNSHON, E. R.
BOBBY OWEN
1 Information received 1933
2 Death among the sunbathers 1934
3 The crossword mystery 1934
4 Mystery villa 1934
5 Death of a beauty queen 1935
6 Death comes to Cambers 1935
7 The Bath mysteries 1936
8 The mystery of Mr.Jessup 1937
9 The dusky hour 1937
10 Dictator's way 1938
11 Comes a stranger 1938
12 Suspects nine 1939
13 Murder abroad 1939
14 Four strange women 1940
15 Ten sar clues 1941
16 The dark garden 1941
17 Diabolical candelabra 1942
18 The Conqueror Inn 1943
19 Night's cloak 1944

20 Secrets can't be kept 1944
21 There's a reason for everything 1945
22 It might lead anywhere 1946
23 Helen passes by 1947
24 Music tells all 1948
25 The house of Godwinsson 1948
26 So many doors 1949
27 Everybody always tells 1950
28 The secret search 1951
29 The golden dagger 1951
30 The attending death 1952
31 Strange ending 1953
32 Brought to light 1954
33 Dark is the clue 1955
34 Six were present 1956

PURSER, P.
COLIN PANTON
1 The twentymen 1968
2 Peregrination 22 1969
3 The Holy Father's navy 1971

PUZO, M.
1 The Godfather 1969
2 Godfather II
3 The Sicilian 1985

QUANTRILL, M.
THE GOTOBED TRIPTYCH
1 Gotobed dawn 1959
2 Gotobedlam 1961
3 John Gotobed alone 1963

QUANTUM LEAP
1 Too close for comfort
2 Carny knowledge
3 The wall
4 Search and rescue
5 Random measures

QUARTERMAIN, H.
RAVEN
1 The diamond hook 1970
2 The man who walked in diamonds 1971
3 Rock of diamond 1972
4 The diamond hostage 1975

QUARTON, M.
1 Breakfast the night before 1991
2 Saturday's child 1993
   N.F. *Autobiography of an Irish childhood*

QUEEN, E.
ELLERY QUEEN
1 The Roman hat mystery 1929
2 The French powder mystery 1930

3 The Dutch shoe mystery 1931
4 The Greek coffin mystery 1932
5 The Egyptian cross mystery 1932
6 The American gun mystery 1932
7 The Siamses twin mystery 1933
8 The adventures of Ellery Queen 1934
9 The Chinese orange mystery 1934
10 The Spanish cape mystery 1935
11 Halfway house 1936
12 The door between 1937
13 The devilto pay 1938
14 The four of hearts 1938
15 The dragon's teeth 1939
16 The new adventures of Ellery Queen 1940
17 Calamity town 1942
18 There was an old woman 1943
19 The murderer is a fox 1945
20 Cat of many tails 1947
21 The casebook of Ellery Queen 1948
22 Ten days wonder 1948
23 Double double 1949
24 Origin of evil 1951
25 The king is dead 1952
26 The scarlet letters 1953
27 Inspector Queen's own case 1956
28 The finishing stroke 1957
29 Queen's Bureau of Investigation 1959
30 The player on the other side 1963
31 And on the eighth day 19
32 Queen's full 1966
33 Face to face 1967
34 The house of brass 1968
35 Q.E.D. 1969
36 When fell the night 1970
37 The last woman in his life 1970
38 A fine and private place 1971
39 Dead man's tale 1977

QUENNELL, P.
1 The marble foot 1976
2 The wanton chase 1980
3 Customs and characters 1982
   N.F. *Autobiography*

QUEST, E.
DET. CHIEF INSPECTOR KATE MADDOX
1 Death walk 1989
2 Cold coffin 1990
3 Model murder 1991
4 Deadly deceit 1992

QUEST, R.
PETER QUENTIN
1 The Cerberus murders 1969
2 Murder with a vengeance 1970

3 Death of a sinner 1971

QUIGLEY, J.
1 King's Royal 1976
2 Queen's Royal 1977

QUINN, P.
PETE RILEY
1 Once upon a private eye 1968
2 Twice upon a crime 1969
3 Thrice upon a killing spree 1970
4 The big game 1971
5 The fatal complaint 1972

QUINNELL, A. J.
CREASY
1 Man on fire 1987
2 The perfect kill 1992
3 The blue ring 1993
4 Black horn 1994

QUINTON, A.
DET.INSPECTOR JAMES ROLAND
1 To mourn a mischief 1989
2 Death of a dear friend 1990
3 A fatal end 1992
4 A little grave 1993
5 The sleeping and the dead 1994

QUOGAN, A.
MATTHEW PRIOR
1 The fine art of murder 1989
2 The touch of a vanished hand 1990

RADFORD, E. M. & A.
DR.MANSON
1 Inspector Manson's success
2 Murder jigsaw
3 Crime pays no dividends
4 John Kyeling died
5 Who killed Dick Whittington?
6 Murder to live
7 Murder isn't cricket
8 Look in on m urder 1955
9 The heel of Achilles 1956
10 Death on the Broads 1958
11 Death of a frightened editor 1959
12 Death at the Chateau Noir 1959
13 Murder on my conscience 1960
14 Death's inheritance 1960
15 Death takes the wheel 1961
16 From information received 1962
17 A cosy little murder 1963
18 Murder of three hosts 1963
19 The hungry killer 1964
20 Mask of murder 1965
21 Murder magnified 1965
22 Death of a gentleman 1966

23 Nor reason for murder 1966
24 Jones's little murders 1967
25 Middlefold murders 1967
26 The safety first murders 1068
27 Trunk call for murder 1968
28 Death of an Ancient Saxon 1968
29 Death of a peculiar rabbit 1969
30 Two ways to murder 1969
31 Murder is a ruby red 1969
32 The greedy killers 1970
33 Dead water 1971
34 Death has two faces 1972

RADLEY, S.
DET.SUPT.QUANTRILL
1 Death and the maiden 1980
2 The Chief Inspector
3 A talent for destruction 1982
4 Blood on the happy highway 1984
5 Fate worse than death 1985
6 Who saw him die? 1987
7 This way out 1989
8 Cross my heart and hope to die 1992
9 Fair game 1994

RAINE, K.
1 Farewell, happy fields 1973
2 The land unknown 1975
3 The lion's mouth 1977
N.F. Autobiography

RAMSAY, D.
LIEUT. MEREDITH
1 Deadly discretion 1971
2 A little murder music 1972
3 No cause to kill 1973
4 You can't call it murder 1977

RANDALL, A. A.
ROGER PATTEN
1 Ride a tiger 1965
2 Flashpoint 1966

RANDALL, R.
1 The Drayton legacy 1986
2 The potter's niece 1987
3 The rival potters 1990

RANDISI, R. J.
MILES JACOBY
1 Eye in the ring 1984
2 The Steinway collection 1985
3 Full contact 1986

RANKIN, I.
INSPECTOR REBUS
1 Knots and crosses 1991
2 Hide and seek 1991
3 Wolfman 1992
4 A good hanging (short stories) 1992
5 Strip Jack 1992
6 The black book 1993
7 Mortal causes 1994

RANKIN, R.
1 The book of ultimate truths 1993
2 Raiders of the lost car park 1994
3 The greatest show off earth 1994

RANKIN, R.
ARMAGEDDON
1 Armageddon 1990
2 They came and ate us 1991
3 The suburban book of the dead 1992

RANKIN, R.
BRENTFORD TRILOGY
1 The anti-Pope
2 The Brentford triangle
3 East of Ealing
Paperback only

RANKINE, J.
FLETCHER
1 Interstellar 2-5 1969
2 One is one 1970
3 The Plantos affair 1971
4 The ring of Garamas 1972
5 The Bromium phenomenon 1976
Science fiction

RANKINE, J.
SPACE CORPORATION
1 Never the same door
2 Moon of Triopus
3 The Fingalnan conspiracy 1973
Science fiction

RANSOME, S.
SCHUYLER COLE
1 False bounty 1948
2 The deadly Miss Ashley 1950
3 Lilies in her garden grew 1951
4 Tread lightly, angel 1952
5 Drag the dark 1953
6 Deadly bedfellows 1955
7 The tragic acquittal 1955
8 Night drop 1956
9 So deadly my love 1958
10 The men in her death 1959
11 I'll die for you 1959

RATHBONE, J.
COLONEL NURI ARSLAN
1 Diamonds bid 1969
2 Handout 1970
3 Triptrap 1972

RATHBONE, J.
JAN ARGAND
1 The Eurokillers 1979
2 Base case 1981
3 Watching the detectives 1983

RATTRAY, S.
HUGO BISHOP
1 Knight sinister 1951
2 Queen in danger 1952
3 Bishop in check 1953
4 Rook's gambit 1954
5 Pawn in jeopardy 1955

RAVEN, S.
1 The old gang 1988
2 Is anyone there? 1990
N.F. Autobiography

RAVEN, S.
ALMS FOR OBLIVION
1 The rich pay ,late 1964
2 Friends in low places 1965
3 The sabre squadron 1966
4 Fielding Gray 1967
5 The Judas boy 1968
6 Places where they sing 1970
7 Sound the retreat 1971
8 Come like shadows 1972
9 Bring forth the body 1974
10 The survivors 1976

RAVEN, S.
THE FIRST BORN OF EGYPT
1 Morning star 1984
2 The face of the waters 1985
3 Before the cock crow 1986
4 New seed for old 1988
5 Blood of my bone 1989
6 In the image of God 1990
7 The troubadour 1992

RAVENLOFT
1 Vampires of the mists, by C.Golden
2 Knight of the black rose, By J.Lowder
3 Dance of the dead, by C.Golden
4 Heart of midnight, by R.J.King
5 Tapestry of dark souls, by E.Bergstrom
6 Carnival of fear, by J.R.King
7 I,Straub, by P.N.Elrod

8 The enemy within, by C.Golden
9 Mordenheim, by C.Williamson
Paperback horror

RAWN, M.
DRAGON PRINCE
1 Dragon prince 1989
2 The star scroll 1990
3 Sunrunner's file 1993
Fantasy

RAWN, M.
DRAGON STAR
1 Stronghold 1992
2 The dragon token 1993

RAYMOND, D.
FACTORY SERIES
1 He died with his eyes open 1984
2 The devil's home on leave 1985
3 How the dead live 1986
4 I was Dora Suarez 1990
5 Dead man upright 1993
6 Not till the red fog rises 1994

RAYMOND, E.
1 The story of my days 1968
2 Please you, draw near 1969
3 Good morning, good people 1970
N.F. Autobiography

RAYMOND, E.
A LONDON GALLERY
1 We, the accused 1935
2 The marsh 1937
3 Gentle Greaves 1949
4 The witness of Canon Welcome 1950
5 A chorus ending 1951
6 The Kilburn tale 1947
7 Child of Norman's End 1934
8 For them that trespass 1944
9 Was there love once?
10 The corporal of the guard 1943
11 A song of the tide 1940
12 The chalice and the sword 1952
13 To the wood no more 1954
14 The Lord of Wensley 1956
15 The old June weather 1957
16 The city and the dream 1958
17 Our late member 1972

RAYNER, C.
GEORGE BARNABAS
1 First blood 1993
2 Second opinion 1994

RAYNER, C.
POPPY CHRONICLES
1 Jubilee 1987
2 Flanders 1988
3 Flapper 1989
4 Blitz 1990
5 Festival 1991
6 Sixties 1992

RAYNER, C.
THE PERFORMERS
1 Gower Street 1973
2 The Haymarket 1974
3 Paddington Green 1975
4 Soho Square 1976
5 Bedford Row 1977
6 Long Acre 1978
7 Charing Cross 1979
8 The Strand 1980
9 Chelsea Reach 1982
10 Shaftesbury Avenue 1983
11 Piccadilly 1985
12 Seven Dials 1986
A family saga set in the 19th and 20th centuries

RAYNER, W.
THE DEVIL'S PICTURE BOOK
1 Wheels of fortune 1979
2 Knave of swords 1980

READ, MISS
1 A fortunate grandchild 1982
2 Time remembered 1986
N.F. Autobiography

READ, MISS
FAIRACRE
1 Village school 1954
2 Village diary 1956
3 Storm in the village 1960
4 Miss Clare remembers 1962
5 Over the gate 1964
6 Village Christmas 1966
7 Fairacre festival 1969
8 Tyler's Row 1972
9 Further afield 1974
10 No holly for Miss Quinn 1976
11 Village affairs 1977
12 The white robin 1979
13 Village centenary 1980
14 Summer at Fairacre 1984
15 Mrs.Pringle 1989
16 Changes at Fairacre 1991
17 Farewell to Fairacre 1993
'Chronicles of Fairacre' 1989, 'Christmas at Fairacre' 1991, and 'Fairacre roundabout' 1992 are omnibus volumes.

READ, MISS
THRUSH GREEN
1 Thrush Green 1960
2 Winter in Thrush Green 1961
3 News from Thrush Green 1970
4 Battles at Thrush Green 1975
5 Return to Thrush Green 1978
6 Gossip from Thrush Green 1981
7 Affairs at Thrush Green 1983
8 At home in Thrush Green 1985
9 The school at Thrush Green 1987
10 Friends at Thrush Green 1990
11 Celebrations at Thrush Green 1992

REEMAN, D.
BLACKWOOD FAMILY
1 Badge of glory 1982
2 The first to land 1984
3 The horizon 1993

REES, G.
1 A bundle of sensations 1960
2 A chapter of accidents 1971
N.F. Autobiography

REEVE, L-D.
ANNE BOLEYN
1 The early years 1980
2 The royal suitor 1981

REEVES-STEVENS, J.
THE CHRONICLES OF GALEN SWORD
1 Shifter
2 Nightfeeder
3 Black hunter
Paperback fantasy-horror

REICHERT, M. Z
LAST OF THE RENSHAI
1 Last of the Renshai 1993
2 The Western wizard 1993
3 Child of thunder 1994

REID, P. R.
1 The Colditz story 1953
2 The latter days 1955
3 Colditz:the full story 1984
4 Colditz:the german story, by
   R.Eggers 1961
5 The diggers of Colditz, by
   J.Champ & C.Burgess 85
6 Padre at Colditz,by J.E.Platt 1985
7 Tunnelling into Colditz,by
   J.Rogers 1986
8 Colditz last stop, by J.Pringle 1988
   *N.F. War stories about the prison
   camp. 1 & 2 were published in one
   volume, 'Colditz' in 1962*

REILLY, H.
INSPECTOR MCKEE
1 McKee of Centre Street 1934
2 Dead man control 1937
3 All concerned notified 1939
4 The dead can tell 1940
5 Murder in Shinbone Alley 1940
6 Death demands an audience 1940
7 Mourned on Sunday 1941
8 The opening door 1945
9 Murder on Angler's Island 1948
10 Silver leopard 1949
11 The farm house 1950
12 Staircase 4 1950
13 Murder at Arroways 1952
14 The velvet hand 1955
15 Not for me, Inspector 1960
16 Follow me 1961
17 The day she died 1963
18 Murder rides the express 1964

RENAULT, M.
ALEXANDER THE GREAT
1 Fire from heaven 1971
2 The Persian boy 1972
3 Funeral games 1981

RENAULT, M.
THESEUS
1 The King must die 1960
2 The bull from the sea 1962

RENDELL, R.
INSPECTOR WEXFORD
1 Put on by cunning 1981
2 From Doon with death 1965
3 A new lease of death 1967
4 Wolf to the slaughter 1968
5 The best man to die 1969
6 A guilty thing surprised 1970
7 No more dying then 1971
8 Murder being once done 1972
9 Some lie and some die 1973
10 Shake hands for ever 1975
11 A sleeping life 1978
12 Make death love me 1979
13 The speaker of Mandarin 1983
14 An unkindness of ravens 1985
15 The veiled one 1988
16 Kissing the gunner's daughter
   1992
17 Simisola 1994

REVELLI, G.
1 Commander Amanda Nightingale
   1969
2 Resort to war 1970

REYNOLDS, W. J.
NEBRASKA
1 Nebraska quotient 1986
2 Moving targets 1987
3 Money trouble 1988
4 Things invisible 1989
5 Naked eye 1990

RHEA, N.
1 Constable on the hill 1979
2 Constable on the prowl 1980
3 Constable around the village 1981
4 Constable across the moors 1982
5 Constable in the dale 1983
6 Constable by the sea 1985
7 Constable along the lane 1986
8 Constable through the meadow 1988
9 Constable at the double 1988
10 Constable in disguise 1989
11 Constable among the heather 1990
12 Constable at the double 1992
13 Constable around the green 1993
14 Constable beneath the trees 1994
N.F. Autobiography of a Yorkshire policeman Televised as 'Heartbeat', and 1, 2, & 5 published as 'The Heartbeat Omnibus' in 1992. 4 and 11 were reprinted with the prefix 'Heart- beat' in 1993

RHEA, N.
DET.SUPT.MARK PEMBERTON
1 False alibi 1991
2 Grave secrets 1992
3 Family ties 1994

RHINEHART, L.
1 The dice man 1971
2 The search for the dice man 1993

RHODES, D.
GUILHELM DE COURDEVAL
1 Next, after Lucifer 1988
2 Adversary 1989

RHODES, E.
1 Madeleine 1989
2 The house of Bonneau 1990

RICCI, N.
1 Lives of the saints 1991
2 In a glass house 1994

RICE, A.
CHRONICLES OF THE VAMPIRES
1 Interview with the vampires 1985
2 The vampire Lestat 1987
3 The Queen of the damned 1989

4 Tale of the bodythief 1993

RICE, A.
MAYFAIR FAMILY
1 The witching hour 1991
2 Lasher 1993
3 Taltos 1994

RICHARDS, A.
1 Ennal's Point 1977
2 Barque whisper 1979

RICHARDS, D. A.
1 Nights below Station Street 1988
2 Evening snow will bring such peace 1990
3 For those who hunt the wounded down 1993

RICHARDS, J.
1 The donkey walk 1968
2 Donkey in danger 1970

RICHARDSON, R.
AUGUSTUS MALTRAVERS
1 The Latimer Mercy 1987
2 Bellringer Street 1988
3 The book of the dead 1989
4 The dying of the light 1990
5 Sleeping in the blood 1991
6 The Lazarus tree 1992

RICHMOND, SIR A.
1 Twenty-six years 1963
2 Another sixty years 1965
N.F. Autobiography

RICHTER, C.
AMERICAN PIONEER TRILOGY
1 The trees 1940
2 The fields 1946
3 The town 1950

RIDLEY, S.
1 Nurse in danger 1963
2 Nurse in doubt 1964
3 Nurse in the South Seas 1965
4 Nurses and ladies 1967
5 Nurse in the mutiny 1970

RIFKIN, S.
MCQUAID
1 McQuaid
2 The snow rattlers
3 McQuaid in August

RIGBY, R.
1 The hill 1974
2 Hill of sand 1981

RIGBY, R.
PRIVATE JOHNNY JACKSON
1 Jackson's war 1967
2 Jackson's peace 1974
3 Jackson's England 1976

RILEY, J. M.
MARGARET OF ASHBURY
1 A vision of light 1990
2 In pursuit of the green lion 1991

RILEY, P.
JAMES SINCLAIR & JERRY WEINBERG
1 Serious misconduct 1993
2 Serious intent 1994
Medical thrillers

RILEY, S.
1 The black Madonna 1992
2 Garland of straw 1993
A family saga set during the English Civil War

RIPLEY, A.
CHARLESTON
1 Charleston
2 Return to Charleston
3 On leaving Charleston
Paperback historical novels about the American Civil War

RIPLEY, M.
FITZROY MACLEAN ANGEL
1 Just another angel 1988
2 Angel touch 1989
3 Angel hunt 1990
4 Angels in arms 1991
5 Angel city 1994

RIPPON, M.
INSPECTOR YGREC
1 Behold the druid weeps 1972
2 The ninth tentacle
3 The hand of Solange 1985

RIVERS, C.
1 Virgins 1984
2 Girls forever brave and true 1986

RIVKIN, J. F.
SILVERGLASS
1 Silverglass
2 Web of wind
Paperback fantasy

RIX, B.
1 My farce from my elbow 1974
2 Farce about face 1989
N.F.

ROBARDS, K.
1 Island flame 1985
2 Sea fire 1986
Bodice rippers

ROBB, C.
OWEN ARCHER
1 The apothecary rose 1994
2 The Lady Chapel 1994
Medieval mysteries.

ROBBINS, H.
HOLLYWOOD TRILOGY
1 The dream of merchants 1951
2 The carpetbaggers 1956
3 The inheritors 1964

ROBERSON, J.
CHRONICLES OF THE CHEYSULI
1 Shapechangers
2 The song of Homana
3 Legacy of the sword
4 Track of the white wolf
5 A pride of princes
6 Daughter of the lion
Paperback fantasy

ROBERTS, A. V.
1 Louisa Elliott 1989
2 Liam's story 1991

ROBERTS, C. S.
HERITAGE COAST
1 The running tide 1987
2 Upon stormy downs 1988
3 A wind from the sea 1989
4 A seagull crying 1989
5 The savage shore 1993
6 An end to summer 1994

ROBERTSON, C.
DET.SUPT.BRADLEY
1 Time to kill 1961
2 Conflict of shadows 1962
3 The frightened widow 1963
4 Dead on time 1964
5 Sinister moonlight 1965
6 Killer's mask 1966
7 Double take 1967
8 Twice dead 1968
9 The devil's cloak 1969
10 The green diamonds 1970

ROBERTSON, C.
PETER GAYLEIGH
1 The temple of dawn 1940
2 The amazing corpse 1941
3 Zero hour 1942
4 Alibi in black 1945

5 Explosion 1945
6 Two must die 1946
7 Dark knighyr 1946
8 Devil's lady 1947
9 Knave's castle 1948
10 Call Peter Gayleigh 1948
11 Sweet justice 1949
12 Death wears red shoes 1950
13 Dusky limelight 1950
14 Peter Gayleigh flies high 1957
15 Demon's moon 1951
16 The tiger's claw 1951
17 Smuggler's moon 1954
18 A lonely place to die 1956

ROBERTSON, C.
VICKY MACBAIN
1 The tiger's claw 1951
2 Venetian mask 1954
3 The Eastlake affair 1956
4 Who rides a tiger 1957
5 The golden triangle 1959
6 Night trip 1960
7 You can keep the corpse 1961
8 Murder sits pretty 1961

ROBERTSON, D.
BELGATE TRILOGY
1 The land of lost content 1985
2 A year of winter 1987
3 Blue remembered hills 1987
Published in one vol. under the first title 1988

ROBERTSON, D.
BELOVED PEOPLE
1 The beloved people 1992
2 Strength for the morning 1993
3 Towards Jerusalem 1993

ROBERTSON, J.
1 Any fool can be a pig farmer 1975
2 Any fool can be a dairy farmer 1980
3 Any fool can be a countryman 1983
4 Any fool can be a villager 1984
5 Any fool can be a yokel 1985
6 Any fool can be a country lover 1986
7 Any fool can keep a secret 1987
8 Any fool can see a vision 1988
9 Any fool can be independent 1989
N.F. Autobiography

ROBINS, P.
DICK & TAMILY
1 The long wait 1964
2 The constant heart 1965

3 The uncertain joy 1966

ROBINSON, D.
1 The Eldorado network
2 Artillery of lies 1991

ROBINSON, K. S.
MARS TRILOGY
1 Red Mars 1992
2 Green Mars 1993

ROBINSON, PETER
INSPECTOR BANKS
1 Gallows view 1988
2 A dedicated man 1989
3 A necessary end 1989
4 The hanging valley 1990
5 Past reason hated 1991

ROCHE, E.
FORTUNE AND POWER
1 The Berg family fortune 1985
2 New money 1986

ROCHRE, R. FRISON-
SIMON SOKKI
1 The raid 1964
2 The last migration 1967

ROCK, P.
1 Passing bells 1981
2 Circles of time 1982
3 A future arrived 1985

ROE, C. F.
DR.JEAN MONTROSE
1 The Lumsden baby 1989
2 Death by fire 1990
3 Bad blood 1991
4 Deadly partnership 1991
5 Fatal fever 1992
6 A death in the family 1993

ROGERS, R.
1 Sweet savage love 1982
2 Dark fires 1982
3 Lost love, last love 1981

ROHAN, M. S.
THE SPIRAL
1 Chase the morning 1990
2 The gates of noon 1992

ROHAN, M. S.
THE WINTER OF THE WORLD
1 The anvil of ice 1986
2 The forge in the forest 1987
3 The hammer of the sun 1988

ROHMER, S.
FU MANCHU
1 The mysterious Dr. Fu Manchu
2 The devil doctor
3 The Si-Fan mysteries
4 Daughter of Fu Manchu
5 The rturn of Dr.Fu Manchu
6 The insidious Dr.Fu Manchu
7 The hand of Dr. Fu Manchu
8 The mask of Fu Manchu
9 The bride of Fu Manchu
10 President Fu Manchu
11 The drums of Fu Manchu
12 The island of Fu Manchu
13 The shadow of Fu Manchu
14 Emperor Fu Manchu
15 Re-enter Dr. Fu Manchu 1957
16 The wrath of Fu Manchu 1973

ROHMER, S.
SUMURU
1 Sins of Sumuru
2 Slaves of Sumuru
3 Virgin in flames
4 The moon is red
5 Sand and satin
6 Sinister Madonna 1956

ROLPH, C. H.
1 London particulars 1980
2 Further particulars 1987
N.F. Autobiography of a criminologist

RONAN, T.
1 Deep of the sky 1962
2 Pack horse and pearling boat 1964
3 Once there was a bagman 1966
N.F. Life in Australia

ROOME, A.
1 A real shot in the arm 1989
2 A second shot in the arm 1990

ROOSEVELT, ELLIOTT
WHITE HOUSE MYSTERIES
1 Murder and the First Lady 1984
2 The Hyde Park murder 1985
3 Murder at the Palace 1987
4 The White House pantry murder 1987
5 Murder in the Oval Office 1990
6 Murder in the West Wing 1994
7 A Royal murder 1994

ROSCOE, M.
JOHNNY APRIL
1 Death is a round black ball 1954
2 Riddle me this 1955
3 A slice of hell 1955

4 One tear for my grave 1956

ROSEN, R.
HARVEY BLISSBERG
1 Strike three,you're dead 1985
2 Fadeaway
3 Saturday night dead 1989

ROSENBERG, J.
GUARDIANS OF THE FLAME
1 The sleeping dragon
2 The sword and the chain
3 The silver crown
4 The heir apparent
5 The warrior lives
Paperback fantasy

ROSS, A.
MARK FARROW
1 The Manchester thing 1970
2 The Huddersfield job 1971
3 The London assignment 1972
4 The Dunfermline affair 1973
5 The Bradford business 1974
6 The Amsterdam diversion 1974
7 The Leeds fiasco 1975
8 The Edinburgh exercise 1975
9 The Ampurias exchange 1976
10
11 The Burgos contract 1978
12 The Congleton lark 1979
13 The Hamburg switch 1980
14 The Menwith tangle 1982
15 The Darlington jaunt 1985
16 The Tyneside ultimatum 1988

ROSS, C.
1 The haunted seventh
2 When the devil was sick

ROSS, CAMERON
ALISTAIR DUNCAN
1 Case for compensation 1980
2 Villa plot,counterplot 1981
3 The scaffold 1981

ROSS, D. F.
WAGONS WEST
1 Independence
2 Nebraska
3 Wyoming
4 Oregon
5 Texas
6 California
7 Colorado
8 Nevada
9 Washington
10 Montana 1992
11 Dakota 1992

12 Utah 1992
13 Idaho 193
14 Missouri 1993
15 Mississippi 1994
16 Louisiana 1994
17 Tennessee 1994
18 Illinois 1994
Dates are for hardback editions

ROSS, I.
PAUL SHAW
1 Rocking the boat 1990
2 Beverley Hills butler 1991
3 How green was my valet 1992

ROSS, I. T.
BEN GORDON
1 Requiem for a schoolgirl 1960
2 Murder out of school 1961
3 Old students never die 1963
4 The man who would do anything 1964
5 Teacher's blood 1965

ROSS, JEAN
1 Under a glass dome
2 The garden by the river

ROSS, JONATHAN
CHIEF INSPECTOR ROGERS
1 The blood running cold 1968
2 Diminished by death 1968
3 Dead at first hand 1969
4 The deadest thing you ever saw 1969
5 Here lies Nancy Frail 1970
6 The burning of Billy Topper 1974
7 I know what it
8 A rattling of old bones 1978
9 Dark blue and dangerous 1981
10 Death's head 1982
11 Dead eye 1983
12 Dropped dead 1984
13 Burial deferred 1985
14 Fate accomplished 1987
15 Sudden departures 1988
16 A time for dying 1989
17 Daphne dead and done for 1990
18 Murder be hanged 1992
19 The body of a woman 1994

ROSS, K.
JULIAN KESTREL
1 Cut to the quick 1993
2 A broken vessel 1994

ROSS, S.
CIVIL WAR
1 Vagabond treasure 1957

2 The sword is king 1958
3 Drum and trumpet sound! 1960

ROSSITER, J.
1 The manipulators 1973
2 The villains 1974

ROSSITER, J.
ROGER TALLIS
1 The murder makers 1969
2 The deadly green 1970
3 A rope for General Dietz 1972
4 The golden virgin 1975

ROSTEN, L.
1 The education of Hyman Kaplan
2 The return of Hyman Kaplan
3 O Kaplan, my Kaplan 1979

ROTH, J.
1 Radetzky march
2 The Emperor's tomb 1984
Not directly linked, but the characters are related

ROTH, L.
1 I'll cry tomorrow
2 Beyond my worth
N.F. Autobiography

ROTH, P.
ZUCKERMANN
1 The ghost writer 1979
2 Zuckermann unbound 1981
3 The anatomy lesson 1984
4 The Prague orgy 1985
5 The counterlife 1987

ROTHEART, M.
HENRY V
1 Cry 'God for Harry' 1972
2 Cry 'God for Glendower' 1973

ROTHENSTEIN, SIR J.
1 Summer's lease 1964
2 Brave day, hideous night 1966
3 Time's thievish progress 1970
N.F. Autobiography

ROTHWELL, H. T.
MICHAEL BROOKS
1 Exit a spy 1967
2 Dive deep for danger 1968
3 Duet for three spies 1968
4 No honour among spies 1969
5 No kisses from the Kremlin 1969

ROUGVIE, C.
ROBERT BELCOURT
1 Medal for Pamplona 1963
2 Tangier assignment 1965
3 The Gredos reckoning 1966
4 When Johnny died 1967

ROWLANDS, B.
MELISSA CRAIG
1 A little gentle sleuthing 1990
2 Finishing touch 1991
3 Over the edge 1992
4 Exhaustive enquiries 1993

ROWLEY, L.
THE FENRILLE BOOKS
1 The war for eternity
2 YThe black ship
3 The founder
4 To a highland nation

ROWLEY, L.
THE VANG
1 The battlemaster
2 The military farm
Paperback fantasy

ROWSE, A. L.
1 A Cornish childhood 1942
2 A Cornishman at Oxford 1965
3 A Cornishman abroad 1979
N.F. Autobiography

ROYCE, K.
SPIDER SCOTT & INSPECTOR BULMAN
1 The XYY man 1970
2 The concrete boot 1971
3 The miniatures frame 1972
4 Spider underground 1974
5 Trap Spider 1974
6 The crypto man 1984
7 The Mosley receipt 1985
8 No way back 1986
9 The Ambassador's son 1994

ROYSTON, J.
1 The Penhale heiress 1988
2 The Penhale fortune 1989

RUARK, R.
1 Grenadine Etching 1968
2 Grenadine's spawn 1970

RUBENSTEIN, A.
1 My young years 1973
2 My many years 1980
N.F. Autobiography

RUCK, B.
1 A storyteller tells the truth
2 A smile for the past
3 A trickle of Welsh blood 1967
4 An asset to Wales 1970
5 Ancestral voices 1972
N.F. Autobiography

RUCK, R. J.
1 Place of stones 1970
2 Hill farm story 1966
3 Along came a llama 1978
N.F. Autobiography

RUHEN, C.
NEIGHBOURS
1 Neighbours
2 Indiscretions
3 Home truths 1988
4 Testing times 1989
5 Family matters 1989
6 Special friends 1989
7 Dark secrets 1989
8 Unsolved crimes
9 Cover stories 1990
Based on the TV series

RUNDLE, A.
AMBERWOOD
1 Amberwood 1973
2 Heronbrook 1975
3 Judith Lammeter 1976

RUSH, R.
1 The birthday treat 1983
2 The birthday girl 1983
Horror stories

RUSSELL, D.
THE TAMARISK TREE
1 My quest for liberty and love 1975
2 My school and the years of war 1980
3 Challenge to the Cold War 1985
N.F. Autobiography of the wife of Bertrand Russell

RUSSELL, M.
JIM LARKIN
1 Deadline 1972
2 Concrete evidence 1973
3 Crime wave 1974
4 Phantom holiday 1974
5 Murder by the mile 1975

RUSSELL, R.
DR.STEVEN RUSHTON
1 Go on, I'm listening 1983
2 While you're here, Doctor 1985

RUSSO, R.
1 Mohawk 1986
2 The risk pool 1989
About a small town in New York State

RYAN, C.
1 The longest day 1960
2 The last battle 1966
3 A bridge too far 1974
N.F. A trilogy on WW2

RYAN, F.
DET. INSPECTOR SANDY WORDINGS
1 Sweet summer 1987
2 Tiger, tiger 1988
3 Goodbye, baby blue 1990

RYBAKOV, A.
1 Children of the Arbat 1988
2 Fear 1993

SABBAGH, P.
1 Fanina 1966
2 Fanina, child of Rome 1967

SABERHAGEN, F.
BERSERKER
1 Berserker man
2 Brother Berserker
3 Berserker's planet
4 Berserker blue death
Paperback fantasy

SABERHAGEN, F.
BOOK OF SWORDS
1 The first book of swords
2 The second book of swaords
3 The third book of swords
4 The first book of lost swords:Woundhealer's story
5 The second book of lost swords:Sightbinder's story
6 The third book of lost swords:Stonecutter's story
Paperback fantasy

SACHS, M.
1 Witches' sabbath 1964
2 The hunt 1967

SADDLER, K. A.
DAVE STEVENS
1 The great brain robbery 1965
2 Gilt edge 1966
3 Talking turkey 1967

SADLER, B.
CASCA
1 The eternal mercenary
2 God of death
3 The war lord
Paperback fantasy

SADLER, G.
JUSTUS
1 The lash
2 Bloodwater
3 Black vengeance
Paperback slave saga

SADLER, J.
ANDERSON
1 Arizona blood trail 1981
2 Sonora lode 1982
3 Tamaulipas guns 1982
4 Severo siege 1983
5 Lobo moon 1983
6 Sierra showdown 1983
7 Throw of a rope 1984
8 Manhunt in Chihuahua 1985
9 Return of Amarillo 1986
10 Montana mine 1987
11 Saltillo Road 1987
12 Long gun war 1988
13 Palomino stud 1988
14 Ghost town guns 1990
15 Headed nirth 1992
16 Matamoros mission 1993
17 Hangrope journey 1994

SAHGAL, N.
1 Prison and chocolate cake
2 From fear set free
N.F. Autobiography

SALINGER, J. D.
GLASS FAMILY
1 For Esme with love and squalor 1953
2 Franny and Zooey 1962
3 Raise high the roof beam, carpenters 1963
4 Seymour 1963

SALISBURY, R.
1 Close the door behind you 1982
2 When the boys came out to play 1984
3 Birds of the air 1988
4 Sweet Thursday 1990

SALLIS, S.
RISING FAMILY
1 A scattering of daisies 1985
2 The daffodils of Newent 1985

3 Bluebell windows 1987
4 Rosemary for remembrance 1987

SALTER, E.
INSPECTOR HORNSLEY
1 Death in a mist 1957
2 Will to survive 1958
3 There was a witness 1960
4 Voice of the peacock 1962
5 Once upon a tombstone 1963

SALVATORE, R. A.
DARK ELF TRILOGY
1 Homeland 1990
2 Exile 1991
3 Sojourn 1991

SALVATORE, R. A.
ICEWIND DALE TRILOGY (FORGOTTEN REALMS)
1 The crystal shard
2 Streams of silver
3 The halfing's gem

SALVATORE, R. A.
THE CLERIC QUINTET
1 Canticle
2 In sylvan shadow
3 Night masks
4 The fallen fortress
5 The chaos curse
Paperback fantasy

SAM
1 Sam, by J.Powell 1973
2 Stay single and live forever, by L.Sands 1974
3 Up in the world, by L.Sands 1976
Based on the TV series

SAMPSON, F.
DAUGHTER OF TINTAGEL
1 Wise woman's telling 1989
2 White nun's telling 1989
3 Black smith's telling 1990
4 Taliesin's telling 1991
5 Herself 1992

SAMPSON, G.
PAOLA & GEORGE
1 Drug on the market 1967
2 Playing with fire 1968

SANDEL, C.
1 Alberta and Jacob 1962
2 Alberta and freedom 1963
3 Alberta alone 1964

SANDERS, B.
WARD & SALLY DIGBURN
1 Secret dragnet 1956
2 To catch a spy 1958
3 Code to dishonour 1965
4 Feminine for spy 1967

SANDERS, J.
NICHOLAS PYM
1 A firework for Oliver 1964
2 The hat of authority 1965
3 Without trumpet or drum 1966
4 Cromwell's Cavalier 1968
5 Roundabout retreat 1971

SANDERS, L.
ARCHY MCNALLY
1 McNally's secret 1991
2 McNally's luck 1992
3 McNally's risk 1993
4 McNally's caper 1994

SANDERS, L.
PETER TANGENT
1 Tangent objective 1977
2 Tangent factor 1978

SANDERS, L.
TIMOTHY CONE
1 The Timothy files 1987
2 Timothy's game 1988

SANDFORD, J.
LUCAS DAVENPORT
1 Rules of prey 1989
2 Shadow prey 1990
3 Eyes of prey 1991
4 Silent prey 1992
5 Night prey 1994

SANDISON, J.
AN APOLOGY FOR THE LIFE OF JEAN ROBERTSON
1 Jean in the morning 1969
2 Jean at noon 1971
3 Jean in the twilight 1972
4 Jean towards another day 1975

SANDON, J. D.
GRINGOS
1 Guns across the river
2 Cannons in the rain
3 Fire in the wind
4 Border affair
5 Easy money
6 Mazatlan
7 One too many mornings
8 Wheels of thunder
9 Durango

10 Survivors
   Paperback Westerns

SANGSTER, J.
JOHN SMITH
1 Private I
2 Foreign exchange

SANGSTER, J.
KATY TOUCHFEATHER:AIR HOSTESS
1 Touchfeather 1969
2 Touchfeather, too 1970

SAROYAN, W.
1 Mama I love you 1956
2 Papa you're crazy 1957

SAS SERIES
1 Soldier A:behind Iraqui lines 1993
2 Soldier B:heroes of the South
   Atlantic 1993
3 Soldier C: secret war in Arabia
   1993
4 Soldier D:the Colombian cocaine
   war 1993
5 Soldier E: sniper fire in Belfast
   1993
6 Soldier F: guerrillas in the jungle
   1993
7 Soldier G:the desert raiders 1994
8 Soldier H:the headhunters of
   Borneo 1993
9 Soldier I:eighteen years in the elite
   force 1994
10 Soldier J: Counter-insurgency in
   Aden 1994
11 Soldier K:mission to Argentina
   1994
12 Soldier L: the Embassy siege 1994
13 Soldier O:the Bosnian inferno 1994
14 Soldier P: night fighters in France
   1994
   All by Shaun Clarke, except for 4 &
   11, by D. Monnery, and 9, by
   M. P. Kennedy. SAS Omnibus(Books
   1-3) published in hardback 1994

SATTERTHWAIT, W.
JOSHUA CROFT
1 At ease with the dead 1991
2 A flower in the desert 1992
3 The death card 1994

SAUL, R.
FIELD
1 The next best thing 1986
2 The paradise eater 1988

SAVA, G.
1 The healing knife 1937
2 The lure of surgery 1955
   N.F. Autobiography

SAVA, G.
PETER SLAVINE
1 A boy in Samarkand 1950
2 Caught by revolution 1952
3 Flight from the palace 1953
4 Pursuit in the desert 1955

SAVAGE, A.
BARRINGTON FAMILY
1 The eight banners 1992
2 The last bannerman 1993

SAVARIN, J. J.
GORDON GALLAGHER
1 Waterhole 1983
2 Wolf run 1984
3 Windshear 1985
4 Naja 1986
5 The Quiraing list 1988

SAVARIN, J. J.
LEMMUS, A TIME TRILOGY
1 Waiters on the dance 1972
2 Children of lemmus 1972
3 Beyond the Outer Mirr 1973

SAVILLE, A.
BERGERAC
1 Bergerac and the fatal weakness
2 Bergerac and the Jersey Rose
3 Bergerac and the moving fever
4 Bergerac and the traitor's child
   Paperbacks based on the TV series.

SAWKINS, R.
JOHN SNOW
1 Snow on high ground 1966
2 Snow in Paradise 1967
3 Snow along the border 1968

SAXON, P.
THE GUARDIANS
1 Dark ways of death 1966
2 Through the dark curtain 1967
3 The curse of Rathlaw 1968
4 Vampires of Finisterre 1968
5 The killing bone 1968

SAXTON, J.
NEYLER FAMILY
1 The pride 1983
2 The glory 1983
3 The splendour 1984
4 Full circle 1985

SCANLON, N.
QUINN
1 Quinn 1975
2 Quinn and the desert oil 1976

SCANNELL, D.
1 Mother knew best 1976
2 Dolly's war 1976
3 Dolly's mixture 1977
N.F. Autobiography

SCANNELL, D.
BRIGHT FAMILY
1 Polly Bright 1984
2 Jet Bright 1985

SCANNELL, V.
1 Drums of morning 1992
2 Argument of kings 1987
3 The tiger and the rose 1971

SCARBOROUGH, E.
ARGONIAN SERIES
1 The song of sorcery
2 The unicorn creed
3 Bronwyn's bane
Paperback fantasy

SCHIDDEL, E.
1 The devil in Buck's County 1962
2 Scandal's child 1963
3 Devil' summer 1965

SCHMIDT, D.
TWILIGHT OF THE GODS
1 The first name
2 Groa's other eye
3 Three trumps sounding

SCHMITZ, J. H.
TELZEY AMBERDOM
1 The eternal frontiers 1974
2 The Telzey toy 1976
3 The lion game 1976

SCHOLEFIELD, A.
1 A view of vultures 1966
2 Great elephant 1967

SCHOLEFIELD, A. T.
DET.SUPT.GEORGE MACRAE &
DET.SGT.LEOPOLD SILVER
1 Dirty weekend 1990
2 Thief taker 1991
3 Never die in January 1992
4 Threats and menaces 1993
5 Don't be a nice girl 1994

SCOPPETTONE, S.
LAUREN LAURANO
1 Everything you have is mine 1993
2 I'll be leaving you always 1994

SCOTT, A.
1 Scott free 1986
2 Scott goes south 1988
N.F. Travel

SCOTT, B.
STEVE MACLAREN
1 Prayer mat 1967
2 The secret of the elephant 1968
3 A hell of a spot 1971

SCOTT, BRAD
WALT SLADE
1 Death's harvest
2 Texas death
3 Pecos law
4 Thunder trail
5 Blood on the moon
6 Six-gun fury
7 Rider of the mesquite trail
8 Curse of dead men's gold
9 Lead and flame
10 The border terror
11 Outlaw roundup
12 Red road to vengeance
13 Haunted valley
14 The sky riders
15 Boom town riders
16 The river raiders
Paperback Westerns

SCOTT, D.
1 Typhoon pilot
2 One more hour 1989
N.F. Autobiography of a fighter pilot

SCOTT, J.
DET.INSPECTOR ROSHER
1 The poor old lady
2 A better class of business 1976
3 A shallow grave 1977
4 A clutch of vipers 1979
5 The gospel lamb 1980
6 A distant view of death 1981
7 An uprush of mayhem 1982
8 The local lads 1982
9 A death in Irish Town 1983
10 All the pretty people 1983
11 A knife between the ribs 1986

SCOTT, J. M.
1 Snowstone
2 The silver land

SCOTT, MARY
1 Breakfast at six 1955
2 Dinner doesn't matter 1957
3 Tea and biscuits 1962
4 A change from mutton 1965
5 Turkey at twelve 1968
6 Haven't we met before? 1970
7 If I don't, who will? 1971
8 Shepherd's pie 1972
9 Strangers for tea 1975
10 Board but no breakfast 1978
N.F. Life in new Zealand

SCOTT, MARY
FREDDIE
1 Families are fun 1963
2 No sad songs 1964
3 Freddie 1965

SCOTT, MICHAEL
TALES OF THE BARD
1 Magician's law
2 Demon's law
3 Death's law
Paperback fantasy

SCOTT, P.
THE RAJ QUARTET
1 The jewel in the crown 1966
2 The day of the scorpion 1968
3 The towers of silence 1971
4 Division of the spoils 1975

SCOTT, SHEILA
1 I must fly 1971
2 On the top of the world 1973
N.F. Autobiography

SCOTT, SUTHERLAND
SEPTIMUS DODD
1 Murder is infectious 1936
2 The influenza mystery 1938
3 Murder in the mobile unit 1944
4 Operation urgent 1946
5 Blood in their ink 1947
6 The mass radiography murders 1947
7 Tincture of murder 1951
8 Diagnosis:murder 1954
9 Dr.Dodd's experiment 1955

SCYOC, S. J.
1 Darkchild
2 Bluesong
3 Starsilk
Paperback science fiction

SEAFARER
CAPTAIN FIREBRACE
1 Captain Firebrace 1953
2 Firebrace and the 'Java Queen' 1956
3 Firebrace and Father Kelly 1957
4 Smuggler's pay for Firebrace 1959

SEAGRAVE, G. S.
1 Burma surgeon
2 Burma surgeon returns
3 My hospital in the hills
N.F. Autobiography

SEATON, S.
INSPECTOR MARTIN LAIDMAN
1 Don't take it to heart 1955
2 Dust in your eye 1957

SECOMBE, F.
1 How green was my curate 1988
2 A curate for all seasons 1990
3 Goodbye curate 1992
4 Hello vicar 1993
5 A comedy of clerical errors 1994
N.F. Autobiography

SEDLEY, K.
ROGER THE CHAPMAN
1 Death and the Chapman 1991
2 The Plymouth cloak 1992
3 The hanged man 1993
4 The holy innocents 1994
Elizabethan murder mysteries

SEGAL, O.
1 Love story 1970
2 Oliver's story 1977

SEGER, M.
1 Sarah 1988
2 Elizabeth 1989
3 Catherine 1989
A trilogy about sisters in the American Civil War

SELA, O.
NICK MAASTEN
1 The bearer plot 1972
2 The Portuguese fragment 1974

SELLERS, M.
CALOSTE FISHER
1 Leonardo and others 1980
2 From eternity to here 1981
3 Cache on the rocks 1982

SELVON, S.
THE LONELY LONDONERS
1 The lonely Londoners 1956
2 Moses ascending 1975
3 Moses imagrating 1983

SELWYN, F.
SERGEANT VERITY
1 Cracksman on velvet 1974
2 Sergeant Verity and the Imperial diamond 1975
3 Sergeant Verity presents his compliments 1977
4 Sergeant Verity and the blood royal 1979
5 Sergeant Verity and the swell mob 1981

SEMYONOV, J.
1 Tass is authorised to announce 1987
2 Intercontinental knot 1988

SERAFIN, D.
SUPT. LUIS BERNAL
1 Saturday of glory 1979
2 Madrid underground 1982
3 Christmas rising 1982
4 The body in Cadiz Bay 1985
5 Port of light 1987
6 The angel of Torremolinos 1988
Detective stories set in Spain

SERLING, R.
1 The President's plane is missing 1978
2 Air Force One is haunted 1986

SETTLE, M. L.
BEULAH QUINTET
1 The long road to Paradise [Prisons] 1974
2 O Beulah land 1956
3 Know nothing 1960
4 The scapegoat 1980
5 The killing ground 1983
About the life and social change in America from the settlers in Cromwellian times to 1980. Reprinted in paperback in 1988, with a change of title for vol. 1

SEUFFERT, M.
MIKE HUBBARD
1 Hand of a killer 1967
2 Trespassers will die 1968
3 Devil at the door 1969

SEVERN, R.
JEFF CASS
1 Stalk a long shadow
2 Game for hawks
3 The killing match

SEWART, A.
DET.INSPECTOR EVANS
1 Loop current 1980
2 The turn up 1981

SEWART, A.
DET.SGT.CHAMBERLAYNE
1 In that rich earth 1981
2 A romp in green heat 1981
3 Smoker's cough 1982
4 Drink! for once dead 1983
5 Dead man drifting 1984

SEYMOUR, A.
1 The land where I belong 1970
2 Fragrant the fertile earth 1971
N.F. Autobiography of a farmer

SEYMOUR, ANN
ANNE BOLEYN
1 Maid of destiny 1970
2 The bitter chalice 1972

SEYMOUR, ARABELLA
1 The sins of Rebeccah Russell 1988
2 The end of the family 1990

SEYMOUR, JEANETTE
PURITY
1 Purity's passion
2 Purity's ecstasy
3 Purity's shame

SEYMOUR, JOHN
1 On my own terms
2 The fat of the land
N.F. Autobiography

SHADBOLT, M.
FERDINAND WILDBLOOD
1 Season of the Jew 1986
2 Monday's warriors 1990
3 The house of strife 1993

SHADOWRUN
1 Never deal with a dragon,by N.Findley
2 Choose your enemies carefully, by N.Findley
3 Find your own truth,by R.N.Charrette
4 2XS, by N.Findley
5 Changeling, by C.Kubasik

6 Never trust an elf, by
  R.N.Charrette
7 Streets of blood, by C.Sargent
8 Shadowplay, by N.Findley

SHAH, D. K.
PARIS CHAN
1 As crime goes by 1991
2 Dying cheek to cheek 1992

SHAKESPEARE, L. M.
JAMES ROSS-GILBERT
1 Utmost good faith 1988
2 The gentlemen's Mafia 1989
  *Financial thrillers set in Lloyds of
  London*

SHANE, B.
1 Railhead
2 Iron rails
3 Rails west
  Paperback Westerns

SHANNON, D.
LUIS MENDOZA
1 Extra kill 1962
2 The ace of spades 1963
3 Knave of hearts 1963
4 Death of a busybody 1963
5 Double bluff 1964
6 Case pending 1964
7 Mark of murder 1965
8 Root of all evil 1966
9 The death-bringers 1966
10 Death by inches 1967
11 Coffin corner 1967
12 With a vengeance 1968
13 Chance to kill 1969
14 Rain with violence 1969
15 Kill with kindness 1969
16 Schooled to kill 1970
17 Crime on their hands 1970
18 Unexpected death 1971
19 Whim to kill 1971
20 The ringer 1972
21 Murder with love 1972
22 With intent to kill 1973
23 No holiday for crime 1974
24 Spring of violence 1974
25 Crime file 1975
26 Deuces wild 1976
27 Streets of death 1977
28 Cold trail 1978
29 Felony at random 1979
30 Felony file 1980
31 Murder most strange 1981
32 The motive on record 1982
33 Exploit of death 1983
34 Destiny of death 1985

35 Chaos of crime 1986
36 Blood count 1987
  *Nos. 1-5 were published under the
  author name, Elizabeth Linington*

SHANNON, DORIS
ROBERT FORSYTH
1 Death for a doctor 1986
2 A death for a dancer 1987
3 Death for a dreamer 1991
4 Death for a double 1992
5 Death for a dietician
6 Death for a darling
7 Death for a dilettante
  5-7 not published in UK

SHARAM, N.
WHITE DOG TRILOGY
1 The white earth 1986
2 The white arrow 1987
3 White rage 1988

SHARP, A.
JOHN MOSELY
1 A green tree in Gedde 1966
2 The wind shifts 1967
3 The apple pickers 1969

SHARP, M.
1 The eye of love 1961
2 Martha in Paris 1962
3 Martha, Eric and George 1964

SHARPE, T.
1 Riotous assembly 1971
2 Indecent exposure 1972

SHARPE, T.
WILT
1 Wilt 1977
2 The Wilt alternative 1979
3 Wilt on high 1984

SHATNER, W.
JAKE CARDIGAN
1 Tekwar 1990
2 Teklords 1991
3 Teklab 1992
4 Tek vengeance 1993

SHAW, B.
1 Who goes here? 1977
2 Warren Peace 1993

SHAW, B.
ASTRONAUTS
1 The ragged astronauts 1986
2 The wooden spaceships 1988

SHAW, B.
ORBITSVILLE
1 Orbitsville
2 Orbitsville departure 1983
3 Orbitsville judgement 1990

SHAW, I.
JORDACHE FAMILY
1 Rich man, poor man 1970
2 Beggarman, thief 1977

SHAW, S.
PHILIP FLETCHER
1 Murder out of tune 1988
2 Bloody instructions 1991
3 Dead for a ducat 1992
4 The villain of the earth 1994

SHEA, K.
THE SARACEN
1 Land of the infidel
2 The Holy War

SHEA, R.
SHIKE
1 Time of the dragons 1981
2 Last of the Zinja 1982
Set in Japan during the war against the Khans

SHEA, R. & WILSON, R. A.
ILLUMINATUS
1 Eye of the pyramid
2 The golden apple
3 Leviathan
Paperback science fiction

SHEARS, S.
1 Tapioca for tea 1970
2 Gather no moss 1972
3 The seventh commandment 1973
4 Other people's children 1978
N.F. Autobiography

SHEARS, S.
ANNIE PARSONS
1 Annie Parsons 1978
2 Annie's boys 1979
3 Annie's kingdom 1980

SHEARS, S.
COURAGE
1 Child of gentle courage 1973
2 Courage in darkness 1974
3 Courage to serve 1974
4 Courage in war 1976
5 Courage in parting 1977

SHEARS, S.
FRANKLIN FAMILY
1 The village 1984
2 Family fortunes 1985
3 The young generation 1986
4 Return to Russets 1990

SHEARS, S.
LOUISE
1 Louise 1975
2 Louise's daughters 1976
3 Louise's inheritance 1977

SHEARS, S.
THE NEIGHBOURS
1 The neighbours 1982
2 The neighbours' children 1983

SHEARS, S.
THOMAS
1 The sisters 1988
2 Thomas 1989
3 Son of Thomas 1991

SHECKLEY, R.
HUNT
1 Victim prime 1987
2 Tenth victim 1966
3 Hunter/victim 1988
Science fiction

SHEFFIELD, C.
HERITAGE UNIVERSE
1 Summertide 1990
2 Divergance 1991
3 Transcendance 1992

SHELBY, G.
CANNAWAYS
1 The Cannaways 1978
2 The Cannaway concern 1981

SHELBY, G.
THIRD CRUSADE
1 The knights of dark renown 1968
2 The Kings of vain intent 1970

SHELBY, G.
WILLIAM MARSHAL
1 The devil is loose 1972
2 The wolf at the door 1975

SHELDON, S.
1 The other side of midnight 1975
2 Memories of midnight 1990

SHELYNN, J.
NED PARKER
1 A place called Purgatory 1978

2 The night marches 1978
3 The Cuoto snatch 1979
4 For a girl called Isiah 1979
5 The Judas factor 1980
6 Joker in a stacked deck 1981

SHELYNN, J.
SAM CLAYTON
1 The affair at Cralla Voe 1978
2 A fall of snow 1980
3 Epilogue for Selena 1980

SHEPHARD, E. H.
1 Drawn from memory 1957
2 Drawn from life 1961
N.F. Autobiography

SHEPHERD, S.
DET. INSPECTOR RICHARD
MONTGOMERY
1 Thinner than blood 1991
2 A lethal fixation 1993
3 Nurse Dawes is dead 1994

SHERWOOD, JOHN
CELIA GRANT
1 Green trigger fingers 1984
2 A botanist at bay 1985
3 The mantrap garden 1986
4 Flowers of evil 1987
5 Menacing groves 1988
6 A bouquet of thorns 1989
7 The sunflower plot 1990
8 The hanging garden 1992
9 Creeping Jenny 1993
10 Bones gather no moss 1994
Thrillers about a horticulturalist

SHERWOOD, JOHN
MR. BLESSINGTON
1 The disappearance of
Dr.Bruderstein 1949
2 Mr.Blessington's plot 1951
3 Ambush for Anatol 1952
4 Vote for poison 1956

SHERWOOD, V.
1 Bold breathless love
2 Real reckless love
3 Wild wilful love
4 Rich radiant love
Paperback bodice rippers

SHERWOOD, V.
LOVESONG
1 The beauty and the English lord
1987

2 The beauty and the buccaneer
1987
Bodice rippers

SHERWOOD, V.
THIS TOWERING PASSION
1 The lovers 1991
2 The mistress 1991

SHIPLEY, R.
MILLARD FAMILY
1 Wychwood 1989
2 Echoes of Wychwood 1991

SHIPWAY, G.
1 The Paladin 1972
2 The wolf time 1973

SHIPWAY, G.
AGAMEMNON
1 Warrior in bronze 1977
2 King in splendour 1979

SHORT, A.
1 The heritors 1977
2 Clatter vengeance 1979

SHORT, A.
CHRISTIE FAMILY
1 The first fair wind 1984
2 The running tide 1986
3 The dragon seas 1988
*Novels about the Scottish fishing
industry*

SHORT, A.
SILVERCAIRNS
1 Silvercairns 1990
2 Rainbow Hill 1991
3 Willowbrae 1992

SHULMAN, S.
1 Francesca the Florentine 1971
2 The Madonna of the shadows 1973

SHUPP, M.
DESTINY MAKERS
1 With fate conspire
2 Morning of creation
3 Soldier of another fortune
4 Death's grey land

SHWARTZ, S.
HEIRS TO BYZANTIUM
1 Byzantium's crown
2 The woman of flowers
3 Queensblade
Paperback fantasy

SIBLEY, P.
1 High wald to Wandlemere 1973
2 Ravens in winter 1974

SILKE, J. R.
DEATH DEALER
1 Prisoner of the horned helmet
2 Lords of destruction
3 Tooth and claw
4 Plague of knives

SILLIPHANT, S.
JOHN LOCKE
1 Steel tiger 1986
2 Bronze bell 1987

SILLITOE, A.
1 The death of William Posters 1965
2 A tree on fire 1967
3 The flame of life 1979

SILLITOE, A.
MICHAEL CULLEN
1 A start in life 1970 (rev. ed. 1979)
2 Life goes on 1986

SILLITOE, A.
SEATON FAMILY
1 The open door 1990
2 The key to the door 1961
3 Saturday night and Sunday
  morning 1958

SILVERBERG, R.
MAJIPOOR
1 Lord Valentine's castle 1981
2 Majipoor chronicles 1982
3 Valentine Pontifex 1984

SILVERBERG, R.
NEW SPRINGTIME
1 At winter's end 1988
2 The Queen of springtime 1989

SILVERBERG, R. & GARRETT, R.
1 The shrouded planet
2 The dawning light

SILVERMAN, D.
JOHN MUNG
1 The fall of the Shogun 1986
2 The black dragon 1988
3 Shishi 1989
4 Tairo:the great elder 1990

SILVERWOOD, R.
SUPT. CAWTHORNE
1 Deadly daffodils 1968
2 Dying for a drink 1971

3 The illegitimate spy 1972

SIMENON, G.
INSPECTOR MAIGRET
1 Maigret sets a trap 1965
2 Maigret on the defence 1966
3 The patience of Maigret 1966
4 Maigret and the headless corpse
  1967
5 Maigret and the Nahour case 1967
6 Maigret's pickpocket 1968
7 Maigret has doubts 1968
8 Maigret takes the waters 1969
9 Maigret and the Minister 1969
10 Maigret hesitates 1970
11 Maigret's boyhood friend 1970
12 Maigret and the wine merchant
  1971
13 Maigret and the killer 1971
14 Maigret and the madwoman 1972
15 Maigret and the flea 1972
16 Maigret and Monsieur Charles
  1973
17 Maigret and the dosser 1973
18 Maigret and the millionaire 1974
19 Maigret and the gangsters 1974
20 Maigret and the loner 1975
21 Maigret and the man on the
  Boulevard 1975
22 Maigret and the black sheep 1976
23 Maigret and the ghost 1976
24 Maigret's Christmas 1976
25 Maigret and the spinster 1977
26 Maigret and the Hotel Majestic
  1977
27 Maigret in exile 1978
28 Maigret and the toy village 1978
29 Maigret's rival 1979
30 Maigret in New York 1979
31 Maigret and the coroner 1980
  *Only those published in England are
  listed. The full sequence appears in
  earlier editions of 'Sequels'.*

SIMMONS, D.
1 Hyperion 1990
2 The fall of Hyperion 1991

SIMMONS, W. M.
DREAMLAND
1 In the net of dreams
2 When dreams collide

SIMON, R. L.
MOSES WINE
1 The big fix 1974
2 Wild turkey 1976
3 Peking duck 1979

SIMONS, R.
INSPECTOR WACE
1 The houseboat killings 1959
2 A frame for murder 1960
3 Murder joins the chorus 1969
4 Gamble with death 1960
5 The killing chase 1961
6 Silver and death 1963
7 Bullet for a beast 1964
8 Dead reckoning 1965
9 The veil of death 1966
10 Taxed to death 1967
11 Death on display 1968
12 Murder first class 1969
13 Reel of death 1970
14 Picture of death 1973

SIMPSON, D.
INSPECTOR LUKE THANET
1 The night she died 1980
2 Six feet under 1982
3 Puppet for a corpse 1983
4 Close her eyes 1984
5 Last seen alive 1985
6 Dead on arrival 1986
7 Element of doubt 1987
8 Suspicious death 1988
9 Dead by morning 1989
10 Doomed to die 1991
11 Wake the dead 1992
12 No laughing matter 1993

SIMPSON, J.
1 Touching the void 1988
2 This game of ghosts 1993
N.F. Autobiography of a mountaineer

SIMPSON, M.
MAYAN STEVENSON
1 Anywhere but here 1990
2 The lost father 1992

SIMS, G.
NICHOLAS HOWARD
1 The terrible door 1964
2 Sleep no more 1966
3 The last best friend 1967
4 The sand dollar 1969

SINCLAIR, A.
ALBION TRYPTYCH
1 Gog 1967
2 Magog 1972
3 King Ludd 1988

SINCLAIR, A.
BUMBO
1 The breaking of Bumbo 1959
2 Beau Bumbo 1985

SINCLAIR, A.
EMPIRE QUARTET
1 The far corners of the earth 1991
2 The strength of the hills 1992

SINCLAIR, J.
1 Warrior Queen 1977
2 Canis the warrior 1979
About Boudicca and the Romans.

SINDEN, D.
1 A touch of the memoirs 1982
2 Laughter in the second act 1985
N.F. Autobiography

SINGER, I. B.
1 the manor 1968
2 The estate 1970

SITWELL, SIR O.
1 Left hand, right hand 1945
2 The scarlet tree 1946
3 Great morning 1948
4 Laughter in the next room 1949
5 Noble essences 1950
6 Tales my father taught me 1961
N.F. Autobiography

SJOWALL, M. & WAHLOO, P.
INSPECTOR MARTIN BECK
1 Roseanna 1968
2 The man on the balcony 1969
3 Thge man who went up in smoke 1970
4 The laughing policeman 1971
5 The fire engine that disappeared 1972
6 Murder at the Savoy 1972
7 The abominable man 1973
8 The locked room 1974
9 Cop killer 1975
10 The terrorists 1977

SKELTON, C. L.
1 MacLarens 1979
2 Sweethearts and wives 1980

SKELTON, C. L.
HARDACRE FAMILY
1 Hardacres
2 Hardacres luck 1985

SKELTON, P.
1 The charm of hours 1971
2 The promise of days 1972
3 The blossom of months 1974

SKIDMORE, I.
1 Island fling 1981

2 The magnificent Evan
Humorous novels about a Welsh island

SKINNER, P.
1 Ursula 1985
2 Hello Pat 1989

SKIRROW, D.
JOHN BROCK
1 It won't get you anywhere 1966
2 I was following this girl 1967
3 I'm trying to give it up 1968

SKVORECKY, J.
DANNY SMIRICKY
1 The engineer of human souls
2 The miracle game 1991

SKVORECKY, J.
LIEUTENANT BORUVKA
1 The mournful demeanour of Lieutenant Boruvka 1988
2 Sins for Father Knox 1989
3 The end of Lieutenant Boruvka 1990
4 The return of Lieutenant Boruvka 1990

SLOVO, G.
KATE BEIER
1 Morbid symptoms 1984
2 Death by analysis 1986
3 Death comes staccato 1987
4 Catnap 1994

SMEETON, M.
1 Once is enough 1959
2 Sunrise to windward 1966
N.F. Sailing.

SMITH, D. W.
DET.CHIEF INSPECTOR HARRY FATHERS
1 Father's law 1986
2 Serious crimes 1987
3 The fourth crow 1989

SMITH, DODIE
1 Look back with love 1974
2 Look back with mixed feelings 1978
3 Look back with astonishment 1979
4 Look back with gratitude 1986
N.F. Autobiography

SMITH, E.
1 Memories of a country girlhood
2 Seven pennies in my hand

3 Many fingers in the pie
4 Never too late
N.F. Paperback autobiographies, set in Leicester

SMITH, E. E. 'DOC'
FAMILY D'ALEMBERT
1 The Imperial stars
2 Strangler's moon
3 The clockwork traitor
4 Getaway world
5 The bloodstar conspiracy
6 The purity plot
7 Plant of treachery
8 Eclipsing boundaries
9 The Omicron invasion

SMITH, E. E. 'DOC'
LENSMAN
1 Triplanetary 1955
2 First lensman 1957
3 Galactic patrol 1971
4 grey lensman 1971
5 Second stage lensman 1972
6 Children of the lens 1972
7 Masters of the vortex 1972
8 Dragon lensman, by D.E.Kyle
9 Lensman from Rigel,by D.E.Kyle

SMITH, E. E. 'DOC'
LORD TEDRIC
1 Lord Tedric
2 THe Space pirates
3 The Black Knights of the Iron Sphere
4 Alien realms

SMITH, E. E. 'DOC'
SKYLARK
1 The Skylark of Space
2 Skylark three
3 The Skylark of Valeron
4 Skylark Duquesne

SMITH, E. E. 'DOC'
SUBSPACE
1 Subspace explorers
2 Subspace encounter

SMITH, EVELYN E.
SUSAN MELVILLE
1 Miss Melville regrets 1987
2 Miss Melville returns 1988
3 Miss Melville rides a tiger 1992

SMITH, F. E
1 Rage of the innocent 1987
2 In presence of my foes 1988

SMITH, F. E.
1 A meeting of stars 1986
2 A clash of stars 1987
3 Years of the fury 1989

SMITH, F. E.
633 SQUADRON
1 633 Squadron 1956
2 Operation Rhine Maiden 1975
3 Operation Crucible 1977
4 OPeration Valkyrie 1978
5 Operation Cobra 1981
6 Operation Titan 1982
7 Operation crisis 1990
8 Operation Thor 1994

SMITH, F. E.
SAFFRON
1 Saffron's war
2 Saffron's army

SMITH, F. M.
1 Surgery at Aberffrwd 1981
2 A GP's progress to the Black
  Country 1984
  N.F. Autobiography of a doctor

SMITH, G. N.
SABAT
1 The graveyard vulture
2 The blood merchants
3 Cannibal cult
4 The druid connection
  Paperback horror stories

SMITH, G. N.
THIRST
1 The thirst
2 The plague
  Paperback horror stories

SMITH, JOAN
LORETTA LAWSON
1 A masculine ending 1987
2 Why aren't they screaming? 1988
3 Don't leave me this way 1992
4 What men say 1993

SMITH, M. C.
ARKADY RENKO
1 Gorky Park 1981
2 Polar star 1989
3 Red Square 1992

SMITH, MARTIN
ROMAN GREY
1 Gypsy in amber 1975
2 Canto for a gypsy 1975

SMITH, S.
NOREEN SPINKS
1 Flies 1990
2 Dosh 1991

SMITH, W.
BALLANTYNE FAMILY
1 A falcon flies 1980
2 Men of men 1981
3 The angels weep 1982

SMITH, W.
COURTNEY FAMILY
1 The burning shore 1985
2 Power of the sword 1986
3 Rage 1987
4 A time to die 1989
5 Golden fox 1990
  *About the descendants of Sean
  Courtney*

SMITH, W.
SEAN COURTNEY
1 When the lion feeds 1965
2 The sound of thunder 1966
3 A sparrow falls 1977

SMYTH, SIR J.
1 Beloved cats 1963
2 Blue Magnolia 1964
3 Ming 1966
  N.F. About the author's Siamese cats

SNOW, C. P.
STRANGERS AND BROTHERS
1 A time of hope 1938
2 Strangers and brothers 1940
3 The conscience of the rich 1958
4 The light and the dark 1947
5 The masters 1957
6 The new men 1961
7 Homecomings 1956
8 The affair 1960
9 The corridors of power 1964
10 The sleep of reason 1968
11 Last things 1970
12 In their wisdom 1972

SNYDER, M.
THE QUEEN'S QUARTER
1 New moon
2 Sadar's keep

SOLDIER OF FORTUNE
1 Valin's raiders, by T.Williams
2 The Korean contract, by
  D.Armstrong 1994
3 The Vatican assignment, by
  J.Halliday 1994

4 Operation Nicaragua, by C.Pullen 1994

SOLZHENITSYN, A.
1 August 1917 1972
2 Lenin in Zurich 1976
Novels about the Russian Revolution

SOMERS, J. [D. LESSING]
1 Diary of a good neighbour 1983
2 If the old could 1984
Published in one vol. 1985 as Doris Lessing

SOMERS, P.
HUGH CURTIS & MOLLIE BROWN
1 Beginner's luck 1957
2 Operation piracy 1958
3 The shivering mountain 1959

SOMTOW, S. P.
1 Rivverrun 1993
2 Armorica 1994

SOMTOW, S. P.
TIMMY VALENTINE
1 Vampire junction 1991
2 Valentine:return to Vampire Junction 1992

SORIANO, O.
1 A funny dirty little war 1983
2 Winter quarters 1989

SOUBIRAN, A.
THE STORY OF JEAN NERAC
1 The doctors 1953
2 The healing oath 1954
3 Bedlam 1956

SOUTHWORTH, L.
INSPECTOR TOM ANDERSON
1 Felon in disguise 1967
2 The corpse on London bridge 1969

SOYINKA, W.
1 Ake:years of childhood 1985
2 Isara:a voyage round Essay 1990
N.F. Autobiography

SPACE 1999
1 Breakaway, by E.C Tubb
2 Moon odyssey, by J.Rankine
3 Space guardians, by B.Ball
4 Collision course, by E.C.Tubb
5 Lunar attack, by J.Rankine
6 Astral quest, by J.Rankine
7 Alien seed, by E.C.Tubb
8 Android planet, by J.Rankine

9 Rogue planet, by E.C.Tubb
10 Earthfall, by E.C.Tubb
11 Mindbreaks of Space, by M.Butterworth
Based on the TV series

SPAIN, N.
MIRIAM BIRDSEYE
1 Cinderella goes to the morgue 1950
2 R in the month 1950
3 Not wanted on voyage 1951
4 Out damned tot 1952

SPANIER, G.
1 It isn't all mink 1968
2 And now it's sables 1970
N.F. Autobiography

SPEAKMAN, F. J.
1 A keeper's tale 1962
2 A forest by night 1965
3 Out of the wild 1967
N.F. Autobiography of a gamekeeper

SPEDDING, A.
A WALK IN THE DARK
1 The road and the hills 1988
2 A cloud over water
3 The streets of the city
Fantasy. 2 & 3 in paperback

SPENCER, C.
SIMPSON FAMILY
1 Anarchists in love 1965
2 The tyranny of love 1967
3 Lovers in war 1969
4 Victims of love 1978

SPENCER, S.
TAYLOR FAMILY
1 Salt of the earth 1993
2 Up our street 1994

SPERBER, M.
1 The wind and the flame 1952
2 To dusty death 1954
3 The lost boy 1956

SPICER, B.
CARNEY WILDE
1 The dark light 1949
2 Blues for the prince 1952
3 The golden door 1952
4 Blacksheep run 1952
5 Shadow of fear 1953
6 The taming of Carney Wilde 1955
7 Exit, running 1960

SPICER, M.
LADY JANE HILDRETH
1 Cotswold manners 1990
2 The Cotswold murders 1991
3 The Cotswold mistress 1992

SPILLANE, M.
MIKE HAMMER
1 I, the jury 1952
2 The big kill 1952
3 The long wait 1953
4 Kiss me deadly 1953
5 The snake 1964
6 The twisted thing 1966
7 The body lovers 1967
8 Survival zero 1970
9 The killing man 1990

SPILLER, A.
CHIEF INSPECTOR DUCK MALLARD
1 You can't get away with murder
  1948
2 And thereby hangs 1948
3 Brief candle 1949
4 Phantom circus 1950
5 Murder without malice 1954
6 Murder is a shady business 1954
7 Black cap for murder 1955
8 Brains trust for murder 1955
9 Ring twice for murder 1955
10 The black rat 1956
11 It's in the bag 1956
12 Murder on a shoestring 1958

SPRAGUE DE CAMP, L.
1 The incompleat enchanter
2 The castle of iron
3 The enchanter compleated

SPRAGUE DE CAMP, L.
THE RELUCTANT KING
1 The goblin tower
2 The clocks of Iraz
3 The unbeheaded king
  Paperback fantasy

SPRING, H.
1 Hard facts 1944
2 Dunkerley's 1950
3 Time and the hour 1957

SPRING, M. H.
1 Memories and gardens 1964
2 Frontispiece 1969
  N.F. Autobiography

SPRINGER, N.
SEA KING TRILOGY
1 Madbond

2 Mindbond

SPRINGER, N.
THE BOOK OF ISLE
1 The white hart 1984
2 The silver sun 1984
3 The sable moon 1985
4 The black beast 1985
5 The golden swan 1985
  Fantasy

SPURLING, H.
1 Ivy when young 1974
2 Secrets of a woman's heart 1984
  *N.F. Biography of Ivy Compton-
  Burnett*

ST. ALBANS, DUCHESS OF
1 Mimosa and the mango 1974
2 The road to Bordeaux 1976
3 Uncertain wings 1977
  N.F. Autobiography

ST. AUBYN, E.
PATRICK MELROSE
1 Never mind 1992
2 Bad news 1992
3 Some hope 1994

ST. LAURENT, C.
BERNADETTE
1 Algerian adventure
2 Toujours Bernadette

ST. LAURENT, C.
CHERIE
1 Caroline Cherie 1959
2 Caroline in Italy 1960
3 The loves of Caroline Cherie 1960
4 Caroline Cherie and Juan 1961
5 The intrigues of Caroline Cherie
  1962

ST. LAURENT, C.
CLOTILDE
1 Clotilde 1959
2 Encore Clotilde 1960

STABLEFORD, B.
1 The werewolves of London 1990
2 The angel of pain 1991

STABLEFORD, B.
ASGARD TRILOGY
1 Journey to the centre
2 Invaders from the centre
3 The centre almost told

STABLEFORD, B.
HOODED SWAN
1 Halcyon drift 1973
2 Rhapsody in black 1974
3 Promised land 1975

STABLEFORD, B.
THE DAEDALUS MISSION
1 The Florians
2 Critical theshold
3 Wildeblood's empire
4 City of the sun

STACY, R.
DOOMSDAY WARRIOR
1 Doomsday warrior
2 Red America
3 The last American
4 Bloody America
5 America's last declaration
6 American rebellion
7 American defiance
8 American glory
Paperback

STALL, M.
DANIEL LACEY
1 The killing mask 1981
2 The wet job 1982

STALLMAN, R.
THE BEAST
1 The orphan
2 The captive
3 The book of the beast

STALLWOOD, V.
KATE IVORY
1 Death and the Oxford box 1993
2 Oxford exit 1994

STAMP. T.
1 Stamp album 1987
2 Coming attractions 1988
3 Double feature 1989
N.F. Autobiography of the actor

STAND, M.
BILL RICE
1 Murder in the camp 1963
2 Escape from murder 1964
3 Death came with darkness 1965
4 Death came with flowers 1965
5 Death came in Lucerne 1966
6 Death came with diamonds 1967
7 Diana is dead 1968
8 Death came to Lighthouse Steps 1968
9 Death came to the studio 1969

10 Death came too soon 1970

STANLEY, G.
ARAKI
1 A death in Tokyo 1990
2 The ivory seal 1991

STANTON, M.
1 The heavenly horse from the outermost west 1989
2 Piper of the gates of dawn 1989

STAPLES, M. J.
ADAMS FAMILY
1 Down Lambeth way 1988
2 Our Emily 1989
3 King of Camberwell 1990
4 Missing person 1994

STAR TREK
1 Star Trek,by J.Blish
2 Star Trek 2
3 Star Trek 3
4 Star Trek 4
5 Star Trek 5
6 Star Trek 6
7 Star Trek 7
8 Star Trek 8
9 Star Trek 9
10 Star Trek 10
11 Star Trek 11
12 Star Trek 12
13 Star Treg log 1,by A.D.Foster
14 Star Trek log 2
15 Star Trek log 3
16 Star Trek log 4
17 Star Trek log 5
18 Spock must die,by J.Blish
19 Spock Messiah,by T.R.Cogswell
20 The galactic whirlpool,by D.Gerrold
21 Mudd's angels, by J.A.Lawrence
22 Planet of judgment,by J.Haldeman
23 The new voyages,by S.Marshak
24 The new voyages 2
25 Death's angels,by K.Sky
26 The entropy effect,by V.N.MacIntyre
27 The wrath of Khan,by V.N.MacIntyre
28 Web of the Romulans by M.S.Murdock
29 The Klingon gambit,by R.E.Vardeman
30 The search for Spock,by V.N.MacIntyre
31 Uhura's song, by J.Kagan
32 The covenant of the crown,by H.Weinstein

33 Mutiny on the 'Enterprise', by R.E.Vardeman
34 Corona,by G.Bear
35 The final reflection,by J.M.Ford
36 Dwellers in the crucible,by M.W.Bonnano 1987
37 Mindshadow, by J.M.Dillard 1987
38 Pawns and symbols, by M.Larson 1987
39 Ishmael, by B.Hambly 1987
40 Killing time, By.D.Van Hise 1987
41 The voyage home, by V.N.McIntyre 1987
42 Shadow lord, by L.Yep 1987
43 The Prometheus design,by S.Marshak & Culbreath1986
44 Triangle,by S.Marshak and M.Culbreath 1986
45 Black fire, by S.Cooper 1986
46 The abode of life, by L.Correy 1986
47 The tears of the singers, by M.Snodgrass 1986
48 Spock's world,by Diane Duane 1989
49 The final frontier, by J.M.Dillard 1989
50 The lost years, by J.M.Dillard 1990
51 Prime directive, by J.Reeves-Stevens 1991
52 The disinherited, by R.Greenberger 1992
53 Probe, by M.W.Bonnana 1992
54 Ice trap, by L.A.Graf 1992
55 The undiscovered country,by J.M.Dillard 1992
56 Sanctuary, by J.Vornholt 1992
57 Windows on a lost world, by V.E.Mitchell 1993
58 Shadows on the sun,by M.J.Friedman 1993
59 Best destiny,by D.Carey 1992
60 The starship trap,by M.Gilder 1993
61 Firestorm, by L.A.Graf 1993
62 Sarek, by A.C.Crispin 1994
63 The Patrian transgressor, by S.Hawke 1994
64 Price of the phoenix 1994
65 Cross road, by B.Hambly
Mostly paperback, but some hardbacks published

STAR TREK
DEEP SPACE NINE
1 Emissary, by J.M.Dillard
2 The siege, by P.David
3 Bloodletter, by K.W.Jeter
4 The big game, by S.Scholfield
5 Fallen heroes, by D.A.Hugh
6 War child, by E.Friesner

STAR TREK
STAR TREK ADVENTURES
1 The galactic whirlpool, by D.Gerrold
2 Perry's planet, by J.Haldeman
3 The starless world
4 Planet of judgement, by J.C.Haldeman
5
6 Trek to Madonna, by S.Goldin

STAR TREK
THE NEXT GENERATION
1 Encounter at Farpoint
2 Ghost ship
3 The Peacekeepers
4 The children of Hamlin
5 Survivors
6 Strike zone
7 Power hungry
8 Masks
9 The Captain's honour
10 A call to darkness
11 A rock and a hard place
12 Gulliver's fugitives
13 Doomsday world
14 The eyes of the beholders
15 Exiles
16 Fortune's light
17 Contamination
18 Boogeymen
19 Q in law
20 Perchance to dream
21 Spartacus
22 Chains of command
23 Imbalance
24 War drums, by J.Vornholt 1992
25 Nightshade
26 Grounded, by D.Bishop 1992
27 The Romulan prize, by S.Hawke 1992
28 Reunion, by M.J. Friedman 1992
29 Imzadi, by P.David 1992
30 Guises of the mind, by R.Neason 1993
31 Foreign foes, by D.Galanteur
32 Dark mirror, by D.Duane
33 Here there be dragons, by J.Peel
34 The devil's heart, by C.Carter 1993
35 Sins of commission, by S.Wright 1994
36 Q-squared, by P.David 1994
37 All good things, by M.J.Friedman 1994
Those without authors and dates have not all been published yet in the UK

235

STAR WARS
1 Star wars,by G.Lucas
2 Splinter of the mind
3 The Empire strikes back,by D.Glut
4 Han Solo at Stars End,by B.Daley
5 Han Solo's revenge, by B.Daley
6 Han Solo and the lost legacy,by B.Daley
7 Return of the Jedi,by J.Khan
8 Lando Calrissian and the Mindharp of Sharu
9 Lando Calrissian and the flamewind of Oseon
10 Lando Calrissian and the starcave of Thonboka
11 Heir to the Empire, by T.Zahn 1991
12 Dark force rising, by T.Zahn 1992
13 The last command, by T.Zahn 1993
14 The truce at Bakura, by K.Tyers 1994
15 The courtship of Princess Leia,by D.Wolverton1994
8-10 are by L. N. Smith 11-15 are in hardback.

STAR WARS
JEDI ACADEMY
1 Jedi search, by K.J.Anderson 1994
2 Dark apprentice, by K.J.Anderson 1994

STARK, R.
ALAN GROFIELD
1 The dame 1967
2 The damsel 1968
3 The blackbird 1969
4 Lemons never lie 1971

STARK, R.
PARKER
1 The score 1967 (retitled 'Point Blank')
2 The hunter 1963
3 The man with the getaway face (The steel hit)1963
4 The outfit 1963
5 The mourner (Killtown) 1965
6 The jugger (Made in the USA) 1965
7 The seventh (The split) 1966
8 The handle (Run lethal) 1966
9 The rare coin score 1967
10 The green eagle score 1967
11 The black ice score 1968
12 The sour lemon score 1969
13 Slayground 1971
14 Deadly edge 1971

15 Plunder squad 1972
16 Butcher's moon 1974
Most are published only in USA. UK dates are 1985-

STARLING, J.
1 Alice in reflection 1987
2 Emily in waiting 1988

STASHELT, C.
COSMIC WARLOCK
1 A warlock in spite of himself
2 A wizard in Bedlam
3 King Kobold

STATHAM, F. P.
1 The Roswell women 1989
2 Roswell legacy 1990

STAYNES, J. & STOREY, M.
DET. SUPT. BONE
1 Goodbye,Nanny Gray 1987
2 A knife at the opera 1988
3 Body of opinion 1988
4 Grave words 1991
5 The late lady 1991
6 Bone idle 1993

STEED, N.
JOHNNY BLACK
1 Black eye 1989
2 Black mail 1990

STEED, N.
PETER MARKLIN
1 Tin-plate 1986
2 Die-cast 1987
3 Chipped 1988
4 Wind up 1990
5 Boxed-in 1991
6 Dead cold 1992
Thrillers about a dealer in tin-plate toys

STEIN, A. M.
MATT ERRIDGE
1 Never need an enemy
2 Home and murder
3 Blood on the stars
4 I fear the Greeks
5 Faces of death
6 Deadly delight
7 Executioner's rest
8 Snare Andalucia
9 Kill is a four-letter word
10 Alp murder
11 The finger
12 Lock and key
13 Coffin country

14 Lend me your ear
15 Body search
16 Nowhere?
17 The rolling heads
18 One dip dead
19 The cheating butcher
20 A nose for it
21 A body for a buddy 1981
22 Hangman's row 1982
23 The bombing run 1983
24 The garbage collector 1986

STEIN, A. M.
TIM MULLIGAN & ELSIE HUNT
1 Death meets 400 rabbits 1953
2 Moonmilk and murder 1955
3 Shoot me dacent 1957

STEIN, S.
GEORGE THOMASSY
1 The magician 1983
2 Other people 1984
3 The touch of treason 1985

STEINBECK, J.
1 Cannery Row 1945
2 Sweet Thursday 1954

STEPHENS, R.
BREW GINNY
1 The man who killed his brother 1980
2 The man who risked his partner 1985
3 The man who tried to get away 1990

STERLING, S.
FIRE MARSHAL BEN PEDLEY
1 Where there's smoke 1946
2 Alarm in the night 1949
3 The hinges of hell 1956
4 Candle for a corpse 1958
5 Fire on Fear Street 1959

STERLING, S.
GIL VINE
1 Alibi baby 1955
2 Dead right 1957
3 Dead to the world 1958
4 The body in the bag 1960

STEVENS, G.
DAVE HASLAM
1 Provo 1993
2 Kennedy's ghost 1994

STEVEN
AYRTON FAMILY
1 Amberwell 1954
2 Summerhills 1956

STEVENSON, D. E.
BARBARA BUNCLE
1 Miss Buncle's book 1937
2 Miss Buncle married 1939
3 The two Mrs.Abbotts 1944

STEVENSON, D. E.
DRUMBERLEY
1 Vittoria Cottage 1949
2 Music in the hills 1950
3 Winter and rough weather 1951

STEVENSON, D. E.
KATHARINE WENTWORTH
1 Katharine Wentworth 1964
2 Katharine's marriage 1965

STEVENSON, D. E.
MRS.TIM
1 Mrs.Tim 1946
2 Mrs.Tim carries on 1947
3 Mrs.Tim gets a job 1947
4 Mrs.Tim flies home 1952

STEVENSON, D. E.
SARAH MORRIS
1 Sarah Morris remembers 1967
2 Sarah's cottage 1968

STEVENSON, R. L.
TREASURE ISLAND
1 Treasure Island 1883
2 The adventures of Long John Silver 1977
3 Return to Treasure Island, by D.Judd 1977
4 The adventures of Ben Gunn, by R.F.Delderfield
5 Silver's revenge, by R.Leeson 1978
  The Last Will and Testament of Robert Louis Stevenson', by S. LLewellyn 1981 is a pendant

STEVENSON, ROBERT
1 Highland vet 1976
2 Vets rush in 1976
3 Vets rush out 1979
  N.F. Autobiography

STEWART, C.
1 The residency 1962
2 Jethro's daughters 1964

STEWART, D.
THE SEQUENCE OF ROLES
1 The round mosaic 1965
2 The pyramid inch 1966
3 The Mamelukes 1967

STEWART, F.
INSPECTOR NEWSOM
1 Deadly nightcap 1966
2 Blood relations 1967

STEWART, J. I. M.
A STAIRCASE IN SURREY
1 Young Patullo 1975
2 Gaudy 1974
3 The memorial service 1976
4 The Madonna of the Astrolabe 1977
5 Full term 1978

STEWART, MARY
MERLIN AND ARTHUR
1 The crystal cave 1972
2 The hollow hills 1973
3 The last enchantment 1979
4 The savage day 1984

STEWART. A.
1 Temps
2 Eurotemps
Paperback s. f.

STIRLING, J.
CLARE KELSO
1 Lantern for the dark 1992
2 Shadows on the shore 1993

STIRLING, J.
HOLLY BECKMAN
1 Deep well at noon 1979
2 Blue evening gone 1981
3 The gates of midnight 1983

STIRLING, J.
NICHOLSON FAMILY
1 The good provider 1988
2 The asking price 1989
3 The wise child 1990
4 The welcome light 1991

STIRLING, J.
PATTERSON FAMILY
1 Treasures on earth 1985
2 Creature comforts 1986
3 Hearts of gold 1987
Set in 18th & 19th century Scotland

STIRLING, J.
STALKER FAMILY
1 The spoiled earth 1975
2 The hiring fair 1976
3 The dark pasture 1978
About a Scottish family in the 19th century.

STOCKS, M.
1 My commonplace book 1970
2 Still more commonplace 1973
N.F. Autobiography

STOKER, B.
DRACULA
1 Dracula
2 Dracula's guest
3 The Dracula archives,by R.Rudorff 1971
4 Dracula's diary,by M.Geare & M.Corby 1982
5 Dracula,my love,by P.Tremayne 1983
6 Dracula's children,by R.Chetwynd-Hayes 1987
7 House of Dracula, by R.Chetwynd-Hayes 1987
8 Dracula unbound, by B.Aldiss 1991
9 The ultimate Dracula; ed. by B.Preiss 1992
10 Anno Dracula, by K.Newman 1992
11 Covenant with the vampire, by J.Kalogridis 1994
12 Secret life of Laszlo Count Dracula,by R.Anscombe

STOKES, D.
1 Voices in my ear 1980
2 More voices in my ear 1981
3 Innocent voices in my ear 1983
4 Whispering voices in my ear 1985
N.F. Autobiography of a medium

STOREY, A.
THE SECOND COMING
1 The rector 1970
2 The centre holds 1973
3 The Saviour 1978

STORM, J.
SARAH VANESSA
1 Dark emerald 1951
2 Bitter rubies 1952
3 Deadly diamond 1953

STORY, J. T.
ALBERT ARGYLE
1 Live now, pay later 1961

2 Something for nothing 1963
3 The urban district lover 1964

STORY, J. T.
HORACE SPURGEON FENTON
1 Hitler needs you 1970
2 One last mad embrace 1969

STOTT, M.
1 Forgetting's no excuse 1973
2 Before I go 1985
   N.F. Autobiography

STOUT, R.
NERO WOLFE
1 Fer-de-lance 1934
2 The league of frightened men 1935
3 The rubber band 1936
4 The red box 1937
5 Some buried Caesar 1939
6 Over my dead body 1940
7 Black orchids 1940
8 Where there's a will 1940
9 Not quite dead enough 1944
10 Too many cooks 1945
11 The silent speaker 1946
12 Too many women 1947
13 More deaths than one 1948
14 Trouble in triplicate 1949
15 The second confession 1950
16 Three doors to death 1950
17 Even in the best families 1951
18 Curtains for three 1952
19 Murder by the book 1952
20 Triple jeopardy 1953
21 Out goes she 1953
22 The golden spiders 1954
23 Three men out 1954
24 The final deduction 1955
25 Before midnight 1955
26 The black mountain 1955
27 Three witnesses 1956
28 Might as well be dead 1957
29 Three for the chair 1958
30 If death ever slept 1959
31 Crime and again 1959
32 Champagne for one 1959
33 Murder in style 1960
34 Three at Wolfe's door 1960
35 Too many clients 1961
36 Homicide trinity 1962
37 Gambit 1963
38 The mother hunt 1964
39 Trio for blunt instruments 1964
40 A right to die 1965
41 The doorbell rang 1966
42 Death of a doxy 1967
43 The father hunt 1969
44 Death of a dude 1970

45 Please pass the guilt 1974
46 A family affair 1976
   For further titles see
   GOLDSBOROUGH, R.

STRAITON, E.
1 Animals are my life 1979
2 A vet at large 1982
3 Positively vetted 1983
4 A vet on the set 1985
   N.F. Autobiograp

STRAKER, J. F.
DAVID WRIGHT
1 A coilof rope 1962
2 Final witness 1963

STRAKER, J. F.
INSPECTOR PITT
1 Postman's knock 1953
2 Pick up the pieces 1954
3 The ginger horse 1955
4 A gun to pay with 1956
5 Goodbye, Aunt Charlotte 1958

STRAKER, J. F.
JOHNNY INCH
1 Sin and Johnny Inch 1968
2 Tight circle 1970
3 A letter for obi 1971
4 The goat 1972

STRANGE, O.
SUDDEN
1 Sudden
2 Dudden gold-seeker
3 Sudden outlawed
4 Sudden makes war
5 Sudden rides again
6 Sudden takes the trail
7 Sudden plays a hand
8 Sudden strikes back
9 Sudden troubleshooter
10 Sudden at bay
11 Sudden - Apache fighter
12 Sudden - dead or alive
   8-12 were written by F. H. Christian

STRANGER, J.
DOG SERIES
1 Three's a pack 1980
2 Two for joy 1982
3 A dog in a million 1984
4 Dog days 1986
   N.F. The author

STRATTON, A.
1 The lady 1986
2 Gina 1988

STREATFEILD, N.
1 The vicarage family 1963
2 Away from the vicarage 1965
3 Beyond the vicarage 1971
N.F. Autobiography

STREET, PAMELA
1 The millrace 1983
2 The way of the river 1984
3 Many waters 1985
4 Unto the fourth generation 1985

STRESHINSKY, S.
1 Hers the kingdom 1981
2 Gift of the golden mountain 1989

STRONG, T.
SAS
1 Whisper who dares 1983
2 The fifth hostage 1984

STUART, A.
VLADIMIR GULL
1 Snap judgment 1976
2 Vicious circles 1978
3 Force play 1980

STUART, I.
DAVID GRIERSON
1 Death from disclosure 1979
2 End on the rocks 1981
3 The garb of truth 1982
4 Thrilling sweet and rotten 1983
5 A growing concern 1987

STUART, V.
CAPT.ALEX SHERIDAN
1 Like victors and lords 1964
2 Mutiny in Meerut 1974
3 Massacre at Cawnpore 1974
4 The battle of Lucknow 1975
5 The heroic garrison 1975

STUART, V.
COMMANDER PHILIP HAZARD
1 The valiant sailors 1967
2 The brave captains 1968
3 Black Sea frigate 1971
4 Hazard in 'Huntress' 1972
5 Hazard of 'Circassia' 1973
6 Shannon's brigade 1976
7 Sailors on horseback 1978

STUART, V.
THE AUSTRALIANS
1 The exiles 1981
2 The settlers 1981
3 The traitors 1982
4 The explorers 1983

5 The adventurers 1983
6 The colonists 1984
7 The gold-seekers 1985
8 The patriots 1986
9 The Empire builders 1987
10 The seafarers 1988
11 The nationalists 1989
12 The imperialists 1990

STUBBS, J.
BRIEF CHRONICLES
1 Kit's Hill 1979
2 The ironmaster 1981
3 The Vivian inheritance 1982
4 The Northern correspondent 1984

STUBBS, J.
INSPECTOR LINOTT
1 Dear Laura 1973
2 The painted face 1974
3 The golden crucible 1976

STURROCK, J.
THE BOW STREET RUNNER
1 Village of rogues 1972
2 A wicked way to die 1973
3 The wilful lady 1975
4 A conspiracy of poisons 1977
5 Suicide most foul 1981
6 Captain Bolton's corpse 1982
7 The Pangersbourne murders 1984

STYLES, S.
MR.FITTON
1 A sword for Mr.Fitton 1975
2 Mr.Fitton's commission 1977
3 Baltic convoy 1979
4 The quarterdeck ladder 1982
5 The lee shore 1986
6 Gun-brig captain 1987
7 H.M.S. Cracker 1988
8 A ship for Mr.Fitton 1992
9 The independent cruise 1992
10 Mr.Fitton's prize 1993
11 Mr.Fitton and the Black Legion
   1994

SUGERMAN, D.
1 No-one gets out of here alive 1980
2 Wonderland Avenue 1989

SULITZER, P. L.
1 Hannah 1988
2 The empress 1989

SUMMERS, R.
1 Killigrew clay 1986
2 Clay country 1987

3 Family ties 1988
   A family saga set in the clay-mines in Cornwall

SUMNER, R.
NELL GWYN
1 Mistress of the streets 1975
2 Mistress of the boards 1977
3 Mistress of the King 1979

SUNLEY, M.
1 The quiet earth 1990
2 Fields inthe sun 1991
3 Sons of toil 1992
   Novels about farming in the Yorkshire Dales

SUTHREN, V.
EDWARD MAINWARING
1 Royal Yankee 1987
2 The golden galleon 1989
3 Admiral of fear 1991

SUTHREN, V.
PAUL GALLANT
1 The black cockade 1979
2 A King's ransom 1980

SUTTON, J.
BEL AIR GENERAL
1 Bel Air General 1987
2 The price of life 1988
3 Masks and faces 1988
4 Vital signs
5 Critical condition
   Novels set in a Californian hospital 4 & 5 in paperback only

SVEVO, L.
1 Confessions of Zeno 1930
2 Further confessions of Zeno 1969

SWANTON, E. W.
1 Sort of a cricket person 1976
2 Follow on 1977
   N.F. Cricketing memoirs

SWINNERTON, F.
1 The woman from Sicily 1956
2 A tigress in Prothero 1958
3 The Grace divorce 1960
4 Quadrille 1965

SWINSON, A.
SERGEANT CORK
1 Sergeant Cork's casebook 1968
2 Sergeant Cork's second casebook 1969

SWITHIN, A.
THE PERILOUS QUEST FOR LYONESSE
1 Princes of Sandastre
2 The lords of the stoney mountains
3 The winds of the wastelands
4 The nine gods of Safaddne

SYLVESTER, M.
WILLIAM WARNE
1 A dangerous a
2 A lethal vintage 1988
   Thrillers about a wine merchant

SYMONS, J.
SHERIDAN HAYNES
1 The Blackheath poisonings 1978
2 Sweet Adelaide 1980
3 The Detling murders 1982
4 A three-pipe problem
5 The Kentish Manor murders 1988

TALBOT, M.
AUSTRALIAN SAGA
1 To the ends of the earth 1987
2 A wilful woman 1989

TANGYE, D.
1 A gull on the roof 1964
2 A cat in the window 1965
3 A drake at the door 1966
4 A donkey in the meadow 1967
5 Lama 1969
6 Cornish summer 1971
7 Cottage on a cliff 1973
8 A cat affair 1975
9 The way to Minack 1975
10 Sun on the lintel 1976
11 Somewhere a cat is waiting 1977
12 The winding lane 1978
13 When the winds blow 1980
14 The Ambrose rock 1982
15 A quiet year 1984
16 The cherry tree 1986
17 The world of Minack 1991
   N.F. Country life in Cornwall

TANNAHILL, R.
1 The world, the flesh and the devil (1400s) 1985
2 Camerons of Kinveil (1800s) 1988

TANNER, J.
HILLSBRIDGE
1 The black mountains 1983
2 The emerald valley 1985
3 The hills and the valley 1988

TAPPLY, W. G.
BRADY COYNE
1 Death at Charity's Point 1984
2 The Dutch Blue error 1985
3 Follow the sharks 1986
4 A rodent of doubt 1987
5 Dead meat 1987
6 The vulgar boatman 1988
7 A void in hearts 1989
8 Dead winter 1990
9 Client privilege 1991
10 The spotted cats 1992
11 Tight lines 1993
12 The snake eater 1994

TARGET, G. W.
1 The evangelists 1958
2 The teachers 1960
3 The missionaries 1961
4 The shop stewards 1962
5 The Americans 1964
6 The scientists 1966

TARR, J.
THE AVARYAN RISING
1 The hall of the mountain king
2 The lady of Han-Gilen
3 A fall of princes

TARR, J.
THE HOUND AND THE FALCON
1 The Isle of Glass 1986
2 The golden horn 1986
3 The hounds of God 1987
Fantasy

TARSIS, V.
1 The pleasure factory 1967
2 The gay life 1968

TAYLOR, A.
WILLIAM DOUGAL
1 Caroline Miniscule 1983
2 Waiting for the end of the world 1984
3 Our fathers' lies 1985
4 An old school tie 1986
5 Freelance death 1987
6 Blood relation 1990
7 The sleeping policeman 1992
8 Odd man out 1993

TAYLOR, ALICE
1 To school through the fields 1990
2 Quench the lamp 1991
N.F. Autobiography of a life in Ireland

TAYLOR, DAVID
1 Zoo vet 1976
2 Doctor in the zoo 1978
3 Going wild 1980
4 Next panda,please 1982
5 The wandering whale 1984
6 Dragon doctor 1986
N.F. Autobiography of a vet

TAYLOR, DAY
1 The black swan
2 Moss rose

TAYLOR, F.
1 The kinder garden 1991
2 The peacebrokers 1992

TAYLOR, G.
1 Piece of cake 1969
2 Return ticket 1972
N.F. Autobiography

TAYLOR, H. B.
DAVID HALLIDAY
1 The duplicate 1964
2 The triumvirate 1966

TAYLOR, K.
BARD
1 Bard
2 The first long ship
3 The wild sea
4 Raven's gathering
5 Felimid's homecoming

TAYLOR, R.
CHRONICLES OF HAWKLAN
1 The call of the sword
2 The fall of Fyorland
3 The waking of Orthlund
4 Into Narsindal
Paperback fantasy

TAYLOR, R.
NIGHTFALL
1 Farnor 1992
2 Valderen 1993

TAYLOR, S.
1 Lights across the Delaware 1954
2 Farewell to Valley Forge 1955
3 Storm the last rampart 1960
Novels about the American War of Independence

TELL, D.
POPPY DILLWORTH
1 Murder at Red Rock Ranch 1990
2 The Hallelujah murders 1991

TELUSHKIN, J.
RABBI DANIEL WINTER
1 The unorthodox murder of Rabbi Moss 1987
2 The final analysis of Dr.Stark 1988
3 An eye for an eye 1990

TEMPLE, R.
SIMON LEIGH
1 Spy is a dirty word 1970
2 The Schulsinger affair 1971

TENKO
1 Tenko, by A.Masters 1981
2 Last Tenko, by M.Hardwick 1985
3 Tenko reunion, by A.Valery 1985
Paperback. Based on the TV series

TENNANT, E.
1 A house of hospitalities 1987
2 A wedding of cousins 1988

TEPPER, S. S.
JINIAN FOOTSEER
1 Jinian Footseer
2 Dervish daughter
3 Jinian Stareye

TEPPER, S. S.
MARVIN MANYSHAPED
1 The song of Marvin Manyshaped
2 The flight of Marvin Manyshaped
3 The search of Marvin Manyshaped

TEPPER, S. S.
PETER
1 King's blood four
2 Necromancer nine
3 Wizard's eleven
Paperback fantasies. Each trilogy is linked to 'The True Game'.

TERRY, C.
1 King of diamonds 1983
2 The fortune seekers 1985

TEVIS, W.
FAST EDDY
1 The hustler 1960
2 The colour of money 1985

TEY, J.
DET.INSPECTOR ALAN GRANT
1 The man in the queue 1927
2 A shilling for candles 1936
3 The Franchise affair 1948
4 To love and be wise 1950
5 The daughter of time 1951
6 The singing sands 1952

THANE, E.
WILLIAMSBURG
1 Dawn's early light 1943
2 Yankee stranger 1944
3 Ever after 1945
4 The light heart 1947
5 Kissing kin 1948
6 This was tomorrow 1951
7 Homing 1958

THAYER, L.
PETER CLANCY
1 The mystery of the thirteenth floor
2 The unlatched door
3 The puzzle
4 The sinister mark
5 The key
6 Poison
7 Alias Dr.Ely
8 The darkest spot
9 Set a thief
10 Dead men's shoes
11 The last shot
12 The glass knife
13 To catch a thief
14 The Scrimshaw millions
15 Hell-gate tides
16 The counterfeit bill
17 The second shot
18 The death weed
19 Red-handed
20 Murder in the mirror
21 Death in the gorge
22 The last trump
23 The man's doom
24 Ransome racket
25 The strange Sylvester affair
26 Lightning strikes twice
27 Stark murder
28 X marks the spot
29 Guilty
30 Persons unknown
31 Hallowe'en homicide
32 Murder is out
33 Murder on location
34 Accessory after the fact
35 Hanging's too good 1945
36 A plain case of murder 1945
37 Accident, manslaugter or murder 1946
38 Five bullets 1947
39 A hair's breadth 1947
40 The jaws of death 1048
41 Murder stalks the circle 1949
42 Out, brief candle 1950
43 A clue for Clancy 1947
44 Death within the vault 1950
45 Civil root 1951
46 Too long endured 1952

47 Clancy's secret mission 1952
48 The prisoner pleads not guilty 1954
49 No holiday for death 1954
50 Murder on the Pacific 1955
51 Fatal alibi 1959
52 Web of hate 1959
53 Two ways to die 1960
54 Dead on arrival 1960
55 And one cried murder 1962
56 Death walks in shadow 1966

THEROUX, P.
1 The consul's file 1981
2 The London embassy 1982

THEW, L. M.
1 The pit village and the store 1985
2 From store to war 1987
N.F. Autobiography set in a South Yorkshire mining community.

THIRKELL, A.
BARSETSHIRE
1 High Rising 1933
2 Wild strawberries 1934
3 The demon in the house 1934
4 August folly 1936
5 Summer half 1937
6 Pomfret Towers 1935
7 The Brandons 1939
8 Before lunch 1939
9 Cheerfulness breaks in 1940
10 Northbridge Rectory 1941
11 Marling Hall 1942
12 Growing up 1943
13 The headmistress 1945
14 Miss Bunting 1945
15 Peace breaks out 1946
16 Private enterprise 1947
17 Love among the ruins 1948
18 The old Bank House 1949
19 Country chronicle 1950
20 The Duke's daughter 1951
21 Happy returns 1952
22 Jutland Cottage 1953
23 What did it mean? 1954
24 Enter Sir Robert 1955
25 Never too late 1956
26 A double affair 1957
27 Close quarters 1958
28 Love at all ages 1959
29 Three score and ten 1961
The last volume was completed by C. A. Lejeune

THOMAS, C.
FIREFOX
1 Firefox 1977

2 Firefox down 1983
3 Winter hawk 1987

THOMAS, C.
KENNETH AUBREY
1 The bear's tears 1985
2 All the grey cats 1988
3 The last raven 1990
4 A hooded crow 1992
5 Playing with cobras 1993

THOMAS, CHRISTINE
O'NEILL FAMILY
1 Bridie 1989
2 April 1990
3 Hannah 1991

THOMAS, D. M.
SERGEI ROZANOV
1 Ararat 1983
2 Swallow 1984
3 Sphinx 1986
4 Summit 1987
5 Lying together 1990

THOMAS, DONALD
INSPECTOR SWAIN
1 Belladonna 1984
2 The Ripper's apprentice 1986
3 Jekyll, alias Hyde 1988
Detective stories set in Victorian London

THOMAS, G.
DAVID MORTON
1 Deadly perfume 1991
2 Godless icon 1992
3 Voices in the silence 1993
4 Organ hunters 1994

THOMAS, H.
1 As it was 1926
2 World without end 1931
3 Time and again 1978
4 Under storm's wing 1988
N.F. Autobiography

THOMAS, LESLIE
1 This time next week 1974
2 In my wildest dreams 1984
N.F. Autobiography

THOMAS, LESLIE
DANGEROUS DAVIES
1 Dangerous Davies 1976
2 Dangerous in love 1987
3 Dangerous by moonlight 1993

THOMAS, LESLIE
THE VIRGIN SOLDIERS
1 The virgin soldiers 1966
2 Onward, virgin soldiers 1971
3 Stand up, virgin soldiers 1975

THOMAS, R.
MCCORKIE & PADULLO
1 The cold war swap 1970
2 Cast a yellow shadow 1971
3 The backup men 1972

THOMAS, R.
WUDU,LTD.
1 Out on the rim 1988
2 Chinaman's chance 1978
3 Voodoo,Ltd. 1993

THOMPSON, D.
WILDERNESS
1 King of the mountain
2 Lure of the wild
3 Savage rendezvous
4 Blood fury
5 Tomahawk revenge
6 Black Powder justice
7 Vengeance trail
8 Death hunt
9 Mountain devil
10 Blackfoot massacre
11 Northwest passage
12 Apache blood
13 Mountain manhunt
14 Tenderfoot
15 Winterkill
16 Blood truce
17 Trapper's blood
18 Mountain cat
19 Iron warrior
Paperback Westerns

THOMPSON, E. V.
NATHAN JAGO
1 The restless sea 1983
2 Polrudden 1985
3 Mistress of Polrudden 1993
Set in Cornwall in the 18th and 19th centuries

THOMPSON, E. V.
RETALLICK FAMILY
1 Ben Retallick 1980
2 Chase the wind 1977
3 Harvest of the sun 1978
4 Singing spears 1982
5 The stricken land 1986
6 Lottie Trago 1990
Novels about mining in Cornwall and S. Africa

THOMPSON, G.
DADE COOLEY
1 Murder mystery 1981
2 Nobody cared for Kate 1983
3 A cup of death 1988

THOMPSON, GRACE
VALLEY SERIES
1 A welcome in the valley 1989
2 Valley affairs 1990
3 The changing valley 1990
4 Valley in bloom 1993
Novels set in South Wales

THOMPSON, K.
DERAIN FAMILY
1 Great house 1955
2 Mandevilla 1957
3 Sugarbed 1963
4 Richard's way 1965
5 The painted caves 1968

THOMPSON, N.
1 At their departing 1986
2 On their return 1987

THOMPSON, R.
1 No exit from Vietnam 1971
2 Peace is not at hand 1974
N.F. History of the Vietnam War

THOMSON, DAVID
1 Nairn in darkness and light 1987
2 Woodbrook 1974
N.F. Memories of a Scottish childhood

THOMSON, J.
CHIEF INSPECTOR FINCH
1 Not one of us 1972
2 Death cap 1973
3 The long revenge 1974
4 Case closed 1977
5 A question of identity 1978
6 Deadly relations 1979
7 Alibi in time 1980
8 Shadow of a doubt 1981
9 To make a killing 1982
10 Sound evidence 1984
11 A dying fall 1985
12 The dark stream 1986
13 No flowers, by request 1987
14 Rosemary for remembrance 1988
15 The spoils of time 1989
16 Past reckoning 1990
17 Foul play 1991

THORNDYKE, R.
DOCTOR SYN
1 Doctor Syn on the high seas 1936

2 Doctor Syn returns 1935
3 Further adventures of Doctor Syn 1936
4 Courageous exploits of Doctor Syn 1936
5 The amazing quest of Doctor Syn 1938
6 The shadow of Doctor Syn 1944
7 Doctor Syn 1915
Listed in chronological order of reading

THORNE, B.
1 Vienna prelude 1992
2 Prague counterpoint 1992

THORNE, B.
ZION COVENANT
1 Munich signature 1993
2 Jerusalem interlude 1994
3 Danzig passage 1994
4 Warsaw requiem 1994

THORNE, B. & B.
SAGA OF THE SIERRAS
1 Sequoia scout 1991
2 The year of the grizzly 1992

THORNE, N.
1 People of this parish (as R.Ellerbeck) 1991
2 The rector's daughter 1992

THORNE, N.
ASKHAM CHRONICLES
1 Never such innocence 1985
2 Yesterday's promises 1986
3 Bright morning 1986
4 A place in the sun 1987

THORNE, N.
CHAMPAGNE
1 Champagne 1991
2 Champagne gold 1992

THURLEY, J.
1 Household gods 1988
2 Tenements of clay 1989
Not direct sequels, but companion novels

TIBBLE, A.
1 Greenhorn 1973
2 One woman's story 1976
3 Alone 1979
N.F. Autobiography

TIDYMAN, E.
SHAFT
1 Shaft 1971
2 Shaft's big score
3 Shaft has a ball
4 Shaft's carnival of killers
5 Shaft among the Jews 1973
6 The last Shaft 1974

TILLEY, P.
AMTRAK WARS
1 Cloud warrior 1984
2 The first family 1985
3 Iron master 1992
4 Blood river
5 Death bringer
6 Earth-thunder
Paperback fantasy. 'Dark visions', a guide to the Amtrak Wars mission is a pendant to the series.

TIMLETT, P. V.
1 Seedbearers
2 Power of the serpent
3 Twilight of the serpent
Paperback fantasy

TIMLIN, M.
NICK SHARMAN
1 Zip gun boogie 1992
2 The turnaround 1991
3 Take the A-train 1991
4 Gun street girl 1990
5 Romeo's tune 1990
6 A good year for the roses 1988
7 Hearts of stone 1992
8 Pretend we're dead 1994
Paperback private eye stories

TIMMS, E. V.
AUSTRALIAN SAGA
1 Forever to remain 1948
2 Pathway of the sun 1949
3 The beckoning shore 1950
4 The valleys beyond 1952
5 The challenge 1953
6 The scarlet frontier 1954
7 The fury 1955
8 They came from the sea 1956
9 The shining harvest 1957
10 Robina 1958
11 The big country 1959
12 Time and change 1972

TIMPSON, J.
1 Paper trail 1990
2 Sound track 1991

TINNISWOOD, P.
BRANDON FAMILY
1 A touch of Daniel 1969
2 I didn't know you cared 1973
3 Except you're a bird 1974
4 Call it a canary 1985
5 Uncle Mort's North Country 1986
6 Uncle Mort's South Country 1990

TINNISWOOD, P.
THE BRIGADIER
1 Tales from a long room 1981
2 More tales from a long room 1982
3 The Brigadier down under 1983
4 The Brigadier in season 1984
5 Tales from Witney Scrotum 1987

TINNISWOOD, P.
WINSTON
1 Hayballs 1989
2 Winston 1991

TIPPETT, G.
WILSON YOUNG
1 Wilson's gold 1982
2 Wilson's luck 1983
3 Wilson's choice 1983
4 Wilson's revenge 1983
5 Wilson's woman 1993
Westerns

TOD, M.
WOODSTOCK SAGA
1 The silver tide 1994
2 Thesecond wave 1994

TOER, P. A.
1 This earth of mankind 1979
2 Child of all nations 1980

TOLKIEN, J. R. R.
HISTORY OF MIDDLE EARTH
1 The book of lost tales 1 1983
2 The book of lost tales 2 1984
3 The lays of Beleriad 1985
4 The shaping of Middle Earth 1986
5 The lost road 1987
6 The return of the shadow 1988
7 The treason of Isengard 1989
8 The war of the ring 1990
9 Sauron defeated 1992
10 Morgoth's ring 1993
11 The war of the jewels 1994
*A mixture of fiction and fragments
based on Tolkien's notes for 'The Lord
of the Rings', edite by his son*

TOLKIEN, J. R. R.
THE LORD OF THE RINGS
1 The Hobbit 1950
2 The felowship of the Ring 1952
3 The two towers 1954
4 The return of the King 1955
5 The Silmarillion

TOLSTOY, L.
1 War and Peace
2 Count Vronsky's daughter, by
C.Salisbury 1981

TOMALIN, R.
RALPH OLIVER
1 The garden house 1964
2 The spring house 1968

TOMS, P.
CHRONICLES OF PENNYCRESS
1 Mrs.Sherwood's summer 1965
2 Three fountains 1966
3 Cottage on the Green 1967

TORR, I.
1 A time of change 1967
2 Sundown 1969

TORRIE, M.
TIMOTHY HERRING
1 Heavy as lead 1966
2 Late and cold 1967
3 Your secret friend 1968
4 Churchyard salad 1969
5 Shades of darkness 1970
6 Bismark herrings 1971
*Entries also appear under the author's
real name, Gladys Mitchell.*

TOURNEY, L.
MATTHEW STOCK
1 The players
2 Low treason 1984
3 Familiar spirits 1985
4 The Bartholomew Fair murders
1987
*Detective stories set in the 17th
century*

TOVEY, D.
1 Cats in the belfry 1958
2 Donkey work 1962
3 Cats in May 1959
4 Life with Grandma 1964
5 Raining cats and donkeys 1966
6 The new boy 1970
7 Double trouble 1972
8 Making the horse laugh 1974
9 The coming of Saska 1977

10 A comfort of cats 1979
11 Roses round the door 1984
12 Waiting in the wings 1986
N.F. Autobiography

TOWNEND, P.
MCGILL
1 Man on the end of a rope 1960
2 The road to El Suida 1961

TOWNEND, P.
PHILIP QUEST
1 Out of focus 1970
2 Zoom! 1971

TOWNLEY, P.
1 The stone maiden 1986
2 Nearest of kin 1988

TOWNSEND, P.
1 Duel of eagles 1970
2 Duel in the dark 1986
N.F. Wartime experiences of a fighter pilot

TOY, B.
1 A fool on wheels 1955
2 A fool in the desert 1956
3 A fool strikes oil 1957
N.F. Travels in North Sfrica and Arabia

TOYNBEE, P.
THE VALEDICTION OF PANTALOON
1 Pantaloon 1963
2 Two brothers 1964
3 A learned city 1966
4 View from a lake 1968

TRANTER, N.
1 Macbeth the King 1978
2 Margaret the Queen 1979
3 David the Prince 1980
4 True Thomas 1981
5 The Wallace 1975
Not true sequels, but they cover the early history of Scotland, in chronological order, and come before the 'Robert the Bruce' trilogy

TRANTER, N.
JAMES GRAHAM,EARL OF MONTROSE
1 The young Montrose 1972
2 Montrose the Captain-General 1973

TRANTER, N.
JAMES V TRILOGY
1 The riven realm 1984

2 James,by the grace of God 1985
3 Rough wooing 1986

TRANTER, N.
MASTER OF GRAY
1 The Master of Gray 1961
2 The courtesan 1963
3 Past Master 1965
4 Mail Royal 1989

TRANTER, N.
ROBERT THE BRUCE
1 The steps to the empty throne 1969
2 The path of the hero king 1969
3 The price of the King's peace 1971

TRANTER, N.
THE HOUSE OF STEWART
1 Lords of misrule 1976
2 Folly of princes 1977
3 The captive crown 1977
4 Warden of the Queen's March 1989
5 Lion let loose 1967
6 The Unicorn rampant 1984

TRAVEN, B.
THE JUNGLE NOVELS
1 Government 1971
2 The carreta 1970
3 March to Caobaland 1961
4 Trozas
5 The rebellion of the hanged 1952
6 General from the jungle
Not all published in the UK

TRAVERS, B.
1 Vale of laughter 1957
2 A'sitting on a gate 1978
N.F. Autobiography

TRAVERS, H.
DOMINIQUE AUBREY
1 Madame Aubrey and the police 1966
2 Madame Aubrey dines with death 1967

TREACY, S.
1 Shay Scally and Manny Wagstaff 1977
2 Scallywags 1979

TREASE, G.
1 A whiff of burnt boats 1972
2 Laughter at the door 1974
N.F. Autobiography

TREHERNE, J.
DR.JAMES YEO
1 The trap 1985
2 Mangrove chronicles 1986

TREMAYNE, P.
LANKERNE
1 The fires of Lankerne 1979
2 The destroyers of Lankerne 1982
3 Buccaneers of Lankerne 1983

TRENHAILE, J.
STEPAN POVIN
1 A view from the square 1983
2 Nocturne for the general 1985

TRESILLIAN, R.
BLOODHEART
1 Bloodheart 1986
2 Bloodheart royal 1986
3 Bloodheart feud 1987

TRESILLIAN, R.
BONDMASTER
1 Bondmaster 1977
2 Bondmaster Buck 1984
3 Blood of the Bondmaster 1978
4 Bondmaster breed 1979
5 Bondmaster fury 1982
6 Bondmaster's revenge 1983
Novels set on a slave plantation in Dominica, listed in chronological order

TRESILLIAN, R.
FLESH TRADERS
1 Master of Black River 1987
2 Black River affair 1987
3 Black River breed 1987

TREVANION, M.
JONATHAN HEMLOCK
1 The Eiger sanction 1973
2 The Loo sanction 1974

TREVELYAN, R.
PENDRAGON
1 Pendragon -late of Prince Albert's Own 1975
2 His Highness commands Pendragon 1976
3 Pendragon and the Montenegran plot 1977
4 Pendragon and the seeds of mutiny 1979

TREVOR, M.
LUXEMBOURG
1 The fugitives 1973

2 The marked man 1974
3 The enemy at home 1974
4 The forgotten country 1975
5 The treacherous paths 1976
6 The civil prisoner 1977
7 The fortunes of peace 1978
8 Wanton fires 1979

TRIPP, M.
JOHN SAMSON
1 Obsession 1973
2 The once a year man 1977
3 Cruel victim 1979
4 The wife smuggler 1978
5 A woman in bed 1976
6 Going solo 1981
7 One love too many 1983
8 Death of a man-tamer 1987
9 The frightened wife 1987
10 The cords of vanity 1989
11 Video vengeance 1990
12 A woman of conscience 1994

TROLLOPE, J. [AS C. HARVEY]
LEGACY
1 Legacy of love 1991
2 A second legacy 1993

TROW, M. J.
INSPECTOR LESTRADE
1 The adventures of Inspector Lestrade 1985
2 Brigade 1986
3 Lestrade and the hallowed house 1986
4 Lestrade and the Leviathan 1987
5 Lestrade and the brother of death 1987
6 Lestrade and the Ripper 1988
7 Lestrade and the guardian angel 1990
8 Lestarde and the deadly game 1990
9 Lestrade and the gift of the prince 1991
10 Lestrade and the dead man's hand 1992
11 Lestrade and the sign of nine 1992
12 Lestrade and the sawdust ring 1993
13 Lestrade and the mirror of murder 1993
see also Doyle, A. C. Sherlock Holmes

TROY, S.
INSPECTOR SMITH
1 Half way to murder 1955
2 Tonight and tomorrow 1957
3 Drunkard's end 1960

4 Second cousin removed 1961
5 Waiting for Oliver 1961
6 Don't play with the rough boys
  1963
7 Cease upon the midnight 1964
8 No more a'roving 1966
9 Sup with the devil 1968
10 Swift to its close 1969
11 Blind man's garden 1970

TROYAT, H.
SYLVIE
1 Sylvie 1982
2 Sylvie; her teenage years 1987
3 Happiness 1989

TRUMP, I.
KATRINKA KOVAR
1 For love alone 1992
2 Free to love 1993

TRUSS, E. C.
INSPECTOR GIDLEIGH
1 In secret places 1958
2 The hidden men 1959
3 One man's death 1960

TS'AO CHAN HSUEH CHIN
THE STORY OF THE STONE
1 The golden days 1973
2 The crab-flower club 1977
3 The warning voice 1980
4 The debt of tears 1982
5 The dreamer wakes 1986

TUBB, E. C.
DUMAREST SAGA
1 Winds of Gath
2 Derai
3 Toyman
4 Kalin
5 The jester at Scar
6 Lallia
7 Technos
8 Veruchia
9 Mayenne
10 Jendelle
11 Zenya
12 The eye of the Zodiac
13 Eloise
14 Jack of swords
15 Spectrum of a forgotten sun
16 Haven of darkness
17 Prison of night
18 Incident on Ath
19 The Quillian sector
20 Web of sand
21 Iduna
22 The terra data

23 World of promise
24 Nectar of heaven
25 The Terridae
26 The coming event
27 Earth is heaven
28 Melome
29 Angado
30 Symbol of Terra
31 The temple of truth
  *Paperback science fiction 28 & 29,
  and 30 & 31 published as two in one
  vol.*

TUCKER, T.
RICHARD II
1 Woman into wolf 1969
2 The unravished bride 1970

TURNBULL, P.
GLASGOW POLICE DIVISION
1 Deep and crisp and even 1981
2 Dead knock 1982
3 Fair Friday 1983
4 Big money 1984
5 Condition purple 1989
6 Two way cut 1988
7 And did murder him 1991
8 Long day Monday 1992
9 The killing floor 1994

TURNER, B.
SOLDEN
1 Bound to die 1966
2 Sex trap 1968
3 Circle of squares 1969
4 Another little death 1970
5 Solden's woman 1972

TURNER, G.
THE TREELAKE SAGA
1 A stranger and afraid 1964
2 The cupboard under the stairs
  1962
3 Waste of shame 1965
4 Lame dog man 1968

TURNER, GEORGE
1 Beloved son 1978
2 Vaneglory 1981
3 Yesterday
  Science fiction

TURNER, J.
HAISBY
1 The arcade 1990
2 Harbour Hill 1991

TURNER, JAMES
1 Seven gardens for Catherine 1968

2 Sometimes into England 1970
N.F. Autobiography

TURNER, JAMES
NICHOLAS DE LA HAYE
1 The crimson moth 1962
2 Thelong avenues 1964
3 Anna Chevron 1966

TURNER, JAMES
RAMPION SAVAGE
1 Murder at Landred Hall 1954
2 A death by the sea 1955
3 The dark index 1959
4 The glass interval 1961
5 The nettleshade 1962
6 The slate landscape 1964
7 The blue mirror 1965
8 Requiem for two sisters 1968
9 The stone dormitory 1970

TURNER, P.
1 Colonel Shepperton's clock 1964
2 The Grange at High Force 1965

TURNER, S.
1 Over the counter 1962
2 A farmer's wife 1963
3 The farm at King's Standing 1964
N.F.Autobiography

TUROW, S.
'SANDY' STERN
1 Presumed innocent 1988
2 Burden of proof 1990
3 Pleading guilty 1993

TURPIN, A.
GEOFFREY GILLIARD
1 My flat and her apartment 1963
2 The box 1965
3 Beatrice and Bertha 1966
4 Innocent employments 1967
5 Laughing cavalier 1969

TURTLEDOVE, H.
THE TALE OF CRISPOS
1 Krispos rising
2 Krispos of Videssos
Paperback fantasy

TURTLEDOVE, H.
THE VIDESSOS CYCLE
1 The misplaced legion
2 An Emperor for the Legion
3 The Legion of Videssos
4 Swords of the Legion
Paperback fantasy

TUTE, W.
TARNHAM
1 A matter of diplomacy 1969
2 The powder train 1970
3 The Tarnham connection 1971
4 The resident 1973
5 Next Saturday in Milan 1975

TUTTLE, W. C.
HASHKNIFE
1 The medicine man
2 Ghost trails
3 Thicker than water
4 Morgan trail
5 Santa Dolores stage
6 Hashknife of Stormy River
7 Tumbling River range
8 The deadline
9 Arizona ways
10 Hashknife lends a hand
11 Hashknife of the canyon trail
12 Bluffer's luck
13 Hidden blood
14 Trouble trailer
15 Shotgungold
16 Valley of suspicion
17 Doublecrossers of Ghost Tree 1965
18 The payroll of fate 1966
19 The ghost busters 1968

TWAIN, M.
TOM SAWYER AND HUCKLEBERRY
FINN
1 Adventures of Tom Sawyer
2 Adventures of Huckleberry Finn
3 Ton Sawyer abroad
4 Tom Sawyer,detective
5 Tom Sawyer grows up, by
   C.Wood
6 Further adventures of Huck
   Finn,by G.Matthews 1982

TYNDALL, J.
ROGER TURNBULL
1 Death in the Jordan 1970
2 Death in the Lebanon 1971

UHNAK, D.
CHRISTIE OPERA
1 The bait 1969
2 The witness 1970
3 The ledger 1971

ULASI, E.
1 Many things you no understand
   1970
2 Many things begin for change
   1971

UNDERHILL, C.
FANTOM
1 Captain Fantom 1977
2 The forging of Fantom 1979

UNDERWOOD, M.
NICK ATTWELL
1 The juror 1975
2 The fatal trip 1977
3 Murder with malice 1977
4 Crooked wood 1978

UNDERWOOD, M.
RICHARD MONK
1 The man who died on Friday 1967
2 The man who killed too soon 1968

UNDERWOOD, M.
ROSA EPTON
1 A pinch of snuff 1974
2 Anything but the truth 1978
3 Smooth justice 1979
4 Victim of circumstance 1980
5 Crime upon crime 1981
6 Double jeopardy 1981
7 Goddess of death 1982
8 A party to murder 1984
9 Death in camera 1985
10 The hidden man 1985
11 Death at Deepwood Grange 1986
12 The uninvited corpse 1987
13 The injudicious judge 1987
14 Dual enigma 1988
15 A compelling case 1989
16 Rosa's dilemma 1990
17 Dangerous business 1990
18 The seeds of murder 1991
19 Guilty conscience 1992

UPDIKE, J.
BECH
1 Bech:a book 1970
2 Bech is back 1983

UPDIKE, J.
RABBIT
1 Rabbit, run 1961
2 Rabbit redux 1972
3 Rabbit is rich 1982
4 Rabbit at rest 1990

UPFIELD, A. W.
DET.INSPECTOR NAPOLEON
BONAPARTE
1 The house of Cain 1928
2 The Barakee mystery 1929
3 The beach of atonement 1930
4 A royal abduction 1932
5 Gripped by drought 1932

6 Wings above the Diamantia 1936
7 Mr.Jelly's business 1938
8 The bone is pointed 1938
9 The sands of Windee 1939
10 Winds ofevil 1939
11 Bushranger of the skies 1940
12 No footprints in the bush 1944
13 Death of a swagman 1945
14 The devil's steps 1946
15 An author bites the dust 1948
16 The widows ofBroome 1951
17 The mountains have a secret 1952
18 The new shoe 1952
19 Venom house 1953
20 Murder must wait 1953
21 Death of a lake 1954
22 Cake in the hatbox 1954
23 The battling prophet 1956
24 The man of two tribes 1956
25 Bony buys a woman 1957
26 The bachelors of Broken Hill 1958
27 Bony and the mouse 1959
28 Bony and the black virgin 1959
29 The mystery of Swordfish Reef 1960
30 Bony and the Kelly gang 1960
31 Bony and the white savage 1961
32 The will of the tribe 1962
33 Madman's bend 1962
34 The Lake Frome monster 1966

UPSTAIRS, DOWNSTAIRS
1 Upstairs, downstairs, by J.Hawkesworth 1973
2 Rose's story, by T.Brady and C.Bingham 1973
3 Sarah's story, by M.Hardwick 1973
4 Mr.Hudson's story, by M.Hardwick 1973
5 In my lady's chamber, by J.Hawkesworth 1974
6 Mr.Bellamy's story, by M.Hardwick 1974
7 The years of change, by M.Hardwick 1974
8 Mrs.Bridges' story, by M.Hardwick 1975
9 The war to end wars, by M.Hardwick 1976
10 Endings and beginnings, by M.Hardwick 1976
11 On with the dance, by M.Hardwick 1977
12 Thomas and Sarah, by M.Hardwick 1978
13 Two for a spin, by M.Hardwick 1978
Stories adapted from the TV series

UPWARD, E.
EDWARD SEBRILL
1 In the thirties 1968
2 The rotten elements 1969
3 No home but the struggle 1977

URQUHART, M.
1 Frail on the north circular 1962
2 Girl on the waterfront 1962
3 Dig the missing 1963

USHER, F.
AMANDA CURZON & OSCAR SALLIS
1 The man from Moscow 1967
2 No flowers in Braslov 1968
3 The Boston crab 1970

USHER, F.
DAYE SMITH
1 Ghost of a chance 1956
2 The lonely cage 1956
3 Portrait of fear 1957
4 The proce of death 1957
5 Death is waiting 1958
6 First to kill 1959
7 Deathin error 1959
8 Dig my darling 1960
9 Shot in the dark 1961
10 The faceless stranger 1961
11 Fall into my grave 1962
12 Who killed Rosie Gray? 1962
13 Stairway to murder 1964

VACHSS, A.
BURKE
1 Flood
2 Strega
3 Blue Belle 1990
4 Hard candy 1990
5 Blossom 1991
6 Sacrifice 1992
7 Shella 1993

VALENTINE, D.
KEVIN BRYCE
1 Unorthodox methods 1988
2 A collector of photographs 1989
3 Fine distinctions 1991

VALIN, J.
HARRY STONER
1 The lime pit 1980
2 Final notice 1981
3 Dead letter 1982
4 Day of wrath 1983
5 Natural causes 1984
6 Life's work 1988
7 Fire lake 1989
8 The music lovers 1993

VAN DER POST, L.
1 A story like the wind 1972
2 A far off place 1974

VAN GREENAWAY, P.
INSPECTOR CHERRY
1 The Medusa touch 1973
2 Doppelganger 1975
3 The destiny man 1977
4 'Cassandra' Bell 1981
5 The Lazarus lie 1982
6 The killing cup 1987

VAN GULIK, R.
JUDGE DEE
1 The Chinese bell murders 1958
2 The Chinese gold murders 1959
3 The Chinese lake murders 1960
4 The Chinese nail murders 1961
5 The Chinese maze murders 1961
6 The Emperor's pearl 1962
7 The haunted monastery 1963
8 The lacquer screen 1963
9 The red pavilion 1964
10 The willow pattern 1965
11 The monkey and the tiger 1965
12 The phantom of the temple 1966
13 Murder in Canton 1966
14 Judge Dee at work 1967
15 Necklace and calabash 1967
16 Poets and murder 1968

VAN SLYKE, H.
1 The heart listens 1974
2 The mixed blessing 1975

VAN VOGT, A. E.
1 The weapon shops of Isher
2 The weapon makers

VAN VOGT, A. E.
NULL-A
1 The worlds of Null-A 1968
2 The players of Null-A 1970
   Science fiction

VAN WORMER, L.
ALEXANDRA WARING
1 Riverside Drive 1989
2 West End 1991

VANCE, J.
CADWAL CHRONICLES
1 Araminta station 1988
2 Ecce and Old Earth 1992
3 Throy 1993

VANCE, J.
DEMON PRINCES
1 Star king 1968
2 The killing machine
3 Palace of love
4 The face 1980
5 The book of dreams 1982

VANCE, J.
LYONESSE
1 Lyonesse
2 The green pearl
3 Madouc 1990
Paperback fantasy

VANCE, J.
PLANET OF ADVENTURE
1 City of Chasch 1974
2 Servant of the Wankh 1974
3 The Dirdir 1975
4 The Pnume 1975

VANCE, J. H.
SHERIFF JOE BAIN
1 The Fox Valley murders 1966
2 The Pleasant Grove murders 1968

VANDERGRIFF, A.
DAUGHTERS OF THE SOUTH WIND
1 Daughters of the wild country
2 Daughters of the opal skies
3 Daughters of the far islands
4 Daughters of the misty isles
Paperback fantasy

VANNER, L.
1 Rannoch Chase
2 Guardian of Rannoch 1986
Paperback

VARDEMAN, R. E.
SWORDS OF RAEMLLYN
1 Swords of Raemllyn
2 Death's acolyte
3 The beasts of the mist
4 For crown and kingdom
Paperback fantasy. 2-4 published as Swords . . . Book 2 in one vol.

VARDEMAN, R. E.
THE WAR OF POWERS
1 The war of powers
2 Istu awakened
Paperback fantasy

VARLEY, J.
GAE TRILOGY
1 titon
2 Wizard 1981

3 Demon 1984
Paperback fantasy

VAUGHAN, A.
1 Signalman's morning 1981
2 Signalman's twilight 1983
3 Signalman's nightmare 1987
N.F. Autobiography of a railwayman

VELIKOVSKY, I.
AGES IN CHAOS
1 From the Exodus to King Akhnaton 1953
2 The time of Isiah and Homer
3 Rameses II and his time 1979
4 Peoples of the sea 1977
N.F. Cosmography

VENTERS, A.
GIL KENNEDY
1 Kennedy's killing 1982
2 Blood on the rocks 1983

VERNEY, J.
1 Going to the wars 1955
2 A dinner of herbs 1966
N.F. Autobiography

VERNON, E.
1 Practice makes perfect 1971
2 Practise what you preach 1978
3 Getting into practice 1979
N.F. Autobiography of a doctor

VERNON, F.
1 Gentlemen and players 1984
2 Privileged children 1982
3 A desirable husband 1987
Novels about Edwardian family life

VERNON, T.
FAT MAN
1 Fat man on a bicycle 1981
2 Fat man on a Roman road 1983
3 Fat man in the kitchen 1986
4 Fat man in Argentina 1990
N.F. Travels in search of adventure and recipes

VICKERS, B.
1 Fed up to the top attic 1984
2 Life golden in time 1985
N.F. Life in Victorian Bridlington

VIDAL, G.
1 Myra Breckinridge 1968
2 Myron 1975

VIDAL, G.
WASHINGTON TRILOGY
1 Burr 1973
2 1876 1976
3 Washington DC 1967

VINES, F.
1 The lonely shore 1959
2 So wild the sea 1961

VINGE, J.
1 The snow queen 1980
2 The summer queen 1992
Paperback science fiction

VINGE, V.
1 The peace war
2 Marooned in real time
Paperback science fiction

VINTER, M.
1 All these shall perish 1970
2 Rat in a trap 1071
3 The wounds of treason 1972

VIVIS, A.
STRATHANNAN
1 Daughters of Strathannan 1992
2 The Lennox women 1993
3 The rowan tree 1994

VOINOVICH, V.
1 Life and adventures of Private
  Ivan Chomkin 1978
2 Pretender to the throne 1981
*Novels about Russia during and after
WW2*

VOLLMANN, W. T.
SEVEN DREAMS
1 The ice-shirt 1990
2 Fathers and crows 1992
3 The rifles 1994
*The author calls it a history of North
America.*

VOSS BARK, C.
MR.HOLMES
1 Mr.Holmes at sea 1962
2 Mr.Holmes goes to ground 1963
3 Mr.Holmes and the fair Armenian
  1964
4 Mr.Holmes and the love bank
  1964
5 The Shepherd file 1966
6 See the living crocodiles 1967
7 The second red dragon 1968

VYVYAN, C. C.
1 Roots and stars 1962
2 Journey up the years 1966
N.F. Autobiography

WADDELL, M.
OTLEY
1 Otley 1965
2 Otley pursued 1966
3 Otley forever 1967
4 Otley victorious 1969

WAHLOO, P.
CHIEF INSPECTOR JENSEN
1 Murder on the 31st floor 1969
2 The steel spring 1970

WAIN, J.
1 Where the rivers meet 1988
2 Comedies 1990
3 Hungry generations 1994

WAINWRIGHT, J.
1 Death in a sleeping city 1966
2 Ten steps to the gallows 1966
3 Evil intent 1966
4 The crystallised carbon pig 1967
5 Talent for murder 1967
6 The worms must wait 1968
7 Web of silence 1968
8 Edge of extinction 1968
9 The darkening glass 1969
10 The takeover men 1969
11 The big tickle 1969
12 Prynter's devil 1970
13 Freeze thy blood less coldly 1970
14 The last buccaneer 1971
15 Dig the grave and let him die 1971
16 Night is a time to die 1972
17 Requiem for a loser 1972
18 A pride of pigs 1973
19 High class kill 1973
20 A touch of malice 1973
21 Kill the girls and make them cry
   1974
22 The hard hit 1974
23 Square dance 1974
24 Death of a big man 1975
25 Landscape with violence 1975
26 Coppers don't cry 1975
27 Acquittal 1976
28 Walther P.38 1976
29 Who goes next? 1976
30 The bastard 1976
31 Pool of tears 1977
32 A nest of rats 1977
33 The day of the peppercorn kill
   1977
34 The jury people 1978

35 Thief of time 1978
36 Death certificate 1978
37 A ripple of murders 1978
38 Brainwash 1979
39 Tension 1979
40 Duty elsewhere 1979
41 Take murder 1979
42 The eye of the beholder 1980
43 Dominoes 1980
44 A kill of small consequences 1980
45 Venus fly trap 1980
46 The tainted man 1980
47 All on a summer's day 1981
48 An urge for justice 1981
49 Anatomy of a riot 1982
50 Blayde RIP 1982
51 Distaff factor 1982
52 Their evil ways 1983
53 Spiral staircase 1983
54 All through the night 1985
55 Clouds of guilt 1985
56 Forgotten murders 1987
57 A very parochial murder 1988
58 The man who wasn't there 1989
*Novels about police work in the North
of England*

WAINWRIGHT, J.
DAVIS
1 Davis doesn't live here anymore
1970
2 The pig got up and slowly walked
away 1971
3 My word you should have seen us
1972
4 My God how the money rolls in
1972
5 The devil you don't 1974

WALDER, D.
1 Bags of swank 1964
2 The short list 1965
3 The House party 1966

WALDRON, S.
STEVE ESSEX
1 Leap before you look 1968
2 Hot ice 1969

WALKER, A.
MISS CELIE AND MISS SHUG
1 The colour purple 1983
2 The temple of my familiar 1987
3 Possessing the secret of joy 1992

WALKER, D.
DOUGAL TROCHAR
1 Winter of madness 1964
2 Black Dougal 1973

WALKER, D.
GEORDIE BLACK
1 Geordie 1966
2 Come back Geordie 1968

WALKER, L.
MONTGOMERIES OF PEPPER TREE BAY
1 Six for heaven 1953
2 Shining river 1955
3 Waterfall 1956 (reissued as 'The
bell branch'1971
4 Ribbons in her hair 1957
5 Pepper Tree Bay 1959
6 Monday in summer 1961

WALKER, P. N.
CARNABY-KING
1 Carnaby and the hi-jackers 1967
2 Carnaby and the jail breakers 1968
3 Carnaby and the assassins 1968
4 Carnaby and the conspirators 1969
5 Carnaby and the saboteurs 1970
6 Carnaby and the eliminators 1971
7 Carnaby and the demonstrators
1972
8 Carnaby and the infiltrators 1974
9 Carnaby and the kidnappers 1976
10 Carnaby and the counterfeiters
1980
11 Carnaby and the campaigners
1984

WALKER, P. N.
PANDA ONE
1 Panda One on duty 1977
2 Panda One investigates 1978
3 Witchcraft for Panda One 1979
4 Siege for Panda One 1980
*See also the series written under the
pseudonym of Nicholas RHEA*

WALLACE, R.
ESSINGTON HOLT
1 To catch a forger 1988
2 An axe to grind 1989
3 Paint out 1990
4 Finger play 1991

WALLER, L.
WOODS PALMER
1 The banker 1968
2 The family 1969
3 The American 1971
4 The Swiss account 1976
5 Game plan 1983
6 Embassy 1987
7 Deadly sins 1992

WALMSLEY, L.
1 Foreigners 1935
2 Three fevers 1932
3 Sally Lunn 1938
4 Phantom lobster 1933
5 Love in the sun 1939
6 The golden waterwheel 1946
7 The happy ending 1951
8 Paradise Creek 1963

WALSH, B.
1 Live bait 1981
2 Cheat 1982

WALTON, E.
1 Prince of Annwynn
2 The children of Llyr
3 The song of Rhiannon
4 The island of the mighty
Paperback fantasy

WARBURG, F. J.
1 An occupation for gentlemen 1959
2 All authors are equal 1973
N.F. Autobiography of a publisher

WARD, E.
1 Number one boy 1969
2 I've lived like a lord 1970
N.F. Autobiography

WARD, R. H.
NEIL FALDER
1 The conspiracy 1964
2 The wilderness 1962
3 The offenders 1963

WARDMAN, F.
INSPECTOR CLOUSEAU
1 The return of the Pink Panther 1977
2 The Pink Panther strikes again 1977

WARHAMMER
1 Konrad, by D.Ferring
2 Shadowbreed, by D.Ferring
3 Warblade,by D.Ferring
4 Drachenfeld, by J.Yeovil

WARHAMMER
40000
1 Space marine, by I.Watson
2 Inquisitor, by I.Watson
3 Harlequin, by I.Watson 1994

WARNER, R.
JULIUS CAESAR
1 The young Caesar 1959

2 Imperial Caesar 1960

WARREN, C. H.
1 Happy countryman 1939
2 England is a village 1940
3 The land is yours 1943
4 Miles from anywhere 1944
5 Adam was a ploughman 1947
6 Scythe in the apple tree 1953
7 Content with what I have 1967
N.F. Rural life in Essex

WARREN, R.
1 Where no mains flow 1955
2 A lamb in the lounge 1959
N.F. Autobiography

WARREN, V.
BRANDON
1 Brandon takes over 1953
2 Brandon in New York 1954
3 Brandon returns 1954
4 Bullets for Brandon 1955
5 No bouquets for Brandon 1955

WARRINER, T.
AMBO,MR.SCOTTER & THE
ARCHDEACON
1 Method in his murder 1950
2 Ducats in her coffin 1951
3 Death's dateless night 1952
4 The doors of sleep 1955
5 Death's bright angel 1956
6 She died, of course 1958
7 Heavenly bodies 1960

WARRINGTON, F.
BLACKBIRD SERIES
1 A blackbird in silver
2 A blackbird in darkness
3 A blackbird in amber
4 A blackbird in twlight
Paperback fantasy

WATERHOUSE, K.
BILLY LIAR
1 Billy Liar 1961
2 Billy Liar on the moon 1975

WATSON, CLARISSA
PERSIS WILLUM
1 The fourth stage of Gainsborough Brown 1978
2 The bishop in the back seat 1981
3 Runaway 1986

WATSON, COLIN
FLAXBOROUGH
1 Coffin, scarcely used 1963

2 Bump in the night 1964
3 Hopjoy was here 1965
4 Lonely heart 4122 1967
5 Charity ends at home 1968
6 The Flaxborough crab 1969
7 Broomsticks over Flaxborough 1972
8 The naked nuns 1975
9 One man's meat 1977
10 Blue murder 1979
11 Plaster sinners 1980
12 Whatever's been going on at Mumblesby? 1982

WATSON, I.
1 The book of the river 1983
2 The book of the stars 1984
3 The book of being 1985
Science fiction

WATSON, I.
MANA
1 Lucky's harvest 1994
2 The fallen moon 1994

WATSON, S.
1 In the twinkling of an eye
2 The mark of the beast

WATT-EVANS, L.
LORDS OF DUS
1 Lure of the basilisk
2 The seven altars of Dusarra
3 The sword of Bheleu
4 The book of silence
Paperback fantasy

WAUGH, H.
CHIEF OF POLICE FELLOWS
1 Road block 1960
2 Sleep long my love 1961
3 Born victim 1962
4 Thelate Mrs.D 1962
5 That night it rained 1962
6 Last seen wearing 1962
7 Death and circumstances 1963
8 The missing man 1964
9 Prisoner's plea 1964
10 End of a party 1965
11 Pure poison 1966
12 The con game 1967

WAUGH, H.
FRANK SESSIONS
1 Finish me off 1969
2 The young prey 1970

WAUGH, H.
SIMON KAYE
1 The Glenna Powers case 1981
2 The Doria Rafe case 1982
3 The Billy Cantrell case 1982
4 The Nerissa Claire case 1983
5 The Veronica Dean case 1984
6 The Priscilla Copperthwaite case 1986

WAWN, F. T.
1 The masterdillo
2 The road to the stars

WAY, P.
CRISPIN BRIDGE
1 Super Celeste 1979
2 Icarus 1980
3 Belshazzar's feast 1982

WAYNE, J.
1 Brown bread and butter in the basement 1977
2 The purple dress 1979
N.F. Autobiography

WEALE, A.
LONGWARDEN SERIES
1 All my wordly goods 1988
2 Time and chance 1989

WEATHERHEAD, J.
PROFESSOR DAVID CONNELL
1 A force of innocence 1966
2 The sacred shaft 1967

WEAVER, M.
1 Wolf dreams 1987
2 Nightreaver 1988
3 Blood fang 1989

WEBSTER, E.
BENNI SOLDANO
1 Cossack hide-out 1981
2 Red alert 1982
3 The Venetian spy-glass 1982
4 Madonna of the black market 1983
5 Million dollar stand-in 1983
6 The Verratoli inheritance 1983

WEBSTER, JACK
1 A grain of truth 1981
2 Another grain of truth 1988
N.F. Autobiography of a Scots journalist

WEBSTER, JAN
1 Collier's Row 1976
2 The Saturday city 1978

3 Beggarman's country 1979

WEIDMAN, J.
BENNY KRAMER
1 Fourth Street East 1971
2 Last respects 1972
3 Tiffany Street 1974

WEINSTEIN, H. & CRISPIN, A. C.
V
1 V 1984
2 East coast crisis 1985
3 The alien swordmaster, by
  S.Sucharitkus
4 Prisoners and pawns
  Based on the TV series

WEIR, M.
1 Shoes were for Sunday 1969
2 Best foot forward 1972
3 A toe on the ladder 1973
4 Stepping into the spotlight 1975
5 Walking into the Lyon's den 1977
6 One small footprint 1980
7 Spinning like a peerie 1986
8 A gangin' fits aye getting 1988
  N.F. Autobiography

WEIS, M.
STAR OF THE GUARDIANS
1 The lost king 1991
2 King's jest 1991
3 King's sacrifice 1992

WEIS, M. & HICKMAN, T.
DEATH GATE CYCLE
1 Dragon wing 1990
2 Elven star 1991
3 Fire sea 1991
4 Serpent mage 1992
5 The hand of chaos 1993
6 Into the labyrinth 1994

WEIS, M. & HICKMAN, T.
DRAGONLANCE CHRONICLES
1 Dragons of Autumn twilight
2 Dragons of winter night
3 Dragons of Spring dawning

WEIS, M. & HICKMAN, T.
DRAGONLANCE LEGENDS
1 Time of the twins
2 War of the twins
3 Test of the twins

WEIS, M. & HICKMAN, T.
DRAGONLANCE TALES
1 The magic of Krynn

2 Kender, gully dwarves and
  gnomes
3 Love and war
  *Paperback fantasy. The books have
  become a cult, and have pendants in
  the form of atlases, etc.*

WEIS, M. & HICKMAN, T.
ROSE OF THE PROPHET
1 The will of the wanderer
2 The paladin of the night
3 The prophet of Akhran

WEIS, M. & HICKMAN, T.
THE DARKSWORD TRILOGY
1 Forging the darksword
2 Doom of the darksword
3 Triumph of the darksword

WEISS, D.
MOZART
1 Sacred and profane 1969
2 The assassination of Mozart 1970

WELCH, P.
HELEN BLACK
1 Murder by the book 1990
2 Still waters 1991
3 A proper burial 1993

WELCOME, J.
1 Bellary Bay 1979
2 A call to arms 1985

WELCOME, J.
RICHARD GRAHAM
1 Run for cover 1959
2 Hard to handle 1964
3 Wanted for killing 1965
4 Hell is where you find it 1967
5 On the stretch 1967
6 Go for broke 1972

WELLMAN, M. W.
SILVER JOHN
1 Who fears the devil 1975
2 The old gods waken 1979
3 After dark
4 The lost and the lurking 1982
  Supernatural stories

WELLS, A.
THE BOOKS OF THE KINGDOMS
1 The wrath of Ashar
2 The usurper
3 The way beneath
  Paperback fantasy

WELLS, M.
THE EXPATRIATES
1 The expatriates 1987
2 The silk king 1987
3 The tycoon 1988

WELLS, T.
DETECTIVE KNUT SEVERSON
1 A matter of love and death 1966
2 What should you know of dying?
   1967
3 Dead by the light of the moon
   1968
4 Murder most fouled up 1968
5 Die quickly dear mother 1969
6 The young can die protesting 1970
7 Dinky died 1971
8 What to do until the undertaker
   comes 1972
9 The lotus affair 1973
10 How to kill a man 1973
11 A die in the country 1974
12 Brenda's murder 1974
13 Have mercy upon us 1975
14 Hark hark the watchdogs bark
   1976
15 A creature was stirring 1977

WENDORF, P.
THE PATTERAN TRILOGY
1 Larksleve 1985
2 Blanche 1986
3 Bye bye blackbird 1987

WENSBY-SCOTT, C.
THE PERCY TRILOGY
1 Lion of Alnwick 1980
2 Lion dormant 1983
3 Lion invincible 1984

WENTWORTH, P.
MISS SILVER
1 Grey mask 1928
2 The case is closed 1937
3 Lonesome road 1939
4 Danger point 1942
5 The Chinese shawl 1943
6 Miss Silver intervenes 1944
7 The clock strikes twelve 1945
8 The key 1946
9 The traveller returns 1948
10 Pilgrim's Rest 1948
11 Latter End 1949
12 Spotlight 1949
13 The eternity ring 1950
14 The case of William Smith 1950
15 Miss Silver comes to stay 1951
16 The catherine wheel 1952
17 The Brading collection 1952

18 Through the wall 1952
19 The ivory dagger 1953
20 Anna, where are you? 1953
21 The watersplash 1953
22 Ladies' Bane 1954
23 Out of the past 1955
24 Vanishing point 1955
25 The silent pool 1955
26 The Benevent treasure 1956
27 Poison in the pen 1956
28 The listening eye 1957
29 The gazebo 1957
30 The fingerprint 1958
31 The Alington inheritance 1959
32 The girl in the cellar 1960
33 Miss Silver detects 1961

WEST, C.
PAUL CROOK
1 Funnel web 1988
2 Stonefish 1990
3 Little ripper 1991
4 Stage fright 1993

WEST, E.
1 Hovel in the hills 1977
2 Garden in the hills 1980
   *N.F. Describes how the author created
   a garden in a remote part of Wales.*

WEST, J.
JESS AND ELIZA BIRDWELL
1 The friendly persuasion 1946
2 Except for thee and me 1969

WEST, M.
VATICAN TRILOGY
1 The shoes of the fisherman
2 Clowns of God
3 Lazarus 1990

WEST, P.
ALLEY JAGGERS
1 Alley Jaggers 1970
2 I'm expecting to live quite soon
   1971
3 Bela Lugosi's white Christmas
   1971

WEST, R.
AUBREY FAMILY
1 The fountain overflows 1957
2 This real night 1984
3 Cousin Rosamund 1985
   *Volume 3 was published after the
   author's death*

WESTHEIMER, D.
1 Von Ryan's express 1969

2 Von Ryan's return 1979

WESTLAKE, D. E.
1 The fugitive pigeon 1965
2 The busy body 1966
3 The spy in the ointment 1967

WESTLAKE, D. E.
JOHN DORTMUNDER
1 Hot rock 1969
2 Bank shot 1972
3 Jimmy the kid 1975
4 Nobody's perfect 1978
5 Why me?
6 Good behaviour 1987

WESTON, C.
KRUG & CASEY
1 Poor, poor Ophelia 1973
2 Susannah screaming 1975
3 Rouse the demon 1976

WETERING, J VAN DE
ADJUTANT GRIJPSTRA AND SGT.DE GIER
1 Outsider in Amsterdam 1976
2 Tumbleweed 1976
3 Corpse on the dyke 1977
4 Death of a hawker 1977
5 The Japanese corpse 1978
6 The blond baboon 1978
7 The Maine massacre 1979
8 The mind murders 1981
9 The streetbird 1984
10 The rattle-rat 1986
11 Hard rain 1987
12 The Adjutant's cat and other stories 1988
Detective stories set in Holland

WHALLEY, P.
HARRY SOMMERS
1 Robbers 1986
2 Bandits 1986
3 Villains 1987

WHARTON, M.
1 The missing Will 1984
2 A dubious codicil 1991
N.F. Autobiography

WHEATLEY, D.
DUC DE RICHLIEU
1 Three inquisitive people 1931
2 The forbidden territory 1933
3 The devil rides out 1935
4 The golden Spaniard 1938
5 Strange conflict 1941
6 Code-word golden fleece 1946

7 The second seal 1944
8 Dangerous inheritance 1965
9 Gateway to hell 1970

WHEATLEY, D.
GREGORY SALLUST
1 The scarlet impostor 1942
2 Faked passports 1943
3 The black baroness 1944
4 V for vengeance 1946
5 Come into my parlour 1947
6 The island where time stands still 1954
7 Traitor's gate 1958
8 They used dark forces 1964
9 The white witch of the South seas 1967

WHEATLEY, D.
JULIAN DAY
1 The quest of Julian Day 1939
2 The sword of fate 1944
3 Bill for the use of a body 1964

WHEATLEY, D.
ROGER BROOK
1 The launching of Roger Brook 1947
2 The shadow of Tyburn Tree 1948
3 The rising storm 1952
4 The man who killed the King 1953
5 The dark secret of Josephine 1958
6 The rape of Venice 1959
7 The sultan's daughter 1963
8 The wanton princess 1966
9 Evil in a mask 1969
10 The ravishing of Lady Mary Weare 1970
11 The Irish witch 1973
12 Desperate measures 1974

WHEATLEY, D.
THE TIME HAS COME
1 The young man said 1978
2 Drink and ink 1979
3 My secret war 1980
N.F. Autobiography

WHEELER, D.
EDWIN MOULD
1 Mould 1967
2 An unimpeachable source 1970

WHEELER-BENNETT, SIR J.
1 Knaves, fools and heroes 1974
2 Special relationships 1975
N.F. Autobiography

WHELPTON, E.
1 The making of a European 1974
2 The making of an Englishman 1976
N.F. Autobiography

WHITAKER, B.
JOHN ABBOT
1 Of nice and murder 1968
2 A matter of blood 1969
3 The chained crocodile 1970
4 The man who wasn't there 1971

WHITE, A.
AYSGILL FAMILY
1 The homeward tide 1981
2 The vanishing land 1982
3 The years of change 1983

WHITE, A.
COMMANDOS
1 The long day's dying 1965
2 The long night's walk 1966
3 The long watch 1968
4 The long drop 1969
5 The long midnight 1972
6 The long fuse 1973
7 The long summer 1975
8 The long silence 1976

WHITE, A.
INSPECTOR ARMSTRONG
1 Armstrong 1973
2 Death in duplicate 1974
3 Death in darkness 1975

WHITE, A.
RAVENSWYKE
1 Ravenswyke 1979
2 The homeward tide 1981

WHITE, EDMUND
1 A boy's own story 1985
2 The beautiful room is empty 1988

WHITE, J.
BEN ESCOBIE
1 The Persian oven 1987
2 California exit 1987

WHITE, J. D.
ROGER KELSO
1 Young Mr. Kelso 1963
2 Brave Captain Kelso 1959
3 Kelso of the 'Paragon' 1969
4 Captain of Marine 1960
5 The princess of Persia 1961
6 Commodore Kelso 1967
7 Fair wind to Malabar 1973

8 A wind in the rigging 1973
9 A spread of sail 1975
In chronological order

WHITE, J. D.
SEBASTIAN KETTLE
1 The Leipzig affair 1974
2 The Salzburg affair 1977
3 The Brandenburg affair 1979

WHITE, JAMES
SECTOR GENERAL
1 Hospital station 1986
2 Ambulance ship 1986
3 Star surgeon 1987
4 Hospital station 1987
5 Sector General 1988
6 Star healer 1989
7 Futures past 1989
8 Code blue emergency 1990
Science fiction. 3 is in paperback

WHITE, S.
PENHALIGON
1 The English Captain 1976
2 Clear for action 1977
3 His Majesty's frigate 1979

WHITE, STEPHEN
DR. ALAN GREGORY
1 Privileged information 1992
2 Private practices 1993

WHITEHEAD, B.
YORK CYCLE OF MYSTERIES
1 Playing God 1988
2 The girl with red suspenders 1990
3 The Dean it was that died 1991
4 Sweet death, come softly 1992

WHITING, C.
COMMON SMITH, V.C.
1 The Baltic run 1993
2 In Turkish waters 1994
3 Death on the Rhine 1994

WHITING, C.
DESTROYERS
1 Operation Africa 1974
2 Operation Stalag 1974
3 Operation Caucasian Fox 1974
4 Operation II Duce 1974
5 Operation Kill Ike 1975
6 Operation Werewolf 1976

WHITING, C
MAJOR JOHN BOLD
1 Bugles at dawn 1990
2 Sabres in the sun 1991

WHITING, C.
T FORCE
1 The big breakout 1978
2 Massacre at Metz 1979
3 Highway through hell 1979

WHITMAN, C.
INSPECTOR LONDON & SERGEANT
GRAY
1 Doctor death 1969
2 Death out of focus 1970
3 Death suspended 1971

WHITTAKER, J.
1 The raking of the embers 1982
2 The flame in the morning 1984
Novels set in 19thC Australia

WHITEMORE, E.
JERUSALEM QUARTET
1 Sinai tapestry 1978
2 Jerusalem poker 1978

WHITTLE, T.
EDWARD VII
1 Bertie 1974
2 Edward 1975

WHITTLE, T.
QUEEN VICTORIA
1 The young Victoria 1971
2 Albert's Victoria 1972
3 The widow of Windsor 1973

WHYTE, B.
1 Yellow on the broom 1979
2 Red rowans and wild honey 1990
N.F. Autobiography

WIAT, P.
BLACK BOAR SAGA
1 Raven in the wind 1978
2 Lord of the Black Boar 1975
3 Sword of Woden 1975
4 Tree of Vortigern 1976
5 The Atheling 1977
6 Westerfalca 1979
7 Lord of the wolf 1980

WIAT, P.
CHARLTON MEAD
1 The mistletoe bough 1981
2 Bride of darkness 1982
3 Wychwood 1982

WIAT, P.
EDWARD III TRILOGY
1 Queen gold 1985
2 The grey goose-wing 1985

3 The whyte swan 1986

WIAT, P.
GREY FAMILY
1 Five gold rings 1982
2 Children of the spring 1983

WIAT, P.
HOWARD SAGA
1 Maid of gold 1971
2 Like as the roaring waves 1972
3 Wear a green kirtle 1987
4 The Queen's fourth husband 1976
5 Lion without claws 1976
6 Yet a lion 1978

WIAT, P.
PLANTAGENETS
1 The hammer and the sword 1992
2 The lovers 1993

WIAT, P.
WILMINGTON
1 The fourposter 1979
2 Shadow of Samain 1980

WIAT, P.
WYATT SAGA
1 Master of Blandeston Hall 1973
2 The heir of Allington 1973
3 Sound now the passing bell 1973
4 Knight of Allington 1974
5 Rebel of Allington 1977
6 My lute be still 1977

WIDEMAN, J. E.
1 Damballah 1984
2 Hiding place 1984
3 Sent for you yesterday 1984
*Novels set in a Black ghetto in
Pennsylvania*

WIGG, T. I. G.
1 For the sons of gentlemen 1960
2 A job with the boys 1959

WILCOX, C.
LIEUT. FRANK HASTINGS
1 The lonely hunter 1971
2 The disappearance 1972
3 Dead aim 1972
4 Hiding place 1973
5 Long day down 1974
6 Aftershock 1974
7 The watcher 1977
8 Power plays 1981
9 Mankiller 1982
10 Victims 1986
11 Swallows's fall 1987

WILCOX, J.
1 Modern Baptists 1984
2 North Gladiola 1985
3 Miss Undine's living room 1987
Novels set in Tula Springs, Louisiana

WILDE, J.
1 Love's tender fury 1982
2 Love me Marietta 1983
Bodice rippers

WILES, J.
1 The grand trunk road 1972
2 Delhi is far away 1974
N.F. Travel

WILHELM, K.
CHARLIE MEIKLEJOHN &
CONSTANCE LEIDL
1 The Hamlet trap 1987
2 Smart house 1989
3 The dark door 1990
4 Sweet, sweet poison 1991

WILKINSON, B.
GEOFFREY MILDMAY
1 Proceded at will 1949
2 Run, mongoose 1951
3 Last clear chance 1954
4 Night of the short knives 1965

WILLEFORD, C.
HOKE MOSELEY
1 Miami blues 1985
2 New hope for the dead
3 Sideswipe 1988

WILLIAMS, ALAN
1 The Beria papers 1972
2 Gentleman traitor 1974

WILLIAMS, ALAN
RUPERT QUINN
1 The long run south 1960
2 Barbouze 1962

WILLIAMS, D.
FIGHTER
1 Bluebirds over 1982
2 Vendetta 1982

WILLIAMS, D.
MARK TREASURE
1 Unholy writ 1974
2 Treasure by degrees 1977
3 Murder for Treasure 1979
4 Treasure up in smoke 1978
5 Copper, gold and treasure 1982
6 Treasure preserved 1983
7 Advertise for Treasure 1984
8 Wedding Treasure 1985
9 Murder in Advent 1985
10 Treasure in roubles 1986
11 Divided Treasure 1987
12 Treasure in Oxford
13 Holy Treasure 1989
14 Prescription for murder 990
15 Treasure by post 1991
16 Planning on murder 1992
17 Banking on murder 1993

WILLIAMS, D.
TANK
1 Tank 1985
2 Fortress Eagle 1986
3 Sugar sugar 1987
War stories set in North Africa

WILLIAMS, E. M.
1 Pig in paradise 1966
2 Valley of animals 1967
3 The Pant Glas story 1970
*N.F. The author's life with her
animals*

WILLIAMS, EMLYN
1 George 1961
2 Emlyn 1973
N.F. Autobiography

WILLIAMS, G.
AMAZING CHRONICLES OF THE
MICRONAUTS
1 Micronaut world
2 Revolt of the Micronauts
Paperback science fiction

WILLIAMS, J.
LEGENDARY MURDERS
1 A copper snare 1981
2 The murder triangle 1982
3 Images of death 1984
4 Portrait of the dead 1985

WILLIAMS, MARY
1 Carnecrane 1980
2 Return to Carnecrane 1981

WILLIAMS, P. O.
PELBAR
1 The ends of the circle
2 The breaking of North Wall
3 The dome in the forest
4 The fall of the shell
Paperback fantasy

WILLIAMS, R.
1 Border country 1962

2 Second generation 1964
3 Fight for manhood 1979

WILLIAMS, R.
PEOPLE OF THE BLACK MOUNTAINS
1 The beginning 1989
2 Eggs of the eagle 1990

WILLIAMS, TAD
MEMORY, SORROW AND THORN
1 The dragonbone chair 1989
2 Stone of farewell 1990
3 To green angel tower 1993

WILLIAMS, TIMOTHY
COMMISSARIO TROTTI
1 Converging parallels 1982
2 The puppeteer 1985
3 Persona non grata 1987
4 Black August 1992

WILLIAMSON, A.
DET. SUPT. YORK
1 Funeral march for Siegfried 1979
2 Death of a theatre filly 1980

WILLIAMSON, H. R.
CATHERINE DE MEDICI
1 The Florentine woman 1969
2 The last of the Valois 1970
3 Paris is worth a Mass 1971

WILLIAMSON, H. R.
PASSING OF THE PLANTAGENETS
1 The butt of Malmsey 1969
2 The marriage made in blood 1968
3 A matter of martyrdom 1969
4 The Cardinal in exile 1969
5 The Cardinal in England 1970

WILLIAMSON, HENRY
A CHRONICLE OF ANCIENT SUNLIGHT
1 Dark lantern 1951
2 Donkey boy 1952
3 Young Philip Maddison 1953
4 How dear is life 1954
5 A fox under my cloak 1957
6 The golden virgin 1957
7 Love and the loveless 1958
8 A test of destruction 1960
9 The innocent moon 1961
10 It was the nightingale 1962
11 The power of the dead 1963
12 The phoenix generation 1965
13 A solitary war 1966
14 Lucifer before sunrise 1967
15 The gale of the world 1969

WILLIAMSON, P.G.
FIRSTWORLD CHRONICLES
1 Dinbig of Khimmur 1991
2 The legend of Shadd's torment 1993
3 From enchantery

WILLIS, T., LORD
ROSIE CARR
1 Spring at the 'Winged Horse' 1983
2 The green leaves of summer 1988
3 The bells of Autumn 1991

WILLIS, W.
1 The seven little sisters 1960
2 An angel on each shoulder 1963
3 The hundred lives of the ancient mariner 1967
N.F. Autobiography

WILMOTT, P.
1 Growing up in a London village 1979
2 A green girl 1983
N.F. Autobiography

WILSON, A. N.
1 Unguarded hours 1978
2 Kindly light 1979

WILSON, A. N.
LAMPITTS
1 Incline our hearts 1989
2 Bottle in the smoke 1990
3 Daughters of Albion

WILSON, B.
CASSANDRA REILY
1 Gaudi afternoon 1992
2 Trouble in Transylvania 1993

WILSON, B.
PAM NILSEN
1 Murder in the collective 1986
2 Sisters of the road 1987
3 The dog collar murders 1989

WILSON, C.
CHIEF INSPECTOR GREGORY SALTFLEET
1 The schoolgirl murder case 1974
2 The Janus murder case 1984

WILSON, C.
GERALD SORME
1 Ritual in the dark 1960
2 Man without a shadow 1963
3 The god of the labyrinth 1970

WILSON, C.
SPIDER WORLD
1 The tower 1987
2 The delta 1987
3 The magician 1992
Science fiction

WILSON, D.
ROBERT DUDLEY
1 Bear's whelp 1979
2 Bear rampant 1981

WILSON, F. P.
THE LANAGUE CHRONICLES
1 Wheels within wheels 1978
2 An enemy of the state 1980
Publishd as 1 vol. in 1992

WILSON, F. P.
THE NIGHTWORLD CYCLE
1 The keep 1981
2 The tomb 1984
3 The touch 1986
4 Reborn 1990
5 Reprisal 1991
6 Nightworld 1992
Horror stories

WILSON, G. M.
INSPECTOR LOVICK
1 Murder on Monday 1963
2 Shot at dawn 1964
3 The devil's skull 1965
4 The headless man 1966
5 Cake for Caroline 1967
6 Do not sleep 1968
7 Death in buttercups 1969
8 A deal of death caps 1970
9 The bus ran late 1971
10 She kept on dying 1972

WILSON, I.
GREGORY FLAMM
1 But not for love 1962
2 That feeds on men 1963
3 Lillies that fester 1964
4 Empty tigers 1965

WILSON, J.
ISLAND CHRONICLE
1 Weep in the sun 1976
2 Troubled heritage 1977
3 Mulatto 1978

WILSON, R.
SCHRODINGER'S CAT
1 The universe next door
2 The trick top hat

3 Homing pigeons
Paperback science fiction

WILSON, SANDRA
LADY CECILY PLANTAGENET
1 Less fortunate than fair 1970
2 The Queen's sister 1973
3 The Lady Cecily 1974

WILSON, STEVE
1 Dealer's move 1979
2 Dealer's war 1980
3 Dealer's wheels 1982

WILSON, T. E.
BIG TOM HOLDER
1 The newcomers 1981
2 Yellow fever 1982
3 Harvest of gold 1983
Set in New Zealand

WILSON, T. R.
1 Master of Morholm 1986
2 The ravished earth 1988
3 Straw tower 1990

WILTSE, D.
BECKER
1 A prayer for the dead 1992
2 Close to the bone 1993
3 The edge of sleep 1994

WILTZ, C.
NEAL RAFFERTY
1 The killing circle 1981
2 A diamond before you die 1988

WINGATE, J.
1 Frigate 1980
2 Carrier 1981
3 Submarine 1982

WINGFIELD, R. D.
INSPECTOR JACK FROST
1 Frost at Christmas 1989
2 A touch of Frost 1990
3 Night Frost 1992

WINGROVE, D.
CHUNG KUO
1 The middle kingdom 1989
2 Broken wheel 1990
3 The white mountain 1991
4 Stone within 1992
5 Beneath the tree of heaven 1993
6 White moon, red dragon 1994

WINGS, M.
EMMA VICTOR
1 She came too late 1986
2 She came in a flash 1988

WINSLOW, P. G.
SUPT. MERLIN CAPRICORN
1 Death of an angel 1974
2 The Brandenburg hotel 1976
3 The Witch Hill murders 1977
4 Coppergold 1978
5 The counsellor heart 1979
6 The Rockefeller gift 1982

WINSOR, D.
TAVY MARTIN
1 Red on Wight 1973
2 The death convention 1974

WINTON, J.
1 We joined the Navy 1969
2 We saw the sea 1960
3 Down the hatch 1961
*N.F. Adventures of a group of
submariners*

WINWARD, W.
1 The Canaris fragments 1983
2 The last and greatest art 1983

WODEHOUSE, P.G.
1 Performing flea 1953
2 Over seventy 1957
N.F. Autobiography

WODEHOUSE, P.G.
BLANDINGS CASTLE
1 Something fresh 1915
2 Leave it to Psmith 1923
3 Blandings Castle 1935
4 Summer lightning 1929
5 Heavy weather 1933
6 Lord Emsworth and others 1927
7 Full moon 1947
8 Pigs have wings 1952
9 Service with a smile 1962
10 Galahad at Blandings 1965
11 A pelican at Blandings 1969
12 Sunset at Blandings (unfinished)
1977

WODEHOUSE, P. G.
JEEVES AND WOOSTER
1 My man Jeeves 1917
2 The inimitable Jeeves 1923
3 Carry on Jeeves 1925
4 Very good, Jeeves 1930
5 Thank you Jeeves 1934
6 Right-ho Jeeves 1934

7 Code of the Woosters 1938
8 Joy in the morning 1946
9 The mating season 1949
10 Ring for Jeeves 1953
11 Jeeves and the feudal spirit 1954
12 Jeeves in the offing 1960
13 Stiff upper lip, Jeeves 1963
14 Jeeves and the tie that binds 1971
15 Aunts aren't gentlemen 1974
*Published in five omnibus volumes,
1990-93*

WOLWODE, L.
1 Beyond the bedroom wall 1987
2 Born brothers 1990
Companion volumes

WOLD, A. L.
1 Jewels of the dragon
2 Crown of the serpent
3 Lair of the Cyclops
Paperback fantasy

WOLF, J.
1 The road to Avalon 1989
2 Born of the sun 1990
3 The edge of light 1991

WOLFE, G.
1 Soldier of the mist 1986
2 Soldier of Arete 1990

WOLFE, G.
BOOK OF THE LONG SUN
1 Nightside 1993
2 Lake of the long sun 1994
3 Calde of the long sun 1994

WOLFE, G.
THE BOOK OF THE NEW SUN
1 Shadow of the torturer 1980
2 The claw of the conciliator 1981
3 The sword of the Lictor 1982
4 The citadel of the Autarch 1983
5 The urth of the New Sun 1987

WONGAR, B.
1 Waig 1987
2 Karan 1987
3 Gabo Djara 1988
A trilogy about Australian Aborigines

WOOD, B.
1 Wolf King 1991
2 The lost prince 1992

WOOD, B.
LUTE
1 Minstrel's lute 1987

2 Satanic lute 1987

WOOD, C.
JOHN ADAM
1 John Adam - Samurai 1971
2 John Adam in Eden 1972

WOOD, CHRISTOPHER
1 Taiwan 1983
2 A dove against death 1983

WOOD, JAMES
1 Tipple in the deep 1968
2 Beer for Christmas 1970
3 A drop of himself 1972
N.F. Autobiography

WOOD, JAMES
INSPECTOR JUMBO COLLINS
1 North Beat 1973
2 North kill 1975

WOOD, JAMES
JAMES FRAZER
1 The sealer 1960
2 The 'Liza Bastian' 1962
3 Bay of seals 1963
4 Fire Rock 1965
5 The Friday run 1966
6 Three blind mice 1968
Stories about a Scottish trawler

WOOD, R. S.
1 The Riding Officer 1987
2 The rose of St. Keverne 1989
Novels about smuggling in Cornwall

WOOD, T.
RED BENNETT
1 Dead in the water 1984
2 The killing cold 1984
3 Dead centre 1985
4 Fool's gold 1986
5 The killing cold 1987
6 Corkscrew 1988
7 When the killing starts 1989
8 On the inside 1990
9 Flashback 1992
10 Snow job 1993

WOODHOUSE, M.
GILES YEOMAN
1 Treefrog 1970
2 Rock baby 1971
3 Mama doll 1972
4 Blue bone 1973
5 Moon hill 1975

WOODHOUSE, M. & ROSS, R.
1 The Medici guns 1974
2 The Medici emerald 1975
3 The Medici hawks 1977

WOODHOUSE, S.
DR. ALEXANDER FRENCH
1 Season of mists 1984
2 Peacock's feather 1989
3 Native air 1990

WOODMAN, R.
NATHANIEL DRINKWATER
1 An eye of the fleet (1780) 1981
2 A King's cutter (1797) 1983
3 A brig of war (1798) 1983
4 Bomb vessel (1801) 1984
5 The corvette (1803) 1985
6 1805 1985
7 Baltic mission (1807) 1986
8 A private revenge (1808-9) 1989
9 The flying squadron (1811) 1992
10 In distant waters (1812) 1988
11 Under false colours (1812) 1991

WOODS, S.
AMANDA ROBERTS & JOE DONELLI
1 Reckless
2 Body and soul
3 Stolen moments
4 Ties that bind

WOODS, S.
ANTONY MAITLAND
1 Bloody instructions 1961
2 Malice domestic 1962
3 The taste of fears 1963
4 Error of the moon 1963
4 Trusted like the fox 1964
6 This little measure 1964
7 The windy side of the law 1965
8 Though I know she lies 1965
9 Enter certain murderers 1966
10 Let's choose executioners 1966
11 The case is altered 1967
12 And shame the devil 1967
13 Knives have edges 1968
14 Past praying for 1968
15 Tarry to be hanged 1969
16 An improbable fiction 1970
17 Serpent's tooth 1971
18 The knavish crown 1971
19 They love not poison 1972
20 Yet she must die 1973
21 Enter the corpse 1973
22 Done to death 1974
23 A show of violence 1975
24 My life is done 1976
25 The law's delay 1977

26 A thief or two 1977
27 Exit murderer 1978
28 This fatal writ 1979
29 Proceed to judgment 1979
30 They stay for death 1980
31 Weep for her 1980
32 Cry guilty 1981
33 Dearest enemy 1981
34 Enter a gentlewoman 1982
35 Villains by necessity 1982
36 Most grievous murder 1982
37 Call back yesterday 1983
38 The lie direct 1983
39 Where should he die 1983
40 The bloody book of law 1984
41 Murder's out of tune 1984
42 Defy the devil 1984
43 An obscure grave 1985
44 Away with them to prison 1985
45 Put out the light 1985
46 Most deadly hate 1986
47 Nor live so long 1986
48 Naked villainy 1986

WOOLEY, P.
GUINEVERE AND ARTHUR
1 Child of the northern spring
2 Guinevere, Queen of the summer
   stars 1992

WOUK, H.
1 The winds of war 1965
2 War and remembrance 1978

WREN, M. K.
CONAN FLAGG
1 Curiosity didn't kill the cat 1975
2 A multitude of sins 1976
3 Oh, bury me not 1978
4 Nothing's certain but death 1978
5 Wake up darlin' Corey 1984

WREN, M. K.
THE PHOENIX LEGACY
1 Sword of the lamb
2 Shadow of the swan
3 House of the wolf
   Paperback fantasy

WRIGHT, A. T.
ISLANDIA
1 Islandia 1942
2 The Islar, by M. Saxton 1969
3 The two kingdoms
4 Havoc in Islandia, by M. Saxton
   1984
   Fantasy

WRIGHT, D.
THREADED DANCES SEQUENCE
1 The parrot cage 1990
2 Never such innocence 1991
3 Dreams of another day 1992
4 The tightrope walkers 1993

WRIGHT, E.
CHARLIE SALTER
1 The night the gods smiled 1983
2 Smoke detector 1984
3 Death in the old country 1985
4 A single death 1986
5 A body surrounded by water 1987
6 A question of murder 1988
7 A sensitive case 1989
8 Final cut 1991
9 A fine Italian hand 1992
10 Death by degrees 1993

WRIGHT, L. R.
KARL ALBERG
1 The suspect
2 Sleep while I sing
3 Chill rain in January 1990
4 Fall from grace 1992

WRIGHT, P.
1 I am England 1987
2 That near and distant place 1988

WRIGHT, W.
BART CONDOR
1 Suddenly you're dead 1964
2 Blood in the ashes 1964
3 A hearse waiting 1965
4 Until she dies 1965
5 Blonde target 1966
6 Two faces of death 1987

WRIGHT, W.
PAUL CAMERON
1 Shadows don't bleed 1967
2 The sharp edge 1968

WRIGHTSON, P.
THE BOOK OF WIRRUN
1 The ice is coming 1977
2 The dark bright water 1979
3 Behind the wind 1981
   Fantasy. Published in one vol. 1987

WURTS, J.
CYCLE OF FIRE
1 Storm warden 1989
2 Keeper of the keys 1989
3 Shadowfane 1990

WURTS, J.
WARS OF LIGHT AND SHADOWS
1 The curse of the Mistwraith 1993
2 The ships of Merior 1994

WYLIE, J.
ISLAND AND EMPIRE
1 Dark fire
2 Echoes of flame
3 The last augary

WYLIE, J.
SERVANTS OF ARK
1 The first named
2 Centre of the circle
3 The mage-born child
Paperback fantasy

WYLIE, J.
THE UNBALANCED EARTH
1 Dreams of stone
2 The lightless kingdom
3 The age of chaos
Fantasy, originally in paperback, but published as one hardback volume in 1991

WYLIE, J.
DR. QUARSHIE
1 The killer breath 1980
2 Skull still bone 1975
3 The butterfly flood 1977
4 To catch a viper 1978
5 Death is a drum 1979
6 A tiger in red weather 1981
7 The long dark night of Baron Samedi 1982

WYNDHAM, J.
1 Love is blue 1986
2 Love lessons 1984
3 Anything once 1992

WYNDHAM, U.
1 Astride the wall 1988
2 Laughter and the love of friends 1989
N.F. Autobiography

YEH, CHUN-CHAN
QUIET ARE THE MOUNTAINS
1 The mountain village 1988
2 The open fields 1988
3 A distant journey 1989

YEOVIL, J.
DARK FUTURE
1 Demon download

2 Dark future
Paperback fantasy

YERBY, F.
1 The man from Dahomey
2 The darkness at Ingraham Crest 1981

YORK
JONAS WILDE
1 The eliminator 1965
2 The co-ordinator 1966
3 The predator 1968
4 The deviator 1969
5 The dominator 1970
6 The infiltrator 1970
7 The expurgator 1971
8 The assassinator 1972
9 The captivator 1973
10 The fascinator 1975

YORK, A.
MUNROE TALLENT
1 Tallent for trouble 1976
2 Tallent for disaster 1978

YORKE, K.
1 A woman's place 1983
2 The pair bond 1984

YORKE, M.
DR. PATRICK GRANT
1 Dead in the morning 1970
2 Silent witness 1971
3 Grave matters 1973
4 Mortal remains 1974
5 Cast for death 1976

YOSHIKAWA, E.
MUSASHI
1 The way of the Samurai
2 The art of war
3 The way of the sword
4 The Bushido code

YOUNG, GAVIN
1 Slow boats to China 1981
2 Slow boats home 1985
N.F. Travel

YUILI, P. B.
JAMES HAZELL
1 Hazell plays Solomon 1974
2 Hazell and the three-card trick 1975
3 Hazell and the menacing jester 1976

ZAREMBA, E.
HELEN KEREMOS
1 A reason to kill 1989
2 Beyond hope 1989
3 Work for a million 1990
4 Uneasy lies 1992

ZELAZNY, R.
CHANGELING SAGA
1 Changeling
2 Madwind

ZELAZNY, R.
THE KINGDOM OF AMBER
1 Nine princes in Amber 1973
2 The guns of Avalon 1974
3 The sign of the unicorn 1977
4 The hand of Oberon 1978
5 The courts of chaos 1979
6 Trumps of doom 1981
7 Blood of Amber 1982
8 Sign of chaos 1986
9 Knight of shadows 1991
10 Prince of chaos 1993

ZILAHAY, L.
DUKAY FAMILY
1 The donkeys 1949
2 The angry angel 1953
3 A century in scarlet 1966

ZIMMERMAN, B.
QUINN PARKER
1 Thicker than water 1992
2 Blood under the bridge 1993
3 Full-bodied red 1994

ZINKIN, T.
1 Odious child 1970
2 Weeds grow fast 1973
   N.F. Autobiography

ZUIKERMAN, S.
1 From apes to warlords 1978
2 Monkeys, men and missiles 1988
   N.F. Autobiography

INDEX OF SERIES AND CHARACTERS

Titles of the most popular series and names of leading characters are listed alphabetically in this index. It is by no means comprehensive, but it may prove useful in identifying fictional characters or the titles of series. Details of individual items in a series are to be found in the main text, under the author's name.

Title/character	Author	Title/character	Author
Accursed Kings series	Druon, M.	Bognor, Simon	Heald, T.
Adams family	Staples, M.J.	Bolitho, Richard	Kent, A.
Adkins, Harry	Foxall, R.	Bonaparte, Inspector	Upfield A.W
Alexandria quartet	Durrell, L.	Bone, *Supt.* Robert	Staynes &
Alien	Foster, A.D.		Storey
Alleyn, *Inspector*	Marsh, N.	Bond, James	Fleming, I.
Alms for oblivion	Raven, S.	Book of Isle	Springer, N.
Alvarez Inspector	Jeffries, R.	Bostock family	Darby, C.
Angel	Ripley, M.	Bourne	Ludlum, R.
Angelique	Golon, S.	Bradley, *Dame* Beatrice	Mitchell , G.
Appleby, Sir John	Innes, M.	Brandon family	Tinniswood, P.
Appletree saga	Pearce, M.E.	Brandsetter, Dave	Hansen, J.
Apprentice Adept	Anthony, P.	Brannigan, Kate	McDermid, V.
Archer, Lew	Macdonald, R.	Bray, Nell	Linscott, G.
Argand, Jan	Rathbone, J.	Bridges over time	Anand, V.
Argyll.Jonathan	Pears, I.	Brothers of Gwynedd	Pargeter, E.
Arrow, Steve	Mantell, L.	Brook, Roger	Wheatley, D.
Asch, Gunner	Kirst, H.H.	Browne, *Det. Chief*	
Askham chronicles	Thorne, N.	*Inspector*	Bell, P.
Athelstan, Brother	Harding, P.	Bunting, Mr.	Greenwood, R.
Aubrey, Jack	O'Brian, P.	Burke	Vachss, A.
Aubrey, Kenneth	Thomas, C.	Cable, Brevet	Callison, A.
Audley, David	Price, A.	Cadfael, *Brother*	Peters, E.
Australians, The	Stuart, V.	Cain, Jenny	Pickard, N.
Aveyard, *Superintendent*	Fraser, |J.	Calder, Keith	Hammond, G.
Aysgill family	White, A.	Cameron, RN	McCutchan, P.
Bailey, Bill	Cookson, C.	Camillo, Don	Guareschi, G.
Balkan trilogy	Manning, O.	Campion, Albert	Allingham, M.
Banks, *Inspector*	Robinson, P.	Canopus in Argos	Lessing, D.
Barforth family	Jagger, B.	Capricorn, Merlin	Winslow, P.G.
Baron, The	Creasey, |J.	Carlyle, Carlotta	Barnes, L.
Barsetshire series	Thirkell, A.	Carmichael, Nurse	Cohen, A.
Basnett, Andrew	Ferrars, E.	Carnaby series	Walker, P.N.
Bassett, Det.Chief		Carrick, Webb	Knox, B.
Inspector	Burden, P.	Castang, Henri	Freeling, N.
Bawtry, Sam	Enefer, D.	Casteel family	Andrews, V.
BelAir General	Sutton, J.	Castle Rising	Cradock, F.
Belgariad, The	Eddings, D.	Catherine	Benzoni, J.
Belgate trilogy	Robertson, D.	Chambrun, Pierre	Pentecost, J.
Bencolin, Henri	Carr, J.D.	Changewinds	Chalker, J.H.
Bennet, Reid	Wood, T.	Chee, Jim	Hillerman, T.
Beulah Land	Coleman, L.	Chelmarsh, Dorian	
Birthgrave series	Lee, T.	Fairweather	Hardwick, M.
Black Boar series	Wiat, P.	Children of the North	Powers, M.S.
Blackoaks	Carter, A.	Children of violence	Lessing, D.
Black Widowers	Asimov, I.	Chronicles of an age of	
Blackshirt	Graeme, B.	Darkness	Cook, H.
Blackstone	Falkirk, R.	Chronicles of ancient	
Blaise, Modesty	O'Donnell, P.	sunlight	Williamson, H.
Blake, Jonathan	Chance, J.N.	Chronicles of Hawklan	Taylor, R.
Bliss, Vicky	Peters, E.	Clachan series	Armstrong, S.

Tag/character	Author	Title/character	Author
Claudia series	Franken, R.	Duffy	Kavanagh, D.
Cluster	Anthony, P.	Dumarest saga	Tubb, E.C.
Cody	Brierley, D.	Duncton chronicles	Horwood, W.
Coffin, *Inspector*	Butler, G.	Dune	Herbert, F.
Conan the Barbarian	Howard, R.	East Enders	Miller, H.
Corbett, Hugh	Doherty, P.C.	Eightyseventh Precinct	McBain, E.
Cordwainers	Gower, I.	Eisengrin trilogy	Davies, R.
Cornelius, Jerry	Moorcock, M.	Elenium	Eddings, D.
Courage series	Shears, S.	Eliot family	Goudge, E.
Courtney family	Smith, W.	Epton, Rosa	Underwood, M.
Coyne, Brady	Tapply, W.G.	Erridge, Matt	Stein, A.M.
Craddocks of		Everard, Nick	Fullerton, A.
Shallowford	Delderfield, R.F.	Fairacre series	Miss Read
Craigallan family	Barclay, T.	Fairlyden	Kirkwood, G.
Crawford of Lymond	Dunnett, D.	Falco	Davis, L.
Cribb, *Sergeant*	Lovesey, P.	Falcon family	Darby, C.
Crichton, Tessa	Morice, A.	Falcon series	Benzoni, J.
Crook, Paul	West.C.	Falconhurst	Onstott, K.
Crook, Arthur	Gilbert, A.	Falkenstein, Jesse	Egan, L.
Crow, Inspector	Lewis, R.	Family d'Alambert	Smith, E.E.
Cunningham, John	Hammond, G.	Fansler, Kate	Cross, A.
Dalgleish, Adam	James, P.D.	Faro, Jeremy	Knight, A.
Dalziel, Supt.	Hill, R.	Farrow, Mark	Ross, A.
Dancers at the end of		Fell, Gideon	Carr, J.D.
time	Moorcock, M.	Fen, Gervase	Crispin, E.
Dancing Gods	Chalker, J.L.	Finch, Inspector	Thomson, J.
Dando	Clive, W.	Finchley, Mr.	Canning, V.
Daniels, Charmian	Melville, J.	First born of Egypt	Raven, S.
Darkover series	Bradley, M.Z.	Fitton, Mr.	Styles, S.
Dawlish, Patrick	Creasey, J.	Flandry, Lieut.	Anderson, P.
Daughters of England	Carr, P.	Flannery, Jimmy	Campbell, R.
Death Gate Cycle	Weis, M.	Flashman	Fraser, G.M.
Death merchants	Rosenberger, J.	Flax of Dream series	Williamson, H.
Decker, Pete	Kellerman, F.	Flaxborough chronicles	Watson, C.
Deene, Carolus	Bruce, L.	Fletch	McDonald, G.
Delancy, Richard	Parkinson, J.N.	Flynn family	Glover, J.
Delaware, Alex	Kellerman, J.	Flynn, Inspector	McDonald, G.
Department Z	Creasey, J.	Flynn, Xavier	Braine, J.
Derain family	Thompson, K.	Foundation	Asimov, I.
Desert Commandos	Landsborough,	Foxearth trilogy	Oldfield, P.
	G.	Frazer, Tim	Durbridge, F.
Destiny of Eagles	Carnegie, S.	Freer, Felix	Ferrars, E.
Devlin, Brock	Mitchell, S.	Gaunt, Jonathan	MacLeod, R.
Devlin, Harry	Edwards, M.	Gautier, *Inspector*	Grayson, R.
Devlin, Liam	Higgins, J.	Gently, *Supt.*	Hunter, A.
Didier, Auguste	Myers, A.	Gently, Dirk	Adams, D.
Discworld	Pratchett, T.	Ghote, *Inspector*	Keating, H.R.F.
Dobie, Professor	Cory, D.	Gideon, *Commander*	Creasey, J.
Dollengager family	Andrews, V.	Gollantz saga	Jacob, N.
Dorsai	Dickson, G.R.	Gor series	Norman, J.
Dowling, Father	McInerny, R.	Gordon, Lindsay	McDermid, V.
Dragon series	McCaffrey, A.	Gorodish and Alba	Delacorta
Dragon Prince	Rawn, M.	Grady, Emma	Cox, J.
Dragonard	Gilchrist, R.	Grafton, Jake	Coonts, S.
Drenai saga	Gemmel, D.	Graham, Davina	Anthony, E.
Drinkwater, Nathaniel	Woodman, R.	Grants of Rothiedrum	Fraser, C.S.
Duddleswell, Father	Boyd, N.	Gurney	Llewellyn, S.

Tag/character	Author	Title/character	Author
Habsburg series	Hamilton, J.	Kessler, Rolf	Hutson, S.
Haggard series	Nicole, C.	Kincaid family	Kennedy, A.
Halfhyde, *Lieut.*	McCutchan, P.	King, Willow	Cooper, N.
Halley, Sid	Francis, D.	Kingdom of Amber	Zelazny, R.
Halloran, Meg	LaPierre, J.	Kinsfolk	Cowper, R.
Hamilton	Cookson, C.	Kirov saga	Harrod-Eagles,
Harding	Melville-Ross,		C.
	A.	Koesler, Father	Kienzle, R.
Harpur, Colin	James, B.	Kramer, *Lieut.*	Maclure, J.
Harris, Mrs	Gallico, P.	Kruger, Herbie	Gardner, J.
Harris, Paul	Black, G.	Lacey, Meg	Bowers, E.
Harris, Sam	Cronin, M.	Lambert, John	Gregson, R.
Havoc	Healey, B.	Lampitts	Wilson, A.N.
Hawkmoon	Moorcock, M.	Landon, Arnold	Lewis, R.
Hawkwood, *Sir* John	Cole, H.	Landover series	Brooks, T.
Hawksmoor	Armitage, A.	Larkin family	Bates, H.E.
Hazard, Commander	Stuart V.	Lavette family	Fast, H.
Hazell, James	Venables, T.	Lawson, Loretta	Smith, J.
Hefferman, Hooky	Meynell, L.	Leaphorn, Joe	Hillerman, T.
Helliconia trilogy	Aldiss, B.	Lensman series	Smith, E.E.
Helm, Matt	Hamilton, D.	Lestarde, *Inspector*	Trow, M.J.
Heron family	Belle, P.	Levant trilogy	Manning, O.
Heron saga	Oldfield, P.	Lewker, Abercrombie	Carr, |G.
Hilton family	Nicole, C.	Lightbringer trilogy	Lee, T.
Hogg, Miss	Lee, A.	Lisle, Darina	Laurence, J.
Holland, Mark	Myers, P.	Lloyd, *Inspector*	McGown, J.
Holmes, Sherlock	Doyle A.C.	Lomax, Jacob	Allegretto, M.
Homecoming	Card, O.S.	Lorimer family	Melville, A.
Honeybath	Innes, M.	Louise	Shears, S.
Hope, Matthew	McBain, E.	Love, Jason	Leasor, J.
Hornblower	Forester, C.S.	Lovejoy	Gash, J.
Horne, Adam	Hill, P.	Lubbock, John	Cooper, B.
Horowitz, Jacob and		Lucia	Benson, E.F.
Helen	Delman, D.	Ludlow, Harry	Donachie, D.
House for the season	Chesney, M.	Lugh the Harper	Finney, P.
Howard saga	Wiat, P.	Lynley, Thomas	George, E.
Howard, Jeri	Dawson, J.	McAllister	Chisholm, M.
Howarths of Kit's Hill	Stubbs, J.	McCone, Sharon	Muller, M.
Hoyland, Tamara	Mann, J.	McGarr, *Chief Inspector*	Gill, B.
Hurricane Squadron	Jackson, R.	McGee, Travis	Macdonald, J.D.
Illuminatus	Shea, R.	McGuire, Kelly	Hennessey, M.
Incarnations of		McPherson, Elizabeth	McCrumb, S.
Immortality	Anthony, P.	M.A.S.H.	Hooker, R.
Jackson, 'Jacko'	Palmer, F.	Maddox, *Sergeant*	Blaisdell, A.
Jalna	De la Roche, M.	Maddox, Kate	Quest, E.
Joan, Sister	Black, V.	Maigret, *Inspector*	Simenon, G.
Jury, Richard	Grimes, M.	Maitland, Antony	Woods, S.
Kaplan, Hyman	Rosten, L.	Majipoor	Silverberg, R.
Kaywana series	Mittelholzer, E.	Mallen family	Cookson, C.
Kelling, Sarah	Macleod, C.	Mallett, Dan	Parrish, F.
Kelly, Homer	Langton, J.	Mallin & Coe	Ormerod, R.
Kelly, John	Clancy, T.	Malloreon	Eddings, D.
Kelso, Roger	White, J.D.	Mamur Zapt	Pearce, M.
Keltiad	Kenealy, P.	Margery family	Bassett, R.
Kemp, Lennox	Meek, M.R.D.	Marianne	Benzoni, J.
Kent family	Jakes, J.	Marlowe, Philip	Chandler, R.
Kenworthy, Supt.	Hilton, J.B.	Marple, Miss	Christie, A.

275

Tag/character	Author	Title/character	Author
Martian series	Burroughs, E.R.	Peacock series	Gordon, K.
Mary Ann Shaughnessy	Cookson, C.	Peckover, Harry	Kenyon, ǀM.
Mason, Perry	Gardner, E.S.	Pel, Inspector	Hebden, M.
Masters, Chief Inspector	Clark, D.	Pellucidar series	Burroughs, E.R.
Masuto, Masao	Cunningham,	Pendragon	Trevelyan, R.
	E.V.	Pengarron	Cook, G.
Matthew and Son	Kenworthy, C.	Penhaligon series	White, A.
Maxim, Harry	Lyall, G.	Pentecost family	Malpass, E.
McGann family	Nicole, C.	Percy trilogy	Wensby-Scott,
Men at war	Baldwin, A.		C.
Mendoza , Luis	Shannon, D.	Performers	Rayner, C.
Merivale, Sir Henry	Carr, J.D.	Peroni, Inspector	Holme, T.
Miami Vice	Grave, S.	Perrin, Reginald	Nobbs, D.
Middleton-Brown,		Peters, Toby	Kaminsky, S.
David	Charles, K.	Philis	Perry, R.
Millhone, Kinsey	Grafton, S.	Pink, Melissa	Moffat, G.
Minder	Masters, A.	Pink Panther	Waldman, F.
Mission Earth	Hubbard, L.R.	Pitt, Charlotte and	
Mongo mysteries	Chesbro, G.C.	Thomas	Perry, A.
Montgomery family	Deveraux, J.	Pitt, Dirk	Cussler, C.
Montrose, Dr.Jean	Roe, C.F.	Plantagenet saga	Plaidy, J.
Morgan, Rain	Grant-Adamson,	Plantagenets	Dymoke, J.
	L.	Poirot, Hercule	Christie, A.
Morse, Det.Chief		Poldark series	Graham, W.
Inspector	Dexter, C.	Pollard, Det.	
Mortdecai, Charlie	Bonfiglioli, K.	Superintendent	Lemarchand E.
Mosley, Detective		Pollifax, Mrs.	Gilman, D.
Inspector	Greenwood, J.	Poppy chronicles	Rayner, C.
Muffin, Charlie	Freemantle, B.	Porridge	Clement, D.
Mulcahaney, Norah	O'Donnell.L.	Potter, Brock	Maling, A.
Music of Time, The	Powell, A.	Powers, Georgina	Danks, D.
Myth	Asprin, R.	Pratt, Henry	Nobbs, D.
Necroscope	Lumley, B.	Preston, Mark	Chambers, P.
Neighbours	Ruhan, C.	Pringle, Mr.	Livingston, N.
Neylor family	Saxton, J.	Prism Pentad	Denning, T.
Niccolo, House of	Dunnett, D.	Probyn, Julia	Bridge, A.
November Man	Granger, B.	Pym, Mrs.	Morland, N.
Nugent family	Burton, B.	Quantrill, Det.	
Oakes, Blackford	Buckley, W.F.	Superintendent	Radley, S.
Oakes, Boysie	Gardner, J.	Quatermass	Kneale, N.
Ogilvie, James	McNeil, D.	Quiller	Hall, A.
Omaran saga	Cole, A.	Quist, Julian	Pentecost, H.
Omen	Howard, J.	Rackstraw	Hardwick, M.
Onedin Line	Abrahams, C.	Rainwood family	Bromige, I.
Otani, Superintendent	Melville, J.	Raj quartet	Scott, P.
Palfrey, Dr.	Creasey, J.	Rama	Clarke, A.C.
Palmer-Jones, George	Cleeves, A.	Ramage	Pope, D.
Pamplemousse, M.	Bond, M.	Rambo	Morrell, D.
Panda One	Walker, P.N.	Ramsay, Inspector	Cleeves, A.
Panzer Platoon	Lutz, G.	Raven	Mackenzie, D.
Pargeter, Mrs.	Brett, S.	Raven, Richard	Griffin, J.
Paris, Charles	Brett, S.	Reachfar series	Duncan, J.
Parker	Stark, R.	Rebus, John	Rankin, I.
Parsons, Annie	Shears, S.	Resnick, Charlie	Harvey, J.
Pascoe, Inspector	Hill, R.	Rhanna	Fraser, C.S.
Paton, Crispin	Draper, A.	Rhodenbarr, Bernie	Block, L.
Peabody, Amelia	Peters, E.	Richlieu, Duc de	Wheatley, D.

Tag/character	Author	Title/character	Author
Riftwar saga	Feist, R.	Squadron	Holden, M.
Ripley	Highsmith, P.	Stahl, Otto	Kessler, L.
Riverworld saga	Farmer, P.J.	Stainless Steel Rat	Harrison, H.
Roger the Chapman	Sedley, K.	Stainton, Alec	Murray, S.
Rogers, *Chief Inspector*	Ross, J.	Starbuck, Nathaniel	Cornwell, B.
Roper, *Det.*		Star Lord saga	Buffery, J.
Superintendent	Hart, R.	Star requiem	Cole A.
Roper, Ian	Bolitho, J.	Star Trek	see title
Roselynde chronicles	Gellis, R.	Star Wars	see title
Rostnikov, Porfiry	Kaminsky, S.	Starsky and Hutch	Franklin, M.
Rowan series	Darby, C.	Stephanie	Gobineau, M.
Rumpole	Mortimer, J.	Stevenson family	Macdonald, M.
Runestaff series	Moorcock, M.	Stoner, Harry	Valin, J.
Russell, Charles	Haggard, W.	Storm Troop series	Kessler, L.
Ryan, Father 'Blackie'	Greeley, A.N.	Strathannan	Vivis, A.
Ryan, Jack	Clancy, T.	Summer wine chronicles	Clarke, R.
Sabre series	Darby, C.	Sutton Place	Lampitt, D.
Sackett	L'Amour, L.	Swann saga	Delderfield, R.F.
Saint, The	Charteris, L.	Sweyneseye	Gower, I.
Sallust, Gregory	Wheatley, D.	Syn, Doctor	Thorndike, R.
Salter, Charlie	Wright, E.	Tallentire family	Bragg, M.
Samson, Bernard	Deighton, L.	Tallon, Jack	Ball, J.
Savage family	Masters, J.	Tamuli	Eddings, D.
Savage, Mark	Payne, L.	Tanner, Alex	Donald, A.
Sawyer, Pete	Albert, M.	Tanner, Evan	Block, L.
Saxon, Ludovic	Cassells, J.	Tanner, John	Greenleaf, S.
Scarpetta, Kay	Cornwell, P.D.	Tansey, *Det. Chief*	
School for Manners	Chesney, M.	*Inspector*	Penn, J.
Scudder, Matthew	Block, L.	Tarzan	Burroughs, E.R.
Scully	Bleasdale, A.	Tedric, Lord	Smith, E.E.
Seaton family	Sillitoe, A.	Temple, Paul	Durbridge, F.
Sector General	White, J.	Thane and Moss	Knox, B.
Secret Army	Brason, J.	Thanet, Luke	Simpson, D.
Seeton, Miss	Carvic, H.	Thatcher, JohnPutnam	Lathen, E.
Sensual life	Croft-Cooke, R.	Thomas Covenant	Donaldson, S.R.
Sidhe legends	Flint, K.C.	Thongor	Carter, L.
Shaft	Tidyman, E.	Thorne, *Inspector*	Penn, J.
Shannara	Brooks, T.	Thrush Green	Miss Read
Shapiro, Frank	Bannister, J.	Tibbett, Henry	Moyes, P.
Shard, Simon	McCutchan, P.	Tibbs, Virgil	Ball, J.
Sharpe, Richard	Cornwell, B.	Tildy Crawford	Fraser, S.
Shaw, Commander	McCutchan, P.	Toff, The	Creasey, J.
Sheridan, Alex	Stuart, V.	Tramont series	Barclay, T.
Shore, Jemima	Fraser, A.	Travers, Ludovic	Bush, C.
Sidel, Isaac	Charyn, J.	Treasure, Mark	Williams, D.
Silver, Maud	Wentworth, P.	Trethowan, Perry	Barnard, R.
Sipstrassi tales	Gemmell, D.	Trotter, Tilly	Cookson, C.
633 Squadron	Smith, F.E.	Tweed	Forbes, C.
Skylark series	Smith, E.E.	Unwin, Miss	Hervey, E.
Slade, Anthony	Gribble, L.	Urgent, Mark	Forde, N.
Slider, Bill	Harrod-Eagles,	Valentine, Claudia	Day, M.
	C.	Van der Valk, Piet	Freeling, N.
Sloan, *Inspector*	Aird, C.	Varallo, Vic	Egan, L.
Small, Rabbi	Kemelman, H.	Virginian series	Fletcher, I.
Smiley, George	Le Carre, J.	Walker, Amos	Estleman, L.D.
Soul Rider	Chalker, J.H.	Wanawake, Penny	Moody, S.
Spenser	Parker, R.B.	Ward, Eric	Lewis, R.

Tag/character	Author	Title/character	Author
Webb, *Chief Inspector*	Fraser, A.	Winter King's war	Dexter, S.
Weavers	Baker, D.	Winter, *Lieut.* Jason	Gaston, B.
Wellworld saga	Chalker, J.L.	Witchworld	Norton, A.
Wentworth, Lyon	Forrest, R.	Wolfe, Nero	Stout, R.
West, Inspector	Creasey, J.	World of the Alfar	Boyer, E.H.
Wexford, *Chief Inspector*	Rendell, R.	Wotan Panzer series	Kessler, L.
Wheel of Time	Jordan, R.	Wyatt saga	Wiat, P.
Whiteoaks	De la Roche, M.	Wycliffe, *Det.Superinten-*	
Williamsburg series	Thane, E.	*dent*	Burley, W.J.
Willing, Basil	McCloy, H.	Xanth	Anthony, P.
Willows and Parker	Gough, L.	Yellowthread Street	Marshall, W.L.
Wimsey, Peter	Sayers, D.L.	York Cycle of Mysteries	Whitehead, B.
Windmill Hill	Evans, S.	Yorke, Edward	Pope, D.
Wings of gold	Cruise, T.E.	Yorke, Ned	Pope, D.
Wintercombe	Belle, P.	Zen, Aurelio	Dibdin, M.